D1255145

Tone *A Linguistic Survey*

Tone *A Linguistic Survey*

Edited by

Victoria A. Fromkin

Department of Linguistics
University of California, Los Angeles
Los Angeles, California

Academic Press
New York   San Francisco   London
A Subsidiary of Harcourt Brace Jovanovich, Publishers

ACADEMIC PRESS, INC.
111 Fifth Avenue, New York, New York 10003

United Kingdom Edition published by
ACADEMIC PRESS, INC. (LONDON) LTD.
24/28 Oval Road, London NW1 7DX

Library of Congress Cataloging in Publication Data

Main entry under title:

Tone: a linguistic survey.

Includes bibliographies and indexes.
1. Tone (Phonetics)--Addresses, essays, lectures.
I. Fromkin, Victoria.
P223.T6   414   77–92239
ISBN 0–12–267350–6

Contents

List of Contributors

Numbers in parentheses indicate the pages on which the authors' contributions begin.

Stephen R. Anderson (133), *Department of Linguistics, University of California, Los Angeles, Los Angeles, California 90024*

Victoria A. Fromkin (1), *Department of Linguistics, University of California, Los Angeles, Los Angeles, California 90024*

Jackson T. Gandour (41), *Department of Audiology and Speech Sciences, Purdue University, West Lafayette, Indiana 47907*

Jean-Marie Hombert (77), *Department of Linguistics, University of California, Los Angeles, Los Angeles, California 90024*

Larry M. Hyman (257), *Department of Linguistics, University of Southern California, Los Angeles, California 90007*

William R. Leben (177), *Department of Linguistics, Stanford University, Stanford, California 94305*

Charles N. Li (271), *Department of Linguistics, University of California, Santa Barbara, Santa Barbara, California 93107*

James D. McCawley (113), *Department of Linguistics, University of Chicago, Chicago, Illinois 60637*

John J. Ohala (5), *Department of Linguistics, University of California, Berkeley, Berkeley, California 94720*

Russell G. Schuh (221), *Department of Linguistics, University of California, Los Angeles, Los Angeles, California 90024*

Sandra A. Thompson (271), *Department of Linguistics, University of California, Los Angeles, Los Angeles, California 90024*

List of Contributors

Preface

The chapters in this volume concern the phonetics and phonology of tone from both a synchronic and a diachronic point of view. The idea for such a "state of the art" volume arose in the course of discussions in the tone seminar connected to the UCLA Tone Project, a research endeavor supported for the last several years by a National Science Foundation grant (75-07158). I would therefore like to thank the NSF and all the faculty and students who have contributed to this volume in one way or another, either as writers of chapters or as critics and researchers whose findings have been incorporated into the discussions. Special thanks go to the non-UCLA scholars for their major contributions, and to Dr. Martin Mould for his painstaking efforts on the language and general indexes.

It is hoped that this volume will stimulate further research (and debate) on tonal phenomena and how such should be incorporated into a general theory of language. Because of the growing recognition of the major role played by tone in human language, however, one can predict an increase in the number of descriptive and theoretical studies on tone.

We believe that this volume can also serve as a text in phonology courses and seminars, since there is no other single volume or collection of papers or readings which has the breadth of coverage on tone contained here.

Introduction

VICTORIA A. FROMKIN

Given that a major goal for linguistic theory is to define the notion "possible human language," and since the majority of the world's languages are tone languages, a viable theory of language must provide answers to at the least the following questions:

1. What are the physiological and perceptual correlates of tone?
2. How do tonal and nontonal features interact?
3. What are the necessary and sufficient universal tone features?
4. Should tone be represented segmentally or suprasegmentally in the lexicon?
5. What is the nature of tone rules, and are they similar to and/or different from other phonological rules?
6. What is the nature of historical tone changes, and why do tones develop (tonogenesis)?
7. How do children acquire the tone systems and tone rules of their first languages; what are the similarities and differences, if any, between tonal and nontonal phonological acquisition?

The chapters in this volume attempt to summarize what is known in answer to each of these questions. Chapters I and II, by Ohala and Gandour, respectively, are concerned with the first question. Hombert, in Chapter III, shows that both production mechanisms and perception must be considered in attempting to answer Question 2. The authors of these first three chapters present results of their own experiments as well as referring to the experimental research of other phoneticians, physiologists, and psychologists. These first three chapters provide the phonetic (in the broad sense) basis for phonological tonal phenomena. Speech mechanisms from the speakers' and the hearers' sides must serve as necessary but not sufficient constraints on linguistic

1

Tone: A Linguistic Survey

systems, including the tonal aspects of such systems, since "only those aspects of the physical signal which we can perceive and only differences in sound which we can produce can be candidates" for contrastive elements (Fromkin 1977).

Anderson, in Chapter V, in discussing the answer to Question 3, shows clearly that the physical and physiological aspects of tone alone cannot resolve questions concerning, for example, the number of possible contrastive tones which are possible in a language, or the question being debated among tonologists on whether contour tone features are required in **any** language. Similarly, the case presented by Leben in Chapter VI in favor of a suprasegmental representation of tones does not depend on the physical analysis but on linguistic evidence. He provides a number of detailed descriptive studies in support of his hypothesis.

In Chapter VII, Schuh not only summarizes the kinds of tone rules found in languages, he also seeks to constrain such rules, and he further discusses the important syntactic function played by tone in a number of the world's languages (particularly those in Africa), showing once more the intricate interdependence of "levels" found in grammars.

Hyman, in Chapter VIII, presents a number of general and specific principles which he suggests constrain historical tone change. It is just such universal principles which are required in our attempt to delimit the class of possible human languages and the grammars which generate them. Clearly such languages must be learnable, and in the final Chapter IX, Li and Thompson summarize the unfortunately few studies which have investigated how such languages are learned or acquired by children. They also suggest a number of questions which need resolution; hopefully these will stimulate further investigations of tone acquisition in many diverse languages.

All the chapters are both "state of the art" summaries of what has been discovered to date and of the opinions held by different linguists and are also reports on studies—experimental, descriptive, and theoretical—conducted by the individual authors. Each chapter presents new material, some never before published. The ideas put forth, in many cases, are controversial. It is therefore not surprising that there should be differences of opinion among the authors. It can almost be predicted that new controversies will arise on the basis of the opinions expressed here. But such is in the best traditions of science.

McCawley's Chapter IV will undoubtedly lead to both debate and further research. One might think that in a volume devoted to tonal phenomena, the question which serves as the title for his chapter, "What is a tone language?" need not even be asked, let alone be controversial. Yet, despite the fact that linguists have been discussing and describing tone languages for hundreds of years, there does not seem to be an agreed on definition of a tone language. Nor is there any common set of criteria for classifying languages according to how pitch (an auditory phenomenon) and fundamental frequency (an acoustic phenomenon) are used. Most linguists, however, have differentiated tone from intonation, although both utilize pitch and fundamental frequency to contrast meanings.

Beach in his classic paper of 1924, provided a definition of tone which was so broad as to include a language like English as a tone language because it uses pitch contrastively due to the role played by intonation. But his paper does attempt an explicit definition of tone, a classification of tones, and a typology of tone languages. In referring to Beach's earlier work, Pike (1948) suggests that it is "preferable . . . to keep tonal and intonational types distinct in nomenclature [p. 3]." Pike (1975) discusses the "overlapping" classification problem, stating that "tone and intonation were never held in sharp, dichotomous partition—in the tonal material, word tone was recognized for Norwegian, for example, and in languages of typical tonal style, one found intonational overlay as a separate system." He goes on to say that although "in the main they were treated separately in the early materials, . . . various later discoveries began to put pressure on this system [Pike 1975: 2]."

The pressures on the system were considered by McCawley in a paper presented in 1964. In this paper McCawley emphasizes that "what is basic to the role of pitch in a tone language is not its contrastiveness but its lexicalness. In his chapter in this volume he considers this notion in greater detail, refines his definition, further discusses the similarities and/or differences between "pitch accent" and "tone" languages and whether they should be dichotomized into separate classes, and makes a number of radical proposals concerning the representation of tone and tone rules which will undoubtedly provoke much discussion.

One might question why there is any concern at all for the classification of languages into, for example, intonation, pitch accent, and tone languages. It is not the case that we are interested in classification for itself. In any science a natural classification of objects is based on the relevant characteristics of the things under investigation and group together objects which possess fundamental similarities. In such natural classifications, the determining characteristics are associated, frequently, with other characteristics of which they are logically independent. Thus Schuh in his chapter in this book attempts to show that "the different types of tone rules between African and Asian languages . . . may reflect the difference in language typology in the two areas [p. 251]." That is, given the correct set of typological criteria other important predictions may follow. The concepts by means of which we seek to establish a "natural system" are definitely chosen with a view to attaining systematic explanations and not merely descriptive import.

> The devising of a classification is, to some extent, as practical a task as the identification of speciments, but at the same time it involves more speculation and theorizing, [for] a natural system . . . is one which enables us to make the maximum number of prophesies and deductions. [Huxley 1940: 20].

Thus, once we are able to arrive at the proper criteria for answering the question "What is a tone language?" other "prophesies and deductions" should follow. The chapters in this volume go a long way toward providing such natural classifications of tones and tone rules as well.

The chapters in this book are neither the first nor the last word on the topic of tone. It is interesting that out of the 551 entries in "An Annotated Bibliography of Tone" (Maddieson 1974), 397 have been written since 1960. This reflects the growing interest in the subject. We are happy to add one more reference to the growing body of literature on the phonetics and phonology of tone, knowing that this will be one of many more such volumes to appear in the future.

REFERENCES

Beach, D. 1924. The science of tonetics and its application to Bantu languages. *Bantu Studies, 2*(2), 75–106.

Fromkin V. A. 1977. Some questions regarding universal phonetics and phonetic representations. In A. Juilland (Ed.), *Linguistic studies offered to Joseph Greenberg.* Saratogo, California: Anma Libri. Pp. 365–380.

Huxley, J. 1940. *The new systematics.* Oxford: Oxford University Press.

Maddieson, I. (Ed.). 1974. An annotated bibliography of tone. *UCLA Working Papers in Phonetics, 28.*

McCawley, J. D. 1964. What is a tone language? Paper presented to meeting of Linguistic Society of America, Indiana University, 1 August, 1964.

Pike, K. L. 1948. *Tone languages.* Ann Arbor: University of Michigan Press.

Pike, K. L. 1975. Introduction. In R. M. Brench (Ed.), *Studies in tone and intonation.* Basel, Switzerland: S. Karger. Pp. 1–3.

I

Production of Tone[1]

JOHN J. OHALA

Real languages are not minimal redundancy codes invented by scholars fascinated by the powers of algebra, but social institutions serving fundamental needs of living people in a real world. [In trying to understand] how human beings communicate by means of language, it is impossible for us to discount physical considerations, [i.e.] the facts of physics and physiology [Halle 1954: 79–80].[2]

1. INTRODUCTION

This chapter is offered as a brief review of those aspects of tone production that may be relevant to an understanding of tonal phenomena. It is reasonable that widely attested sound patterns, tonal or not, can be explained to a great extent, if not totally, by reference to the only thing that is common to different linguistic communities, though they be geographically, chronologically, or geneologically remote from each other, namely, the physical mechanisms used in the transmission and reception of speech: the human articulatory and auditory mechanisms, including associated neurological structures. This approach has proven useful in phonology for almost a century (Passy 1890, Rousselot 1891, Haden 1938, Grammont 1965, Lindblom 1972, 1975, Ohala 1971, 1972a, 1974a, 1974b, 1975a, 1975b, 1975c, 1976, Ohala and Lorentz 1977).

It is impossible in the space of one brief chapter to give even the beginnings of a comprehensive review of the production of tone, and, in any case, there are other extensive reviews of fundamental frequency production which serve that purpose: Arnold 1961, Damste 1968, Luchsinger and Arnold 1965, Zemlin

[1] This research was supported in part by the National Science Foundation, and the Committee on Research and the Computing Center of the University of California, Berkeley.

[2] Parts of this quotation have been rearranged from the original without, I think, distorting its sense.

1968, Ohala 1970, Sawashima 1970, Broad 1973, Netsell 1969, Dixit 1975, as well as collections such as Bouhuys 1968 and the extensive bibliography in Di Cristo 1975. I will therefore attempt the following more modest tasks: first, to review very briefly enough of laryngeal anatomy and physiology so that the later parts of this chapter and the other chapters making reference to the production of tone will be understandable even to those with little previous exposure to experimental phonetics; second, to review the more recent and more controversial issues in tone production; third, to provide an introduction to the literature in this area; and fourth, to give the reader some of the facts which have emerged from the various experimental studies on tone production and also to convey a "feel" for how research is done in this area, for it is only with an understanding of the basic research techniques that the reader will be able to evaluate on his own the evidence and claims.

1.1 Terminology

I use the terms "pitch" and "fundamental frequency" (F_0) interchangeably. Both will be taken to mean the rate of vibration of the vocal cords during voice production. When quantified, the units are hertz (Hz). Some cases of tonal contrasts which linguists have described apparently include the distinctive use of other phonetic parameters besides pitch, for example, duration, voice quality, manner of tone offset, and vowel quality. However, I will be concerned only with pitch itself, and not with these other parameters. Subglottal air pressure, P_s, will be mentioned frequently as a determinant of pitch. More properly this should be the difference between subglottal and oral air pressure, i.e., the transglottal pressure drop; however, in most cases of interest (nonobstruents) this would have approximately the same value as subglottal pressure itself, since oral pressure would be near zero. The units for P_s will be centimeters of water (cm H_2O), since the standard way of measuring pressures in the vocal tract is with a U-tube water manometer (see Figure 4). Glottal air flow will also be mentioned as a determinant of pitch. In most cases glottal air flow is directly proportional to P_s and has a similar effect on pitch. There are instances, however, where the two are not necessarily related to each other (namely, when glottal area varies or when the larynx itself moves up or down). In such complex cases the effect of one parameter on pitch may be greater than the other (see Ishizaka and Flanagan 1972).

2. REVIEW OF LARYNGEAL ANATOMY AND PHYSIOLOGY

Functionally, the larynx is a valve and a sound producer. As a valve it regulates the flow of air into and out of the lungs and keeps food and drink out of the lungs. The two functions are accomplished by a relatively complex

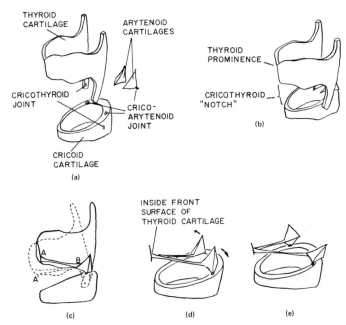

Figure 1. (a) An exploded schematic representation of laryngeal cartilages and their movements. (b) Cartilages as they are normally joined. (c) Manner of rotation of thyroid and cricoid cartilages which cause vocal cords, *AB*, to increase in length, *A′B*. (d) Adducted position of the vocal cords when arytenoid cartilages are tilted inward. (e) Abducted position of the vocal cords when arytenoid cartilages are tilted outwards.

arrangement of cartilages, muscles, and other tissues. The hard structure of the larynx consists of four principal cartilages: the thyroid, the cricoid, and a pair of arytenoid cartilages, as shown schematically in Figure 1 (a—exploded view—and b). The thyroid and cricoid are connected as shown and pivot about a transverse axis. The two arytenoid cartilages are connected to the cricoid cartilage via a ligamentous "hinge" and sit atop its rear rim. Each can rotate on the rim of the cricoid in such a way as to bring their front projections towards or away from the midline (see Figure 1d and e).

The two vocal "cords" or, more appropriately, the vocal folds, are basically ligaments which stretch between the inner lower front surface of the thyroid cartilage and the front faces of the separate arytenoid cartilages (see Figure 1 d and e). It is the rotation of the arytenoid cartilages which enables the vocal cords to be brought together towards the midline for voicing or breath-holding (adducted) or to be separated from each other (abducted). With the cords adducted and the arytenoid cartilages fixed with respect to the cricoid cartilage, rotation of the thyroid and cricoid cartilages with respect to each other causes the vocal cords to change their length: Bringing these two cartilages' front edges together lengthens and stretches the cords; increasing the separation of the front edges shortens and slackens the cords (see Figure 1c). As will be discussed below, this is the primary mechanism for changing the tension of the cords and thus the pitch of voice.

The muscles which cause the movements of the laryngeal cartilages and of the larynx as a whole are quite numerous and are attached in ways that are difficult to explain fully in prose. The schematic representation of some of these muscles and their attachments in Figure 2 (a–c) may be sufficient to make this aspect of laryngeal anatomy clear. Some of the categorizations or cover terms generally used when speaking of these muscles are:

1. The adductor muscles: the lateral cricoarytenoid, the vocalis (that part of the more complex thyroarytenoid muscle—not shown in the figures—which runs parallel to the vocal cords), and the interarytenoid muscles. These close off the laryngeal opening.

2. The abductor muscle: the posterior cricoarytenoid, which draws the vocal cords apart.

3. The tensor muscle: the cricothyroid, which, by drawing the front edges of the thyroid and cricoid cartilages closer together, lengthens and tenses the vocal cords.

4. The strap muscles: the sternohyoid, sternothyroid, and thyrohyoid (also the omohyoid, not shown in the figures), which are in front of the larynx and which attach directly or indirectly to the larynx and to portions of the skeletal frame enabling them to move the larynx as a whole up or down or, within limits, forward or backward. (Such movements are most noticeable during yawning and swallowing.) Some believe that the strap muscles may also be able to affect movements of the thyroid cartilage with respect to the cricoid (see below).

5. The constrictor and other pharyngeal muscles which connect to the larynx from the rear via the pharyngeal walls and which can, like the strap

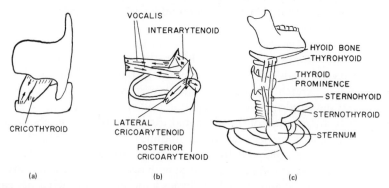

Figure 2. Schematic representation of the laryngeal muscles and the movements they accomplish: (a) cricothyroid muscle; (b) lateral cricoarytenoid, vocalis, posterior cricoarytenoid, and interarytenoid muscles; (c) strap muscles: sternothyroid, thyrohyoid, and sternohyoid muscles.

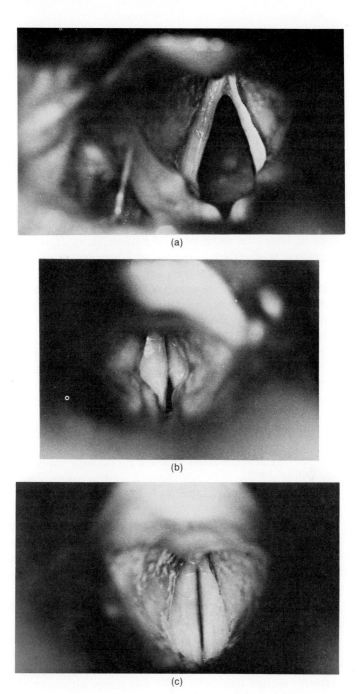

Figure 3. Photographs (by the author and Ralph Vanderslice) of the larynx taken with a laryngoscope. In these views the front of the larynx is at the top. (a) The vocal cords (the white bands) in the abducted position for normal breathing (cf. Figure 1e). The "knobby" structures at the base of the vocal cords are the fleshy covering of the arytenoid cartilages. (b) Low-pitched phonation. (c) High-pitched phonation.

muscles, affect the position of the larynx as a whole and also the closure or constrictions of the laryngeal passage giving out onto the pharynx.

The first three groups are also referred to collectively as the intrinsic laryngeal muscles, and the remaining ones as the extrinsic laryngeal muscles, although occasionally some writers include the cricothyroid in the latter category. Like most structures in the body, all of these muscles, except the interarytenoid, are symmetrically paired, one on the right and one on the left, even though it is common to speak of the cricothyroid "muscle" rather than "muscles."

It is fairly easy to detect on oneself the rotation of the thyroid and cricoid cartilages—or at least one result of it, the diminishing of the cricothyroid space—by applying one's finger to the "notch" between the cartilages (easily felt through the skin) as one raises the pitch of voice. The stretching and the abduction/adduction of the vocal cords is also relatively easy to view in oneself with the help of a laryngoscope (which is just a small mirror placed at a 45° angle on a thin handle). The photographs in Figure 3 (a–c) were taken using a homemade laryngoscope.

In a thin person's neck it is possible to see the outline of some of the strap muscles, particularly the sternohyoid—especially if the individual, lying supine, attempts to lift up his head. There is as yet no easy way to visualize the other muscles, even with a laryngoscope.

3. BRIEF HISTORY OF RESEARCH ON PITCH REGULATION

The role of the larynx and trachea in sound production has been recognized for millenia (Allen 1953), although detailed and accurate descriptions of laryngeal anatomy were not available until the work of Vesalius (1543). And it was not until even more recently that experimental evidence was offered to show that the vocal cords produce the sound of voicing by means of their vibration, which in turn interrupts (i.e., "chops up") the air stream passing through the glottis into the vocal tract proper, and that it was lengthening and consequent tensing of the cords which changed the rate of vibration, i.e., the pitch of voice (Ferrein 1741, Willis 1833).

The great German physiologist, Johannes Müller, more than anyone else can be credited with putting our knowledge of laryngeal physiology on a firm empirical basis, in that not only did he verify (and quantify) many earlier claims about the action of the larynx in sound production, but he also un- covered many new details as well (Mueller 1851). Many of his studies were done using freshly excised human larynges, sometimes with most of the rest of the vocal tract attached (see Figure 4). By adding known weights to strings attached (via pulleys) to various parts of the larynx, he simulated the action of certain laryngeal muscles, and by blowing into a tube connected to the trachea (the exact pressure of which was measured by a U-tube water manometer), he simulated the pulmonic air flow. He showed that although the primary mecha- nism for raising pitch was the tensing of the vocal cords via the cricothyroid

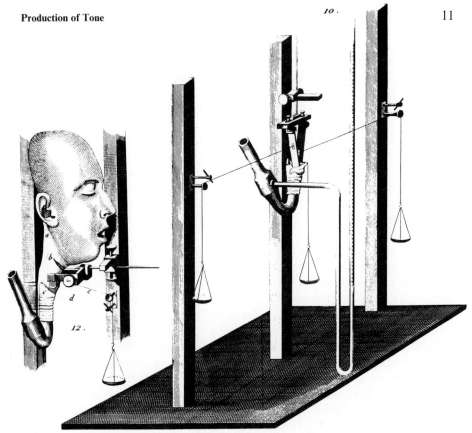

Figure 4. The laboratory set-up Müller used in his studies with excised larynges to quantify the effect of muscular pull and air flow on various parameters of the voice, including pitch (from Mueller 1851).

muscle, it was also possible to change pitch by varying P_s; in this case pitch varied at the rate of about 4.5 Hz/cm H_2O.

Although Müller was not the first to use this technique, he was perhaps the first to use it carefully and to get reliable quantitative data from it. Experimentation with excised larynges has continued to yield important data which increase our understanding of laryngeal mechanisms used in speech (e.g., van den Berg and Tan 1959, Furukawa 1967, Anthony 1968, Baer 1975).

Of course, excised larynges cannot duplicate every aspect of the living larynx, and this leaves open the possibility that studies based on them exclusively may have missed some very fundamental aspects of normal laryngeal behavior. At least Raoul Husson thought so. In his 1950 dissertation he challenged the prevailing views on the mechanisms of vocal cord vibration and pitch regulation by claiming that each vibration of the cords was accomplished by a separate contraction of the adductor muscles, i.e., for a F_0 of 400 Hz these muscles would supposedly contract at the rate of 400 twitches/sec. This was called the **neurochronachtic** theory; the traditional view was called the

myoelastic aerodynamic theory (van den Berg 1958). In support of his theory Husson and his followers claimed to have recorded (via electromyography, EMG) contractions of the vocalis muscle having the same rate as the vibrations of the vocal cords. Also, in another study they reported that they found vocal cord vibration in the absence of any air flow through the glottis (in a tracheotomized patient whose pulmonic air was diverted out through the hole in his trachea by a tube). The arguments and counterarguments, evidence and counterevidence offered on both sides were quite complex, but in the end the neurochronachtic theory was disproved. It was shown, for example, that what was interpreted as individual contractions of the vocalis in the above-mentioned EMG studies were actually movement artifacts caused by the vibration of the EMG needle inserted in the vibrating vocal cord. Moreover, the vocal cord vibrations supposedly found in the absence of glottal air flow were shown to be caused by a probable leakage of air around the tube diverting the tracheal air flow, such that there was some slight glottal air flow causing the vibrations after all. An additional piece of evidence supporting the myoelastic aerodynamic theory was the fact that a push on the chest of a person phonating will produce a sudden involuntary increase in P_s and a consequent increase in F_0. This phenomenon, which shows that aerodynamic factors can affect pitch (as Müller had also shown on excised larynges), is familiar to anyone who has attempted to converse or sing while driving over a bumpy road. By 1971 the neuro-chronachtic theory was judged long dead and so much a nonissue that Abramson (1972) chided Lafon for bothering to devote a good part of his plenary address at the 7th International Congress of Phonetic Sciences to a refutation of Husson's claims.

Insofar as a model, whether implemented mechanically or by a computer program, represents a manifestation of a theory, it can be said that all important aspects of the myoelastic aerodynamic theory of vocal cord vibration have been successfully duplicated and, in that sense, verified by a number of very successful vocal cord models (Wegel 1930, Ishizaka and Flanagan 1972, Flanagan, Ishizaka, and Shipley 1975).

In retrospect, Husson's theory seems highly unlikely, given what was known at the time about laryngeal physiology and about muscular contractions in general. Nevertheless some of the most imaginative and technologically advanced studies on laryngeal physiology were made as a result of the dispute between the two theories (see, e.g., Fabre 1957, Isshiki 1959, van den Berg and Tan 1959, Faaborg-Andersen 1957, 1965). This is consistent with the view that two (or more) clearly defined competing theories can be very beneficial to a scientific field (Feyerabend 1968, Derwing 1973).

4. RECENT ISSUES IN LARYNGEAL PHYSIOLOGY

Although the earlier research indicated that the pitch of voice could be varied both by adjustments in the tension of the vocal cords and by changes in the aerodynamic conditions at the glottis, there were—inevitably—many questions concerning pitch control for which there were no clear answers:

1. Are the mechanisms of dynamic pitch control used in speech the same as those used in singing and steady-state phonation (the only conditions investigated in the earlier work)?
2. Are both of the above-mentioned mechanisms of pitch control used in speech, and, if so, what is the relative contribution of each?
3. Is pitch lowered simply by relaxing the pitch-raising muscles, or is there a separate (active) pitch-lowering mechanism?
4. What is the role of the commonly observed larynx height variations in pitch variations? Or, more generally, what is the role of the extrinsic laryngeal muscles in pitch control?
5. What causes the small systematic variations in pitch found near specific speech segments?

4.1 The "Larynx versus Lungs" Controversy

One study which triggered a detailed investigation of these questions was the MIT dissertation of Philip Lieberman (1967b) and other articles based on it (e.g., Lieberman 1967a, 1968). Briefly, he claimed that variation of pitch in speech was accomplished not by the action of the laryngeal muscles but by variations in P_s (except in the case of the pitch rise at the end of yes–no questions, where he allowed that the laryngeal muscles were responsible).[3] This claim was based on recordings from three speakers of the voice signal and the P_s during various types of utterances. His data were similar to the top two parameters shown in Figure 7 (the third parameter in the figure will be considered later). Such records (and many that were published previously, e.g., Smith 1944, Ladefoged 1963) often show a certain synchronization between the momentary pitch rise on the stressed syllable (cf. *bombed* in the second sentence) and a momentary increase in the P_s function. Likewise, the terminal falling pitch such as that in Sentence 1 in the figure was observed to coincide with falling P_s. Lieberman had no records of the activity of the laryngeal muscles and assumed that in general they maintained a constant level of tension in the vocal cords, except, of course, in the case of the terminal rises on yes–no questions, such as that in the third sentence in the figure, where there is

---

[3] Lieberman claimed that this was the "archetypal" manner of pitch control in speech. He also allowed that "alternate articulatory maneuvers" could be used to vary pitch, for example, use of the laryngeal muscles. So formulated, his hypothesis is nonempirical, since there is no conceivable data that could falsify it (see also Ohala and Ladefoged 1970, Ohala 1970). For example, Lieberman considered his hypothesis that P_s causes F_0 as verified even though he himself admitted that a majority of his subjects, two out of three, gave evidence of using these so-called "alternate articulatory maneuvers."

no correlation between pitch and P_s and thus where P_s cannot be invoked as a cause of the pitch change. He also obtained simultaneous values of F_0 and P_s at various points in his data where he assumed that the laryngeal muscles maintained a constant level of activity and thus arrived at "calibrations" of the effect of P_s on F_0 that ranged from 16 to 22 Hz/cm H_2O.[4]

Lieberman intended his "P_s causes F_0" hypothesis to apply to pitch changes on stressed syllables and sentence-final elements. He did not apply it to tone or to pitch accent (such as occur in Chinese and Japanese) and in fact, called for further research to decide how pitch was varied in such cases. He did suggest, however, that the shape of "allotones" that appear on stressed syllables or at the end of sentences in Chinese are due to the same factors which shape pitch variation in nontonal languages, i.e., P_s variations. There have also been some attempts by others to explain certain aspects of tonal sound patterns by reference to Lieberman's hypothesis, e.g., terracing in African tone languages (Painter 1971, 1974).

Although no one had yet made direct recordings of the activity of the laryngeal muscles during speech when Lieberman's dissertation appeared, the dominant opinion among phoneticians and speech scientists was not in agreement with his claims. Rather, they thought that the pitch of voice during speech was in all cases, yes–no questions or not, controlled by the laryngeal muscles and that the effect of P_s on pitch (certainly real enough, as Müller had shown a century ago) was too small to account for the major part of the observed pitch variations (Sweet 1877, Scripture 1902, Stetson 1928, Wegel 1930, Pressman and Kelemen 1955, Ladefoged 1963, Öhman and Lindqvist 1966, Zemlin 1968, Proctor 1968). There were a number of reasons for this belief:

1. Larynx height follows pitch variations.

It was commonly observed that the larynx moves up and down in the neck during the pitch changes in speech and singing, and it was thus assumed that in some way the larynx contributed to these pitch changes (Herries 1773, Scripture 1902, Critchley and Kubik 1925).

2. Different consequences of laryngeal versus pulmonic paralysis.

Clinical observations suggested that paralysis or other loss of the use of some of the laryngeal muscles commonly resulted in defective use of pitch in speech (Critchley and Kubik 1925, Sokolowsky 1943, Sonninen 1956, Arnold

---

[4] As I have pointed out elsewhere (Ohala 1977a), the values Lieberman gives for $\Delta F_0/\Delta P_s$ are questionable even in the absence of data on laryngeal activity. My own analysis of his data showed that if he had indeed followed the measurement procedures he specified in his book, the values would be more like 28–33 Hz/cm H_2O. These are absurdly high values, of course, and clearly reveal that the assumption behind the measurements, namely, that the laryngeal muscles maintained a constant level of activity, is false. The skeptical reader may, if he cares to, check this for himself, since all the relevant raw data are published in Lieberman 1967b.

1961, Luchsinger and Arnold 1965). On the other hand, respiratory paralysis apparently did not result in any defect in the use of pitch in speech (Peterson 1958).

3. Electromyographic studies of laryngeal function.

Direct EMG recordings during steady state phonation showed the laryngeal muscles, especially the cricothyroid, to be very highly correlated with the pitch level produced (Katsuki 1950, Faaborg-Andersen 1957, 1965, Sawashima, Sato, Funasaka, and Totsuka 1958, Arnold 1961, Kimura 1961). Hirano, Koike, and von Leden (1967) also found the sternohyoid active for low pitch and extremely high pitch. It was therefore assumed that these results could be extrapolated to speech conditions. It should be mentioned here that as a technique for gathering data on muscle activity, EMG is rather simple in concept but extremely difficult to use in practice, especially on the muscles of the larynx. It consists of inserting small electrodes (thin needles or wires) into the muscle of interest and then amplifying and recording the small spikelike voltage variations they pick up from the contracting muscle. The chief problem is making sure the electrodes end up in the intended muscle, which is particularly difficult in the case of the larynx since so many muscles are crowded into such a small space. For example, we may guess that the "cricothyroid" muscle which Zenker (1964) found to be active during low pitch and during jaw opening—an unusual pattern for this muscle—was actually the sternohyoid muscle for which these patterns are more expected. The sternohyoid lies over the cricothyroid (see also Faaborg-Andersen 1964). Nevertheless, used carefully it can give us reliable information on the activity of specific muscles, as is evident from the similar results obtained in independent studies (see below).

4. Calibrations of the extent of P_s influence on F_0.

Calibrations of the effect of P_s on F_0, where some care was taken to ensure that the vocal cords maintained a constant level of activity, yielded values of $\Delta F_0/\Delta P_s$ (i.e., rate of change of pitch with respect to the change in P_s) of 2–5 Hz/cm H_2O in the pitch range used in speech. The calibrations of $\Delta F_0/\Delta P_s$ were obtained by the push-on-the-chest technique described above. Figure 5 (data from Öhman and Lindqvist 1966) shows the kind of raw data obtained from such investigations. The close temporal coincidence of the F_0 and P_s curves is a reasonable assurance that the F_0 change was caused in a purely automatic way by the P_s increase and not by the speaker reacting to the push on the chest. Figure 6 shows how the data can be analyzed, by plotting the F_0 variation as a function of the P_s variation. The slope of such plots, then, equals $\Delta F_0/\Delta P_s$. In Figure 6 the slope is 2.9 Hz/cm H_2O. Having obtained such calibrations Ladefoged (1963) and Öhman and Lindqvist (1966) applied them to their records of P_s and F_0 during connected speech in order to factor out those pitch variations that could be attributed to P_s. By far the major part

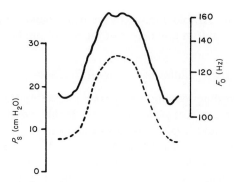

Figure 5. Synchronized variations in pitch, F_0 (solid line), and subglottal air pressure, P_s (broken line) during a sudden push on the speaker's chest (redrawn from data given by Öhman and Lindqvist 1966).

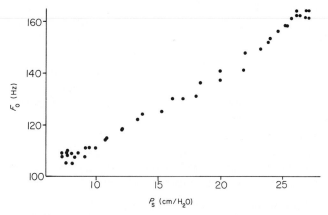

Figure 6. Variations in fundamental frequency, F_0, plotted as a function of variations in subglottal air pressure, P_s, during a sudden push on the speaker's chest (data from Figure 5). From such data it can be deduced that P_s can influence F_0 at the rate of about 2.9 Hz/cm H_2O (the slope of the line passing through the data points as determined by the least squares method).

of the recorded pitch variations had to be attributed to factors other than P_s, i.e., to laryngeal factors. For example, for a stress-related pitch rise of 50–100 Hz—quite common in normal speech—no more than 5–10 Hz of the rise could be due to P_s variations. Öhman and Lindqvist also commented that "the f_0 changes during stressed syllables do not correlate well with the stress-induced [P_s] changes either in phase or in amplitude [p. 4]."

Lieberman did not review most of this evidence and made no attempt to reconcile his claims with the fraction he did review except to dismiss Öhman and Lindqvist's findings as applying to singing not to speech.

Although Lieberman (1968) declared his hypotheses "verified," the overwhelming bulk of research done on the topic since 1967 has not supported his innovative claims and has instead supported the traditional view of the primacy of the larynx in pitch control. New evidence was obtained, as well as refinements and elaborations of the existing types of data. These were:

1. Larynx height correlates with pitch.

Vanderslice (1967) recorded vertical laryngeal movements and P_s during connected speech and showed the former to be better correlated with pitch than was P_s. Quantitative data showing good correlation between larynx height and pitch were obtained by many investigators (Ohala 1972b, Ewan and Krones 1974, Ewan 1976, Shipp 1975a, 1975b, Shipp and Izdebski 1975, Kakita and Hiki 1976). There is undoubtedly some individual variation in this, however, since Lindqvist, Sawashima, and Hirose (1973) and Gandour and Maddieson (1976), each studying a single subject, failed to find substantial correlation between these two parameters. Looking at all the relevant studies, however, there are still more cases where the correlation was found than where it was not. It is reasonable to conclude, then, that the larynx, at least in part by its vertical movements, actively participates in the control of pitch in speech whether it is found on pitch falls or pitch rises, on nonterminal or sentence-terminal elements.

2. Further calibrations of $\Delta F_0 / \Delta P_s$.

Additional calibration of the effect of P_s on pitch were made using refined techniques, including monitoring the activity of the laryngeal muscles during the induced pressure changes (Netsell 1969, Ohala and Ladefoged 1970, Ohala 1970, Lieberman, Knudson, and Mead 1969, Hixon, Mead, and Klatt 1971, Baer 1976, Okamura, Gould, and Tanabe 1976).[5] Table 1 summarizes these and earlier such determinations of $\Delta F_0 / \Delta P_s$. The studies employing excised larynges generally yield higher values than do those involving living subjects, Lieberman's (1967b) study excepted, of course. This is probably due to the excised larynges lacking normal muscle tonus (van den Berg and Tan 1959). Lieberman et al.'s (1969) upper limit of 10 Hz/cm H_2O is substantially lower than that originally claimed by Lieberman. Curiously, Hixon et al. (1971), using the same technique and one of the same subjects involved in the study of Lieberman et al., could not replicate those earlier findings, i.e., did not find values as high as 10 Hz/cm H_2O. Although there may be methodological problems with all of these calibration techniques, there is scant evidence from them to support Lieberman's claim that P_s could be responsible for all or even most of the observed pitch variations in speech. It follows, then, that other factors, presumably the laryngeal muscles, must be causing the pitch changes.

---

[5] Okamura et al. (1976) do not report their results in a way which allows them to be converted to Hz/cm H_2O. However, their data seem much like that of Hixon et al. (1971).

TABLE 1

Values of $\Delta F_o/\Delta P_s$ (in Hz/cm H_2O) from Various Studies

Source	Normal voice	High pitch and falsetto
Mueller (1851)[a]	4.3 ~ 4.5	10 ~ 16
Isshiki (1959)	3.3	
van den Berg and Tan (1959)[a]	5 ~ 13	17 ~ 20
Ladefoged (1963)	5	
Öhman and Lindqvist (1966)	2.9	
Furukawa (1967)[a]	8[b]	
Anthony (1968)[a]	6 ~ 8	
Lieberman, Knudson, and Mead (1969)	3 ~ 10	9 ~ 18
Netsell (1969)	3.5 ~ 9.4	
Ohala and Ladefoged (1970)	2 ~ 4	7 ~ 10
Ohala (1970)	2 ~ 8	
Hixon, Mead, and Klatt (1971)	2 ~ 4	
Baer (1976)	3 ~ 5	
Lieberman (1967)	16 ~ 22	

[a] Used excised larynges.
[b] Average slope of one F_o versus P_s plot.

3. P_s not independent of laryngeal activity.

It was pointed out (by Isshiki 1969, Ohala 1970, 1975a, 1976, van Katwijk 1971, 1974) that P_s variations can be caused in part by changes in glottal and oral impedance, i.e., by anything which would cause reduced air flow, e.g., obstruent closures, reduced mean glottal area, such as occurs during pitch increases (Sonesson 1960, Ishizaka and Flanagan 1972), or increased percentage of closed time in the glottal area function, such as occurs during voice intensity increases (Sonesson 1960, Flanagan 1965). This point has long been well known among speech scientists (Stetson 1928, Peterson 1957, Strenger 1958, Isshiki 1964, Yanagihara and von Leden 1966, Öhman and Lindqvist 1966, Ladefoged 1968, Zemlin 1968, Benguerel 1970, Netsell 1973).

A related fact which no doubt reflects the increase of glottal impedance with increasing pitch is that the minimum pressure drop necessary to maintain voicing is greater for high pitch than for low pitch (Mueller 1851, Isshiki 1959).

Thus, not only is it improbable that P_s variations could cause much of the observed pitch change in speech, it is probable that to some extent the P_s variations are themselves caused by laryngeal activity.

For this reason it is not surprising that good correlations are occasionally found between speech intensity (which is unquestionably causally correlated with P_s) and pitch (Lieberman 1967a, Zee and Hombert 1976), but, again, rather than the correlation implying that one of the parameters causes variation in the other, it reflects the fact that both are heavily influenced by a third parameter, laryngeal activity.

4. Electromyography of laryngeal muscles during speech.

Electromyographic studies of the activity of the laryngeal muscles during speech in a variety of languages (tone, "pitch accent," nontone) showed that they were centrally involved in pitch changes, no matter what type of pitch change was involved. (Ohala and Hirano 1967, Öhman, Mårtensson, Leandersson, and Persson 1967, Fromkin and Ohala 1968, Hirano, Ohala, and Vennard 1969, Hirano and Ohala 1969, Netsell 1969, Lieberman, Sawashima, Harris, and Gay 1970, Ohala 1970, 1972b, Garding, Fujimura, and Hirose 1970, Simada and Hirose 1970, 1971, Erickson and Abramson 1972, Sawashima, Kakita, and Hiki 1973, Atkinson 1973, Fischer-Jørgensen 1974, Collier 1975, Maeda 1975, Shipp 1975a, Erickson and Atkinson 1976, Atkinson and Erickson 1976, Erickson, Liberman, and Niimi 1976). In agreement with the earlier findings for singing, the cricothyroid muscle was found to be the primary force for raising pitch although the lateral cricoarytenoid and vocalis also assisted. In addition, in many studies the sternohyoid and sternothyroid were shown to be active during pitch lowering. (The involvement of the strap muscles in pitch change is not surprising, of course, given the evidence cited above that larynx height varies with pitch.) Typical EMG records are shown in Figures 7, 8, and 9. The pitch and P_s parameters in Figure 7 were discussed earlier; the third parameter shown is the cricothyroid activity. It can be seen that in the

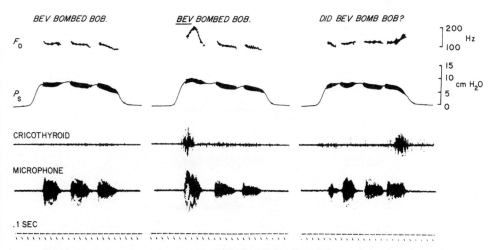

Figure 7. From the top: fundamental frequency (F_0), subglottal air pressure (P_s), cricothyroid activity, microphone signal and .1 sec time standard during three utterances.

first sentence, where there is no pitch rise, this muscle is not active. However, considerable activity is evident during the pitch rises in the other two sentences. Moreover, the degree of activity during the terminal rise in the third sentence, the question, where the involvement of the laryngeal muscles has never been questioned, is of about the same magnitude as the degree of activity associated with the pitch rise on the stressed syllable in the second sentence, where Lieberman would have predicted the laryngeal muscles would show no change in level of activity.

Figure 8 shows F_0 and the activity of the cricothyroid and the sternohyoid muscles. Again, during the rise in pitch on *Bev* the cricothyroid is active, but during the lowered pitch after the rise the cricothyroid is inactive and the sternohyoid shows increased activity. Since the sternohyoid attaches at its upper end to the hyoid bone, it is also occasionally involved in such segmental activities as jaw opening and tongue retraction (Ohala and Hirose 1969). This has led some researchers to discount the role of the sternohyoid in pitch control and to suggest that its activity in such records may be associated only with segmental gestures (Lieberman 1970, Harris 1970). This issue is easily resolved by recording the activity of this muscle during pitch changes in the absence of any segmental gestures, e.g., while humming. Figure 9 (from Ohala 1972b) shows data gathered under such conditions. It shows the sternohyoid active during the lowering of pitch and during the maintenance of low pitch. This finding was recently replicated by Atkinson and Erickson (1976).

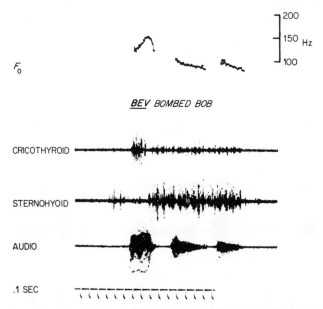

Figure 8.   From the top: fundamental frequency (F_0), cricothyroid activity, sternohyoid activity, microphone signal (audio), and .1 sec time standard during the utterance "**Bev** bombed Bob."

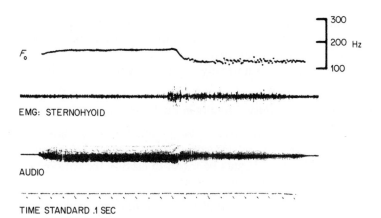

F_0

300

200 Hz

100

EMG: STERNOHYOID

AUDIO

TIME STANDARD .1 SEC

Figure 9. From the top: fundamental frequency (F_0), sternohyoid activity, microphone signal (audio), and .1 sec time standard during a sudden voluntary change in F_0 while the subject phonated with jaw closed.

I should emphasize that the sternohyoid and sternothyroid muscles, although certainly involved in pitch lowering, are not necessarily the only or even the primary muscles responsible for it. This conclusion is based on the fact that these muscles often show no marked activity in speech until after a pitch contour has begun to lower (Sawashima, Kakita, and Hiki 1973, Erickson and Atkinson 1976). Other muscles may be involved in initiating the fall. The main point is that laryngeal muscles do contribute to pitch lowering in speech.

Although there are still reasonable grounds to dispute the involvement of any particular extrinsic muscle in pitch lowering during speech, it would appear necessary that **some** extrinsic muscle(s) be involved in lowering pitch in certain cases where the simple relaxation of the pitch-raising muscles—a possibility raised by Harris (1970)—would not be sufficient. Specifically, there is evidence that as an individual gradually raises pitch, the cricothyroid begins to show activity only at a level of pitch considerably above his lowest pitch, e.g., at 120 or 140 Hz in a male speaker capable of reaching 75–80 Hz. In order to reach such lower pitch levels—quite common in speech—relaxation of the cricothyroid would not help.

5. Investigations of pulmonic activity in speech.

Studies of the pulmonic respiratory muscles and changes in lung volume, although still quite scanty, failed in many cases to show the kind of pulmonic activity during pitch rises on stressed syllables which would be expected if Lieberman's hypothesis were correct. Ladefoged (1967) reports that in an extensive EMG study of the respiratory muscles, increased activity was found on stressed syllables, whether these were emphatically stressed or not. However, Munro and Adams (1971) and van Katwijk (1971, 1974) failed to replicate this finding, except that van Katwijk did find increased activity on emphatically stressed syllables. In a very preliminary plethysmographic study (measurement of lung volume) involving only three subjects, I invariably found increased lung volume decrement (indicative of extra expiratory activity) only on emphatically stressed, not on normally stressed syllables (Ohala 1977a).

4.2 The Role of the Extrinsic Muscles in Pitch Control

Yet to be satisfactorily resolved is the question of exactly how the extrinsic laryngeal muscles and the related correlation of larynx height and pitch are involved in pitch control. It may be useful to classify the various opinions on this question into the following categories:

1. They (the extrinsic muscles) play at most only an ancillary role in pitch regulation.
2. They play a central role by changing (lengthening and/or shortening) the vocal cords.
3. They play a central role in some other way than by changing vocal cord length.

Sokowlowsky (1943) and Faaborg-Andersen (1964), among others, have espoused (1). Sokowlowsky feels the extrinsic muscles move the larynx about in the neck in order to allow the intrinsic muscles to do their task more efficiently. However, he does not go into detail on this point. It is also the "received opinion" among voice teachers that singers should not shift the position of their larynx to change pitch (Luchsinger and Arnold 1965). This is undoubtedly true, but it need not apply to ordinary speech.

The second view has been advocated by (among others) Sonninen (1956, 1968), Zenker and Zenker (1960), Zenker (1964), Lindqvist (1972), and Erickson, Liberman, and Niimi (1976). Zenker and Zenker suggest a variety of ways the extrinsic muscles could change vocal cord length, whereas the others generally focus on a specific muscle or group of muscles which might perform the task: Sonninen on the sternothyroid, Lindqvist on the pharyngeal constrictors, and Erickson et al. on the supralaryngeal muscles which attach to the hyoid bone. All of these hypotheses are quite promising and require further research to test them.

In 1972 I presented evidence for the third position, suggesting that it was the **vertical**, not simply the anterior–posterior tension of the vocal cords which could affect pitch. Conceivably the vertical stretching of the soft tissues of the larynx may cause the vocal cords to be free of overlying tissues (the false vocal cords) and in that way allow freer and more rapid vibration. Another possibility is that vertical stretching thins and vertical compression thickens the cords, thereby affecting their rate of vibration. Stevens (1975) suggests that the vertical shifts of the larynx may create changes in the vocal cord properties which would affect their sensitivity to P_s. Shipp and Haller (1972), Shipp

(1975a, 1975b), and Ewan (1976) are also advocates of the "vertical tension" hypothesis. Clearly more evidence is needed to test this hypothesis.

Whatever might be the way in which vertical larynx shifts affect pitch, there is evidence that this mechanism is less directly involved in pitch raising than in pitch lowering. Ohala and Ewan (1973) sampled pitch and larynx position (using the "thyroumbrometer" (Ewan and Krones 1974), a photoelectric device which tracks the shadow of the laryngeal contour cast on it) while subjects execute rapid pitch changes. Figure 10 shows a sample of the data. In Figure 11 the average larynx height (from several tokens similar to that in Figure 10 as produced by one subject) is plotted against the F_0. Both of these figures show first of all the good correlation between larynx height and pitch; however, they also show a slight phase shift between the two during the pitch

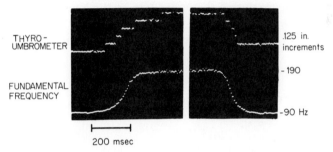

Figure 10. Synchronized variations in fundamental frequency (F_0) and larynx height (transduced by the thyroumbrometer) during a sudden F_0 increase (on the left) and a sudden F_0 decrease (on the right) (from Ohala and Ewan 1973).

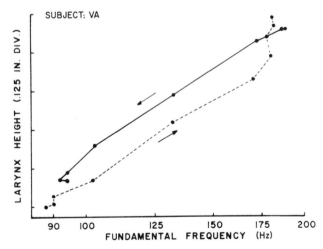

Figure 11. Larynx height plotted as a function of fundamental frequency, F_0, during rapid changes in F_0 (from tokens similar to that in Figure 10) (from Ohala and Ewan 1973).

rise—i.e., after the target high pitch is reached during the rising contour, the larynx continues to rise. In the case of the falling contour, the two parameters are more closely synchronized. Similar records presented by Kakita and Hiki (1976) show the same thing. This may mean that the cricothyroid is the primary pitch raiser, with secondary (and somewhat delayed) assistance from the muscles that raise the larynx; for pitch lowering, though—at least for rapid drops in pitch—the larynx height mechanism may be primary.

Further support for the "vertical tension" hypothesis comes from cases of bilateral cricothyroid paralysis in which patients are still able to vary pitch (although over a more restricted range, of course). In one such case, lateral X-rays taken at two different pitches revealed that there was no change in the rotation of the thyroid and cricoid cartilages with respect to each other—and thus we may presume no anterior–posterior stretching of the vocal cords—but the larynx was higher during the production of the higher pitch (Luchsinger and Arnold 1965).

More evidence relevant to these questions will be presented in the next sections.

5. FIRST STEPS TOWARD EXPLAINING UNIVERSAL TONE PATTERNS

Although the study of laryngeal physiology and the study of the way tones pattern in languages are both relatively far along, the application of the physiological research to questions in tonology is very recent and therefore somewhat primitive. There are more unanswered questions in this area than there are answered ones. Nevertheless we may take some consolation in the fact that the questions are highly specific and the various hypotheses offered as answers to the questions are generally explicit and detailed enough to be testable.

In the phonological literature, there is considerable evidence that tones interact with certain classes of speech segments in very specific ways (see Chapter III, by Hombert, this volume, as well as Hyman 1973, Hombert 1975, and Hombert, Ohala, and Ewan 1976). As Hombert discusses in Chapter III, in seeking explanations for these interactions what we need to show is that in the process of producing (intentionally) certain speech sounds or sequences of speech sounds, conditions are created which (unintentionally) affect other speech sounds in a purely mechanical way, that is, due to the physical constraints of our sound producing or sound receiving mechanisms (see Ohala 1974a, 1975b for elaborations of this point). Such unintentional distortions of the speech signal can, in time, be reinterpreted as intended parts of the signal and even outlive the original sounds which fostered their development. Thus it must have been with the nasal vowels in languages such as

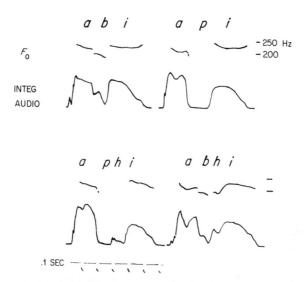

Figure 12.   Fundamental frequency (F_0) and the integrated, rectified microphone signal during four Hindi nonsense words; .1 sec time standard at bottom (from Ohala 1974a).

French and Hindi. Originally we may suppose the vowels were unintentionally nasalized due to a purely mechanical assimilation to adjacent nasal consonants; when the nasal consonants dropped out the nasalization remained on the vowels.

Since the interaction between tone and segments is fully covered in Chapter III of this volume, I will restrict my discussion to two aspects of this question. The first concerns the commonly observed phenomenon that voiceless oral obstruents produce high tone (or a higher variant of a tone) on the following vowel, whereas voiced oral obstruents produce low tone (or a lower variant) on the following vowel (Haudricourt 1961, Cheng 1973). The second question I will discuss concerns the influence of vowels on pitch. There will be some overlap between my discussions here and those in Chapter III, but to insure an understanding of the earlier part of this chapter this discussion is necessary.

5.1 Interaction of Tone and Oral Obstruents

The different effects on tone produced by voiceless and voiced oral obstruents are manifested phonetically today even in nontonal languages,[6] e.g., Hindi, as is evident in the pitch curves in Figure 12. The figure shows the

---

[6] Hombert (1975) and Jeel (1975) provide good reviews of the literature (as well as original contributions) on F_0 differences after voiced/voiceless stops.

pitch and speech intensity for Hindi nonsense words /abi/, /api/, /aphi/, and
/abhi/. It is clear that the pitch at the onset of the second vowel is slightly
higher after the two voiceless stops, lower after the two voiced stops. Diachronically this effect has given rise to the introduction or multiplication of
tones (Hombert 1975). In fact Punjabi has tones today, presumably due to the
influence of an earlier consonant system similar to the one Hindi has.

We do not yet know the reason for this effect of the voicing distinction on
pitch, although considerable progress has been made on the problem in the
last few years. An early explanation for it was that the aerodynamic conditions
created by the voiceless/voiced obstruents, i.e., high air flow after voiceless,
especially voiceless aspirated, obstruents, and low air flow after voiced obstruents caused the high and low pitches, respectively (Ohala 1973). This was
an appealing hypothesis in part because it explained why these consonants
should affect the following, not the preceding vowel. However, there are apparently serious problems with the hypothesis. First, the differing aerodynamic
conditions present at obstruent release last for only a few milliseconds after
voicing begins, whereas the effect of these consonants on the pitch of the
following vowels is known to last for 100 msec or more (Hombert 1975).
Moreover, although the air flow differences between voiceless and voiced obstruents is as described above at the moment of release, there is some evidence
that by the time voicing starts, glottal air flow after voiceless aspirated stops
may in fact be **less** than that at vowel onset after a voiced stop. (This is evident
in data published by Isshiki and Ringel 1964, van Hattum and Worth 1967.)
In any case, the P_s is less at vowel onset following an aspirated stop as opposed
to a voiced or voiceless unaspirated stop. This is shown in Figure 13 where
the P_s and microphone signal are given for two utterances identical except for
the medial stops. P_s builds up (from the level on the vowels) during the closed
portions of both stops. At release of the voiced stop the P_s remains at this high
level and then gradually returns to normal. After the release of the aspirated
stop, however, the P_s decreases markedly (due to the rapid outflow of air) and
then gradually builds back up at vowel onset. But P_s is lower at vowel onset

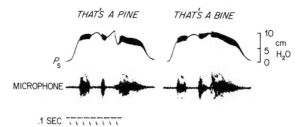

Figure 13.   From the top: subglottal air pressure (P_s), microphone signal, and .1 sec time
standard during two utterances (from Ohala 1975a).

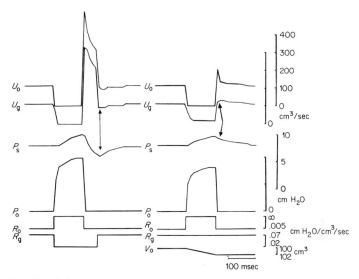

Figure 14. Simulation of aerodynamic events during two VCV utterances. On the left C = voiceless aspirated stop; on the right C = voiced stop. Upper four output parameters: oral airflow (V_o), glottal airflow (U_g), subglottal air pressure (P_s), and oral air pressure (P_o); three input parameters: oral constriction air resistance (R_o), glottal resistance (R_g), oral volume (V_o) (from Ohala 1975a).

after the /ph/ than the /b/. P_s data in other studies reveal the same basic pattern (Ladefoged 1963, Ohala and Ohala 1973).[7]

These relationships between stop type and the air flow and P_s at vowel onset are also predicted by an aerodynamic model of speech (Ohala 1975a, 1976). The input and output of the model for intervocalic voiced and voiceless aspirated stops are given in Figure 14. In the figure, the bottom three curves, oral resistance (R_o), glottal resistance (R_g), and oral volume (V_o) (not given for the voiceless aspirated stop), are the independent parameters, i.e., the input to the model and the top four curves; oral air flow (U_o), glottal air flow (U_g), subglottal air pressure (P_s), and oral air pressure (P_o) are the dependent parameters, i.e., the output of the model. Stop closure occurs when the oral resistance becomes infinite. The main difference between the two stop types is the presence versus the absence of glottal opening (reduction of glottal resistance) when the oral closure occurs. The above-mentioned relations of

[7] A further, if indirect, indication of the reality of this difference in P_s after voiced and voiceless stops can be found in the various reports that vowels have greater intensity following voiced as opposed to voiceless aspirated stops (House and Fairbanks 1953, Lehiste and Peterson 1959). This makes sense only when we realize that voice intensity is largely a function of P_s and that the P_s on vowels will vary as a function of the type of stop preceding as described above.

glottal air flow and P_s at vowel onset may be seen by comparing the values of the relevant curves at the points marked by arrows.[8]

Given these fairly substantial problems with the aerodynamic hypothesis, it seems best to look for explanations in terms of how vocal cord state could be differentially affected by voiced and voiceless obstruent articulation. Two such hypotheses have been proposed.

Halle and Stevens (1971) note that the degree of stiffness of the vocal cords can determine whether or not voicing will occur, i.e., stiff vocal cords will inhibit and slack vocal cords will facilitate voicing. They suggest that it is the vocal cords' stiffness and slackness during voiceless and voiced stops, respectively, which also affects the pitch of surrounding vowels. This is an interesting and innovative hypothesis because traditionally either vocal cord abduction or the reduction of the transglottal pressure drop have been cited as necessary and sufficient conditions for cessation of voicing during voiceless stops (and there is ample evidence that these two conditions do occur during voiceless obstruents). But there are some problems with the hypothesis, as discussed in Hombert's chapter and in Anderson's chapter, this volume.

A second hypothesis suggests itself from the fairly well-established fact that larynx height is slightly higher for voiceless than voiced stops (Jespersen 1889 Hudgins and Stetson 1935, Ewan and Krones 1974, Ewan 1976; further references on this point are given by Slis and Cohen 1969). If it is then true, as suggested above, that, other things being equal, vocal cord tension varies with larynx height, the different pitch on vowels following the different obstruents is accounted for. Presumably the lower larynx during voiced stops is a consequence of the need of the vocal tract to expand in order to accommodate more air in the oral cavity so that it can maintain the positive transglottal pressure drop necessary for voicing. In Figure 14 it can be seen that oral volume (V_o), one of the input parameters to the aerodynamic model, increases during the simulated voiced stop. This turned out to be necessary in order to maintain the glottal air flow necessary for voicing. Without this volume increase P_o would become equal to P_s (and thus the transglottal pressure drop and glottal air flow would fall to zero) within 20 msec of the stop closure onset.

---

[8] It may be worth mentioning that when originally working on this problem, it was the predictions of the model regarding the differences in air flow after stops which were discovered first, and only then was the literature searched to try to verify the predictions—and, as mentioned, some support was found for them. This is one function of models: to tell us what to look for, to reveal to us the logical consequences of our assumptions, so that by comparing the model's predictions with "real" data we can see whether those assumptions are reasonable or not. Some may think model making is a futile exercise since one can only get out of a model whatever one puts into it, and therefore its output ought to be known beforehand. This is not necessarily the case, however. As Simon (1969) notes, simulation studies can provide new knowledge because "even when we have correct premises, it may be very difficult to discover what they imply. All correct reasoning is a grand system of tautologies, but only God can make use of that fact. The rest of us must painstakingly and fallibly tease out the consequences of our assumptions [p. 15]."

Data which tend to support this reasoning were presented by Ewan (1976), who found the difference in larynx height between voiced and voiceless stops to be greater at stop release than at stop onset. Furthermore he showed that this difference in larynx height persists for some time (more than 100 msec) into the following vowel. All of this is compatible with the fact that stops affect the pitch of following not preceding vowels and that the pitch perturbations last for over 100 msec.

There is, unfortunately, at least one problem with this hypothesis, too. Namely, given that the data suggest that the larynx is actively depressed for voiced stops vis-à-vis sonorants, it should be the case that pitch on vowels after voiced stops is also perturbed downwards in comparison with that for sonorants. However, this latter prediction is not borne out: The available data suggest that pitch following voiced stops is substantially similar to that following sonorants and that it is the pitch following voiceless stops that is perturbed upwards (Lea 1972, Hombert 1975, Jeel 1975). A great deal of research is currently going on to attempt to resolve these problems.

5.2 The Influence of Vowels on Pitch

It has been noted for over 50 years that, other things being equal, the average pitch of vowels shows a systematic correlation with vowel height, that is, the higher the vowel, the higher the pitch (Crandall 1925, House and Fairbanks 1953, Lea 1972). The difference in pitch between high and low vowels may be as much as 25 Hz. Although such a pitch perturbation is of the same order of magnitude as that caused by consonants, there are remarkably few instances in which vowels are claimed to have triggered the development of tones. I suspect the reason for this lies in the constraints of the auditory system and not in the articulatory system (see speculations on this in Hombert, this volume, and Hombert *et al.* 1976). Nevertheless the mechanism causing this pitch perturbation is of interest since it may provide additional evidence on some of the hypothesized ways pitch can be changed other than by action of the intrinsic laryngeal muscles.

Two hypotheses are currently entertained as explanations for this effect. One, the "coupling" hypothesis, suggests that during the production of relatively close, constricted vowels, the acoustic impedance of the vocal tract is high enough to "dictate" to the vocal cords the frequencies they can vibrate at, namely, at or very close to the resonant frequencies of the vocal tract. Since high, close vowels have low first resonances—closest to the F_0 of voice— they would be expected to have the greatest effect on pitch (Lieberman 1970, Atkinson 1973). An early mathematical model of the vocal cords' vibration constructed by Flanagan and Landgraf (1968) did reveal such interaction between vocal cord vibration and the vocal tract, but in later, more sophisticated models this phenomenon was far less evident (Ishizaka and Flanagan 1972).

According to the "tongue pull" hypothesis (Ladefoged 1964, Lehiste 1970), the tongue, in articulating a high close vowel, somehow pulls on the vocal cords and causes greater tension in them, thus raising the pitch slightly. Ohala and Eukel (1976) attempted to test the two hypotheses by measuring the effect on the average pitch of vowels when speakers utter them with and without small wooden blocks propping open their jaws. Earlier research by Lindblom and Sundberg (1971a) showed that speakers can utter acoustically normal high vowels even with their jaws propped open by compensatorily bunching their tongues up more and thus presumably increasing the pull of the tongue on the structures it is connected to, including the larynx. Thus the test allows one of the hypothesized causal factors, tongue pull, to vary while the other causal factor, vocal tract impedance, remains constant. An enhancement of the pitch difference between high and low vowels when speaking with propped open jaw would support the tongue-pull hypothesis; no such enhancement would support the coupling hypothesis.

In fact, the pitch difference was enhanced. This was taken as support of the tongue-pull hypothesis, and therefore may be taken as further support for the hypothesis discussed above that the pitch of voice can be controlled in part by varying the vertical tension of the vocal cords. (See Ohala and Eukel 1976 for more details of the test and for further arguments in support of the conclusion.)[9]

5.3 Falling versus Rising Tones

There are intriguing reports in the tonal literature that falling tones behave differently than rising tones, namely, that they are more numerous in tonal inventories of languages (Cheng 1973), that the pitch interval between the tonal sequence low–high is more likely to be reduced than the interval between a high–low sequence (Hyman 1973a), that falling contours must cover a greater pitch range than a rising contour in order to be perceived with a given level of "prominence" (Black 1970, 't Hart 1975). (For further evidence of such asymmetries see also Hombert 1975.) The perceptual data may simply reveal listeners' "knowledge" of an articulation-caused asymmetry between rising and falling pitch contours, or it could be the reverse: The asymmetry may be of auditory origin, and speakers may modify their articulation to accommodate the listener.

[9] To keep this review as balanced as possible, I should note that objections have been raised against the tongue-pull hypothesis, too. One of these is that larynx height is in certain cases **inversely** related to vowel height, just the opposite of what would be expected if the tongue were pulling on the larynx during high vowels (Ladefoged, DeClerk, Lindau, and Papcun 1972, Atkinson 1973). It is not feasible to review the details of this minor dispute here. Arguments can be found in Ohala 1972b, 1977b, and Ohala and Eukel 1976 as to why this counterevidence to the tongue-pull hypothesis may be irrelevant to this issue.

Some studies by Ohala and Ewan (1973) and Sundberg (1973), although they do not reveal the exact causes of the effect, do suggest that it is at least articulatory in nature. (This does not rule out the possibility that it is both articulatory and auditory in nature.) Briefly, both studies showed that speakers are able to produce a falling pitch over a given pitch interval much faster than a rising pitch over the same interval. (In Sundberg's study this was true only of speakers with no voice training.) This effect is evident in Figure 10, which is from the study by Ohala and Ewan.

Of course, we should be cautious in attempting to apply these results to speech and to tone production, but they may indicate that since falling tones can be produced faster than rising tones, they make better tonal contrasts— are perceptually more salient—and for that reason are found in greater number in languages. Also, since they can be accomplished quicker, they might be less likely than rising tones to "spill over" onto the next syllable. This is an area where more research is needed.

5.4 Downdrift

Most (all?) languages exhibit a gradual fall in pitch from the beginning to the end of an utterance, that is, over a stretch of speech that has been called variously a "phonological phrase," a "breath group," or a "syntagm." (This need not apply to questions, however.) In many tone languages this results in successive tones becoming phonetically lower and lower in pitch until, at the end of the phrase, the high tones could be phonetically as low or even lower than the low tones at the beginning of the phrase. This is called "downdrift" in African languages but is evident in nontone languages as well (Collier 1972, Weitzman 1970). Breckenridge (1977) has, in fact, recently demonstrated the auditory reality of downdrift (or the "declination effect," as she calls it) in English. Listeners judged the peaks of two pitch prominences in a synthesized sentence to be equal even though the second was a few hertz lower than the first. The causes or origins of downdrift are not known, but it is possible to consider the following three hypotheses for it.

Maeda (1975) suggests that the larynx progressively lowers during a single breath group as a result of its linkage to the sternum which should lower as lung volume decreases, and that given the correlation between larynx height and pitch, this movement should cause a gradual lowering of pitch. Ewan (1976) showed, however, that the larynx normally moves upwards during expiration (on which speech is superimposed), not downwards.

One might also suppose that a gradual reduction in P_s due to the pulmonic system's having to work harder (against the elastic recoil force of the lungs and thorax) to maintain a positive P_s as lung volume decreases might cause a gradual lowering of pitch. This hypothesis encounters the same difficulty noted above for Lieberman's hypothesis, namely, that the magnitude of the observed downdrift usually exceeds what could be accounted for by P_s variations.

A third hypothesis—one which I personally believe in—is that the effect is due to active laryngeally caused changes in vocal cord tension, and that it is not an "automatic" effect at all, but is purposeful. This is superficially reasonable because the gradual pitch decrement in utterances serves a useful linguistic purpose in signaling clause and sentence boundaries. We might say (with apologies to Voltaire) that if downdrift were not purposeful to start out with, speakers would soon enough make it so since it is so useful in speech. Moreover, there is some evidence in favor of this hypothesis, namely, that the rate of pitch decrement is inversely proportional to the length of the utterance it spans (Weitzman 1970, Hirose 1971, Collier 1972, Silverstein 1976). This would be a very amazing finding if the slow pitch fall were a purely mechanical effect determined by decreasing lung volume or the like—in which case the rate should be about the same no matter how long the utterance—on the other hand, it is a very reasonable finding if it is actively and purposefully controlled by the speaker. This still leaves open, of course, the question of how this apparently universal pattern originated.

REFERENCES

Abramson, A. C. 1972. Discussion of plenary address by J.-C. Lafon. In A. Rigault and R. Charbonneau (Eds.), *Proceedings of the 7th International Congress of Phonetic Sciences*. The Hague: Mouton. Pp. 25–26.

Allen, W. S. 1953. *Phonetics in ancient India*. Oxford Univ. Press.

Anthony, J. K. F. 1968. Study of the larynx II. *Work in Progress, 2*, 77–82.

Arnold, G. E. 1961. Physiology and pathology of the cricothyroid muscle. *Laryngoscope, 71*, 687–753.

Atkinson, J. E. 1973. Aspects of intonation in speech: Implications from an experimental study of fundamental frequency. Unpublished Ph.D. dissertation, University of Connecticut.

Atkinson, J. E., & Erickson, D. E. 1976. The function of strap muscles in speech: Pitch lowering or jaw opening. *Journal Acousical Society of America, 60*, S65.

Baer, T. 1975. Investigation of phonation using excised larynxes. Unpublished dissertation, MIT.

Baer, T. 1976. Effects of subglottal pressure changes on sustained phonation. *Journal of the Acoustical Society of America 60*, S65.

Benguerel, A. P. 1970. Some physiological aspects of stress in French. *Natural Language Studies*. University of Michigan Phonetics Laboratory, *4*.

van den Berg, Jw. 1958. Myoelastic-aerodynamic theory of voice production. *Journal Speech and Hearing Research, 1*, 227–244.

van den Berg, Jw., & Tan, T. S. 1959. Results of experiments with human larynxes. *Practica Oto-Rhino-Laryngologica, 21*, 425–450.

Black, J. W. 1970. The magnitude of pitch inflection. In B. Hala, M. Romportl, & P. Janota (Eds.), *Proceedings of the 6th International Congress of Phonetic Sciences, Prague, 7–13 September 1967*. Prague: Czechoslovak Academy of Sciences. Pp. 177–181.

Bouhuys, A. (Ed.). 1968. Sound production in man. *Annals of the New York Academy of Sciences*, *155*(1).

Breckenridge, J. 1977. The declination effect. *Journal of the Acoustical Society of America*, *60*, S90.

Broad, D. J. 1973. Phonation. In F. D. Minifie, T. J. Hixon, & F. Williams (Eds.), *Normal Aspects of Speech, Hearing, and Language*. Englewood Cliffs: Prentice-Hall. Pp. 127–167.

Cheng, C. C. 1973. A quantitative study of tone in Chinese. *Journal of Chinese Linguistics*, *1*, 93–110.

Collier, R. 1972. *From pitch to intonation*. Ph.D. dissertation, University of Louvain.

Collier, R. 1975. Physiological correlates of intonation patterns. *Journal of the Acoustical Society of America*, *58*, 249–255.

Crandall, I. B. 1925. The sounds of speech. *Bell System Technical Journal*, *4*, 586–622.

Critchley, M., & Kubik, C. S. 1925. The mechanism of speech and deglutition in progressive bulbar palsy. *Brain*, *48*, 492–534.

Damste, P. H. 1968. X-ray study of phonation. *Folia Phoniatrica*, *20*, 65–88.

Derwing, B. L. 1973. *Transformational grammar as a theory of language acquisition*. Cambridge University Press.

Di Cristo, A. 1975. Soixante-et-dix ans de recherches en prosodie. *Travaux de l'Institut de Phonétique d'Aix-en-Provence, Etudes phonétiques*, *1*.

Dixit, R. P. 1975. Neuromuscular aspects of laryngeal control: With special reference to Hindi. Unpublished Ph.D. dissertation, University of Texas.

Erickson, D., & Abramson, A. S. 1972. Electromyographic study of the tones in Thai. *Status Reports on Speech Research*, Haskins Laboratories, *SR-31/32*, 231–236.

Erickson, D., & Atkinson, J. E. 1976. The function of the strap muscles in speech. *Status Reports on Speech Research*, Haskins Laboratories, *SR 45/46*, 205–210.

Erickson, D. M., Liberman, M. Y., & Niimi, S. 1976. The geniohyoid and the role of the strap muscles in pitch control. *Journal of the Acoustical Society of America 60*, S63.

Ewan, W. G. 1976. Laryngeal behavior in speech. Unpublished Ph.D. dissertation, University of California, Berkeley.

Ewan, W. G., & Krones, R. 1974. Measuring larynx movement using the thyroumbrometer. *Journal of Phonetics*, *2*, 327–335.

Faaborg-Andersen, K. 1957. Electromyographic investigation of intrinsic laryngeal muscles in humans. *Acta Physiologica Scandinavica*, *41*, Suppl. 140.

Faaborg-Andersen, K. 1964. Electromyography of the laryngeal muscles in man. In D. W. Brewer (Ed.), *Research potentials in voice physiology*. State Univ. of New York. New York: University Publishers, Inc. Pp. 105–123.

Faaborg-Andersen, K. 1965. *Electromyography of laryngeal muscles in humans: Technics and results*. Basel: Karger.

Fabre, P. 1957. Un procédé électrique percutane d'inscription de l'accolement glottique au cours de la phonation: Glottographie de haute fréquence. Bulletin, Académie Nationale de Médecine, *141*, 66–69.

Fant, G. 1960. *Acoustic theory of speech production*. The Hague: Mouton.

Ferrein, A. 1741. De la formation de la voix de l'homme. *Mémoires d'Académie Royale des Sciences*, *51*, 409–442.

Feyerabend, P. K. 1968. How to be a good empiricist: A plea for tolerance in matters epistemological. In P. H. Nidditch (Ed.), *The philosophy of science*. Oxford Univ. Press. Pp. 12–39.

Fischer-Jørgensen, E. 1974. Electromyographic investigation of Danish consonants, stress, and stød. *Annual Report of the Institute of Phonetics, Univ. of Copenhagen*, *8*, 203–206.

Flanagan, J. L. 1965. *Speech analysis, synthesis, and perception*. New York: Academic Press.

Flanagan, J. L., Ishizaka, K., & Shipley, K. L. 1975. Synthesis of speech from a dynamic model of the vocal cords and vocal tract. *Bell System Technical Journal*, *54*, 485–506.

Flanagan, J. L., & Landgraf, L. 1968. Self-oscillating source for vocal tract synthesizers. *IEEE Transactions on Audio*, *16*, 57–64.

Fromkin, V. A., & Ohala, J. 1968. Laryngeal control and a model of speech production. *Preprints of the speech symposium, Kyoto.* (Reprinted in *UCLA Working Papers in Phonetics, 10,* 98–110.)

Fujimura, O., & Lindqvist, J. 1971. Sweep-tone measurements of vocal-tract characteristics. *Journal of the Acoustical Society of America, 49,* 541–558.

Furukawa, M. 1967. A study of the mechanism of phonation using excised larynges [in Japanese]. *Oto-Rhino-Laryngological Clinic, Kyoto, 60,* 145–181.

Gandour, J., & Maddieson, I. 1976. Measuring larynx height in Standard Thai using the crico-thyrometer. *UCLA Working Papers in Phonetics, 33,* 160–190.

Garding, E., Fujimura, O., & Hirose, H. 1970. Laryngeal control of Swedish word tone: A preliminary report of an EMG study. *Annual Bulletin,* Research Institute of Logopedics and Phoniatrics, *4,* 45–54.

Grammont, M. 1965. *Traité de phonétique* (2nd ed.). Paris: Librairie Delagrave.

Greenberg, J. H. 1970. Some generalizations concerning glottalic consonants, especially implosives. *International Journal of American Linguistics, 36,* 123–145.

Haden, E. G. 1938. The physiology of French consonant changes. *Language Dissertations, 26.*

Halle, M. 1954. Why and how do we study the sounds of speech? In H. J. Mueller (Ed.), *Report of the 5th Annual Round Table Meeting on Linguistics and Language Teaching.* Washington, D.C.: Georgetown Univ. Pp. 73–83.

Halle, M., & Stevens, K. N. 1971. A note on laryngeal features. *Quarterly Progress Report,* Research Laboratory of Electronics, MIT, *101,* 198–213.

Hanson, R. J. 1975. Fundamental frequency dynamics in VCV sequences. Paper delivered at 8th International Congress of Phonetic Sciences, Leeds, August.

Harris, K. S. 1970. Physiological aspects of articulatory behavior. *Status Reports on Speech Research,* Haskins Laboratories, *SR 23,* 49–68.

't Hart, J. 1975. Discriminability of the magnitude of pitch movements in speech-like signals. Paper delivered at 8th International Congress of Phonetic Sciences, Leeds, August.

Haudricourt, A. G. 1961. Bipartition et tripartition des systèmes de tons dans quelques langues d'Extrême Orient. *Bulletin de la Société Linguistique de Paris, 56,* 163–180.

Herries, J. 1773. *The elements of speech.* London. (Reprinted: Meuston: The Scolar Press, 1968.)

Hirano, M., Koike, Y., & von Leden, H. 1967. The sternohyoid muscle during phonation. *Acta Oto-Laryngologica, 64,* 500–507.

Hirano, M., & Ohala, J. J. 1969. Use of hooked-wire electrodes for electromyography of the intrinsic laryngeal muscles. *Journal of Speech and Hearing Research, 12,* 362–373.

Hirano,, M., Ohala, J. J., & Vennard, W. 1969. The function of laryngeal muscles in regulating fundamental frequency and intensity of phonation. *Journal of Speech and Hearing Research, 12,* 616–628.

Hirose, M. 1971. On Japanese pitch accent: An acoustic analysis. *Monthly Internal Memorandum.* Phonology Laboratory, Berkeley, May, pp. 16–40.

Hixon, T. J., Mead, J., & Klatt, D. H. 1971. Influence of forced transglottal pressure changes on vocal fundamental frequency. *Journal of the Acoustical Society of America, 49,* 105.

Hombert, J. M. 1975. Towards a theory of tonogenesis: An empirical, physiologically, and perceptually-based account of the development of tonal contrasts in language. Unpublished Ph.D. dissertation, University of California, Berkeley.

Hombert, J. M., Ohala, J. J., & Ewan, W. G. 1976. Tonogenesis: Theories and queries. *Report of the Phonology Laboratory,* Berkeley, *1,* 48–77.

House, A. S., & Fairbanks, G. 1953. The influence of consonant environment upon the secondary acoustical characteristics of vowels. *Journal of the Acoustical Society of America, 25,* 105–113.

Hudgins, C., & Stetson, R. H. 1935. Voicing of consonants by depression of larynx. *Archives Néerlandaises de Phonétique Expérimentale, 11,* 1–28.

Husson, R. 1950. Etudes des phénomènes physiologiques et acoustiques fondamentaux de la voix chantée. *Revue Scientifique, 88,* 67–112; 131–146; 217–235.

Hyman, L. M. (Ed.). 1973a. Consonant types and tone. *Southern California Occasional Papers in Linguistics, 1.*

Hyman, L. 1973b. The role of consonant types in natural tonal assimilation. In L. Hyman (Ed.), Consonant types and tone. *Southern California Occasional Papers in Linguistics, 1,* 151–179.

Ishizaka, K., & Flanagan, J. L. 1972. Synthesis of voiced sounds from a two-mass model of the vocal cords. *Bell System Technical Journal, 51,* 1233–1268.

Isshiki, N. 1959. Regulatory mechanism of the pitch and volume of voice. *Oto-Rhino-Laryngological Clinic,* Kyoto, *52,* 1065–1094.

Isshiki, N. 1964. Regulatory mechanism of voice intensity variation. *Journal of Speech and Hearing Research, 7,* 17–29.

Issihiki, N. 1969. Remarks on mechanisms for vocal intensity variations. *Journal of Speech and Hearing Research, 12,* 669–672.

Isshiki, N., & Ringel, R. 1964. Air flow during the production of selected consonants. *Journal of Speech and Hearing Research, 7,* 233–244.

Jeel, V. 1975. An investigation of the fundamental frequency of vowels after various Danish consonants, in particular stop consonants. *Annual Report of the Institute of Phonetics, Univ. of Copenhagen, 9,* 191–211.

Jespersen, O. 1889. *The articulations of speech sounds represented by means of analphabetic symbols.* Marburg in Hessen: N. G. Elwert.

Kagaya, R., & Hirose, H. 1975. Fiberoptic electromyographic and acoustic analyses of Hindi stop consonants. *Annual Bulletin,* Research Institute of Logopedics and Phoniatrics, *9,* 27–46.

Kakita, Y., & Hiki, S. 1976. Investigation of laryngeal control in speech by use of thyrometer. *Journal of the Acoustical Society of America, 59,* 669–674.

Katsuki, Y. 1950. The function of the phonatory muscles. *Japanese Journal of Physiology, 1,* 29–36.

van Katwijk, A. 1971. Subglottal pressure and linguistic stress. *IPO Annual Progress Report,* Eindhoven, *6,* 31–34.

van Katwijk, A. 1974. Accentuation in Dutch: An experimental study. Ph.D. dissertation, Utrecht Univ.

Kimura, N. 1961. Electromyographic study of the extrinsic muscles of the larynx. *Oto-Rhino-Laryngological Clinic,* Kyoto, *54,* 481.

Ladefoged, P. 1963. Some physiological parameters in speech. *Language and Speech, 6,* 109–119.

Ladefoged, P. 1964. *A phonetic study of West African Languages.* Cambridge Univ. Press.

Ladefoged, P. 1967. *Three areas of experimental phonetics.* Oxford Univ. Press.

Ladefoged, P. 1968. Linguistic aspects of respiratory phenomena. In A. Bouhuys (Ed.), *Sound production in man. Annuals of the New York Academy of Sciences, 155*(1), 141–151.

Ladefoged, P. 1971. *Preliminaries to linguistic phonetics.* Chicago Univ. Press.

Ladefoged, P., DeClerk, J., Lindau, M., & Papcun, G. 1972. An auditory–motor theory of speech production. *UCLA Working Papers in Phonetics, 22,* 48–75.

Lea, W. A. 1972. Intonational cues to the constituent structure and phonemics of spoken English. Ph.D. dissertation, Purdue Univ.

Lehiste, I. 1970. *Suprasegmentals.* MIT Press.

Lehiste, I., & Peterson, G. E. 1959. Vowel amplitude and phonemic stress in American English. *Journal of the Acoustical Society of America, 31,* 428–435.

Lieberman, P. 1967a. Intonation and the syntactic processing of speech. In W. Wathen-Dunn (Ed.), *Models for the perception of speech and visual form.* Cambridge, Mass.: MIT Press. Pp. 314–319.

Lieberman, P. 1967b. *Intonation, perception, and language.* Cambridge, Mass.: MIT Press.

Lieberman, P. 1968. On the structure of prosody. *Zeitschrift für Phonetik, Sprachwissenschaft, und Kommunikationforschung, 21,* 157–163.

Lieberman, P. 1970. A study of prosodic features. *Status Reports on Speech Research,* Haskins Laboratories, *SR-23,* 179–208.

Lieberman, P. 1975. *On the origins of language.* New York: Macmillan.

Lieberman, P., Knudson, R., & Mead, J. 1969. Determination of the rate of change of fundamental frequency with respect to subglottal air pressure during sustained phonation. *Journal of the Acoustical Society of America, 45*, 1537–1543.

Lieberman, P., Sawashima, M., Harris, K. S., & Gay, T. 1970. The articulatory implementation of breath group and prominence: Cricothyroid muscular activity in intonation. *Language, 46*, 312–327.

Lindblom, B. 1972. Phonetics and the description of language. In A. Rigault & R. Charbonneau (Eds.), *Proceedings of the 7th International Congress of Phonetic Sciences, Montreal, 22–28 August 1971*. The Hague: Mouton. Pp. 63–98.

Lindblom, B. 1975. Experiments in sound structure. Plenary address, 8th International Congress of Phonetic Sciences, Leeds, August.

Lindblom, B., & Sundberg, J. 1971a. Neurophysiological representation of speech sounds. *Proceedings of the 15th World Congress of Logopedics and Phoniatrics, Buenos Aires*.

Lindblom, B. E. F., & Sundberg, J. E. F. 1971b. Acoustical consequences of lip, tongue, jaw, and larynx movement. *Journal of the Acoustical Society of America, 50*, 1166–1179.

Lindqvist, J. 1972. A descriptive model of laryngeal articulation in speech. *Quarterly Progress and Status Reports*. Speech Transmission Laboratory, Stockholm, *2–3/1972*, 1–9.

Lindqvist, J., Sawashima, M., & Hirose, H. 1973. An investigation of the vertical movement of the larynx in a Swedish speaker. *Annual Bulletin*, Research Institute of Logopedics and Phoniatrics, *7*, 27–34.

Luchsinger, R., & Arnold, G. E. 1965. *Voice–Speech–Language*. Belmont: Wadsworth.

Maeda, S. 1975. Electromyographic study of intonational attributes. *Progress Report*, Research Laboratory of Electronics, MIT, *115*, 261–269.

Mueller, J. *Manuel de physiologie*. 1851. (Trans. from German by A.-J.-L. Jourdan, 2nd ed.) Paris: Chez J.-B. Baillière.

Munro, R. R., & Adams, C. 1971. Electromyography of the intercostal muscles in connected speech. *Electromyography, 11*, 365–378.

Netsell, R. 1969. A perceptual-acoustic-physiological study of syllable stress. Ph.D. dissertation, Univ. of Iowa.

Netsell, R. 1973. Speech physiology. In F. D. Minifie, T. J. Hixon, & F. Williams (Eds.), *Normal Aspects of Speech, Hearing, and Language*. Englewood Cliffs: Prentice-Hall. Pp. 211–234.

Ohala, J. J. 1970. Aspects of the control and production of speech. *UCLA Working Papers in Phonetics, 15*.

Ohala, J. J. 1971. The role of physiological and acoustic models in explaining the direction of sound change. *Project on Linguistic Analysis Reports*, Berkeley, *15*, 25–40.

Ohala, J. J. 1972a. How to represent natural sound patterns. *Project on Linguistic Analysis Reports*, Berkeley, *16*, 40–57.

Ohala, J. J. 1972b. How is pitch lowered? *Journal of the Acoustical Society of America, 52*,124.

Ohala, J. J. 1973. The physiology of tone. In L. Hyman (Ed.), Consonant types and tone. *Southern California Papers in Linguistics, 1*, 1–14.

Ohala, J. J. 1974a. Experimental historical phonology. In J. M. Anderson & C. Jones (Eds.), *Historical linguistics II: Theory and description in phonology*. Proceedings of the 1st International Conference on Historical Linguistics, Edinburgh, 2–7 September 1973. Amsterdam: North Holland. Pp. 353–389.

Ohala, J. J. 1974b. Phonetic explanation in phonology. In A. Bruck, R. A. Fox, & M. W. LaGaly (Eds.), *Papers from the parasession on natural phonology*, Chicago Linguistic Society. Pp. 251–274.

Ohala, J. J. 1975a. A mathematical model of speech aerodynamics. In G. Fant (Ed.), *Speech communication: Proceedings of the Speech Communication Seminar, Stockholm, 1–3 August 1974* (Vol. 2): *Speech production and synthesis by rule*. Stockholm: Almqvist & Wiksell. Pp. 65–72.

Ohala, J. J. 1975b. Phonetic explanations for nasal sound patterns. In C. A. Ferguson, L. M. Hyman, & J. J. Ohala (Eds.), *Nasalfest: Papers from a symposium on nasals and nasalization.* Stanford: Language Universals Project. Pp. 289–316.

Ohala, J. J. 1975c. Conditions for Vowel devoicing and frication. *Journal of the Acoustical Society of America, 58,* S39.

Ohala, J. J. 1976. A model of speech aerodynamics. *Report of the Phonology Laboratory,* Berkeley, *1,* 93–107.

Ohala, J. J. 1977a. The physiology of stress. In L. M. Hyman (Ed.), *Studies in stress and accent. Southern California Occasional Papers in Linguisrics, 4,* 145–168.

Ohala, J. J. 1977b. Speculations on pitch regulation. *Phonetica, 34,* 310–312.

Ohala, J. J., & Eukel, B. W. 1976. Explaining the intrinsic pitch of vowels. *Journal Acoustic Society of America, 60,* S44.

Ohala, J. J., & Ewan, W. G. 1973. Speed of pitch change. *Journal of the Acoustical Society of America, 53,* 345.

Ohala, J. J., & Hirano, M. 1967. Studies of pitch change in speech. *UCLA Working Papers in Phonetics, 7,* 80–84.

Ohala, J. J., & Hirose, H. 1969. The function of the sternohyoid muscle in speech. *Reports of the Autumn 1969 Meeting of Acoustical Society of Japan.* Pp. 359–360. (Reprinted: *Annual Bulletin,* Research Institute of Logopedics and Phoniatrics, 1970, *4,* 41–44.)

Ohala, J. J., & Ladefoged, P. 1970. Further investigation of pitch regulation in speech. *UCLA Working Papers in Phonetics, 14,* 12–24.

Ohala, J. J., & Lorentz, J. 1977. The story of [w]: An exercise in the phonetic explanation for sound patterns. *Proceedings 3rd Annual Meeting of the Berkeley Linguistics Society,* 577–599.

Ohala, M., & Ohala, J. J. 1973. The problem of aspiration in Hindi phonetics. (In Hindi) In *Hindi Bhashavigyan Ank,* Delhi: Central Hindi Directorate, Ministry of Education and Social Welfare, Government of India. Pp. 67–72. (Trans into English and reprinted in *Project on Linguistic Analysis Reports,* Berkeley, 1972, *16,* 63–70; *Annual Bulletin,* Research Institute of Logopedics and Phoniatrics, 1972, *6,* 39–46.)

Öhman, S., & Lindqvist, J. 1966. Analysis-by-synthesis of prosodic pitch contours. *Quarterly Progress and Status Reports,* Speech Transmission Laboratory, Stockholm, *4/1965,* 1–6.

Öhman, S., Mårtensson, A., Leandersson, R., & Persson, A. 1967. Crico-thyroid and vocalis muscle activity in the production of Swedish tonal accents: A pilot study. *Quarterly Progress and Status Reports,* Speech Transmission Laboratory, Stockholm, *2–3/1967,* 55–57.

Okamura, H., Gould, W. J., & Tanable, M. 1976. The role of the respiratory muscle in phonation. In E. Loebell (Ed.), *XVIth International Congress of Logopedics and Phoniatrics, Interlaken 1974.* Basel: Karger. Pp. 351–356.

Painter, C. 1971. Archetypal breath-groups and the motor theory of speech perception: Evidence from a register tone language. *Anthropological Linguistics, 13,* 349–360.

Painter, C. 1974. On the relationship between grammatical units, tonal units, and physiological constraints on the respiratory system in GWA. *Zeitschrift fur Phonetik, Sprachwissenschaft, und Kommunikationforschung, 27,* 302–319.

Passy, P. 1890. *Etudes sur les changements phonétiques.* Paris: Librairie Firmin-Didot.

Peterson, G. E. 1957. Breath stream dynamics. In L. Kaiser (Ed.), *Manual of phonetics.* Amsterdam: North Holland. Pp. 139–148.

Peterson, G. E. 1958. Some observations on speech. *Quarterly Journal of Speech, 44,* 402–412.

Pressman, J., & Kelemen, G. 1955. Physiology of the larynx. *Physiological Reviews, 35,* 506–554.

Proctor, D. F. 1968. The physiologic basis of voice training. In A. Bouhuys (Ed.), *Sound production in man. Annuals of the New York Academy of Sciences, 155* (1), 208–228.

Rousselot, L'Abbé. 1891. *Les modifications phonétiques de langage.* Paris: H. Welter.

Sawashima, M. 1970. Laryngeal research in experimental phonetics. *Status Reports on Speech Research,* Haskins Laboratories, *SR-23,* 69–115.

Sawashima, M., Kakita, Y., & Hiki, S. 1973. Activity of the extrinsic laryngeal muscles in relation to Japanese word accent. *Annual Bulletin*, Research Institute of Logopedics and Phoniatrics, 7, 19–25.

Sawashima, M., Sato, M., Funasaka, S., & Totsuka, G. 1958. Electromyographic study of the human larynx and its clinical application [in Japanese]. *Journal of the Oto-Rhino-Laryngological Society of Japan*, 61, 1357–1364.

Scripture, E. W. 1902. *Experimental phonetics*. New York: Scribners.

Shipp, T. E. 1975a. Vertical laryngeal position during continuous and discrete vocal frequency change. *Journal of Speech and Hearing Research*, 18, 707–718.

Shipp, T. E. 1975b. The apparent functions of vertical larynx position for phonation. Paper delivered at 8th International Congress of Phonetic Sciences, Leeds, August.

Shipp, T. E., & Haller, R. H. 1972. Vertical larynx height during vocal frequency change. *Journal of the Acoustical Soceity of America*, 52, 124.

Shipp, T., & Izdebski, K. 1975. Vocal frequency and vertical larynx positioning by singers and nonsingers. *Journal of the Acoustical Soceity of America*, 58, 1104–1106.

Silverstein, R. O. 1976. A strategy for utterance production in Hausa. *Studies in African Linguistics*, Suppl. 6, 233–241.

Simada, Z., & Hirose, H. 1970. The function of the laryngeal muscles in respect to the word accent distinction. *Annual Bulletin*, Research Institute of Logopedics and Phoniatrics, 4, 27–40.

Simada, Z., & Hirose, H. 1971. Physiological correlates of Japanese accent patterns. *Annual Bulletin*, Research Institute of Logopedics and Phoniatrics, 5, 41–49.

Simon, H. A. 1969. *The science of the artificial*. Cambridge, Mass.: MIT Press.

Slis, I. H., & Cohen, A. 1969. On the complex regulating the voiced–voiceless distinction I & II. *Language and Speech*, 12, 80–102; 137–155.

Smith, S. 1944. *The Danish stød*. Copenhagen: Kaifer.

Sokowlowsky, R. R. 1943. Effect of the extrinsic laryngeal muscles on voice production. *Archives of Otolaryngology*, 38, 355–364.

Sonesson, B. 1960. On the anatomy and vibratory pattern of the human vocal folds. *Acta Oto-Laryngologica*, Suppl. 156.

Sonninen, A. 1956. The role of the extrinsic laryngeal muscles in length adjustment of the vocal cords in singing. *Acta Oto-Laryngologica*, Suppl. 130.

Sonninen, A. 1968. The external frame function in the control of pitch in the human voice. In A. Bouhuys (Ed.), Sound production in man. *Annals of the New York Academy of Sciences*, 155 (1), 68–89.

Stetson, R. H. 1928. *Motor phonetics*. Amsterdam: North Holland.

Stevens, K. N. 1975. Modes of conversion of airflow to sound, and their utilization in speech. Plenary address, 8th International Congress of Phonetic Sciences, Leeds, August.

Strenger, F. 1958. Mesure de la pression d'air sous-glottique, de la pression acoustique, et de la durée de la prononciation des différents sons de langage suédois au cours de la phonation. *Journal Français d'Oto-Rhino-Laryngologie Audio-Phonologie et Chirugie Maxillofaciale*.

Sundberg, J. 1973. Data on maximum speed of pitch changes. *Quarterly Progress and Status Reports*, Speech Transmission Laboratory, Stockholm, *1973/4*, 39–47.

Sweet, H. 1877. *A handbook of phonetics*. Oxford: Clarendon Press.

Vanderslice, R. 1967. Larynx vs. lungs: Cricothyrometer data refuting some recent claims concerning intonation and archetypality. *UCLA Working Papers in Phonetics*, 7, 69–79.

van Hattum, R. J., & Worth, J. H. 1967. Air flow rates in normal speakers. *Cleft Palate Journal*, 4, 137–147.

Vesalius, A. 1543. *De humani corporis fabrica* and [*The*] *epitome* [*of Andreas Vesalius*]. Basel. [*Epitome* trans. into English by L. R. Lind. Cambridge, Mass.: M.I.T. Press, 1969.]

Wegel, R. L. 1930. Theory of vibration of the larynx. *Bell System Technical Journal*, 9, 207–227.

Weitzman, R. S. 1970. Word accent in Japanese. *Studies in the Phonology of Asian Languages*, Univ. of Southern California, *11*.

Willis, R. 1833. On the mechanism of the larynx. *Transactions of the Cambridge Philosophical Society, 4*, 323–352.

Yanagihara, N., & von Leden, H. 1966. The cricothyroid muscle during phonation. *Annals of Otology, Rhinology, and Laryngology, 75*, 978–1006.

Zee, E., & Hombert, J. M. 1976. Intensity and duration as correlates of F_0. *Journal of the Acoustical Society of America, 60*, S44.

Zemlin, W. R. 1968. *Speech and hearing science*. Englewood Cliffs: Prentice Hall.

Zenker, W. 1964. Questions regarding the function of external laryngeal muscles. In D. W. Brewer (Ed.), *Research potentials in voice physiology*. State Univ. of New York. Pp. 20–29.

Zenker, W., & Zenker, A. 1960. Über die Regelung der Stimmlippenspannung durch von aussen eingreifende Mechanism. *Folia Phoniatrica, 12*, 1–36.

II

The Perception of Tone

JACKSON T. GANDOUR

It is of course true in a purely **physical** *sense that all tone languages can be analyzed in terms of register. All this means is that you can't have "movement" without having an A from which you move to B. Hence we may claim necessary priority of points A and B to movement from A to B.* **But** *movement* **from** *A* **to** *B (a physical statement) is not really the same thing as movement* **in a direction** *away from A and toward B. Psychologically, one can have an experience of such movement without being able to "geometrize" in terms of fixed points A and B. [Edward T. Sapir, from his discussion of the psychological possibility of tone contours in a letter written to Kenneth L. Pike dated 14 July 1938 (Pike 1948:8).]*

1. INTRODUCTION

It is generally assumed that the principal phonetic features of **tone** are found in the domain of **pitch**. The term "tone" (linguistic) refers to a particular way in which pitch is utilized in language; the term "pitch" (nonlinguistic, perceptual), on the other hand, refers to how a hearer places a sound on a scale going from low to high without considering the physical properties of the sound. Its primary acoustic correlate is **fundamental frequency**. The term "fundamental frequency" (acoustic) refers to the frequency of repetition of a sound wave of which, when analyzed into its component frequencies, the fundamental is the highest common factor of the component frequencies (Ladefoged 1962). A **tone language**, for the purposes of this review, is a language in which pitch is used to contrast individual lexical items or words. This definition includes the traditional tone languages of Africa and the Far East as well as the marginal tone (or "pitch accent") languages of Europe, and excludes **intonation languages**, like English, in which pitch is used to signal syntactic and/or semantic distinctions at the phrase or sentence level. Admittedly, it is difficult to draw a sharp boundary between tone and nontone languages. Without debating the merits of a particular language taxonomy (see Chapter I),

41

no one would deny that the languages reported on in this review are important for an understanding of **tone perception**, a term which will be used to emphasize the linguistic nature of the perceptual process. It is to be distinguished from **pitch perception**, a term which will be used to refer to the processing of either speech or nonspeech auditory signals.

The aim of this chapter is to survey and evaluate previous research on the phonetics of tone perception and discuss its implications for models of tone perception and linguistic theory in general. Studies that are clearly directed to issues concerning tone perception are included; studies that have investigated pitch perception per se are included if their findings seem to be of relevance to speech perception. Studies that have investigated physiological mechanisms underlying pitch perception are excluded from this review; we will simply note that the function of the ear is to receive the acoustic signal, convert it to electrochemical energy, and transmit the signal via nerve impulses to the brain. Studies that have used "pure tones" as stimuli will receive limited coverage because of the difficulty in extrapolating the findings to perception of complex speech sounds. Generally speaking, emphasis has been placed on those studies that deal with interesting linguistic hypotheses or furnish data crucial for the development of a model of tone perception and an explanatory account of certain tonal phenomena that have been observed in tone languages of the world.

2. ACOUSTIC CORRELATES OF TONE

An act of sensory perception must involve the interpretation of an external physical signal. Several studies have attempted to determine the necessary and sufficient perceptual cues for tones extracted from the physical, acoustic speech signal. These studies have all been completed in relatively recent times, having been made possible with the advent of electronic speech synthesis. Tone languages that have been subjected to this kind of investigation include Thai and Mandarin Chinese from the Far East, Yoruba from West Africa, and Swedish, Norwegian, and Serbocroation from Europe.

2.1 Thai

Thai (Siamese), the national language of Thailand, exhibits five contrastive tones, traditionally labeled mid ( ), low (ˋ), falling (ˆ), high (ˊ) and rising (ˇ).[1] The following set of words illustrate these tones: khaa 'a grass (imperata cylindrica)', khàa 'galangal, a rhizome', khâa 'to kill', khǎa' to engage in

---

[1] As to whether the contour tones, falling and rising, are to be represented phonologically as unitary contours (with contour tonal features) or as sequences of level tones depends on one's theoretical framework. Anderson, in this volume, argues for the "decomposition" on the phonological level of all contour tones.

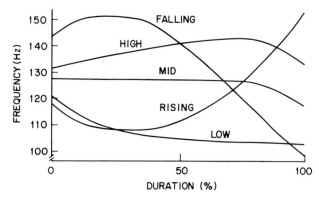

Figure 1. Average fundamental frequency contours (one speaker) of Thai tones on double vowels in prepausal position. Syllables with double vowels were normalized to a duration of 500 msec (adapted from Abramson 1962, by permission of Indiana University Research Center for Language and Semiotic Studies).

trade', and *khăa* 'leg'. Average fundamental frequency contours of the five Thai tones in prepausal position are presented in Figure 1.

It has been shown that Thai listeners can easily identify the tones in real-speech monosyllabic words, even in isolation from any phonetic or linguistic context. Abramson (1962:128) presented four sets of five tonally differentiated real-speech monosyllabic words, produced by a single male speaker, for absolute identification judgments. Most of the subjects (11) identified the tones easily with no errors. Abramson (1975:3–4) replicated the experiment with a different set of monosyllabic words, this time produced by five male and five female speakers, and a larger number of subjects. The overall intelligibility score achieved by the subjects (25) was nearly perfect. Confusion between the mid and low tones accounted for most of the small number of errors; nearly half of these errors, however, were caused by the utterances of one of the ten speakers. Abramson (1976a) found in a similar experiment that the confusion between the mid and low tones was virtually eliminated when the utterances of only one speaker were used for identification tests as compared to composite tests in which the utterances of all the speakers were randomized to prevent adaptation to any one speaker. The mid and low tones, the two Thai tones most vulnerable to confusion, are typically characterized by very little movement of fundamental frequency over time, unlike the falling, high, and rising tones, each of which displays considerable movement of the fundamental frequency (see Figure 1). The mid and low tones were not confused in most of the individual tests, which suggests that the normalization of the tone space could be effected much more easily for an individual speaker.

To test whether Thai listeners could identify each of the tones on the basis of fundamental frequency alone, Abramson (1962:131–134) superimposed synthetic average fundamental frequency contours (see Figure 1) on each of the following real-speech monosyllabic words: *naa* 'field', *nàa* (a nickname), *nâa* 'face', *naá* 'aunt', and *nǎa* 'thick'. Thai subjects (10) easily identified the tones with near-perfect accuracy. This finding suggests that fundamental frequency variation overrides any of concomitant phonetic features of duration or relative amplitude that may be associated with a particular tone. Abramson (1975:5) replicated these perceptual tests, this time using a set of synthetic monosyllables of the type [kha:], with superimposed average fundamental frequency contours. Subjects (38) correctly identified the tones about 93% of the time, indicating that variation in fundamental frequency carries sufficient information for the identification of the Thai tones. That fundamental frequency variation is necessary for the identification of Thai tones is borne out by the results of Abramson's (1972) research on whispered speech in Thai, which indicate that in the context-free setting of isolated words, whispered Thai tones cannot be well identified. Even though certain ideal fundamental frequency contours provide the necessary and sufficient cues for the perception of Thai tones, it is still possible that the concomitant relative amplitude curve may contribute to tonal identification. Abramson (1975:5–8) investigated this possibility be adding synthetic amplitude contours to the set of [kha:] syllables. Under this test condition, Thai listeners (40) were able to correctly identify the tones 96% of the time. Abramson (1975) concludes:

> The overall identifiability of the stimuli moves from 98.6% for real speech through 92.8% for fundamental frequency alone to 96.1% for fundamental frequency plus amplitude, thus suggesting that while fundamental frequency alone is by and large a sufficient cue, its efficacy is enhanced by the addition of amplitude information [pp. 6–8].

Amplitude contours alone, however, are not nearly sufficient for perception of the Thai tones. Abramson (1972:36–37) synthesized a set of real-speech words with a superimposed constant fundamental frequency of 130 Hz. All other concomitant spectral characteristics of these words, including the amplitude contour, were preserved. Identification tests indicated that listeners could not discriminate between the tones at all.

Pike (1948:5) has suggested that a useful distinction may be drawn between level tones and gliding tones. A level tone is one in which, within the limits of perception, the pitch of a syllable does not rise or fall during its production; a gliding tone is one in which the pitch of a syllable has a perceptible rise or fall or some combination of rise and fall. Accordingly, Abramson (1962) suggested that the mid, low, and high Thai tones be regarded as level (= "static" in Abramson's terminology), and that the falling and rising tones be regarded as gliding (= "dynamic" in Abramson's terminology) tones. To investigate the perceptual validity of the distinction between level and gliding tones in Thai, Abramson (1976b) first attempted to determine whether fundamental frequency levels carry enough information for identification of the level tones. Sixteen variants of a syllable of the type [kha:] were generated with superimposed level fundamental frequency trajectories ranging from 152 Hz down to 92 Hz in 4-Hz steps. Thai subjects (37) used only the mid, low, and high tones as identification responses. A peak of 90% identification was achieved for the low tone, about the same as that obtained in the baseline test of a typical low tone; a peak of only 88% was reached for the high tone, as compared to 98% in the baseline test of a typical high tone; and a peak of 73% was reached for the mid tone, as compared to 82% in the baseline test.

Abramson (1976b) further attempted to determine to what extent the responses to level tones would be increased if these tones showed some movement. Sixteen tonal variants of [kha:] were generated, all displaying linear fundamental frequency trajectories starting from a common beginning point of 120 Hz and ending at the same points as in the first test. Thai subjects (31) predominantly used the mid, low, and high tones for their identification responses. Except for the low tone, for which the movement should start somewhat lower in the frequency range, the peaks of percentage identification are higher than those obtained in the first test. The high tone reaches a peak percentage identification of 94%, as compared to 88% in the first test; the mid tone reaches a peak percentage identification of 84% up from 73% in the first test. Based on the results of these two tests (and others), Abramson (1976) concludes that

> fundamental-frequency levels do carry much information in the static tones, although some movement improves them . . . . Although the dichotomy between static and dynamic tones is imprecise, . . . it is still useful as an index to the types of acoustic cues used in the recognition of tones [pp. 126–127].

2.2 Mandarin Chinese

Chinese (Peking Mandarin dialect) exhibits four contrastive tones in its phonological inventory: Tone (‾) high level, Tone 2 (´) high rising, Tone 3 (ˇ) low-dipping and Tone 4 (`) high-falling (Chao 1948:24–25). These tonal contrasts are illustrated in the following set of words: *mā* 'mother', *má* 'hemp', *mǎ* 'horse', and *mà* 'to scold'. Average fundamental frequency contours of the four basic Chinese tones are displayed in Figure 2.

It has been shown that Chinese listeners can readily identify the tones of real-speech monosyllabic words in isolation. Chuang, Hiki, Sone, and Nimura (1972) presented sets of four tonally differentiated Chinese monosyllables, produced by three (two male, one female) native speakers, for absolute identification judgments. Chinese listeners (4) identified the tones easily with no errors. Of the errors, most involved confusions between Tone 2 and Tone 3. This perhaps is not too surprising in light of the physical characteristics of the two tones: Both display rising glides, both start at about the same pitch level, and both have about the same duration (see Figure 2; see also Dreher and Lee 1966). Chuang *et al.* (1972) further point out that considerable variation is

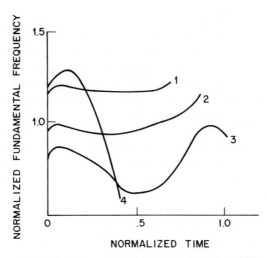

Figure 2. Average fundamental frequency contours (one speaker) of Chinese tones on mono-syllabic words in prepausal position. Fundamental frequency was normalized to the total average fundamental frequency of the four tones; time was normalized to the ratio of the average duration of each tone to the average duration of Tone 3, the longest of the four tones (adapted from Chuang, Niki, Sone, and Nimura 1972, by permission of Akadémial Kiadó).

found across their four speakers with respect to the initial and end glides, which leads them to suggest that "neither the falling and rising contour nor the position of the dip point in tone 3 alone can be the perceptual cues to discriminate tone 3 from tone 2 [p. 299]."

This confusion between Tone 2 and Tone 3 has also been reported in other studies on Chinese tones. Kiriloff (1969) reports an experiment in which adult learners (12) of Mandarin Chinese as a second language made considerably more errors in identifying Tone 2 and Tone 3 than Tone 1 and Tone 4. Klatt (1973:13) and Zue (1976) report an experiment in which native speakers of Mandarin (3) were asked to identify synthetic versions of the four tones (normalized duration) within reduced frequency ranges. When the frequency range was reduced to 2 Hz, it was found that Tone 1 and Tone 4 continued to be identified with near-perfect accuracy, but Tone 2 and Tone 3 were frequently confused. Most of the errors in discrimination tests were also between Tone 2 and Tone 3. Li and Thompson (1976, see also Chapter IX of this volume) found that confusion between Tone 2 and Tone 3 persists to the later stages of the tone acquisition process for Mandarin-speaking children.

Although most of the errors in the Chuang *et al.* (1972) study involved confusions between Tone 2 and Tone 3, the confusions were not symmetrical. Nearly twice as many errors resulted from misidentifying Tone 3 as Tone 2, as from misidentifying Tone 2 as Tone 3. The asymmetry of the perceptual confusions seems difficult to explain in terms of the physical similarity of their fundamental frequency contours, but perhaps is not at all surprising when one considers the phonological relationship that obtains between Tone 2 and Tone 3. Mandarin Chinese has a phonological rule (for discussion of this well-known case of tone sandhi, see Chao 1948 and Cheng 1973a) that neutralizes the distinction between Tone 2 and Tone 3 in the position preceding Tone 3; Tone 3 becomes Tone 2 when it occurs before Tone 3. The following tone sequences are homophonous in connected speech: *fén-chǎng* 'graveyard' and *fěn-chǎng* 'flour factory'. It seems plausible that the direction of perceptual confusion between Tone 2 and Tone 3 reflects this more abstract linguistic relationship. We must exercise a little caution, however, in interpreting the results of the Chuang *et al.* (1972) perception tests, because of the unequal number of confusions caused by each of their four speakers.

Perception tests on synthetic speech (Chuang 1972; Chuang *et al.* 1972) are reported to corroborate that sufficient cues for the discrimination and identification of the four tones in connected speech permit the following representation of the tones: Tone 1 as mid–high flat, Tone 2 as rising from mid–low to mid–high, Tone 3 as low flat with rising end or simply low flat in certain environments, and Tone 4 as falling from high to low, thus indicating that the initial gliding portion of the four tones and the end-gliding portion of Tone 2 are nonsignificant from a perceptual standpoint.

Howie (1972) ran a series of perception tests in which Chinese listeners were asked to identify the four tones under various conditions. One of the stimulus sets consisted of synthetic tones imposed on the real-speech Tone 1 syllable *baō*, yielding a set of four tonally differentiated words: *baō* 'to wrap', *baó* 'hailstone', *baǒ* 'guarantee', and *baò* 'newspaper'. Chinese listeners (12) identified the tones correctly 95% of the time. The results of such identification tests lead Howie to conclude that the synthetic tones represent a valid acoustic description of the Chinese tones in citation forms. Although it is true that Howie found a set of average fundamental frequency contours that furnish sufficient cues for the identification of the tones, it is still possible that alternative acoustic description may yield similar results.

To demonstrate the primacy of fundamental frequency patterns in the identification of the four Chinese tones, Howie generated a set of real-speech citation syllables minimally differentiated by tone (*yīng* 'brain', *yíng* 'camp', *yǐng* 'image', and *yìng* 'hard'), suppressing their original fundamental frequency contours and replacing them with a constant fundamental frequency of 128 Hz. Chinese listeners (6) did poorly in identifying the tones under this condition.

2.3 Yoruba

Yoruba, a Kwa language spoken in Nigeria, has been traditionally analyzed as having three lexically contrastive level tones: high (´), mid ( ), and low (`). These tonal oppositions are exemplified in the following words: *wá* 'to come',

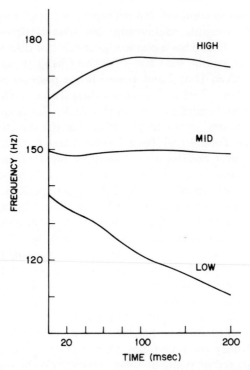

Figure 3. Average fundamental frequency contours (two speakers) of Yoruba tones in word final position (adapted from Hombert 1976a, by permission of author).

wa 'to look', and *wà* 'to exist'. Average fundamental frequency contours of the three Yoruba tones in word-final position are presented in Figure 3.

LaVelle (1974) focused attention on the behavior of the Yoruba low tone in his study of "downdrift," a phenomenon whereby tones show a tendency, to varying degrees, to lower throughout the course of an utterance (for more detailed discussion and analysis of downdrift in West African tone languages, see Schachter and Fromkin 1968, Peters 1973, Hyman 1975, LaVelle 1976, Meyers 1976). Based on acoustical measurements which show that, on di-syllabic words with high–high, mid–mid and low–low tonal patterns, only the final low tone is markedly lower in fundamental frequency than its preceding identical tone, LaVelle posits a linguistic constraint that maintains the maximum perceptual distinctiveness of the high, mid, and low tones. If such a constraint did not operate in Yoruba, he reasons, there would be potential confusion between high–high and high–mid, mid–mid and mid–low, and mid–mid and low–low sequences of tones. In particular, if a final low tone is not lowered, a phonetically low–low sequence of level tones would likely be identified as a mid–mid sequence. In a preliminary perceptual experiment using naturally produced stimuli, LaVelle's expectation was borne out with one native speaker of Yoruba. Although the word-final low tone also displays a falling contour (see Figure 3 above, Figure 9 below), LaVelle assumes that the lowered pitch level of the word-final low tone is the primary perceptual cue distinguishing it from a mid tone in this position. Hombert (1976a:49), on the other hand, suggests that the falling contour is a more important perceptual cue than the level of fundamental frequency.

In perceptual tests using both natural and synthetic stimuli, Hombert (1976b) investigates the relative importance of fundamental frequency, as well as amplitude and duration, as perceptual cues in distinguishing a low tone from a mid tone in word-final position. His acoustical analysis of low–low and low–mid sequence, mid–low and mid–mid sequences indicates that the final low tone displays a lower initial level of fundamental frequency, a falling fundamental frequency contour, a shorter duration (30 msec), and a lower amplitude (6 dB). To test the relative perceptual importance of these various acoustic parameters, his stimulus set consisted of original low–low (ọ̀gọ̀ 'stupid person') and mid–low (ọkọ̀ 'vehicle') words, plus four subsets of synthetic stimuli resulting from modification of the second vowel in the original words. In the first subset, the second vowel had increased amplitude (7 dB); in the second subset, increased duration (50 msec); in the third subset, a level fundamental frequency; in the fourth subset, a combination of increased amplitude, increased duration, and a level fundamental frequency.

Results of listening tests (seven Yoruba subjects) indicate that an increase in duration or amplitude does not cause a shift in identification judgments. This confirms the overriding importance of fundamental frequency as the principal acoustic correlate of Yoruba tones. Shifts in identification judgments, however, do occur with those stimulus subsets exhibiting a final low tone with level fundamental frequency. A low–low tonal sequence (ọ̀gọ̀ 'stupid person') was frequently misidentified as low–mid (ọ̀gọ 'stick'), and mid–low (ọkọ̀ 'vehicle') as mid–mid (ọkọ 'husband'), thus suggesting that the falling contour is the primary perceptual cue of a low tone in word-final position (see Figure 9, p. 70).

While the results of Hombert's perceptual tests are suggestive, they remain inconclusive when one considers that the level fundamental frequency on the second vowel was constructed by repeating the **third** glottal pulse. As can be seen in the production data in Figure 9, level fundamental frequency constructed in this method could potentially bias the experimental outcome. Residual questions notwithstanding, the LaVelle and Hombert studies suggest promising avenues for future research on the perception of sequences of tones.

2.4 Serbocroatian

Unlike the monosyllabic tone languages of Africa and the Far East, the so-called pitch-accent or word-tone languages of Europe do not exhibit lexically

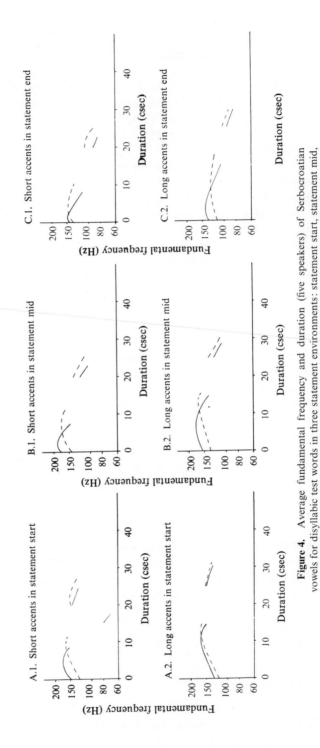

Figure 4. Average fundamental frequency and duration (five speakers) of Serbocroatian vowels for disyllabic test words in three statement environments: statement start, statement mid, and statement end (adapted from Purcell 1972, by permission of Mouton & Co., Publishers).

contrastive pitch on monosyllabic words. Tonal contrasts appear only in certain positions in polysyllabic words. Though it has yet to be fully determined how much perceptual importance to attach to concomitant cues of amplitude and duration, a few perceptual experiments have been completed which seemingly point to the primacy of tone. As stated in Section 1, one may perhaps object to the inclusion of Serbocroatian within a strict tone language taxonomy, but surely not to its selection as a language that exploits tonal contrasts at the word level, which may furnish insights into the perception of tone.

Serbocroatian (a Balto–Slavic language spoken in Yugoslavia) has traditionally been described as having four word tones or accents: (1) short rising, (2) short falling, (3) long rising, and (4) long falling. Purcell's (1971, 1972) acoustical investigations (see also Lehiste and Ivíc 1963) of the word tones in varying sentence environments indicate sizable regular differences in both duration and fundamental frequency between the four traditional accents. By comparison of the average occurrences of short falling with short rising accents and long falling with long rising accents at the start, mid, and end of a statement, differences in the fundamental frequency patterns associated with the rising and falling accents (Figure 4) may be observed.

Purcell (1971) summarizes, as follows:

> Within the accented vowel, the average realization of a falling accent in any of the three statement environments starts higher, peaks earlier and ends lower than does the average realization of a corresponding rising accent in the same statement environment. Within the first postaccentual vowel, the average realization of a falling accent starts, "mids," and ends lower than for a corresponding rising accent [p. 5].

Of these differences in fundamental frequency patterns within the accented syllable and unaccented syllable, Purcell (1975) hypothesized that the relative location of the peak fundamental frequency within the accented vowel (falling tones marked by a peak fundamental frequency located closer to the start of the accented vowel; rising tones marked by a peak fundamental frequency located closer to the end of the accented vowel) was a sufficient perceptual cue for the differentiation of the rising and falling accents.

Synthetic versions of the sequence [ra:di] were generated with 21 different fundamental frequency patterns, intended to approximate the frequency continuum between *radi* (third singular present form of the verb *raditi* 'to work, to do') with a long falling accent and *radi* (second singular imperative form) with a long rising accent. The 21 test stimuli each differed only in the location of the peak fundamental frequency, varied in 10-msec steps within the accented vowel. All of the accented vowels, except for the two stimuli at either extreme of the continuum which peaked at either the start or the end, started at 100 Hz, peaked at 120 Hz and ended at 100 Hz.

Results of identification tests indicate that native speakers of Serbocroatian (20) heard a rising tone (*radi*, second singular imperative form) when the peak fundamental frequency was located near the end of the vowel, a falling tone (*radi*, third singular present form) when the peak fundamental frequency occurred earlier. Purcell concludes that peak fundamental frequency alone is a sufficient cue to distinguish falling from rising tones. This conclusion would appear to be a bit premature since the overall contour covaried with the varying peaks in fundamental frequency.

The transition from falling tone to rising tone judgments was rather abrupt, with falling tone judgments predominant in the first three-quarters of the accented vowel. The preponderance of falling tone judgments suggests perhaps a "perceptual equivalence" between falling and rising tones that departs from strict examination of the physical signal (see Section 4). Speculation aside, while Purcell has demonstrated that the relative location of peak fundamental frequency carries enough information for the differentiation of the falling and rising tones, it remains to be determined whether or not it is the principal cue.

Lehiste and Ivíc (1972) investigated the question of whether or not there was any perceptual significance to differences between the initial and terminal fundamental frequency of the contours associated with the rising and falling accents; that is, is there any perceptual distinction between those contours whose terminal fundamental frequency was higher than the beginning, and those whose fundamental frequency, after an initial rise, dropped below the beginning frequency. Fundamental frequency patterns were superimposed on the synthetic vowel *a*. One "low pitched" set of stimuli had an initial frequency of 117 Hz; another "high pitched" set of stimuli had an initial frequency of 178 Hz. Both sets of stimuli peaked 18 Hz above the initial frequency and ended at frequencies above, equal to, and below the initial frequency. Both Serbocroatian (19) and American English (10) listeners reacted to the higher-pitched stimuli as "rising" and to the lower-pitched stimuli as "falling." Neither group of listeners could hear the difference between the initial and terminal frequencies of a rising–falling fundamental frequency contour. It is possible that these listeners were basing their perceptual judgments on the "average pitch" of the stimuli (see Section 7).

Lehiste and Ivíc (1972) also tested the perception of the long rising and long falling accents, using 44 synthetic variants of *radi*. Variable synthetic fundamental frequency patterns were applied to both the first accented syllable and the post accented syllable. The first set of stimuli had a steeply falling first syllable combined with six level and five falling second syllable contours; the second set had a similar pattern generated with a narrower frequency range; the third set had a level first syllable, and the fourth set a rising first syllable, both combined with the same second syllables as the second set. Serbocroatian listeners (25) could not identify the accent based on the fundamental frequency pattern of the first syllable alone; the fundamental frequency of the second syllable had to be present before listeners agreed in their responses. For a falling first syllable, the second syllable had to acquire a fairly low value before the judgments shifted from random to "falling"; for a level first syllable, the fundamental frequency of the second syllable had to be at least as high as the level of the first to evoke consistent "rising" responses. The same applied to stimuli with a rising first syllable: The rising fundamental frequency alone was not sufficient for consistent "rising" judgments. The second syllable had to have a frequency at least as high as the frequency of the first. In most cases, the shift in response was not between consistent "falling" or "rising," but between either "rising" or "falling" and a random response. Lehiste and Ivíc suggest that "within this set of synthesized words, these features seem to distinguish not between two accents (or two words), but rather between the presence and absence of an identifiable accent (between a word and a non-word) [p. 14]." It would appear that their stimulus set simply did not approximate a continuum between the rising and falling accents. In contrast to Purcell's (1975) findings, it is important to note that Lehiste and Ivíc did not find that **intra**syllabic differences in fundamental frequency furnish sufficient cues to differentiate the rising and falling word tones. The **inter**syllabic fundamental frequency pattern was necessary in order to evoke consistent "falling" and "rising" judgments. Clearly, the last word is not in on the perception of Serbocroatian word tones. Another series of perception tests by Rehder (1968, reported in Percell 1975) seems to indicate both intrasyllabic and intersyllabic effects on "rising" and "falling" tone judgments. Rehder concluded that the important factor for the perception of Serbocroatian word tones was a step up or a step down (approximately 4 Hz) in fundamental frequency in the second half of the stressed vowel or across the boundary between a stressed and a following unstressed vowel.

2.5 Swedish

The Scandinavian languages (Norwegian, Danish, Swedish) are also word-accent languages. A word may carry one of two prosodic patterns: Accent 1 (´) or Accent 2 (`). Monosyllabic words may carry Accent 1 only; a contrast in accent occurs on any nonfinal syllable in words containing more than one syllable. If the last syllable is stressed, there is no accent distinction. An example from Swedish in disyllabic words is *ánden* 'the duck' (from *ande + en*, plus vowel elision) versus *ànden* 'the spirit' (from *and + en*). Wang (lecture given at the LSA Summer Institute, 1973) reports that over 90% of the accentual patterns are predictable and that only a few hundred lexical items need to be marked for tone. According to Garding (1973):

> The Scandinavian accents are lexically not very significant because they are largely predictable from the morphological and phonological structure of the word; . . they do not occur over each syllable but are correlated with stress and juncture. The acoustic nature of the accents varies according to language, dialect and context; . . . where tonal characteristics are predominant for the accent distinction, there are intensity and durational differences as well which cannot be only a consequence of differing pitch patterns [pp. 3–4].

Garding's noncommital stance on the acoustic correlates of the Scandinavian word accents notwithstanding, perception experiments on Southern Swedish by Malmberg (1967) indicate that the distinction between Accent 1 and Accent 2 depends primarily on the characteristics of the fundamental frequency pattern.

In analytical measurements of three possible physical counterparts to the phonological accent distinction in Southern Swedish disyllabic words— (fundamental frequency) the relative location of the peak fundamental frequency from the beginning of the stressed vowel, (intensity) the relative location of the peak intensity in the stressed vowel or difference between intensity peaks in the two syllables, and (duration) the durations of the vowels in the two syllables—Malmberg found that significant differences between Accent 1 and Accent 2 disyllabic words could be obtained with fundamental frequency patterns only. In perception tests using synthetic stimuli, he found that the accentual distinction was lost altogether by removing fundamental frequency variation. This result would seem to be sufficient proof that fundamental frequency variations are indispensable for the accent difference. To determine whether or not fundamental frequency variations alone were sufficient to give a satisfactory impression of Accent 1 and Accent 2, synthetic fundamental frequency patterns were varied as to location of the peak fundamental frequency, approximating the fundamental frequency continuum observed in his analytical measurements, and superimposed on real-speech words. He found that a peak fundamental frequency at 75 msec or later after the beginning of the vowel was heard as Accent 2. Synthesized nonsense words also could be recognized as having one of the two accents if the right frequency curves were applied to them. His attempt to produce recognition of the two accents by means of duration differences in stimuli that had a fixed fundamental frequency pattern was quite unsuccessful. In other experiments, where the fundamental frequency differences were retained, recognition was not affected by reducing intensity differences or even by reversing the intensity curves. Though Malmberg's results clearly point to the primacy of tonal pattern as a perceptual cue, it remains to be determined to what extent concomitant characteristics are essential to the differentiation of the two accents.

Hadding-Koch (1961, 1962) and Jassem (1963) also found that the distinction between the two accents in Southern Swedish depends primarily on fundamental frequency variations. Fintoft and Martony (1964) and Fintoft (1970) found an overriding effect of fundamental frequency in an acoustical and perceptual analysis of Norwegian accents.

3. PERCEPTUAL EFFECTS OF TONE SANDHI

While most of the research on tone perception to date has focused on perceptual cues in citation forms, there is an increasing interest in the perception of tones on juxtaposed syllables in connected speech. As syllables are juxtaposed, tones change their shapes due to the effect of neighboring tones upon one another. This phenomenon, commonly referred to as "tone sandhi," occurs to a greater or lesser extent in all tone languages of the world. The way in which tone sandhi operates, however, differs considerably across linguistic areas. In certain clusters of American Indian languages and in the vast majority of African languages, sequences of tones undergo a form of sandhi that Wang (1967:94) characterizes as "syntagmatic displacement," whereby Tone x is displaced by Tone y or Tone z when Tone y is present elsewhere in the sequence of tones. In the languages of the Sino-Tibetan family and neighboring languages of Southeast Asia, sequences of tones undergo a form of sandhi that Wang characterizes as "paradigmatic replacement," whereby Tone x is replaced by Tone y when it is in some linguistic environments regardless of whether or not Tone y is present elsewhere in the sequence of tones. Hyman and Schuh (1974) discuss the "naturalness" of various kinds of syntagmatic displacement rules found in West African tone languages. It is reported that assimilatory tonal processes usually apply from left to right in these languages. Undoubtedly, the naturalness of these various sandhi processes of syntagmatic displacement and paradigmatic replacement may be partially accounted for in terms of articulatory mechanisms; it also seems reasonable to suppose that perceptual constraints, too, are at play in determining changes in the shapes of tones in connected speech.

Wang and Li (1967) were interested in resolving a long-standing linguistic dispute (Hockett 1947, Martin 1957) in the Peking Mandarin dialect of Chinese concerning the phonological status of Tone 3 when immediately followed by another Tone 3. The question is whether or not Tone 3 and Tone 2 are noncontrastive in the environment immediately preceding a Tone 3—a tonal example of phonological neutralization.

Of the four tones in Mandarin Chinese, Tone 3 has the most diverse shapes:

> In isolated monosyllables [cf. Figure 2, in this chapter] its pitch contour takes on the form of a slight fall in the beginning and, after staying in the low pitch range for about half of its duration, rises to its highest pitch value at the end .... When juxtaposed in speech ... the final rise of tone 3 does not occur when it precedes a tone 1, tone 2, tone 4 or the neutral tone .... Only when a tone 3 precedes another tone 3 is its pitch contour that of a slow and steady rise, similar to that of tone 2 in the same environment .... Since tone 2 also has a slow rising contour ... in the position preceding tone 3, the question is whether or not the tone sequence 3–3 is homophonous with the tone sequence 2–3 [Wang and Li 1967:631].

Test items consisted of 130 pairs of disyllabic utterances minimally differentiated by the tone on the first syllable—one member of the pair had the tone sequence 2–3, the other member had the tone sequence 3–3; for example, *qi-mǎ* 'to ride on a horse' and *qǐ-mǎ* 'at least'. The percentage of correct identification responses for Chinese listeners (14) ranged from 49 to 54, less than chance. Thus, Wang and Li conclude that the phonological distinction between Tone 2 and Tone 3 is neutralized in this environment in connected speech.

We gain further insight into the perceptual cues underlying this case of tone sandhi when we observe the speech of Chinese–English bilinguals. These Chinese speakers often insert English words into Chinese sentences, as in the following: *Haŏ professor bu duō* 'There are not many good professors'. *Haŏ* 'good' is a third-tone word. In the example *Haŏ professor bu duō*, does Tone 3 change to Tone 2 when it precedes the word 'professor'? This is one of the questions that Cheng (1968) investigated in his study of the interpretation of English stresses by Chinese speakers when they speak Chinese with English words inserted. Although perceptual judgments of linguistically significant stress in English (Fry 1955, Lehiste and Peterson 1959, Lehiste 1970) seem to be reflected in at least four acoustical parameters—amplitude, fundamental frequency, vowel quality, and duration—the primary cue is probably fundamental frequency variation (Bolinger 1958). At any rate, we would certainly expect Chinese speakers to pay particular attention to the differences in fundamental frequency in English words. Cheng attempted to find out whether Tone 3 changes to Tone 2 in the position immediately preceding English words with different stresses on the first syllable; for example, *Tā jīntian yoŭ date* 'He has a date today' and *Tā xiǎng retaxyí xià* 'He wants to relax awhile' (Cheng 1968:80, phonetic transcription of stress levels [1, 2, 3, 4] where 1 = primary stress and 4 = reduced stress, based on Chomsky and Miller 1963). Sentences were constructed by using various English words with primary, tertiary, and reduced stress in crucial positions. When Chinese subjects (15) read each sentence at fast tempo, tone sandhi usually took place on Chinese Tone 3 words immediately preceding the English reduced stress, more occurrences of tone sandhi taking place before words with fewer syllables. Tone sandhi did not occur in Chinese third-tone words immediately preceding English primary stress in one, two, three, and four-syllable words, nor did it occur before English tertiary stress in four-syllable words. With an analysis of the four Mandarin Chinese tones in terms of three of Wang's (1967) features—[high], [rising], and [falling]—Cheng is able to specify Tone 3 with one feature [−high]. The English primary, secondary, and tertiary stresses are interpreted as [+high]. Cheng suggests that it is the interpreted [−high] feature that triggers the application of the Chinese tone-sandhi rule.

4. DIFFERENTIAL THRESHOLD FOR PITCH

The differential threshold for pitch perception is of little intrinsic interest to the linguist in and of itself, but information about just discriminable changes in fundamental frequency has important implications for the perception of tone, insomuch as it may help to decide what precision should be attempted in the analysis of fundamental frequency and what limitations should be imposed on pitch perception mechanisms in man. Such data about discriminable changes in fundamental frequency are also relevant to linguistic uses of pitch and may, indeed, provide a partial explanation for the kinds of tonal inventories (Pike 1948, Cheng 1973b) and tonal processes (Hyman and Schuh 1974) that have been observed in the tone languages of the world. Articulatory explanations (e.g., Ohala and Ewan 1973) of tonal phenomena notwithstanding, we must not rule out a priori possible perceptual constraints that may provide a partial explanation of a particular tonal phenomenon.

Considerable attention has been devoted in the literature to just discriminable changes in fundamental frequency (Shower and Biddulph 1931, Boring 1940, Harris 1952, Rosenblith and Stevens 1953, Flanagan and Saslow 1958, Klatt 1973, 't Hart 1974). Some of these studies on pitch discrimination used pure tones as stimuli, and the relevance of their results to speech perception may be seriously questioned in light of the evidence that the subjective pitch of a periodic complex sound depends to a large extent on the periodicity of the waveform regardless of whether there was energy present in the region of the fundamental frequency component or not (Schouten 1940, Miller and Taylor 1948, Flanagan and Guttman 1960, Schouten 1962, Plomp 1966, 1967, Ritsma 1967, Pollack 1969, Houtsma and Goldstein 1970). Klatt (1973), for example, demonstrated that pitch perception is improved slightly when the lower component frequencies and the fundamental are filtered out of the acoustic signal.

Flanagan and Saslow (1958), in their classic study of pitch discrimination, found that just-noticeable differences (JND) in fundamental frequency were approximately .3–.5 Hz in stimuli consisting of synthetic vowels of constant fundamental frequency, and were in general, slightly less than the frequency change discriminate in pure tones of the same frequency and sound-pressure level (Harris 1952). This finding suggests that the presence of harmonic structure provides additional information to the auditory system that is used to estimate pitch. Based on Flanagan and Saslow's results, Lehiste (1970) suggests that "it should be necessary to quantize fundamental vocal frequency on steps of about ±1 Hz in the octave range 80 to 160 Hz, which is the range usually employed by adult male speakers (Fairbanks 1940). Attempted accuracy of measurement should likewise be of the order of ±1 Hz in the fundamental frequency range [p. 64]." But Klatt (1973) correctly points out that "the relevance of the 0.3–0.5 Hz JND figure to speech perception can be questioned;... the experimental conditions under which the fundamental frequency JND was measured did not include the dynamic qualities characteristic of speech [p. 8]."

Klatt's (1973) set of experiments explored the discrimination of fundamental frequency contours in speechlike synthetic stimuli. Subjects (3) listened to a number of 250-msec segments of the synthetic vowel ε, differing only in fundamental frequency. Results indicate that subjects can detect a change of .3 Hz in a constant fundamental frequency contour of 120 Hz (in agreement with Flanagan and Saslow's (1958) original result for synthetic vowels with constant fundamental frequency), but that the JND is an order of magnitude larger

(2.0 Hz) when the fundamental frequency contour has a linear falling slope. It was also found that subjects can detect a change in slope of steep linear falling fundamental frequency contours (corresponding to an initial frequency difference of 4 Hz) and of linear rising and falling fundamental frequency contours with slopes near zero (corresponding to an initial frequency difference of 1.5 Hz). However, as Klatt (1973) himself concedes, "it is not clear whether the subjects base their judgment on rate of change or—for example—on the initial frequency difference between a stimulus pair [p. 72]." More research is required in order to resolve these residual questions. But what is clear, and of interest to the linguist, is the finding that "it is far more difficult to detect an average frequency difference or a difference in rate-of-change of fundamental frequency if the change occurs in a descending ramp fundamental frequency contour [pp. 12–13]." 't Hart (1974) has also investigated the discriminability of fundamental frequency contours in synthetic speech in an attempt to determine how many steps in the size of fundamental frequency movements would be relevant for speech communication. Stimuli consisted of short four-syllable real-speech Dutch utterances that were processed to display contours having a gradual declination line and either a rising or falling slope of varying sizes on the third accented syllable. Native speakers of Dutch (15) were presented with pairs of stimuli that had the same direction of slope, and were asked to report whether one of the two pitch excursions was larger than the other or whether the two pitch excursions were equal. Results indicate that subjects can detect a change of 1.5 semitones in a rising fundamental frequency contour, as compared to 3 semitones in a falling fundamental frequency contour. In other words, changes in the size of pitch rises are easier to discriminate than changes in the size of otherwise identical pitch falls.

While the results of pitch discrimination studies are often difficult to extrapolate to speech perception, the Klatt and 't Hart studies suggest promising avenues for research. A notion of perceptual equivalence between rising and falling pitch movements (small rise = large fall), suggested by the above JND studies on fundamental frequency contours, could provide, in part, a perceptual explanation of the well-known "downdrift" phenomenon among the tone language of West Africa (Schachter and Fromkin 1968, Peters 1973, LaVelle 1976, Meyers 1976), as well as the declination line observed in statement intonational contours (M. Y. Liberman and J. Breckenridge, personal communication).

5. CATEGORICAL PERCEPTION OF TONE

The mode of "categorical perception [Liberman 1957, Liberman, Cooper, Shankweiler, and Studdert-Kennedy 1967]" refers to the phenomenon whereby small steps along an acoustic continuum will produce perceptible differences when they occur between phonetic categories, but not when they occur within a phonetic category. Although the steps along the continuum are well above the nonspeech auditory discrimination threshold, listeners disregard acoustic differences within a category but clearly hear equal acoustic differences between categories. When subjects are asked to discriminate between steps along the acoustic continuum, the listener can do so if he assigns them to different phonetic categories but not if he assigns them to the same phonetic category. In other words, discrimination is dependent on category assignment. The categorical mode of perception is to be distinguished from "continuous perception," a mode in which steps along an acoustic continuum produce no clear-cut category boundaries due to context effects and, further, a mode in which a listener is able to discriminate between steps that he assigns to the same phonetic category. In other words, discrimination is independent of category assignment.

Results of earlier studies seemed to indicate that listeners tend to perceive a continuum categorically if the acoustic variations separate stop consonant categories, but continuously if the "same" acoustic variations separate nonspeech signals or if the acoustic variations separate vowel categories. More recent work, however, has demonstrated that categorical perception is not confined to speech and that continuous perception of vowels is a function of duration and experimental method (for discussion and references, see Lane 1965, Studdert-Kennedy 1974, 1976).

Nonetheless, "the study of categorical perception has . . . revealed functional differences between stop consonants and vowels that are central to the syllabic structure of speech . . . and has provided basic evidence for the distinction between auditory and phonetic levels of processing [Studdert-Kennedy 1974:17]." Granted the perceptual relevance of such studies, the question arises as to how tones are perceived in terms of this dichotomy between continuous and categorical perception.

Abramson (1961) conducted a limited investigation of the categorical perception of Thai tones. The acoustic continuum consisted of five synthetic tonal variants imposed on *naa* that were intended to span the range between the Thai mid (*naa* 'field') and high (*naá* 'aunt') tonal categories (see Figure 1, p. 43). The test design assumed that shape, not height, was the principal acoustical feature distinguishing the Thai mid and high tones. All five tonal variants displayed a falling contour at the end: Tonal Variant 1 had a level fundamental frequency up to the point of fall; Tonal Variants 2–5 had a rising fundamental frequency contour. The tonal variants projected out from a hypothetical initial pivot to the point of fall, each variant separated by 5 Hz at the point of inflection. In the identification tests, Thai subjects (5) assigned the tonal variants to either the mid- or high-tonal categories and displayed a fairly sharp category boundary between Tonal Variants 2 and 3. Discrimination tests included paired 1-step comparisons of the tonal variants arranged in ABX format. At this 1-step level of comparison, it was found that the Thai subjects were slightly better in discrimination at the category boundary (i.e., between Tonal Variants 2 and 3) than American English control subjects.

Though perhaps suggestive of categorical perception, Abramson's results are difficult to interpret because of some uncontrolled variation in the stimuli, individual differences among Thai subjects, discrepancies between the 1-step and 2-step paired comparisons and the rather course 5-step gradation of the acoustic continuum.

In a follow-up study on the categorical perception of tone in Thai, Abramson (1977) used an acoustic continuum consisting of 16 synthetic tonal variants (level fundamental frequency trajectories, ranging from 92 Hz to 152 Hz, super-imposed on *khaa*), which were intended to span the range between the Thai high (*khaá* 'to engage in trade'), mid (*khaa* 'a kind of grass') and low (*khaà* 'galangal') tones. Subjects (33) showed no effect of phoneme categories in their discrimination performance. The results of these experiments are consistent with the view that the perception of Thai tonal categories is not categorical.

Chan, Chuang, and Wang (1975) report (see also Wang 1975) on a categorical perception experiment of Chinese tones. The acoustic continuum consisted of 11 synthetic tonal variants which were intended to span the continuum between Chinese Tone 1 (*ī* 'clothing') and Tone 2 (*í* 'aunt'). The first tonal variant started at 105 Hz and ascended to 135 Hz, the second tonal variant started at 108 Hz and ascended to 135 Hz, the third started at 111 Hz, and so on, until the eleventh stimulus, which was level throughout at 135 Hz. In the beginning portion of the fundamental frequency contours, each of the tonal variants was separated by 3 Hz.

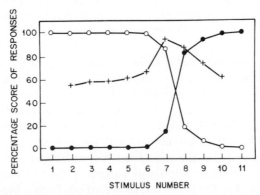

Figure 5. Identification and discrimination functions for Chinese Tone 1 and Tone 2. The open-circle line stands for the identification function of Chinese Tone 2 (*í* 'aunt'); the solid-circle line stands for the identification function of Chinese Tone 1 (*ī* 'clothing'). The plus-line stands for the discrimination function. The ordinate shows both the percentage identification for the identification task and the percentage correct for the discrimination task (adapted from Chan *et al.* 1975, by permission of author).

As can be seen in Figure 5, for the identification test, two untrained Chinese subjects display a sharp category boundary between Tonal Variants 6 and 8; for 2-step ABX discrimination tests, the same two subjects display a peak in discrimination at the category boundary. For three American English control subjects, the category boundary (at Tonal Variant 9) was shifted more toward the level end of the continuum. No peak in discrimination is found at this boundary, but rather a high peak is located between Tonal Variants 9 and 11, thus suggesting that the American English subjects were responding to the psychophysical difference between the level tone and the 10 other tonal variants.

Similar results were obtained for a parallel series of experiments using non-speech stimuli that had the same tonal contours as the speech stimuli. Thus, the preliminary findings of these experiments show that the perception of tone for speech and nonspeech stimuli is categorical to a large extent for native speakers of a tone language. Chan *et al.* suggest that categorical perception of tones for nonspeech stimuli as well as speech stimuli indicates that different processing mechanisms are required than those used for the processing of consonants and vowels.

I would suggest that the phenomenon of categorical perception is not restricted to the linguistic or speech mode, but rather indicates a general auditory sensitivity to acoustic cues that languages happen to exploit to signal differences between phonetic categories. Unless we appeal to an underlying auditory device common to both speech and nonspeech, it would remain sheer coincidence that speech and nonspeech peaks lie at the same place. The differences in scores between speakers of a tone language and speakers of a nontone language would seem to suggest that sensitivity to these cues is heightened as a result of linguistic experience.

However, numerous problems remain in the interpretation of categorical perception experiments on tone. Zue (1976) reports on the categorical perception of Mandarin Chinese tones, with an acoustic continuum consisting of nine tonal variants, intended to span the continuum between Tone 2 and Tone 3. All nine tonal variants, superimposed on the synthetic syllable *bao*, displayed a linear rising fundamental frequency contour (100 to 160 Hz); they differed in the duration (0–400 msec, 50-msec steps) of the beginning steady-state portion up to the point of rise. With this stimulus continuum, both Chinese subjects (3) and American English subjects display a sharp category boundary at Tonal Variant 5, and a peak in discrimination at the category boundary. This result suggests that both groups of subjects simply divided the psychophysical continuum into a "predominantly rising" group of stimuli (Tonal Variants 1–4) and a "predominantly level" group of stimuli (Tonal Variants 6–9). This psychophysical break in the stimulus continuum just happens to coincide with the shapes assumed by Tone 2 and Tone 3 in various sandhi environments. Since Tone 3 does exhibit an essentially flat shape before Tones 1, 2, 4, and the neutral tone, it is perhaps not at all surprising that the Chinese subjects labeled the "predominantly level" group of stimuli as Tone 3.

6. HEMISPHERIC SPECIALIZATION FOR TONAL PROCESSING

There is much evidence to support the claim that the left hemisphere is specialized for language or subsets thereof (for discussion, see Geschwind 1972, Van Lancker 1975, Krashen 1976). An experimental technique commonly used in investigation of speech perception, "dichotic listening," makes it possible to explore the extent to which either the left or right hemisphere is specialized for the processing of auditory signals. In the dichotic-listening paradigm, subjects hear two different auditory signals simultaneously through earphones. When asked to report what he heard in each ear, the responses to the right ear (left hemisphere) are more correct when the stimuli are linguistic in nature, but responses to the left ear (right hemisphere) are more accurate for certain nonlinguistic musical and environmental sounds. Results of dichotic listening experiments (for review of dichotic listening research, see Krashen 1976) generally support the claim that the left hemisphere is not specialized for all auditory stimuli but only those that are linguistic in nature.

Within the dichotic-listening experimental paradigm, Van Lancker and Fromkin (1973) and Van Lancker (1975) took up the question of hemispheric specialization for (nonlinguistic) pitch and (linguistic) tone for native speakers of Thai. One set of stimuli (tone words) consisted of five real-speech Thai words that differed minimally by tone (see Section 2.1), another set (hums) consisted of the five Thai tones hummed without any segmental information. Results from native speakers of Thai (22) indicate that tone words are better heard at the right ear (left hemisphere), while the hums show no ear advantage. Van Lancker and Fromkin conclude that "when pitch is processed linguistically, left-hemisphere specialization occurs as for other language stimuli [p. 107]."

In a similar experiment with speakers of Cantonese, Benson, Smith, and Arreaga (1972) found no right ear advantage in response to tone words. Van Lancker (1975:104), however, points out that the differences in results between Thai and Cantonese study could be attributed to the smaller number of subjects in the Cantonese study and the higher accuracy rate in Cantonese study. Smith and Shand (1974) did find a right ear advantage with a larger number of subjects and with the tone words presented against a background of noise. Thus, it would appear that the left hemisphere is specialized for processing of tones in Cantonese as well as Thai. In a preliminary study of dichotic listening of Yoruba tone words, Curtiss and Lord (1974) were unable to obtain statistically significant results for seven Yoruba speakers. Further testing is necessary before we can evaluate the dichotic-listening results of Yoruba subjects.

7. MULTIDIMENSIONAL SCALING ANALYSIS OF TONE PERCEPTION

> Absolute perceptual identity of two stimuli almost certainly never occurs. What does occur is that two stimuli . . . are perceptually very "similar" and are thus treated "as if" identical. That is, perception acts to group stimuli into more or less homogeneous classes based on degree of similarity [Carroll and Wish 1974a:392].

In multidimensional scaling, the similarity relation between pairs of stimuli is assumed to relate to some form of "distance" defined on dimensions. Direct ratings of similarities or dissimiliarities are generally assumed to measure the psychological distance between the stimuli. These data may be collected for many individual subjects. Typical input data then consists of $n \times n$ stimulus matrices, whose cell values indicate the similarity or dissimilarity of pairs of the n stimuli for m individual subjects (for PARAFAC [Harshman 1970, 1972], the multidimensional scaling method utilized in the perceptual investigations to be discussed below, and INDSCAL [Carroll and Chang 1970, Carroll and Wish 1974a, 1974b, Wish and Carroll 1974]). The output from these multidimensional scaling methods consists of a "group stimulus space"—a configuration of the n stimulus points in an r-dimensional space—and a "subject space"—a configuration of m-individual subject weights in the same r-dimensional space. The weights for each individual subject indicate the relative importance or saliency of each of the r-dimensions. It is primarily by analysis of these subject weights that makes it possible to investigate "individual differences" in perception.

It does seem reasonable to suggest that individuals perceive the world in terms of very nearly the same set of dimensions or perceptual variables but evidently differ enormously with respect to the relative importance (perceptual, cognitive, behavioral) of these dimensions. Such individual differences in the relative importance or saliency of dimensions may be attributed, in part, to the environment (e.g., linguistic environment). With these multidimensional scaling methods that incorporate the notion of individual differences in perception, it is then possible to explore the extent to which an individual's native language influences his perception of speech sounds—of immediate concern here—the perception of tones. To what extent are the dimensions that underlie the perception of tone language-universal? Do particular languages differ in the **number** of features drawn from a common set, or do particular languages differ in the **kind** of features? The studies discussed below have begun such an investigation into the dimensions that underlie the perception of tone.

It is generally acknowledged that one of the primary goals of phonological theory is to develop an empirically grounded set of phonetic features. Considerable disagreement persists, however, between various sets of distinctive features that have been proposed. These sets have differed in both **number** and **nature** of features. Some feature sets have been defined in articulatory terms, others in acoustic terms, while still other sets have included both articulatorily and acoustically based features. The essential nature of phonetic features, their articulatory and perceptual correlates, as well as their level of application in a grammar, present challenging questions for the construction of an empirically based theory of phonology. The aim of Gandour and Harshman's (1978) cross-language multidimensional scaling analysis of tone perception was to bring fresh experimental data to bear on the number and nature of **tone features**—specifically, to determine how many features or dimensions underlie one's perception of tone, what interpretation to assign to the dimensions, and to what extent one's language background influences one's use of the dimensions.

Three languages that differ from one another in the way pitch is used linguistically were chosen for investigation: Thai, Yoruba, and American English. Thai and Yoruba fit into the tone language classification; English does not. Though both Thai and Yoruba are tone languages, they differ in the number and type of lexically contrastive tones (see Sections 2.1 and 2.3). Thai has five contrastive tones, including three level tones and two contour tones;[2] Yoruba has only three contrastive level tones. Although Yoruba does not have lexically contrastive contour tones, surface phonetic rising and falling contour tones do occur, as a result of tonal assimilation rules that operate on sequences of phonologically level tones. A high tone is changed into a rising tone after a low tone; a low tone is changed into a falling tone after a high tone (for further discussion of tone rules, see Ward 1952 and Courtenay 1968). Thus, both Thai and Yoruba have surface phonetic contour tones, but from different sources—in the case of Thai, lexical; in the case of Yoruba, derived by phonological rule. The selection of these three particular languages made it possible to investigate the effect of such differences in phonetic and/or phonological structure on an individual's perception of tone.

The stimulus set used in the experiment contained pitch characteristics commonly reported to be found in tone languages of the world (Pike 1948, Wang 1967), as well as those pitch characteristics apparently used to signal tonal distinctions in Thai and Yoruba. Figure 6 presents a numerical and graphical representation of thirteen tones included in the stimulus set.

Pitch characteristics included three different beginning and ending pitch heights ($1 = 100$ Hz, $3 = 125$ Hz, $5 = 150$ Hz); three level tones versus ten contour tones, five falling and five rising; three different magnitudes of slope; and three different sizes of pitch range traversed (e.g., $15 = 4$-step, $13 = 2$-step, $11 = 0$-step). In addition to these pitch characteristics, nine of the tones were "long" (312 msec) and four were "short" (156 msec). This particular set

---

[2] The decision to assume that Thai has two lexical contour tones was based on the traditional analyses of Thai phonology.

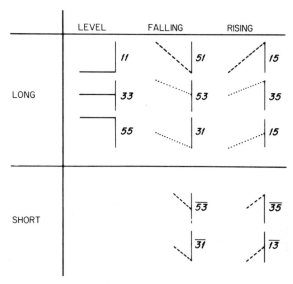

Figure 6. Numeric representation and corresponding graphic representation (after Chao 1930) of the 13 stimulus tones. The ordinate represents a pitch scale ranging from 5 (highest point) to 1 (lowest point), and the abscissa represents time: 55 = "high level," 13 = "low rising," 53 = "high falling," etc. A superscript horizontal bar distinguishes the numeric representations of "short" contour tones from their "long" counterparts. The solid, dashed, and dotted horizontal lines differentiate the 13 stimuli by magnitude of slope.

of thirteen tones also includes seven of Wang's (1967) phonological tones: *11, 33, 55, 53, 31, 35,* and *13*.

Subjects (140:101 Thai, 15 Yoruba, 24 English) were asked to make paired-comparison dissimilarity judgments of these thirteen tones superimposed on a speechlike syllable. PARAFAC estimated the number of linear, orthogonal dimensions underlying the subjects' perceptual judgments of tone and the relative weight or saliency of each dimension for each individual subject.

Results of the PARAFAC analysis indicate that five dimensions, interpretively labeled (1) **average pitch**, (2) **direction**, (3) **length**, (4) **extreme endpoint**, and (5) **slope**, best account for the subjects' perceptual judgments. Figure 7 shows the projection of the thirteen tone stimulus points on each dimension. The dimensions are numbered from left to right in decreasing order of variance accounted for.

Dimension 1, **average pitch**, places the *11* and *55* tones at either end of the axis, *33* near the middle. The clustering of stimuli, in particular *15* and *51* with *33*, clearly supports the interpretation of this dimension. Dimension 2, **direction**, places the five rising and five falling stimuli at opposite ends of the axis, and the three level tones in between. On this dimension, the 4-step interval rising and falling tones are more dissimilar from one another than 2-step interval rising

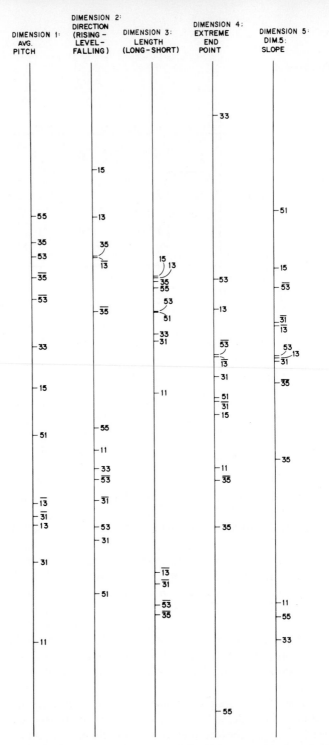

Figure 7. The order and position of the 13 stimulus tones on the five interpreted PARAFAC dimensions. The dimensions are normalized so that the sum of the squared coordinates on each dimension = 1.00.

and falling tones, leading Gandour and Harshman to suggest that for tones opposite in pitch movement, the larger the pitch range, the more dissimilar the tones. Neither the rising nor falling tones cluster according to the pitch height of the beginning or ending point. It is suggested that subjects, on this dimension perceived the tones not as movement **from** a fixed point A **to** a fixed point B, but instead as movement in a direction **away from** A and **toward** B. Linear regression analysis shows that the **direction** dimension closely corresponds to Wang's (1967) phonological feature [±RISING].

Dimension 3, **length**, opposes the nine "long" tones against the four "short" tones. The rising tones (*15, 13, 35*) are seen to be judged longer than their falling counterparts (*51, 31, 53*). The relative position of these rising and falling tones may be related to production data on tonal duration (for review of data, see Gandour 1977), in which vowels or syllables are found to be longer under rising than under falling tones, and perception data (Pisoni 1976; cf. Lehiste 1976), in which vowels under rising tones are perceived to be longer than corresponding vowels under falling tones. The position of the level tones relative to the contour tones, however, does not agree with these other perception data.

Dimension 4, **extreme endpoint**, appears to separate those stimuli containing *1* or *5* endpoints, the extreme ends of the pitch scale, from those stimuli containing a *3* endpoint. The level extreme tones *11* and *55* tend to be perceived as more dissimilar from the nonextreme level tone *33* than do the extreme contour tones from the nonextreme. According to Gandour and Harshman's interpretation, tones at the opposite ends of the physical continuum are more similar psychologically than tones closer to each other on the continuum (e.g., *11* and *55* versus *33*). The dimension **extreme endpoint** is an attempt of PARAFAC to represent this curvature in the perceptual space. It should also be mentioned that multidimensional scaling studies of color perception (Wish and Carroll 1974) and vowel perception (Terbeek and Harshman 1972) also admit the possibility of a nonlinear perceptual space.

Dimension 5, **slope**, orders the stimuli according to magnitude of slope: those stimuli with steepest slope (*51, 15, $\overline{53}$, $\overline{31}$, $\overline{13}$*) at one end of the axis, those stimuli with zero slope (*11, 33, 55*) at the other end, and those stimuli with intermediate slope in the middle. On this interpretation, *35* is the only stimulus tone slightly out of position. The level tones and contour tones show clustering tendencies on this dimension, the former group more tightly clustered than the latter. Linear regression analysis, indeed, shows the **slope** dimension to correspond closely to Wang's binary phonological feature [±CONTOUR].

Of these five dimensions, Gandour and Harshman suggest that two dimensions, **direction** and **slope**, primarily reflect linguistic–phonetic distinctions; two dimensions, **average pitch** and **length**, reflect either linguistic–phonetic or nonlinguistic–auditory distinctions (or both), depending on the language group and the individual subject; and one dimension, **extreme endpoint**, seems to reflect nonlinguistic–auditory properties of the stimulus tones. In addition to a comparison of the clustering patterns of the stimulus tones on each of the dimensions, the linguistic–nonlinguistic interpretation of these five dimensions is evident in a comparison of the mean subject weights or saliency for each language group for each dimension, as shown in Figure 8.

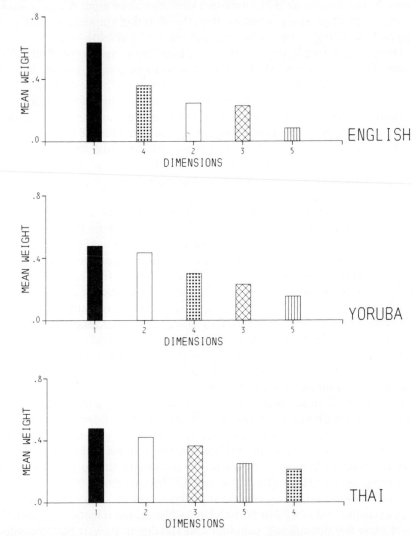

Figure 8.   Mean subject weights for each of the five PARAFAC dimensions for each language group. Dimensions are ordered by mean subject weights from left to right along the abscissa for each language group. Solid-shaded bar stands for Dimension 1, **average pitch**; unshaded bar, Dimension 2, **direction**; cross-hatched bar, Dimension 3, **length**; dotted bar, Dimension 4, **extreme endpoint**; vertical-lined bar, Dimension 5, **slope**.

Dimension 1, **average pitch**, is the most important dimension for all three language groups. Subjects, regardless of language background, emphasized this dimension in making their perceptual judgments, though the English group differs significantly from the Thai and Yoruba groups on the relative importance attached to this dimension. Dimension 2, **direction**, also reveals an interesting separation between Thai and Yoruba, the tone language groups, and English, the nontone language group. The relative perceptual saliency of this dimension, as compared to Dimension 1, is reversed for the language groups: both Thai and Yoruba groups attach significantly more importance to this dimension than English. These cross-language differences in relative perceptual saliency, it is believed, can be accounted for in terms of differences in linguistic structure. The direction of pitch movement, regardless of its level of application in the phonology, obviously carries considerable linguistic information for both Thai and Yoruba speakers and, consequently, was emphasized by those speakers in making their perceptual judgments.

The English group, it should be noted, placed relatively more emphasis on **average pitch** and **extreme endpoint** in comparison with either the Thai or Yoruba groups. Since English is not a tone language, it is not at all surprising that the English group paid relatively little attention to either of the linguistic tone dimensions **direction** and **slope**. The fact that **extreme endpoint** is relatively more important for the English group, as compared to the Thai and Yoruba groups, is further evidence of its nonlinguistic character. There is nothing about the structure of English phonology, in contrast to Thai or Yoruba, that could apparently account for a linguistic interpretation of Dimension 4.

Dimension 5, **slope**, although it accounts for the least amount of variance in the subject's original dissimilarities data, is relatively more salient to Thai and Yoruba, the tone language groups. The fact that Thai and Yoruba also differ in the relative importance attached to Dimension 5 is perhaps related to the occurrence of lexically contrastive level-contour tones in Thai (cf. Hombert 1976b).[3]

This comparison of mean subject weights for **each language group** has revealed significant differences in relative importance attached to these dimensions that appear to be related to the linguistic functions of the dimension(s). Thus, one's language background does have some influence in how tones are perceived. Based on the relative perceptual saliency of the five dimensions combined for **each individual subject**, a discriminant analysis of Thai versus English and Yoruba versus English indicates that the individuals themselves are correctly classified into their respective language group. A discriminant analysis of Thai or Yoruba was not too successful, indicating that, within this five-dimensional tone space, it is easier to distinguish between speakers of a

---

[3] Since we are unsure as to whether Thai does have lexically contrastive level-contour tones, too much importance should not be placed on this suggestion.

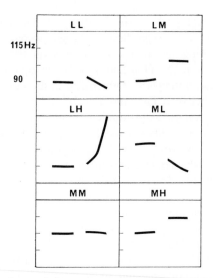

Figure 9. Average fundamental frequency contours (one speaker) of the six Yoruba tone patterns on bisyllabic nouns (from Hombert 1976b, by permission of Department of Linguistics and African Studies Center, University of California, Los Angeles).

tone language and a nontone language than between speakers of two typologically different tone languages.[4]

Hombert (1976b), again using the PARAFAC multidimensional scaling analysis program, investigated the perceptual cues used by Yoruba speakers to distinguish between the six tone patterns of bisyllabic ($V_1 CV_2$) nouns. On V_2, all three lexically contrastive level tones occur (see Section 2.3); on V_1, only low or mid tone occur. Figure 9 shows the average fundamental frequency contours of the six tone patterns.

Phonetically, on V_2, the low tone has a falling contour; the high tone, after a low tone on V_1, has a rising contour.

The stimulus set consisted of two sets of natural-speech minimal pairs, illustrating the 15 possible contrasts in tonal patterns. Yoruba subjects (7) were asked to make paired-comparison (minimal pairs of bisyllabic nouns) judgments of dissimilarity of the tonal patterns.

Results of the PARAFAC analysis indicate two dimensions best account for the Yoruba speakers perceptual judgments. Figure 10 presents the Dimension 1–Dimension 2 plane of the group stimulus space.

Hombert suggests that Dimension 1 is related to direction of pitch movement (falling, level, rising), grouping the six stimulus points into three clusters,

---

[4] See Chapter V by Anderson in this volume for a discussion on the validity of such experiments for decisions regarding the analysis of contour tones as deriving from phonological levels.

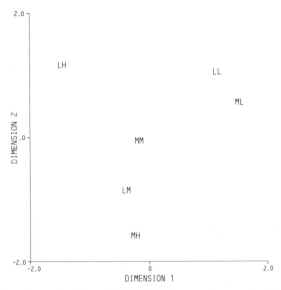

Figure 10. The order and position of the six stimulus tone patterns in the PARAFAC two-dimensional group stimulus space (adapted from Hombert 1976b, by permission of Department of Linguistics and African Studies Center, University of California, Los Angeles).

(1) ML, LL, (2) MM, MH, LM, and (3) LH. The importance of pitch direction in Yoruba speakers' perceptual judgments of tone, using multidimensional scaling techniques, has now been demonstrated with two different stimulus sets (see Gandour and Harshman 1978). This convergence in experimental result is surely not accidental, and thus it reinforces the claim for psychological reality of this perceptual dimension of tone. The interpretation of Dimension 2, as Hombert himself points out, is a bit more complex. The order and position of the six stimulus points first suggest a dimension based on magnitude of slope: LH having the steepest slope on V_2, LL and ML having intermediate slope, and MM, LM, and MH having near-zero slope. On this interpretation, in addition to the slight tendency of clustering of level and contour tones, Dimension 2 bears some resemblance to the **slope** dimension found in Gandour and Harshman's (1978) cross-language study of tone perception. Results of linear regression analysis further indicate that Dimension 1 is also partly determined by the fundamental frequency value of the endpoint of V_2 and that Dimension 2 is also partly determined by the averaged fundamental frequency of V_2 and the difference between fundamental frequency offset of V_1 and onset of V_2 (see Figure 9 above). Thus, it would appear that with a larger number of subjects, a third dimension, based on one of these secondary cues associated with either the first or second dimension, is a likely possibility.

8. CONCLUDING REMARKS

The bulk of previous research on the perception of tone has been directed primarily to the fundamental frequency characteristics of short (monosyllabic or disyllabic) utterances, and it has indeed yielded important information regarding the perception of fundamental frequency contours used to signal tonal distinctions. While the results of this research have been fruitful, the directions for future research seem to lie in the investigation of the perception of fundamental frequency contours in various phonetic and grammatical contexts over longer stretches of speech. By expanding the time domain, questions concerning possible perceptual factors responsible for tonal processes (e.g., tone spreading) that apply in connected speech may be addressed, as well as questions concerning the perceptual effects of the interrelationship between surface constituent structure and various pitch patterns. More research into the relative similarity or dissimilarity of various fundamental frequency contours across several typologically different tone languages should furnish important perceptual information that may partially account for the distribution of tones in synchronic tonal inventories and for diachronic tonal mergers that have taken place in various tone languages, especially those languages and dialects of the Austro–Thai language family. Such research should also provide a better understanding of the underlying dimensions of tone perception required for a general model of tone perception. Hopefully, these suggestions for future research on tone perception will furnish insights into the nature of the interaction between the grammar and the perceptual domain and, ultimately, will furnish a better understanding of the nature of human language.

REFERENCES

Abramson, A. S. 1961. Identification and discrimination of phonemic tones. *Journal of the Acoustical Society of America*, *33*, 842 (abstract).
Abramson, A. S. 1962. The vowels and tones of Standard Thai: Acoustical measurements and experiments. *International Journal of American Linguistics*, *28* (2) (part II). (Also Publication 20.) Bloomington: Indiana University Research Center in Anthropology, Folklore and Linguistics.
Abramson, A. S. 1972. Tonal experiments with whispered Thai. In A. Valdman (Ed.), *Papers in linguistic and phonetics to the memory of Pierre Delattre*. The Hague: Mouton. Pp. 31–44.
Abramson, A. S. 1975. The tones of Central Thai: Some perceptual experiments. In J. G. Harris & J. Chamberlain (Eds.), *Studies in Tai linguistics*. Bangkok: Central Institute of English Language. Pp. 1–16.
Abramson, A. S. 1976a. Thai tones as a reference system. In T. Gething, J. Harris, and P. Kullavanijaya (Eds.), *Tai linguistics in honor of Fang-Kuei Li*. Bangkok: Chulalongkorn University Press. Pp. 1–12.
Abramson, A. S. 1976b. Static and dynamic acoustic cues in distinctive tones. *Haskins Laboratories Status Report on Speech Research*, New Haven, Conn., *SR-47*, 121–127.

Abramson, A. S. 1977. The noncategorical perception of tone categories in Thai. Paper presented at the 93rd Meeting of the Acoustical Society of America, State College, Penn.

Benson, P., Smith, T., & Arreaga, L. 1972. Dichotic listening of lexical tone by speakers of Cantonese and English. Paper presented at the 84th Meeting of the Acoustical Society of America, Miami Beach.

Bolinger, D. L. 1958. A theory of pitch accent in English. *Word, 14*, 109–149.

Boring, E. G. 1940. The size of the differential limen for pitch. *American Journal of Psychology, 53*, 450–455.

Carroll, J. D., & Chang, J. J. 1970. Analysis of individual differences in multidimensional scaling via an n-way generalization of "Eckart-Young" decomposition. *Psychometrika, 35* (3), 283–319.

Carroll, J. D., & Wish, M. 1974a. Multidimensional perceptual models and measurement methods. In E. C. Carterette & M. P. Friedman (Eds.), *Handbook of perception: Psychophysical judgment and measurement* (Vol. 2). New York: Academic Press. Pp. 391–447.

Carroll, J. D., & Wish, M. 1974b. Models and methods for three-way multidimensional scaling. In D. H. Krantz *et al.* (Eds.), *Contemporary developments in mathematical psychology, vol. 2*. New York: W. H. Freeman. Pp. 57–105.

Chan, S. W., Chuang, C. K., & Wang, W. S-Y. 1975. Crosslanguage study of categorical perception for lexical tone. *Journal of the Acoustical Society of America, 58*, 119 (abstract).

Chao, Y. R. 1930. A system of tone letters. *Le Maître Phonétique, 30*, 24–27.

Chao, Y. R. 1948. *Mandarin primer*. Cambridge: Harvard University Press.

Cheng, C. C. 1968. English stresses and Chinese tones in Chinese sentences. *Phonetica, 18*, 77–88.

Cheng, C. C. 1973a. *A synchronic phonology of Mandarin Chinese*. The Hague: Mouton.

Cheng, C. C. 1973b. A quantitative study of Chinese tones. *Journal of Chinese Linguistics, 1* (1), 93–110.

Chomsky, N., & Miller, G. 1963. Introduction to the formal analysis of natural languages. In R. D. Luce, R. R. Bush, & E. Galantis (Eds.), *Handbook of Mathematical Psychology* (Vol. 2). New York: Wiley. Pp. 269–321.

Chuang, C. K. 1972. An acoustical study on the Chinese four tones. Unpublished Ph.D. dissertation [in Japanese], Tohoku University, Sendai, Japan [abstract in English].

Chuang, C. K., Hiki, S., Sone, T., & Nimura, T. 1972. The acoustical features and perceptual cues of the four tones of standard colloquial Chinese. In *Proceedings of the 7th International Congress of Acoustics (Vol. 3)*. Budapest: Akadémial Kiado. Pp. 297–300.

Courtenay, K. 1968. A generative phonology of Yoruba. Unpublished Ph.D. dissertation, UCLA.

Curtiss, S., & Lord, C. 1974. Tone and pitch perception in Yoruba. Unpublished paper, UCLA.

Dreher, J. J., & Lee, P. C. 1966. Instrumental investigation of simple and paired Mandarin tonemes. *DARL Research Communication*, Advanced Research Laboratory, Douglas Aircraft Company. Huntington Beach, California, *13*.

Fairbanks, G. 1940. Recent experimental investigations of vocal pitch in speech. *Journal of the Acoustical Society of America, 11*, 457–466.

Fintoft, K. 1970. *Acoustical analysis and perception of tonemes in some Norwegian dialects*. Oslo: Universitetsforlaget.

Fintoft, K., & Mártony, J. 1964. Word accents in East Norwegian. *Speech Transmission Laboratory: Quarterly Progress Status Report*, Royal Institute of Technology, Stockholm: *3*, 8–15.

Flanagan, J., & Guttman, N. 1960. Pitch periodic pulses without fundamental component. *Journal of the Acoustical Society of America, 32*, 1319–1328.

Flanagan, J., & Saslow, M. 1958. Pitch discrimination of synthetic vowels. *Journal of the Acoustical Society of America, 30*, 435–442.

Fry, D. 1955. Duration and intensity as physical correlates of linguistic stress. *Journal of the Acoustical Society of America, 27*, 765–768.

Fry, D. 1968. Prosodic phenomena. In B. Malmberg (Ed.), *Manual of phonetics*. Amsterdam: North Holland Publishing Co. Pp. 365–410.

Gandour, J. 1977. On the interaction between tone and vowel length: Evidence from Thai dialects. *Phonetica, 34,* 54–65.

Gandour, J., & Harshman, R. 1978. Crosslanguage differences in tone perception: A multi-dimensional scaling investigation. *Language and Speech, 21.*

Garding, E. 1973. The Scandanavian word accents. *Working Papers of the Phonetics Laboratory,* Lund University, Sweden. *8,* 1–119.

Geschwind, N. 1972. Language and the brain. *Scientific American, 226* (4), 76–83.

Hadding-Koch, K. 1961. *Acoustico-phonetics studies in the intonation of Southern Swedish.* Lund, Sweden: Gleerups.

Hadding-Koch, K. 1962. Notes on the Swedish word tones. In A. Sovijävi & P. Aalto (Eds.), *Proceedings of the Fourth International Congress of Phonetic Sciences.* The Hague: Mouton. Pp. 630–638.

Harris, J. D. 1952. Pitch discrimination. *Journal of the Acoustical Society of America, 24,* 750–755.

Harshman, R. A. 1970. Foundations of the PARAFAC procedure: Models and conditions for an "explanatory" multidimensional factor analysis. *UCLA Working Papers in Phonetics, 16.*

Harshman, R. 1972. Determination and proof of minimum uniqueness conditions for PARAFAC 1. *UCLA Working Papers in Phonetics, 22,* 111–117.

't Hart, J. 1974. Discriminability of the size of pitch movements in speech. *Institute for Perception Research Annual Progress Report,* Soesterbera, The Netherlands, *9,* 56–63.

Hockett, C. F. 1947. Peiping phonology. *Journal of the American Oriental Society, 67,* 253–267.

Hombert, J. M. 1975. The perception of contour tones. In C. Cogen, H. Thompson, G. Thurgood, K. Whistler, & J. Wright (Eds.), *Proceedings of the First Annual Meeting of the Berkeley Linguistics Society.* Berkeley: Berkeley Linguistics Society. Pp. 221–232.

Hombert, J. M. 1976a. Consonant types, vowel height, and tone in Yoruba. *UCLA Working Papers in Phonetics, 33,* 40–54.

Hombert, J. M. 1976b. Perception of tones of bisyllabic nouns in Yoruba. *Studies in African Linguistics, Supplement 6,* 109–121.

Houtsma, A. J. M., & Goldstein, J. L. 1970. Aural tracking of musical notes: The problem of the messy fundamental. *MIT Research Laboratories of Electronics Quarterly Progress Report, 98,* 195–203.

Howie, J. M. 1972. Some experiments on the perception of Mandarin tones. In A. Rigault & R. Charbonneau (Eds.), *Proceedings of the 7th International Congress of Phonetic Sciences.* The Hague: Mouton. Pp. 900–904.

Hyman, L. 1975. *Phonology theory and analysis.* New York: Holt, Rinehart and Winston.

Hyman, L., & Schuh, R. 1974. Universals of tone rules: Evidence from West Africa. *Linguistic Inquiry, 5* (1), 81–115.

Jassem, W. 1963. An experiment in word accent perception with synthetic speech. *Speech Transmission Laboratory: Quarterly Progress Report,* Royal Institute of Technology, Stockholm, *1,* 10–12.

Kiriloff, C. 1969. On the auditory perception of tones in Mandarin. *Phonetica, 20,* 63–67.

Klatt, D. 1973. Discrimination of fundamental frequency contours in synthetic speech: Implications for models of pitch perception. *Journal of the Acoustical Society of America, 53,* 8–16.

Krashen, S. 1976. Cerebral asymmetry. In H. Whitaker & M. Whitaker (Eds.), *Studies in neurolinguistics (Vol. 2).* New York: Academic Press. Pp. 157–191.

Ladefoged, P. 1962. *Elements of acoustic phonetics.* Chicago: University of Chicago Press.

Lane, H. 1965. The motor theory of speech perception: A critical review. *Psychological Review, 72,* 275–309.

LaVelle, C. R. 1974. An experimental study of Yoruba tone. *UCLA Working Papers in Phonetics, 27,* 160–170.

LaVelle, C. R. 1976. Universal rules of tone realization. *UCLA Working Papers in Phonetics, 33,* 99–108.

Lehiste, I. 1970. *Suprasegmentals.* Cambridge: MIT Press.

Lehiste, I. 1976. Influence of fundamental frequency pattern on the perception of duration. *Journal of Phonetics, 4* (2), 113–117.

Lehiste, I., & Ivic, P. 1963. Accent in Serbocroatian: An experimental study. *Michigan Slavic Materials, 4.* University of Michigan. Ann Arbor.

Lehiste, I., & Ivic, P. 1972. Experiments with synthesized Serbocroatian tones. *Phonetica, 26,* 1–15.

Lehiste, I., & Peterson, G. 1959. Vowel amplitude and phonemic stress in English. *Journal of the Acoustical Society of America, 31,* 428–435.

Li, C. N., & Thompson, S. 1976. The acquisition of tone in Mandarin-speaking children. *UCLA Working Papers in Phonetics, 33,* 109–130.

Liberman, A. M. 1957. Some results of research on speech perception. *Journal of the Acoustical Society of America, 29,* 117–123.

Liberman, A. M., Cooper, F. S., Shankweiler, D. P., & Studdert-Kennedy, M. 1967. Perception of the speech code. *Psychological Review, 74,* 431–461.

Malmberg, B. 1967. *Structural linguistics and human communication* (2nd ed.). New York: Springer-Verlag.

Martin, S. E. 1957. Problems of hierarchy and indeterminacy in Mandarin phonology. *Bulletin of the Institute of History and Philology,* (Academia Sinica, Taipei), *29,* 209–230.

Meyers, L. 1976. Aspects of Hausa tone. *UCLA Working Papers in Phonetics, 32.*

Miller, G. A., & Taylor, W. G. 1948. The perception of repeated bursts of noise. *Journal of the Acoustical Society of America, 20,* 171–182.

Nabelek, I., Nabelek, A. K., & Hirsh, I. J. 1970. Pitch of tone bursts of changing frequency. *Journal of the Acoustical Society of America, 48,* 536–553.

Ohala, J., & Ewan, W. 1973. Speed of pitch change. *Journal of the Acoustical Society of America, 53,* 345 (abstract).

Peters, A. M. 1973. A new formalization of downdrift. *Studies in African Linguistics, 4,* 139–153.

Pike, K. L. 1948. *Tone languages.* Ann Arbor: University of Michigan Press.

Pisoni, D. B. 1976. Fundamental frequency and perceived vowel duration. Paper presented to the 91st Meeting of the Acoustical Society of America, Washington, D.C.

Plomp, R. 1966. Experiments in tone perception. Institute for Perception, Soesterberg, The Netherlands.

Plomp, R. 1967. Pitch of complex tones. *Journal of the Acoustical Society of America, 41,* 1526–1533.

Pollack, I. 1969. Periodicity pitch for interrupted white noise-factor artifact. *Journal of the Acoustical Society of America, 45,* 237–238.

Purcell, E. T. 1971. The acoustic differentiation of Serbocroatian accents in statements. *Phonetica, 24,* 1–8.

Purcell, E. T. 1972. The acoustic differentiation of Serbocroatian word-tones in statement environments. In A. Rigault & R. Charbonneau (Eds.), *Proceedings of the 7th International Congress of Phonetic Sciences.* The Hague: Mouton. Pp. 997–1003.

Purcell, E. T. 1975. Pitch peak location and the perception of Serbocroatian word tone. Paper presented at the 50th meeting of the Linguistics Society of America.

Rehder, P. 1968. Beiträge zur Erforschung der serbokroatischen Prosodie, die linguistische Struktur der Tonverlaufsminimalpaare. *Slavistische Beiträge, 31.* München: Otto Sagner.

Rosenblith, W. A., & Stevens, K. N. 1953. On the DL for frequency. *Journal of the Acoustical Society of America, 25,* 980–985.

Ritsma, R. 1967. Frequencies dominant in the perception of complex sounds. *Journal of the Acoustical Society of America, 42,* 191–198.

Rosenblith, W. A., & Stevens, K. N. 1953. On the DL for frequency. *Journal of the Acoustical Society of America, 25,* 980–985.

Schachter, P., & Fromkin, V. 1968. A phonology of Akan: Akuapem, Asante, and Fante. *UCLA Working Papers in Phonetics, 9.*

Schouten, J. F. 1940. The perception of pitch. *Philips Technical Review*, 5, 286–294.

Schouten, J. 1962. Existence region of the tonal residue. *Journal of Acoustical Society of America*, 34, 1224–1229.

Shower, E. G., & Biddulph, R. 1931. Differential pitch sensitivity of the ear. *Journal of the Acoustical Society of America*, 3, 275–287.

Smith, T., & Shand, M. 1974. Dichotic perception of initial consonants and lexical tone in Cantonese. Paper presented at the 87th Meeting of the Acoustical Society of America, New York City.

Studdert-Kennedy, M. 1974. The perception of speech. In T. Sebeok (Ed.), *Current trends in linguistics (Vol. 12)*. The Hague: Mouton. (Also in *Haskins Laboratories Status Report on Speech Research*, 1970, *SR-23*, 1–23. New Haven, Conn.).

Studdert-Kennedy, M. 1976. Speech perception. In N. J. Lass (Ed.), *Contemporary issues in experimental phonetics*. New York: Academic Press. Pp. 243–293.

Terbeek, D., & Harshman, R. 1972. Is vowel perception non-Euclidian? *UCLA Working Papers in Phonetics*, 22, 13–19.

Van Lancker, D. 1975. Heterogeneity in language and speech: Neurolinguistic studies. *UCLA Working Papers in Phonetics*, 29.

Van Lancker, D., & Fromkin, V. 1973. Hemispheric specialization for pitch and tone: Evidence from Thai. *Journal of Phonetics*, 1, 101–109.

Wang, W. S-Y. 1967. Phonological features of tone. *International Journal of American Linguistics*, 13, 93–105.

Wang, W. S-Y. 1975. Language change. Paper presented at New York Academy of Sciences Conference on Origins and Evolution of Language and Speech, September.

Wang, W. S-Y., & Li, K-P. 1967. Tone 3 in Pekinese. *Journal of Speech and Hearing Research*, 10, 629–636.

Ward, I. C. 1952. *Introduction to the Yoruba language*. Cambridge: Heffner and Sons.

Wish, M., & Carroll, J. D. 1974. Applications of individual differences scaling to studies of human perception and judgment. In E. C. Carterette & M. P. Friedman (Eds.), *Handbook of perception: Psychophysical judgment and measurement* (Vol. 2). New York: Academic Press. Pp. 449–491.

Zue, V. 1976. Some perceptual experiments on the Mandarin tones. Paper presented at the 92nd Meeting of the Acoustical Society of America, San Diego, California.

III

Consonant Types, Vowel Quality, and Tone[1]

JEAN-MARIE HOMBERT

And Change said "Let the consonants guarding the vowel to the left and the right contribute some of their phonetic features to the vowel in the name of selfless intersegmental love, even if the consonants thereby be themselves diminished and lose some of their own substance. For their decay or loss will be the sacrifice through which Tone will be brought into the world, that linguists in some future time may rejoice [Matisoff 1973a, 73]."

1. INTRODUCTION

This chapter will be devoted to a discussion of the interaction between segments and tone. The effect of the prevocalic consonant types on the fundamental frequency[2] (F_0) and the pitch of the neighboring vowel will be discussed, and, in addition, I will discuss how the vowel quality affects the F_0 and pitch of a vowel. A major motivation for the research on these questions is the attempt to discover an explanation for widely attested historical changes.[3] An

---

[1] I am grateful to the members of the tone seminar at ULCA and the members of the Phonology Laboratory at Berkeley for their help and comments. My special thanks to V. Fromkin, J. Gandour, L. Goldstein, L. Hyman, H. Javkin, P. Ladefoged, I. Maddieson, M. Mazaudon, B. Michailovsky, J. Ohala, and R. Schuh for very helpful discussions and criticisms of this work. This research was supported in part by NSF Grants made to the Phonetics Laboratory, Department of Linguistics, UCLA, and to the Phonology Laboratory, Department of Linguistics, UCB.

[2] The terms **fundamental frequency**, or F_0, **pitch**, and **tone** will be used when referring to articulatory, perceptual, and linguistic entities, respectively.

[3] Explanations of sound changes based on physiological constraints of our articulatory and/or auditory mechanisms have been proposed since the turn of this century. They have received increased attention recently (see Hombert 1975a, Ohala 1974a, 1974b, 1975).

77

understanding of intrinsic effects (i.e., nonintended by the speaker) may provide such an explanation, which implies that the acoustic signal intended by the speaker may become distorted by the time it is perceived by the listener, and that such distortions may give rise to changes over time. The distortions may be due to the action of articulatory constraints which affect the way the sounds are uttered or may be due to auditory constraints which affect the way the sounds are analyzed by the listener's ear. In order to demonstrate that a sound change is phonetically motivated, one has to demonstrate first that these intrinsic perturbations are present in the speech signal (at least in the case of articulatory; motivated sound changes) and, second, that their magnitude is sufficient to be perceived. The historical development of tones (tonogenesis) can result from the reinterpretation by listeners of a previously intrinsic cue after the recession and disappearance of the main cue.[4] The main cue can be an acoustic feature (e.g., voicing) or part of the signal representing a whole segment (e.g., h or ʔ).

In the sections that follow there is some overlap with portions of Chapter I. This is necessary if one is to understand fully the contents of both chapters. In this chapter, however, I will be discussing both the relevant production phenomena and the acoustic (auditory) or perception phenomena, both being important to account for what has been observed in historical change. I will refer to and summarize the findings of previous studies and also report on some of my own experiments which relate to the questions under consideration.

2. EFFECT OF CONSONANT TYPES ON TONE

2.1 Prevocalic Consonants

2.1.1 *Voiced versus Voiceless Stops*

The development of contrastive tones on vowels due to the loss of a voicing distinction on obstruents in prevocalic position is probably the most well documented type of tonogenesis. When such a development occurs, a relatively lower pitch register develops on vowels following the previously voiced series, and a relatively higher pitch is found after the previously voiceless or voiceless aspirated series. This process can lead to a multiplication by two of the number of tones. If the language is atonal, it will have two tones after this development; an already existing two-tone system can be transformed into a four-tone system, and so on. This kind of development is attested extensively in Southeast Asia—in Chinese (Karlgren 1926, Maspero 1912), Karen (Burling 1969,

---

[4] In Hombert (in preparation) the mechanisms underlying the initiation of such sound changes and the switching from the main acoustic cue to the intrinsic (originally secondary) cue are clarified.

TABLE 1

Fundamental Frequencies (in Hz) of Vowels as a Function of the Preceding Consonant as Determined by Three Studies

	p	t	k	b	d	g
House and Fairbanks (1953)	127.9	127.1	127.2	120.9	120.6	122.8
Lehiste and Peterson (1961)	175	176	176	165	163	163
Mohr (1968)	130.7	129.8	131.1	125.1	124.8	125.0

Haudricourt 1946, 1961, Henderson 1973, Jones 1961), Tibeto-Burman (Matisoff 1971a, 1972, 1973a, 1973b, Mazaudon 1977), Austronesian (Blood 1964, cited in Haudricourt 1972b), Tai (Brown 1965, Gandour 1975, Gedney 1973, Li 1954, Sarawit 1973), Miao-Yao (Chang 1973), and Vietnamese (Haudricourt 1954)—as well as in Hottentot languages in South Africa (Beach 1938).

Phonetic studies by House and Fairbanks (1953), Lehiste and Peterson (1961), Mohr (1968), Lea (1973), and Löfqvist (1975), among others, have a bearing on this development of contrastive tones. They show how a voicing distinction in prevocalic position can affect the F_0 of the following vowel. Some of the data from these studies are summarized in Table 1.

Although the number of subjects and the methods used to measure and average the data differ in these studies, it is clear that the F_0 values of vowels after voiceless (aspirated) stops are higher than after voiced stops. Furthermore the results show that these values do not vary in any consistent way as a function of the place of articulation of the stops. Unfortunately, these data give only an averaged or a peak value of F_0, making it impossible to deduce the time course of the F_0 perturbation caused by the preceding consonant.

Experiment I In order to provide the information lacking in the earlier studies summarized in Table 1, I conducted the following experiment. Five subjects without speech disorders or history of hearing pathology whose native language was some form of general American English were used. They each pronounced six CV nonsense words where C = [p, t, k, b, d, g] (and for three subjects [w, m] as well), and V = [i]. The word list spoken consisted of 10 tokens of each test word arranged in random order. Each test word was uttered in the frame "say ____ again." The recording was done in a sound treated room. Measurements were made on a minicomputer after hardware F_0 extraction (Krones 1968). With a reference point at the onset of the vowel, F_0 values were measured at onset and 20, 40, 60, 80, and 100 msec after the onset.

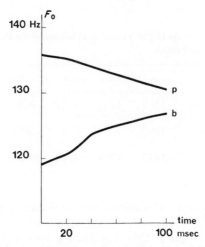

Figure 1. Average fundamental frequency values (in Hz) of vowels **following** American English stops. The curves labeled [p] and [b] represent the values associated with all voiceless and voiced stops, respectively, regardless of place of articulation (five subjects).

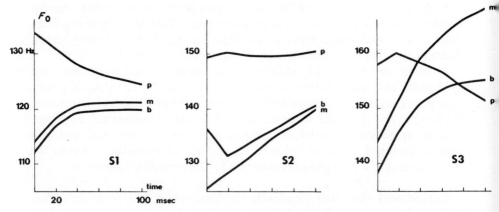

Figure 2. Average fundamental frequency values (in Hz) of vowels following English voiced and voiceless stops and sonorants from three individual speakers.

The results are given in Figures 1 and 2. Figure 1 illustrates F_0 curves on the vowels following the voiced and voiceless stops, averaged over all speakers' samples, and Figure 2 shows the F_0 curves, including those for vowels following sonorants, for three individual speakers.

Although the greatest difference in the F_0 curves in Figure 1 exists at vowel onset, statistical analysis (analysis of variance followed by Duncan's test) reveals that they are still significantly different 100 msec after vowel onset.

These two curves differ from each other in two ways: direction of F_0 change and average relative value. The data in Figure 2 show that individual speakers' F_0 curves exhibit one or both patterns.

The explanations proposed to account for these data (F_0 raising after voiceless consonants versus F_0 lowering after voiced consonants) can be divided into two categories. The first attributes these F_0 perturbations to aerodynamic effects, and the second to differences in vocal cord tension. (See Chapter I for further discussion on these hypotheses.)

Researchers following the first theory (i.e., aerodynamic) would explain the phenomenon in the following terms. After the closure of a voiced consonant, voicing continues, but since the oral pressure increases (because of the closure), the pressure drop decreases, leading to a lower frequency. The fundamental frequency then rises after the release until it reaches the "normal" value of the vowel which is being realized. In the case of a voiceless consonant, since the rate of airflow is supposed to be high, a strong Bernoulli effect will draw the vocal folds together very rapidly; they will be pushed apart very rapidly as well because the subglottal pressure is still high. Consequently, the rate of vibration of the vocal folds will be high at the onset of the vowel and will return gradually to the intrinsic value of the vowel being realized.

The experimental data just presented, as well as earlier studies (Löfqvist 1975), show that a consonant still affects the fundamental frequency of the following vowel at least 100 msec after vowel onset. Proponents of the second theory (vocal cord tension) claim that this perturbatory effect is too long to be attributed to aerodynamic factors. Halle and Stevens (1971) suggest that these intrinsic variations are the result of horizontal vocal cord tension, and they propose the features [stiff] and [slack] vocal cords to capture the relationship between low tone and voiced consonants (where the vocal cords are supposed to be slack in order to facilitate voicing) on the one hand, and high tone and voiceless consonants on the other hand. Studies by Ohala (1972) and Ewan and Krones (1974), as well as more recent work by Ewan (1976), suggest that the F_0 perturbation is caused at least partially by vertical tension (i.e., larynx height).

Both of these explanations (horizontal and vertical tension) fail to account for the fact that postvocalic consonants do not have the same effect on F_0 as prevocalic ones do (however, see below). Lea (1972, 1973) suggests that both voiced and voiceless consonants lower the F_0 of the preceding vowel. Other studies (Mohr 1971, Slis 1966) indicate that postvocalic consonants have an effect on F_0 similar to that of prevocalic consonants, but with a much smaller magnitude. The counterargument presented above, based on different influences of pre- and postvocalic consonants can be weakened if one considers that postvocalic consonants are less "strongly" articulated than their prevocalic counterparts (Slis 1967, Fromkin 1966).

Nevertheless, Halle and Stevens' position is not supported by experimental data; electromyographic recordings by Hirose, Lisker, and Abramson (1973) and Hirose and Gay (1972) do not show obvious differences in the tension of the laryngeal muscles during the production of voiced/voiceless distinctions. Ewan and Krones' claim, however, is in agreement with experimental data showing a correlation between F_0 and larynx height (Ohala 1972, Ohala and Ewan 1973). Ewan and Krones (1974) also show a correlation between voiced sounds and low larynx position as opposed to voiceless sounds and high larynx position. It was also indicated that the larynx was in lower position at the end than at the beginning of a voiced consonant. This suggests that the larynx is actively lowered during a voiced consonant in order to increase the volume of the oral cavity. Warren and Hall (1973) and Bell-Berti (1975) show that this is, at least partially, an active process. If this is the case, one would expect to find a perturbed (lowered) F_0 after voiced consonants, as opposed to a nonperturbed F_0 after sonorants and voiceless consonants. Unfortunately this does not seem to be the case in the data presented in Figure 2, where it is shown that sonorants pattern similarly to voiced obstruents. Although it seems that theories based on muscular tension cannot account for some of the data, we are in an even more difficult situation with theories based only on aerodynamic factors.

Klatt, Stevens, and Mead (1968) present airflow data in which a high rate of airflow lasts only about 50–60 msec into the vowel; comparable but uncalibrated data are presented by Frøkjær-Jensen, Ludvigsen, and Rischel (1971). Moreover, van Hattum and Worth (1967) as well as Isshiki and Ringel (1964) show that oral airflow is momentarily lower after voiceless aspirated consonants than it is after voiced consonants. These data are in agreement with the results of a mathematical model of aerodynamics proposed by Ohala (1976) (see Chapter I). These results seem to favor the theories based primarily on muscular tension.

In the discussion on the effect of obstruents on the F_0 of following vowels, the data presented were from nontonal languages. What these data do not show is the effect of voiced and voiceless consonants at different frequency registers. It is necessary to determine whether the onset frequency of a vowel with a phonologically (and phonetically) low tone will still be affected by a voiced consonant; similarly, we would like to know whether a voiceless consonant will perturb the frequency of a high tone vowel.

Experiment II   In order to find answers to such questions another experiment was conducted. Data on the time course of F_0 variation after voiced and voiceless stops were gathered from two speakers of Yoruba, a language with three contrasting tones: high, mid, and low. The results are given in Figure 3. Each data point represents the average of 70 measurements (see Hombert 1977a for details). The dotted lines represent F_0 of vowels after each series of consonants, and the plain lines represent the averaged frequency of the three Yoruba tones preceded by voiced and voiceless consonants.

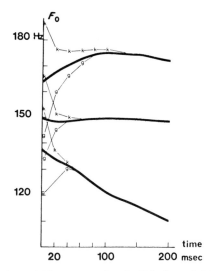

Figure 3. Average fundamental frequency values (in Hz) of vowels following voiced and voiceless velar stops occurring with each of the three Yoruba tones. The thick lines give the average values for both types of stops for each of the three tones (two subjects).

From the data presented in Figure 3, three points can be made:

1. The perturbation caused by a voiced consonant on a following high tone or by a voiceless consonant on a following low tone is greater than the effect of these two series of consonants on a mid tone.
2. The effect of a voiced consonant on a following high tone is greater than the effect of a voiceless consonant on a following low tone.
3. The duration of the perturbations caused by prevocalic consonants on the fundamental frequency of vowels is shorter in Yoruba than in English (cf. Figure 1).

It is interesting to point out that these results are in agreement with Gandour's findings (1974) in his investigation of Thai tones. Gandour found that a shorter part of the vowel was affected by the preceding consonant (about 30 msec for voiceless consonants and about 50 msec for voiced consonants). There may be a tendency in tone languages (which does not exist in nontonal languages) to minimize the intrinsic effect of prevocalic consonants actively—probably in order to render the different tones maximally perceptually distinct.

It was pointed out above that the importance of such "intrinsic" features can only be determined after perceptual studies are conducted. There is evidence from perceptual experiments using synthesized speech that small fundamental frequency perturbations can be used as cues to discriminate between sonorants and voiced obstruents and between voiced and voiceless obstruents (Christovitch 1969, Haggard et al. 1970, Fujimura 1971, Abramson 1975). The perception of stimuli with changing frequency contours has been investigated for pure tones (Brady *et al.* 1961, Heinz *et al.* 1968, Nabelek and Hirsh 1969, Nabelek *et al.* 1970, Pollack 1968, Sergeant and Harris 1962, Tsumura *et al.* 1973) as well as for vowels (Klatt 1973, Rossi 1971). From these studies, however, it is difficult to conclude to what extent the perception of a changing frequency contour would be affected by a steady-state frequency immediately following the contour.

Experiment III In order to obtain these data, the following study was carried out. Ten subjects, native speakers of American English, with normal hearing, participated. Acoustic stimuli consisting of 10 instances of the vowel [i] were synthesized with different fundamental frequency patterns.

As shown in Figure 4, each stimulus was composed of a slope followed by a level tone maintained constant at 120 Hz. The onset frequency was either 110 or 130 Hz (i.e., $F_0 = \pm 10$ Hz). The duration of the slope was varied at 40, 60, 100, 150, and 250 msec. In other words, five stimuli (with F_0 onset = 130 Hz) had a falling fundamental frequency, and five stimuli (with F_0 onset = 110 Hz) had a rising fundamental frequency. The overall duration of each stimulus was fixed at 250 msec. Each time a stimulus was presented, it was followed by a 500 msec pause and a second vowel [i] with a steady-state fundamental frequency. The duration of this vowel was also 250 msec. The level of its fundamental frequency was adjustable by a knob controlled by the subject. The task was to match the pitch of the second vowel to the pitch of the beginning of the first vowel. The rate of stimulus presentation as well as the number of trials for a given presentation were controlled by the subject. Each one of the 10 stimuli was presented three times in a randomized order. The subjects heard the stimuli through earphones at a comfortable level (about 70 dB). The parameter values were chosen in order to simulate the effects of consonants on neighboring vowels.

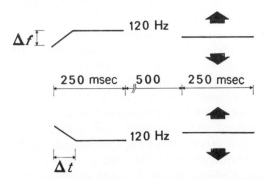

Figure 4.   Schematic representation of the format of stimulus presentation.

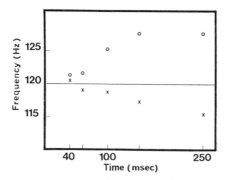

Figure 5. Subjects' responses (i.e., their estimates of starting pitch of tone with initial ramp) plotted as a function of the duration of the ramp. Open circles plot subjects' response to the stimuli with initial falling ramp (130 to 120 Hz); the crosses plot their responses to the stimuli with the initial rising ramp (110 to 120 Hz).

The results are presented in Figure 5; subjects' responses are plotted as a function of the duration of the slope. Responses to stimuli with a falling F_0 at the onset (from 130 to 120 Hz) are indicated by a circle ($\bigcirc$), responses to stimuli with a rising F_0 (from 110 to 120 Hz) are indicated by a cross ($\times$). A statistical analysis of these data (analysis of variance followed by Duncan's test) indicates that the two curves are already perceived as significantly different when the onset slope (from F_0 onset to level F_0) is 60 msec long.

This graph suggests that (*a*) falling patterns (i.e., vowels with fundamental frequency onset below 120 Hz) are perceived more accurately than rising patterns (i.e., vowels with fundamental frequency onset below 120 Hz) and (*b*) the longer the slope, the more accurate the matching; correlation, however, between slope duration and accuracy of matching is not linear.

These results can be explained by forward masking. If we extrapolate the results obtained with steady-state tones to contours, (i.e., masking a higher frequency by relatively lower frequency), we can understand why the onset region of the rising ramp was not accurately perceived, since each frequency was masked by the previous lower frequency (since the frequency is going up). This is not the case for the falling tone in which each frequency is followed by a lower frequency.

Data from the psychoacoustic literature (Brady *et al.* 1961, Heinz *et al.* 1968, Pollack 1968, Nabelek and Hirsh 1969, Nabelek *et al.* 1970, Tsumura *et al.* 1973) can be interpreted as supporting this claim concerning the role of masking in the perception of changing frequency contours. In these experiments, subjects were asked to match the pitch of a steady-state signal with a changing frequency signal. They consistently adjusted their steady-state tone closer to the final point of the contour. This fact already shows the role of masking, which attenuates the effect of the onset region in favor of the offset region, but furthermore there is a tendency to match closer to the final point when the stimulus is a rising contour (as opposed to a falling contour). This indicates, as I have suggested, that the masking of the onset is more effective in the case of rising contours (as opposed to falling contours), and, consequently, this leads to the perception of an averaged pitch closer to the offset frequency. These data are also in agreement with the study of Brady *et al.* (1961) with respect to the role of the rate of frequency change. They found that the matching of a steady-state frequency with a contour frequency is closer to the end point of the contour when the rate of change is high; in other words, the onset region is less salient at high glide rates. This is shown in Figure 5 by responses close to 120 Hz when the slope duration of the stimulus is short (i.e., the rate of frequency change is high). This is also in agreement with Pollack (1968) and Nabelek and Hirsh (1969), whose results indicate that optimum discriminability of relatively small frequency changes is obtained at relatively slow glide rates.

Finally, it should be pointed out that this experiment was limited to the comparison of F_0 differences of vowels following voiced and voiceless obstruents. Further research should investigate the perceptual role of F_0 during voiced consonant immediately preceding vowels versus the absence of F_0 during voiceless consonants.

In Experiments I and II, I showed that the consonantally induced F_0 perturbations on vowels in such nontone languages as English and Swedish persist for some 100 msec after vowel onset. The perceptual data just presented indicate that listeners start hearing significant differences in the F_0 onset of our synthesized stimuli when the slope of the F_0 contour is 60 msec long. Thus, there is at least 40 msec between the time we start hearing the differences and the time the real consonant-related F_0 variations cease to be significantly different. These data, then, allow us to define the narrow limits, both perceptual and articulatory, within which the development of tones from a former voiced/voiceless stop contrast is likely to occur.

2.1.2 Voiced versus Voiceless Sonorants

Haudricourt (1961) claims that in Vietnamese as well as in Tai, the two-way split of the tonal system was not conditioned by a merging of voiceless and voiced series of stops, but rather by the loss of aspiration in the sonorants. He illustrates his point by showing that a tonal split occurred in dialects which have kept the voicing distinction with the stops but which have lost the aspiration in the sonorants as in the case of the Tho dialect of Cao Bang. Similarly, in the Blimaw dialect of Bwe (Karen), aspirated and voiced nasals have merged, phonologizing the tone system. Unfortunately no acoustic data showing the effect of voiced versus voiceless aspirated sonorants on the F_0 of the following vowel are available. It is therefore difficult to validate this change phonetically, as we did in the case of the stop series.

2.1.3 Aspiration

When a language which has voiceless aspirated, voiceless unaspirated, and voiced stops develops two tones from the merging of two of these series, the voiceless unaspirated series generally patterns with the aspirated series, as in Pwo-Karen (Haudricourt 1946, Mazaudon 1977) and most Tai dialects such as Wunning, Chuang, Lung Chow, Nung, Shan, and Black and White Thai (Sarawit 1973). Sometimes, however, the voiceless unaspirated series behaves like the voiced series and has a tendency to give lower tonal reflexes than the unaspirated series, as in Siamese or in Pwo-Karen. Ballard (1975) mentions that in Wu Chiang, tones following the aspirated series are lower than after the unaspirated series.

Similarly, when a language is developing three contrastive tones from three series of stops (voiceless aspirated, voiceless unaspirated, and voiced), there is a tendency to develop higher tones on vowels following the historically voiceless aspirated series, as attested in a Siamese dialect of the Trang province (Haudricourt 1961). However there are some counterexamples to this tendency: In Saek (Sarawit 1973), for instance, there was a tonal split under Prototone A conditioned by the voiceless aspirated/unaspirated series. The tone following the historically aspirated series is lower than after the unaspirated one (*11* versus *24*).[5]

It is often assumed (Hombert 1975a) that voiceless aspirated stops give rise to a higher F_0 at the onset of the following vowel. This claim is supported by data from languages such as Korean (Han 1967, Kim 1968), Thai (Ewan 1976), and Danish (Jeel 1975). However, conflicting data are found from the same as well as other languages. They sometimes show no difference in F_0 onset depending on the preceding consonant, as illustrated by Danish (Fischer-Jørgensen 1968), and sometimes they exhibit the opposite pattern, that is, a higher F_0 after voiceless unaspirated than after voiceless aspirated stops, as in Korean (Kagaya 1974), Thai (Gandour 1974, Erickson 1975), and Hindi (Kagaya and Hirose 1975). In order to provide new data which hopefully will help clarify this issue, an investigation of the two series of voiceless stops in English and French was carried out.

Experiment IV In this experiment two American English speakers (one female and one male) and two French speakers (one female and one male) produced six CV nonsense words [pi, ti, ki, bi, di, gi]. The word list consisted of 10 tokens of each test word arranged in random order, and each test word was uttered in the frame "Say ____ louder" (and "*Dire* ____ *lentement*" for the French frame). No special instructions were given with respect to the speed of reading. The recording was done in a sound treated room. The speech

---

[5] The numbers represent the traditional way of representing tones by Sinologists: *11* = low level tone; *24* = low rising tone.

waveform was sampled at an effective rate of 20,000 Hz. Since most F_0 extractor methods perform poorly in determining the F_0 during the first few cycles, and since these measurements were crucial in our study, we made our measurements directly on the digitized waveform. In order to get maximum accuracy in locating similar points on each consecutive period, high frequencies (above 1 kHz) were filtered out.

An analysis of the data shows that the voice onset time (VOT) values for the French [p, t, k] were shorter than in English (approximatively 15, 30, and 50 msec, respectively, versus 45, 65, and 85 msec for English). As was already noticed by Fischer-Jørgensen (1972) these VOT values from French are longer than one would expect for so-called voiceless unaspirated stops.

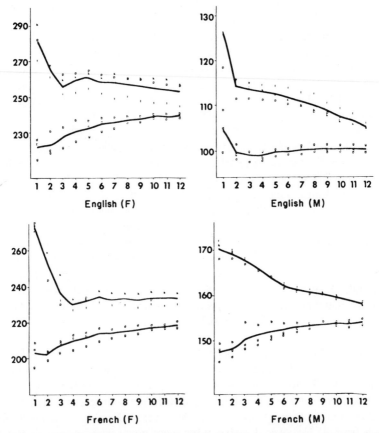

Figure 6. Average fundamental frequency values (in Hz) (vertical axis) of vowels following *p t k* and *b d g* (orthographic) as a function of glottal period (horizontal axis) for two American English speakers (one female and one male) and two French speakers (one female and one male). The upper curve represents average F_0 measurements after *p t k*, the lower curve represents average F_0 measurements after *b d g*.

On the top left graph of Figure 6, the fundamental frequency on the vertical axis is plotted as a function of successive vocal fold cycles on the horizontal axis. The upper line represents the average F_0 after voiceless aspirated stops, the lower line corresponds to the so-called voiced stops. F_0 values corresponding to each individual stop (p, t, k, b, d, g) are represented by corresponding letters on the graph (with the usual orthographic convention). There is the usual fall after the aspirated stops and the usual rise following the voiced stops. The top right graph shows similar data for an English male except for the fact that, even after his so-called voiced stops, the F_0 falls. The bottom left graph shows a French female speaker. The top line shows the comparatively unaspirated stops. But there is still a large fall in F_0. The bottom right graph shows that the French male speaker behaves in substantially the same way. It is clear from these data that there is not a direct correlation between the duration of aspiration after a voiceless consonant and the onset F_0 of the following vowel. English and French voiceless consonants have very similar perturbatory effect on the F_0 of the following vowel, despite the fact that English voiceless stops are far more aspirated.

In order to be able to explain why voiceless aspirated and voiceless unaspirated stops have similar effects on the F_0 of the following vowel, let us examine how the various parameters controlling F_0 are effected by the aspirated versus unaspirated distinction. The first thing that might affect F_0 is the glottal opening. The fact that the glottis is widely open upon release of a voiceless aspirated stop, as opposed to a more closed position for a voiceless unaspirated stop, is irrelevant here. What matters is the relative timing of onset of voicing and glottal adduction. Although the activity of the posterior cricoarytenoid is more important 50 to 100 msec before voice onset (Hirose 1975), there is no evidence that this will affect the rate of vibration of the vocal folds. The vocalis, lateral cricoarytenoid, cricothyroid, and sternohyoid do not seem to be associated with the voiceless aspirated versus voiceless unaspirated distinction, and in most cases these muscles are not involved in the voiced/voiceless distinction either (Hirose and Gay 1972). Consequently, I do not see any reason for a difference in the horizontal tension of the vocal cords for aspirated versus unaspirated sounds. Experimental data show that in Thai and Hindi (Gandour and Maddieson 1976, Ewan 1976, Ewan and Krones 1974) both voiceless aspirated and unaspirated stops have a higher larynx position than their voiced counterparts. But the data are contradictory with respect to the voiceless aspirated/unaspirated series. Let us consider the aerodynamic factors. It has been found in a number of languages such as English (Ladefoged 1967, 1968, 1974, Lieberman 1967, McGlone and Shipp 1972, Murry and Brown, 1975, Netsell 1969), Swedish (Löfqvist 1975), Hindi (Ohala and Ohala 1972, Dixit 1975), and Dutch (Slis 1970) that the respiratory system generates a constant subglottal pressure irrespective of the stop categories (voiced versus voiceless, aspirated versus unaspirated).

It seems that the variations in subglottal pressure can be predicted from glottal and supraglottal adjustments (e.g., glottal opening, mouth opening), even in the case of languages such as Jinghpo (Ladefoged 1971) and Korean (Kim 1965, Lee and Smith 1972) in which different subglottal pressures have been associated with different stop categories. Most experimental data do not show a higher rate of airflow **at vowel onset** depending on the preceding consonant (Isshiki and Ringel 1964, van Hattum and Worth 1967). Klatt, Stevens, and Mead's data (1968) show a slightly higher airflow after the aspirated stop only for a short period of time (about 50 msec).

Although it is true that some data (Subtelny *et al.* 1969) show a higher airflow rate after the aspirated versus the unaspirated series (1070 versus 650 ml/sec) for a significantly longer period of time (over 200 msec after vowel onset), it seems likely that these results reflect the poor frequency response of the flowmeter (warm-wire method) used in this experiment (Kozhevnikov and Chistovitch 1966, Hardy 1967, van den Berg 1962) rather than an actual long-term airflow rate difference caused by the preceding consonant. In fact, Ohala's model of speech aerodynamics (1976) gives a smaller value for airflow at the onset of a vowel following an aspirated stop, as opposed to a higher value after a voiceless unaspirated stop. It does not seem that available airflow data allow us to predict significant differences in F_0 after voiceless aspirated versus unaspirated stops.

It seems then that the parameters controlling the rate of vibration of the vocal folds are not significantly different at the onset of a vowel following a voiceless aspirated stop versus a voiceless unaspirated stop. This explains the data presented at the beginning of this section, where it was shown that English voiceless aspirated stops and French voiceless unaspirated stops had very similar effects on the fundamental frequency of the following vowel. These data also explain why there is no clear tendency to develop a higher (or a lower) tone after voiceless aspirated stops when these stops merge with the voiceless unaspirated series.

2.1.4 Breathy Voiced Consonants

In Punjabi, breathy voiced consonants became voiceless unaspirated, leaving a low tone on the following vowel (Gill and Gleason 1969, 1972, Haudricourt 1971, 1972a, 1973). Data presented by Glover (1970, 1971) on Tibeto-Burman languages indicate that breathy voiced consonants were stronger pitch depressors than (simple) voiced obstruents. In Ndebele, breathy voiced consonants pattern with voiced obstruents in lowering the pitch on following vowels (Ladefoged 1971).

The "seeds" of this phenomenon can be found in Hindi, a nontone language, in that the onset frequency of a vowel after a breathy voiced consonant is markedly lower than that after any other consonant type (Ohala 1974b, Kagaya and Hirose 1975).

The physiological cause of this phenomenon requires more investigation; however, some of the contributory factors can be guessed at. Although the rate of airflow is high upon release of breathy voiced consonants, the vocal cords are not closely adducted, and thus the Bernoulli force should be weak. In addition, during breathy voice there is a less forceful contraction of the laryngeal adductor muscles (Ohala 1973, Hirose, Lisker, and Abramson 1973, Dixit 1975, Kagaya and Hirose 1975), many of which not only act to bring the vocal cords together but also are known to participate in F_0 regulation (Hirano and Ohala 1969, Ohala 1970, Atkinson 1973).

2.1.5 Implosives

Greenberg (1970) indicates that implosives "are always less productive of tone lowering than the corresponding plain voiced stops . . . . [They have] an effect identical with or similar to that of voiceless consonants [p. 133]." In the Loloish group of Lolo-Burmese, the "glottalized" series led to the development of higher tones than the voiceless or voiced series as attested in modern dialects such as Lahu, Lisu, and Sani (Matisoff 1972, Mazaudon 1977). In most Tai dialects, the so-called "preglottalized" series behave like the voiceless series, but in a few cases, as in Lung Ming and in some Pu-yi dialects, the preglottalized series patterned with the voiced series. It is possible to attribute this behavior to the fact that in these dialects the "preglottalized" consonants were in fact ejectives. Available data seem to indicate that ejectives are neutral with respect to tonal development. Phonetic data are badly needed with respect to this class of consonants.

Ohala (1976) presented data from a mathematical model of speech aerodynamics that suggest the plausibility of a claim (attributed to Ladefoged) that the rapidly lowering larynx during implosives generates a very high rate of glottal airflow and in that way raises the F_0 above the normal level. This would only explain a higher pitch for the voicing during the implosive consonant closure itself, however, and would not explain the higher pitch on adjacent vowels.

2.1.6 Prenasalized Stops

In some Miao dialects (Tung-t'ou, Hsiao-chang, Wu-chia), prenasalized stops have produced a tonal split (Chang 1973). In Chichewa (Trithart 1976) and Ngie (Hombert 1976a) there is some evidence that prenasalized voiced stops may have a stronger lowering effect on F_0 than single voiced stops. Here again phonetic data are badly needed to validate these claims made on historical grounds.

2.1.7 Fortis versus Lenis

Haudricourt (1968, 1972a) shows that in Camuhi the merging of a fortis series (old geminates) with the voiceless aspirated series led to a high tone word if these consonants were in word-initial position. Maddieson (1974b) wants to derive the three-tone system of Yoruba from the two-tone system of Niger–Congo through a split conditioned by a fortis/lenis distinction. He claims that fortis stops would be realized with stiffened pharyngeal walls, which would lead to a smaller oral cavity and consequently to a greater drop in F_0. Such developments are very difficult to explain phonetically since they refer to features (fortis and lenis) which are not clearly defined articulatorily. It has been shown that the relationship between [fortis] and extramuscular tension is not always justified (Malécot 1966, 1970). If this fortis/lenis distinction refers to intraoral pressure, then we expect a development similar to the development caused by a voiced/voiceless distinction. If it refers to a length distinction it has been shown by Elugbe and Hombert (1975) that, at least for nasals, this fortis/lenis distinction did not lead to any significant F_0 differences at the onset of the following vowel.

It is therefore not possible at this time to validate or invalidate by phonetic research the claims regarding the role of the fortis/lenis distinction in tonogenesis.

2.2 Postvocalic Consonants

2.2.1 Voiced versus Voiceless Stops

Tonal development from the loss of a voicing distinction in the postvocalic position is extremely rare (if it exists at all). Maran, however, (1971, claims that in certain dialects of Jingpho, tones are completely predictable from the voicing of the final consonant, and he even goes further, predicting the tones from the final segment even when the voicing distinction has disappeared in the surface form. Matisoff (1971b), however, offers a different analysis of Maran's data which does not depend on the voicing of the final consonants affecting the tone of the preceding vowel.

Some studies (Mohr 1968, Slis 1966) indicate that postvocalic consonants have an effect on F_0 similar to that of prevocalic consonants (i.e., voiced consonant lowering versus voiceless consonants raising the F_0 of the vowel) but with a much smaller magnitude. Other studies (Hanson 1975, Lea 1972, 1973) suggest that both voiced and voiceless consonants lower the F_0 of the preceding vowel.

Given the ambiguity of the results of these studies, it is not surprising that there are so few (if any) instances in which the voicing distinction of final consonants gave rise historically to tonal distinctions. That is, since the intrinsic perturbation caused by postvocalic voiced and voiceless consonants on the F_0 of preceding vowels is either similar or random, such perturbations cannot be reinterpreted as tonal contrasts by speakers.

2.2.2 Laryngeals [ʔ] and [h]

The effect of a glottal stop on the pitch of the preceding vowel is widely attested. By the sixth century, glottal stops had disappeared in Vietnamese and were replaced by rising tones (Haudricourt 1954, Matisoff 1973a). In the Lolo-Burmese family, Burmese high tone corresponds to Jingpho glottal stop (Maran 1971), and Lahu high rising tone developed through glottal dissimilation (Matisoff 1970), Mei (1970) has shown that Middle Chinese *shang sheng* (rising tone) comes from a final glottal stop.

The development of a falling tone from a postvocalic [h] has been observed in two cases. Middle Chinese *qu sheng* (falling tone) comes from postvocalic [h] (Pulleyblank 1962, Baron, personal communication). The same origin has been reported for Vietnamese falling tone (Haudricourt 1954, Matisoff 1973a).

Experiment V   In order to evaluate the phonetic processes underlying these developments, an experiment was conducted to show the intrinsic effects of [h] and [ʔ] on the F_0 of the preceding vowel. The subjects in this experiment were four Arabic speakers without speech disorders or history of hearing pathology. They spoke six $C_1 VC_2$ nonsense words placed within the frame *ulu* $C_1 VC_2$ *liyya* ('say $C_1 VC_2$ to me') (C_1 = [m], V = [i, a, u] and C_2 = [h, ʔ]). The word list consisted of 10 tokens of each test word arranged in random order and was read twice. Measurements of F_0 were made on a PDP-12 computer after hardware pitch extraction. Starting from a reference point at the offset of the vowel, F_0 values were measured every 10 msec back to a point 100 msec before the offset. The data obtained from the four subjects are presented in Figure 7, and the results are summarized in Table 2. As seen from this table, F_0 goes up a minimum of 9 Hz before [ʔ] and down 25 Hz before [h]. The two sets of curves are significantly different at least 70 msec before vowel offset. The parameter chosen for the statistical analysis (i.e., the interval between vowel

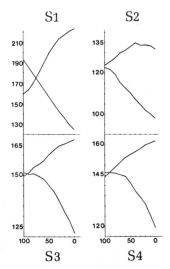

Figure 7.   Average fundamental frequency values (in Hz) of vowels preceding [ʔ] (curves with positive slope) and [h] (curves with negative slope) in Arabic (four subjects).

TABLE 2

**Effect of Postvocalic Laryngeals (h and ʔ) on the F_0
of the Preceding Vowel in Arabic (Four Subjects)**

	Δt msec	Δt_s msec	Δf_h Hz	$\Delta f_ʔ$ Hz
Subject 1	70	70	−50	+48
Subject 2	100	80	−25	+25
Subject 3	90	80	−29	+29
Subject 4	90	80	−27	+27

Key:

Δt = Time interval between the points of intersection of the two F_0 curves and the vowel offset.

Δt_s = The smallest time interval at which the two curves are significantly different.

Δf_h = F_0 difference between F_0 offset of vowel preceding [h] and F_0 value at point of intersection.

$\Delta f_ʔ$ = F_0 difference between F_0 offset of vowel preceding [ʔ] and F_0 value at point of intersection.

offset and intersection of F_0 values) represents the most conservative estimate of statistical significance. If the slope of the curves had been chosen as the parameter, the statistical significance would have been improved.

Experiment VI   In order to determine the extent to which such F_0 variations can be perceived, the following experiment was conducted. Ten subjects, native speakers of American English with normal hearing, participated in the experiment. The stimuli consisted of 30 instances of the vowel [i] synthesized with different fundamental frequency patterns. As shown in Figure 8, the onset

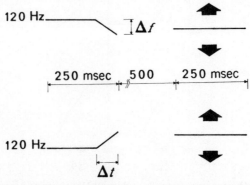

Figure 8.   Schematic represention of the format of stimulus presentation.

frequency was 120 Hz, the frequency difference ΔF between offset and onset frequency was varied, taking the following values: -50, -20, -10, $+10$, $+20$, and $+70$ Hz. The overall duration of the stimulus was fixed at 250 msec. The duration of the rising or falling portion of the stimulus, Δt, was varied between 40, 60, 100, 150, and 250 msec. In other words, 15 stimuli ($3F_0$ offset $\times$ 5 slope durations) had a falling F_0, and 15 stimuli had a rising F_0. Each time the stimulus was presented, it was followed by a 500-msec pause and a second 250-msec vowel [i] with a steady-state F_0. The level of the F_0 of this second vowel was adjustable by a knob controlled by the subject. Each of the 30 stimuli was presented three times in a randomized order. The stimuli were presented over earphones at a comfortable level (about 70 dB). Subjects were asked to match the steady-state F_0 of the second vowel with the F_0 offset of the first vowel.

A statistical analysis of the results shows that the set of synthesized F_0 contours simulating the effect of a following [ʔ] are significantly different ($p < .01$ for paired data and $p < .05$ for grouped data, $1Q$) from the F_0 contours simulating the effect of a following [h] when $\Delta F_? = +10$ Hz and $\Delta F_h = -10$ Hz, and $\Delta t = 40$ msec. For all other greater values of ΔF and Δt, the two F_0 patterns are perceived as significantly different ($p < .01$, $1Q$).

From the Arabic data presented earlier, we concluded that an [h] produces a drop in F_0 (varying from 25 to 50 Hz) on the preceding vowel, while [ʔ] produces a rise in F_0 (from 9 to 48 Hz). It was also shown that these two curves became significantly different at least 70 msec before vowel offset. The perceptual data presented in the preceding paragraph show that F_0 perturbations similar to those caused by [h] and [ʔ] can be perceived even when these perturbations are very small ($\Delta F = \pm 10$ Hz and $\Delta t = 40$ msec).

In summary, it was shown that:

1. [h] and [ʔ] produce significant perturbations on the F_0 of the preceding vowel.
2. These perturbations can be perceived by the auditory system.

The overlap between these two sets of data validate and explain the development of rising and falling tones from the loss of [h] and [ʔ] postvocalically.

3. EFFECT OF TONE ON CONSONANTS

Both the historical and phonetic data discussed above show that consonants can affect tone. On the other hand, it has been claimed that tone does not affect consonants (Hyman 1973b, Hyman 1976a, Hyman and Schuh 1974; but see Maddieson 1974a, 1976a). It certainly is extremely difficult to find a single case in the literature in which it is clear either from the author's presentation or from our own reanalysis that voiceless consonants, for example, became voiced before a low tone, or voiced consonants became voiceless before a high tone. The more widely attested development of postvocalic laryngeals is a much more likely process in these contexts. After a low tone (especially a low falling tone) the vertical displacement of the larynx, which seems to be the main mechanism for F_0 lowering (Ohala, this volume), as well as the relaxation of the cricothyroid muscle, may affect the vibratory conditions sufficiently (Stevens, 1975) to lead to irregular vibrations of the cords, which will be perceived as creakiness (sometimes called laryngealization). This is probably what happened in Kiowa (Sivertsen 1956). Another possibility is that the vibratory conditions deteriorate sufficiently so that voicing stops. If air continues to escape through the open nonvibrating cords, [h] or breathiness can develop. This may be the origin of the breathiness associated with Jingpho low tone (Matisoff, personal communication). After a rising tone (especially after a sharply rising tone) the increased muscular tension of the cords may lead to a glottal closure, which can be reinterpreted as a postvocalic glottal stop as in Jeh (Gradin 1966).

4. EFFECTS OF VOWEL QUALITY ON TONE

A number of scholars attempting to trace the historical development or origin of tone in widely separated languages have suggested that different vowels may give rise to contrasting tones. Thus, Pilczkowa-Chodak (1972) suggests that tone assignment of verbs and of noun plurals in Hausa is largely predictable from the height of the final vowel: A high (versus low) final vowel predicts a high (versus low) tone. This analysis, however, has been criticized by Hausa scholars (Newman 1975, Leben and Schuh, personal communications).

It is also suggested that Middle Chinese words with checked tones (i.e., p, t, k endings) and voiceless initial consonants developed a relatively lower tone when the vowel nucleus was [a] than when it was [ə] (Pulleyblank 1970–1972). In some Cantonese dialects, this tone development has sometimes been analyzed as originating from a length contrast. In the Omei dialect of Mandarin, two tones rearranged themselves depending on vowel height; the "new" high tone regrouping high vowels (Cheung 1973). In Ngizim (Schuh 1971) and in Bade the tone patterns of verbs are partially predictable from the vowel of the first syllable; if the vowel is [a], the verb will have a high tone.

These historical data do not suggest that the development of contrastive tones from vowel height is a .widely attested process; furthermore, the reverse direction of interaction (i.e., low vowels giving rise to high tones) as observed in Ngizim and Bade seems phonetically inexplicable. It would be of interest then if a phonetic explanation for the infrequency of this type of effect could be found.

TABLE 3

Intrinsic Fundamental Frequency of Vowels (in Hz)

		i	*a*	*u*
Black (1949)	(16 subjects)	145.7	132.7	153.0
House and Fairbanks (1953)	(10 subjects)	127.9	118.0	129.8
Lehiste and Peterson (1961)	(5 subjects)	129	120	134
Peterson and Barney (1952)	(33 subjects)	136	124	141

Several studies have shown that American English vowels have an intrinsic fundamental frequency related to their height: High vowels (low F_1) have a higher fundamental frequency than low vowels (Black 1949, House and Fairbanks 1953, Lehiste and Peterson 1961, Peterson and Barney 1952) as shown in Table 3. The same correlation between vowel height and F_0 is found in other languages, such as Danish (Petersen 1976), French (Di Cristo and Chafcouloff 1976), Korean (Kim 1968), and Serbo-Croatian (Ivíc and Lehiste 1963).

Essentially four theories have been proposed to explain why high vowels have a higher intrinsic fundamental frequency than lower vowels. The first theory, proposed by Taylor (1933) and adopted by House and Fairbanks (1953) is called the "dynamo-genetic" theory. Taylor claims that the muscular tension of the tongue, required for the realization of high vowels, is transferred to the muscles of the larynx "via a kind of sympathetic resonance or radiation." This is no longer a viable theory, since we know that electrical insulation in muscles and nerves is good enough to prevent serial contraction of adjacent muscles triggered by osmotic spread of excitability (Atkinson 1973).

The second theory presented by Mohr (1971) relates width of the pharynx and pressure build up behind the point of constriction to explain the fundamental frequency differences between low and high vowels. Since the width of the pharynx is about one-fourth as big for low back vowels as for corresponding high vowels, Mohr tries to relate smaller cavity and constriction further back with higher supraglottal pressure, leading to smaller pressure drop across the glottis and consequently lower fundamental frequency. Unfortunately Mohr's data do not support his own theory.

The next theory, known as the source tract coupling theory (Atkinson 1973, Boë 1972, Flanagan 1965, Flanagan and Landgraf 1968, Lieberman 1970), assumes a possible coupling between the vocal cords and the vocal tract so that a low first formant (characteristic of high vowels) would attract and consequently raise the fundamental frequency. This interaction would be weaker when the first formant is further away from the fundamental frequency (as it is in the case of low vowels). The intrinsic pitch difference between low and high vowels would then be explained. Unfortunately, predictions made by this theory do not receive empirical support. It would predict, for instance, that the difference in pitch between high and low vowels would be reduced when speaking with a helium–air mixture (since a property of helium (or other light gases) is to raise formants and consequently to increase the distance between F_0 and F_1). Beil (1962) showed that this was not the case.

The tongue-pull theory (Ladefoged 1964, Lehiste 1970) is based on the assumption that when the tongue is in high position for the realization of high vowels, it exerts an extra tension transmitted to the larynx via the hyoid bone. This vertical pull increases the tension of the vocal cords (Ohala 1972) and gives rise to a higher pitch for these high vowels. This theory ran into difficulty when Ladefoged, DeClerk, Lindau, and Papçun (1972) provided data showing that tongue height and hyoid bone height were inversely proportional. Although they do not refute the tongue-pull theory, these data show at least that the pulling action is not done through the hyoid bone. Furthermore, if we assume a correlation between larynx height and F_0 (Ohala and Ewan 1973, Ewan and Krones 1974), it seems that the tongue-pull theory would predict that, in a tone language, the F_0 difference would be smaller with vowels realized with high tones as opposed to vowels realized with low tones. Since the larynx is in higher position for high tones than for low tones, we expect that the tension exerted by the tongue will be less. This assumes a linear relationship between tension and larynx elevation (which would have to be tested). Data from Yoruba (Hombert 1977a) and Ewe (Lafage and Hombert, in preparation) show that predictions made by the tongue-pull theory are not verified; in fact, the opposite is found, namely, that the fundamental frequency difference between high and low vowels is more pronounced with high tone than with low tone.

Recently, however, Ohala and Eukel (1976) brought new support in favor of the tongue-pull theory. They showed that an increased pull of the tongue on the laryngeal structures leads to an enhancement of the F_0 difference between high and low vowels. In order to evaluate the extent to which these intrinsic F_0 values were perceived, the following experiment was conducted.

Experiment VII   Ten subjects (five females and five males), all native speakers of American English, participated in this experiment. They were asked to compare the pitch of two synthesized vowels (generated by a software synthesizer) of different quality. Only those who were able to achieve a score of 95% or better in a control experiment involving the comparison of the pitch of two pure tones were selected as subjects. The formant values of the three vowels used in this experiment are given in Table 4. These values are taken from Peterson and Barney (1952), except for the second and third formants

TABLE 4

Formant Values of Synthesized Vowels
i, a, u

	i	*a*	*u*
F_1 (Hz)	270	730	300
F_2 (Hz)	2600	1090	870
F_3 (Hz)	2800	2440	2240

of [i], which were raised in order to sound more speechlike (Delattre, Liberman, Cooper, and Gerstman 1952). Three fundamental frequencies, 115, 120, and 125 Hz (with an accuracy of $\pm .5\%$) were superimposed on each of these three vowels which had a duration of 250 msec (with a rising and decay time of 20 msec). The interval separating the first vowel (V_1) and second vowel (V_2) was 500 msec. The F_0 of the second vowel was either 5 Hz below, equal to, or 5 Hz above the F_0 of the first vowel (in other words, the F_0 range of V_2 was from 110 to 130 Hz). V_1 and V_2 always differed in quality (i.e., there were no i–i, a–a, or u–u sequences). Six repetitions of all possible V_1 and V_2 comparisons were presented (excluding cases where V_1 and V_2 had the same quality), making a total of 324 judgments ($3V_1$ qualities $\times$ $3V_1$ F_0 $\times$ $2V_2$ qualities $\times$ $3V_2$ F_0 $\times$ 6 repetitions). Overall amplitude levels were equalized for the three vowels. Subjects were asked to judge whether the first or the second vowel was higher in pitch (i.e., a two-way forced choice). They were instructed to mark the corresponding vowel on their answer sheet. They had 3 seconds in which to make a response. The experiment was divided into two parts preceded by a short training session in which six pairs were presented. The same stimulus presentation format was adopted in the control experiment in which synthesized vowels were replaced by pure tones. The role of this control experiment was twofold; it was used to determine the accuracy of the subjects' pitch perception and also to investigate the effect of stimulus ordering on the perception of pitch, especially when the two tones had the same frequency.

Since the criterion used to select subjects was quite strict (minimum of 95% correct in the control experiment), they made very few mistakes when the vowels were 5 Hz apart (90% correct or better). As a result, in the following analysis I will only consider the pairs which had identical F_0 on both vowels. The subjects' responses for these pairs are presented in Table 5. From this table, it is clear that the low vowel [a] has a tendency to be judged higher in pitch than the high vowels [i] or [u] (although their fundamental frequencies were in fact equal). Similar results were obtained recently by Chuang and Wang (1976).

TABLE 5

Number of Times Each Vowel Was Judged to Be the Higher in Pitch When Comparing the Pitch of Vowels of Different Quality but Equal Fundamental Frequency (10 Subjects)

$i:a$ comparison ($i-a$ and $a-i$ pairs)	$u:a$ comparison ($u-a$ and $a-u$ pairs)	$u:i$ comparison ($u-i$ and $i-u$ pairs)
$a = 257$	$a = 261$	$i = 185$
$i = 103$	$u = 99$	$u = 175$

These data demonstrate that the effect exists, that the perceived pitch difference between high (low F_1) and low (high F_1) vowels is smaller than their fundamental frequency difference would indicate. However, the origin of this effect has not been demonstrated. Two possibilities should be investigated:

1. It is a low level phenomenon which can be explained by vowel spectra characteristics.
2. It is a higher level phenomenon involving some normalization of fundamental frequency depending on vowel height.

Although a controlled experiment is required in order to accept or reject one of these hypotheses, available relevant experimental data do not seem to favor the first. It has been known for some time that intensity affects pitch perception. Stevens (1935) shows that the pitch of a tone whose frequency is 150 Hz is lowered by as much as 11% when its intensity is raised by 50 dB. More recent data (Cohen 1961) suggest a smaller effect (2–4%). In order to apply these data to vowels, we have to know the frequency region which is the most relevant for pitch perception. Ritsma (1967) indicates that for fundamental frequencies in the range of 100–400 Hz (i.e., the relevant range for speech), the frequency region consisting of the third, fourth, and fifth harmonics plays a dominant role in the perception of pitch. Since the vowels used in this experiment had a F_0 of 115, 120, or 125 Hz, the dominant frequency region is located between 345 (3×115) and 600 Hz (5×125). Since we know (Cohen 1961, Snow 1936, Stevens 1935, Zurmühl 1930) that by increasing loudness we lower the pitch (assuming that we are dealing with a tone below 1000 Hz), the results of Experiment VII would be explained if we could show that the amplitude of the spectrum of [i] or [u] is sufficiently greater than the amplitude of [a] in the relevant frequency region (i.e., approximately 345–600 Hz). In fact, as can be seen from Figure 9, the intensity of [a] is higher than the intensity of [i] or [u] in a major part of this frequency region, and consequently would not explain our results.

The second possibility would imply an interaction between F_0 and vowel quality at a higher neurological level. Since vowel quality and intrinsic F_0 are always produced simultaneously, it is possible that our auditory system subjects

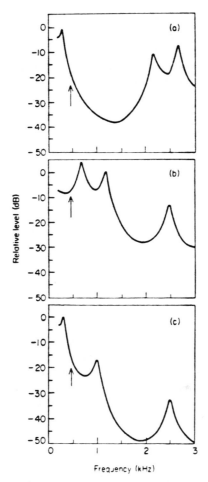

Figure 9. Spectrum of vowels *i, a, u* from top to bottom (after Stevens and House 1961). Arrows indicate dominant frequency region for pitch perception.

the speech signal to some form of normalization having the effect of raising the pitch of low vowels (or lowering the pitch of high vowels). Similar perceptual effects in other systems have been investigated and described; for instance, the size–weight effect by which a small size box is judged heavier than a bigger box of equal physical weight (Birnbaum and Veit 1974). It should be noted that Experiment VII indicates only the direction of the effect. The only quantitative information is that for these selected subjects, under these experimental conditions, the effect was smaller than 5 Hz.

The data presented in Table 3 indicate that the intrinsic variations of fundamental frequency due to vowel height are of the same order of magnitude as the intrinsic differences caused by prevocalic consonants (see Table 1). In fact,

Lehiste (1970) mentions that "the influence of an initial consonant could counterbalance the influence of intrinsic pitch: the average for /kæ/ sequences was 171 Hz, while that of /gi/ sequences amounted to 170 Hz [p. 71]." Since vowel height and prevocalic obstruents seem to cause comparable intrinsic perturbations, one would expect tonal development resulting in vowel merging to be as frequent as tonal development resulting in the loss of some voicing contrast in prevocalic position; and one would expect the development to show that high vowels give rise to high tones and low vowels to low tones. However, historical data illustrating such developments are scanty (see the preceding discussion). Several reasons can be presented to account for this lack of historical development of tones from vowel height:

1. One would expect that such a tonal development would start where the intrinsic differences are maximum; that is, from the merging of low and high vowels. This seems unlikely since even very restricted vowel systems contain *i*, *a*, and *u*.

2. One can also argue that the intrinsic perturbations caused by prevocalic consonants are of a different nature than those caused by vowel height. A voiced (versus voiceless) consonant causes a rising (versus falling) fundamental frequency pattern at the onset of the following vowel. On the other hand, the intrinsic fundamental frequency associated with different vowel qualities is manifested by differences in steady-state fundamental frequency levels. Our auditory system is more "efficient" at detecting changes in varying fundamental frequency signals than differences (of the same magnitude) between two steady-state fundamental frequency signals.

3. Our perception of pitch of vowels can be affected by vowel quality, as was shown earlier.

5. OTHER TYPES OF TONE CHANGES

Independently of the effect of neighboring segments, a tone system can (*a*) increase the number of its tones; (*b*) keep the same number of tones but change the phonetic realizations of existing tones; or (*c*) decrease the number of tones.

5.1 Increase in the Number of Tones

When syllables are lost in a tone language, the tones carried by these syllables are not necessarily lost; they are sometimes recombined with neighboring tones creating new tone shapes. For example, low–high and high–low sequences can become rising and falling tones, respectively, on one syllable after the second syllable is lost. Such changes are commonly found in the Grassfields languages of Cameroun, for instance (Hombert 1976a, Hyman 1972 and in this volume, Hyman and Tadadjeu 1976, Hyman and Voorhoeve 1978, Voorhoeve 1971).

5.2 Changes in the Phonetic Realizations of Tones

5.2.1 Tone Sandhi

The phonetic realizations of certain tones can be influenced by tonal (as well as segmental) contexts. These processes have been described in detail for African languages (Hyman 1973b, 1976b, Chapter VIII, this volume, and Hyman and Schuh 1974) and are also commonly found in Asia (where they are generally referred to as tone sandhi phenomena) (Schuh, Chapter VII, this volume). The phonetic motivations for these sandhi rules are not always obvious anymore.

5.2.2 Redistribution in the Tone Space

The development of new tones from segmental influences in an already complex tone system may lead to the birth of tones very close to each other in the tone space. Under such conditions, these two tones can either merge (see Section 5.3) or move away from each other in the tone space. Their new location can be very different from the original one (Hombert 1977c).

5.2.3 Tone Reversed

A number of languages (e.g., the Chinese dialects of Xi'an, Yangzhou, and Chaozhou, as well as some Loloish languages such as Lahu, Lisu, and Sani) have relatively lower tonal reflexes after historically voiceless consonants and relatively higher tonal reflexes after historically voiced consonants. Some of these cases can probably be explained in terms of reorganizations of tones in the tone space. It is possible that a tone developing from a voiceless consonant found an empty "slot" at a lower location in the space. If all the tones which developed from the voiced consonants are systematically higher than the corresponding tones which developed from voiceless tones, other explanations are needed.

We can speculate both on articulatory and perceptual grounds. First, a possible explanation is that the voiced consonants went through an implosive stage (b → ɓ) before merging with the voiceless series. Since implosives have a tendency to raise the F_0 of the following vowel, it would not be surprising to find lower tonal reflexes on vowels following historically voiceless consonants.

Second, it is possible to speculate on how the intrinsic F_0 perturbations caused by a voiced/voiceless distinction can, for perceptual reasons, lead to completely different tonal developments in Languages A and B. Let us suppose that at the time of the split conditioned by prevocalic voiced/voiceless stops, Language A had a tone system in which the main perceptual cue used to distinguish tones was the onset or the offset or the average pitch of the tone (e.g., a language with level tones only). Let us suppose that speakers of Language B, on the other hand, are using the direction of F_0 change as the main perceptual cue. It becomes easier to understand now why speakers of Language A would reinterpret the intrinsic F_0 shapes after voiced/voiceless consonants [>] as [=], emphasizing that F_0 after voiced consonants is lower than after voiceless consonants, as opposed to Language B, which would reinterpret the same intrinsic F_0 shapes [>] as [X], emphasizing the falling contour after voiceless consonants as opposed to the rising contour after voiced consonants. Now we are at a stage in which at least the second part of the tone originating from the voiced consonants is higher than the corresponding part of the tone originating from the voiceless consonants.

Similar cases of tone reversal have been reported for languages in which tones did not develop from neighboring segments, such as Manya, Loma (Dwyer 1974), Ciluba (Maddieson 1976b), Dangaleat (Fedry 1974), and Chipewyan. Maddieson proposed an explanation based on tonal displacement caused by a high tone morpheme historically added in word-initial position. It would be interesting to see if the same type of explanation would account for the other cases, especially when prefixes are used extensively as in Chipewyan.

5.3 Decrease in the Number of Tones

If two tones are too similar phonetically, they can either move away from each other in the tone space or merge, as happened, for instance, in Vietnamese, Lahu, and numerous Chinese dialects. Sometimes the complexity of a tone system is diminished, not by decreasing the number of tones, but rather by increasing the constraints on possible tone patterns. Such cases are commonly found in Eastern Bantu languages (Schadeberg 1973, Voorhoeve 1973). Because of these constraints, some languages reach a stage where their tonal behavior is very similar to the tonal behavior found in pitch-accent languages (Kalema, 1977). In languages like Swahili and Nyakusa (Kähler-Meyer 1971), the tone system completely disappeared as the result of such processes.

REFERENCES

Abramson, A. S. 1975. Pitch in the perception of voicing states in Thai: Diachronic implications. *Haskins Laboratories Status Reports on Speech Research*, SR-41, 165–174.
Atkinson, J. E. 1973. Aspects of intonation in speech: Implications from an experimental study of fundamental frequency. Unpublished Ph.D. dissertation, Univ. of Connecticut.
Ballard, W. L. 1975. Wu tone sandhi. Paper presented at the 8th International Conference on Sino-Tibetan Languages and Linguistics, Berkeley.
Beach, D. M. 1938. *The phonetics of the Hottentot language*. Cambridge.
Beil, R. G. 1962. Frequency analysis of vowels produced in helium-rich atmosphere. *Journal of the Acoustical Society of America*, 34, 347–349.
Bell-Berti, F. 1975. Control of pharyngeal cavity size for English voiced and voiceless stops. *Journal of the Acoustical Society of America*, 57, 456–461.

van den Berg, J. 1962. Modern research in experimental phoniatrics. *Folia Phoniatrica, 14*, 81–149.
Birnbaum, M. H., & Veit, C. T. 1974. Scale-free tests of an additive model for the size-weight illusion. *Perception and Psychophysics, 16*, 278–282.
Black, J. W. 1949. Natural frequency, duration, and intensity of vowels in readings. *Journal of Speech and Hearing Disorders, 14*, 216–221.
Boë, L. J. 1972. Etude de l'interaction source laryngienne–conduit vocal dans la détermination des caractéristiques intrinsèques des voyelles orales du français. *Bulletin de l'Institut Phonétique de Grenoble, 1*, 25–43.
Brady, P. T., House, A. S., & Stevens, K. N. 1961. Perception of sounds characterized by a rapidly changing resonant frequency. *Journal of the Acoustical Society of America, 33*, 1357–1362.
Brown, J. M. 1965. *From ancient Thai to modern dialects.* Bangkok: Social Science Assoc. Press of Thailand.
Burling, R. 1969. Proto-Karen: A reanalysis. *Occasional Papers of the Wolfenden Society on Tibeto-Burma Linguistics, 1*, 1–116.
Chang, K. 1973. The reconstruction of proto-Miao-Yao tones. *Bulletin of the Institute of History and Philology-Academica Sinica, 44*(4), 541–628.
Cheung, S. H. N. 1973. Tonal redistribution in the Omei dialect. Paper presented at the 6th International Sino-Tibetan Conference, San Diego.
Chistovich, L. A. 1969. Variation of the fundamental voice pitch as a discriminatory cue for consonants. *Soviet Physics-Acoustics, 14*(3), 372–378.
Chuang, C. K., & Wang, W. S. Y. 1976. Influence of vowel height, intensity, and temporal order on pitch perception. *Journal of the Acoustical Society of America, 60*(1), (A), LL 13.
Cohen, A. 1961. Further investigation of the effects of intensity upon the pitch of pure tones. *Journal of the Acoustical Society of America, 33*, 1363–1376.
Delattre, P., Liberman, A. M., Cooper, F. S., & Gerstman, L. J. 1952. An experimental study of the acoustic determinants of vowels. *Word, 8*, 195–210.
Di Cristo, A., & Chafcouloff, M. 1976. An acoustic investigation of microprosodic effects in French vowels. Paper presented at the 14th Conference on Acoustics. High Tatra, Czechoslovakia.
Dixit, R. P. 1975. Neuromuscular aspects of laryngeal control: With special reference to Hindi. Unpublished Ph.D. dissertation, Univ. of Texas, Austin.
Dixit, R. P., & Shipp, T. 1975. A study of subglottal air pressure in Hindi stop consonants. *Journal of the Acoustical Society of America, 58*(1), F11.
Dwyer, D. 1974. Loma: A language with inverted tones. Paper presented at the 5th Conference on African Linguistics, Stanford University.
Elugbe, B., & Hombert, J. M. 1975. Nasals in Ghotuọ: /lenis/ or [short]? *Nasalfest: Papers from a symposium on nasals and nasalization.* Stanford: Language Universals Project. Pp. 167–174.
Erickson, D. 1975. Phonetic implications for an historical account of tonogenesis in Thai. In J. G. Harris & J. R. Chamberlain (Eds.), *Studies in Tai linguistics in honor of W. J. Gedney.* Bangkok: Central Institute of English Language Office of State Universities. Pp. 110–111.
Erickson, D., & Atkinson, J. E. 1975. The function of the strap muscles in speech. *Journal of the Acoustical Society of America, 58*, (1), F4.
Ewan, W. G. 1976. *Laryngeal behavior in speech.* Ph.D. dissertation, Univ. of California, Berkeley.
Ewan, W. G., & Krones, R. 1974. Measuring larynx movement using the thyroumbrometer. *Journal of Phonetics, 2*, 327–335.
Fedry, J. 1974. pátó à l'est, pàtò à l'ouest, ou l'énigme tonale des parlers dangaleat. Paper presented at 11ème Congrès de la Société Linguistique de l'Afrique ociddentale, Yaoundé, Cameroun.
Fischer-Jørgensen, E. 1968. Les occlusives françaises et danoises d'un sujet bilingue. *Word, 24*, 112–153.
Fischer-Jørgensen, E. 1972. p t k et b d g français en position vocalique accentuée. In A. Valdman (Ed.), *Papers in linguistics and phonetics to the memory of Pierre Delattre.* The Hague: Mouton. Pp. 143–200.

Flanagan, J. L. 1965. Recent studies in speech research at Bell Telephone Laboratories. *Proceedings of the 5th International Congress on Acoustics, Liege.*

Flanagan, J. L., & Landgraft, L. L. 1968. Self-oscillating source for vocal-tract synthesizers. *IEEE Transactions: Audio and Electro Acoustics,* AU-16, *1,* 57–64.

Frøkjær-Jensen, B., Ludvigsen, C., & Rischel, J. 1971. A glottographic study of some Danish consonants. In *Form and Substance: Phonetic and linguistic papers presented to Eli Fisher-Jørgensen.* Akademisk Forlag. Pp. 123–140.

Fromkin, V. A. 1966. Neuro-muscular specification of linguistic units. *Language and Speech, 9*(3), 170–199.

Fujimura, O. 1971. Remarks on stop consonants: Synthesis experiments and acoustic cues. In *Form and Substance.* Pp. 221–232.

Gandour, J. T. 1974. Consonant types and tone in Siamese. *Journal of Phonetics,* 1974, *2,* 337–350.

Gandour, J. T. 1975. The features of the larynx: N-ary or binary? *Phonetica, 32,* 241–253.

Gandour, J., & Maddieson, I. 1976. Measuring larynx height in Standard Thai using the cricothyrometer. *UCLA Working Papers in Phonetics, 33,* 160–190.

Gedney, W. 1973. A checklist for determining tones in Tai dialects. In M. E. Smith (Ed.), *Studies in Linguistics in honor of G. L. Trager.* The Hague: Mouton. Pp. 423–437.

Gill, H. S., & Gleason, H. A. 1969. *A reference grammar of Punjabi.* Patiala, India.

Gill, H. S., & Gleason, H. A. 1972. The salient features of the Punjabi language. *Pakha Sanjam, 4,* 1–3.

Glover, W. W. 1970. Gurung tone and higher levels. *Occasional Papers of the Wolfenden Society on Tibeto-Burma Linguistics, 3,* 52–73.

Glover, W. W. 1971. Register in Tibeto-Burman languages of Nepal: A comparison with Mon-Khmer. *Papers in South East Asian Linguistics, 2,* 1–22.

Gradin, D. 1966. Consonantal tone in Jeh phonemics. *Mon-Khmer Studies,* Linguistics Circle of Saigon, *2*(3), 41–53.

Greenberg, J. H. 1970. Some generalizations concerning glottalic consonants, especially implosives. *International Journal of American Linguistics, 36,* 123–145.

Haggard, M., Ambler, S., & Callow, M. 1970. Pitch as a voicing cue. *Journal of the Acoustical Society of America, 47,* 613–617.

Halle, M., & Stevens, K. N. 1971. A note on laryngeal features. *Quarterly Progress Reports,* Research Lab of Electronics, MIT, *101,* 198–213.

Han, M. 1967. *Acoustic features in the manner differentiation of Korean stop consonants. Studies in the Phonology of Asian Languages,* vol. 5. Los Angeles: Acoustic Phonetics Research Lab, University of Southern California.

Hanson, R. J. 1975. Fundamental frequency dynamics in VCV sequences. Paper presented at the 8th International Congress of Phonetic Sciences, Leeds, August.

Hardy, J. C. 1967. Techniques of measuring intraoral air pressure and rate of airflow. *Journal of Speech and Hearing Research, 10,* 650–654.

van Hattum, R. J., & Worth, J. H. 1967. Airflow rates in normal speakers. *The Cleft Palate Journal, 4*(2), 137–147.

Haudricourt, A. G. 1946. Restitution du Karen commun. *Bulletin de la Société Linguistique de Paris, 42,* 103–111.

Haudricourt, A. G. 1954. De l'origine des tons en vietnamien. *Journal Asiatique, 242,* 69–82.

Haudricourt, A. G. 1961. Bipartition et tripartition des systèmes de tons dans quelques langues d'Extrême-Orient. *Bulletin de la Société Linguistique de Paris, 56,* 163–180.

Haudricourt, A. G. 1968. La langue de Gomen et la langue de Touho. *Bulletin de la Société Linguistique de Paris, 63,* 218–235.

Haudricourt, A. G. 1971. On tones in Punjabi. *Pakha Sanjam, 4,* 1–3.

Haudricourt, A. G. 1972a. L'apparition des registres des langues à tons ponctuels. *Proceedings of the 7th International Congress of Phonetic Sciences, Montreal.* Pp. 895–896.

Haudricourt, A. G. 1972b. Two-way and three-way splitting of tonal systems in some Far-Eastern languages. In J. G. Harris & R. B. Noss (Eds.), *Tai Phonetics and Phonology.*

Haudricourt, A. G. 1973. Sur la mutation des occlusives sonores productrices de tons en Indo-Européen. *Bulletin de la Société Linguistique de Paris, 68*, IX–XII.

Heinz, J. M., Lindblom, B., & Lindqvist, J. 1968. Patterns of residual masking for speech-like characteristics. *IEEE Transactions: Audio and Electroacoustics*, AU-16, *1*, 107–111.

Henderson, E. J. A. 1973. Bwe Karen as a two-tone language? An inquiry into the interrelations of pitch tone and initial consonant. Paper presented at the 6th Sino-Tibetan Conference, San Diego.

Hirano, M., & Ohala, J. 1969. Use of hooked-wire electrodes for electromyography of the intrinsic laryngeal muscles. *Journal of Speech and Hearing Research, 12*, 362–373.

Hirose, H. 1975. The posterior cricoarytenoid as a speech muscle. *Research Institute of Logopedics and Phoniatrics, 9*, 47–66.

Hirose, H., & Gay, T. 1972. The activity of the intrinsic laryngeal muscles in voicing control: An electromyographic study. *Phonetica, 25*, 140–164.

Hirose, H., Lisker, L., & Abramson, A. 1973. Physiological aspects of certain laryngeal features in stop production. (Abstract). *Journal of the Acoustical Society of America, 53*, 294–295.

Hombert, J. M. 1975a. Towards a theory of tonogenesis: An empirical, physiologically, and perceptually-based account of the development of tonal contrasts in language. Unpublished Ph.D. dissertation, Univ. of California, Berkeley.

Hombert, J. M. 1975b. Perception of contour tones: An experimental investigation. *Proceedings of the 1st Annual Meeting of the Berkeley Linguistics Society*. Pp. 221–232.

Hombert, J. M. 1976a. Noun classes and tone in Ngie. In L. M. Hyman (Ed.), *Studies in Bantu Tonology. Univ. of Southern California Occasional papers in Linguistics, 3*, 3–21.

Hombert, J. M. 1976b. Perception of bisyllabic nouns in Yoruba. In L. M. Hyman, L. C. Jacobson, & R. G. Schuh (Eds.), *Papers in African Linguistics in Honor of W. E. Welmers. Studies in African Linguistics, 6*, 109–122.

Hombert, J. M. 1976c. Tone space and universals of tone systems. Paper presented at the 51st Annual meeting of the Linguistics Society of America, Philadelphia.

Hombert, J. M. 1977a. Consonant types, vowel height and tone in Yoruba. *Studies in African Linguistics 8*(2), 173–190.

Hombert, J. M. 1977b. Development of tones from vowel height. *Journal of Phonetics, 5*, 9–16.

Hombert, J. M. 1977c. A model of tone systems. *UCLA Working Papers in Phonetics, 36*, 20–32.

Hombert, J. M. In preparation. The mechanism of phonetically motivated sound changes.

Hombert, J. M., Ohala, J. J., & Ewan, W. G. 1976. Tonogenesis: Theories and queries. *Report of the Phonology Lab*, Berkeley, *1*, 48–77.

House, A. S., & Fairbanks, G. 1953. The influence of consonant environment upon the secondary acoustical characteristics of vowels. *Journal of the Acoustical Society of America, 25*, 105–113.

Hyman, L. M. 1972. *A phonological study of Fe ʔfeʔ Bamileke. Studies in African Linguistics*, supp. 4.

Hyman, L. M. (Ed.). 1973a. Consonant types and tone. *Southern California Occasional Papers in Linguistics, 1*.

Hyman, L. M. 1973b. The role of consonant types in natural tonal assimilation. In L. M. Hyman (Ed.), Consonant types and tone. *Southern California Occasional Papers in Linguistics, 1*.

Hyman, L. M. 1976a. On some controversial questions in the study of consonant types and tone. *UCLA Working Papers in Phonetics, 33*, 90–98.

Hyman, L. M. (Ed.). 1976b. Studies in Bantu tonology. *Southern California Occasional Papers in Linguistics, 3*.

Hyman, L. M., & Schuh, R. G. 1974. Universals of tone rules: Evidence from West Africa. *Linguistic Inquiry, 5*, 81–115.

Hyman, L. M., & Tadadjeu, M. 1976. Floating tones in Nlbam-Nkam. In L. M. Hyman (Ed.), Studies in Bantu Tonology. *Southern California Occasional Papers in Linguistics, 3*, 57–111.

Hyman, L. M., & Voorhoeve, J. (Eds.). 1978. *Noun classes in Grassfields Bantu*. Paris: Société d'Etudes Linguistiques et Anthropologiques de France.

Isshiki, N., & Ringel, R. 1964. Air flow during the production of selected consonants. *Journal of Speech and Hearing Research, 7,* 233–244.

Ivíc, P., & Lehiste, I. 1963. Prilozi ispitivanju fonetske i fonoloske prirode akcenata u Savremenom srpskohrvatskom knjizevnom Jeziku. *Zbornik za filogiju i linguistiku, 6* (Noji Sad), 33–73.

Jeel, V. 1975. An investigation of the fundamental frequency of vowels after various Danish consonants, in particular stop consonants. *Annual Report of the Institute of Phonetics, Univ of Copenhagen, 9,* 191–211.

Jones, R. B. 1961. Karen linguistic studies. *University of California Publications in Linguistics, 25*(1).

Kagaya, R. 1974. A fiberoptic and acoustic study of the Korean stops, affricates, and fricatives. *Journal of Phonetics, 2*(2), 161–180.

Kagaya, R., & Hirose, H. 1975. Fiberoptic electromyographic and acoustic analyses of Hindi stop consonants. *Annual Bulletin,* Research Institute of Logopedics and Phoniatrics, *9,* 27–46.

Kähler-Meyer, E. 1971. Niger-Congo, Eastern Bantu. *Current Trends in Linguistics* (The Hague: Mouton), *7,* 307–356.

Kalema, J. 1977. Accent modification rules in Luganda. *Studies in African Linguistics, 8*(2), 127–142.

Karlgren, B. 1926. *Etudes sur la phonologie chinoise. Archives d'Etudes Orientales, 15.*

Kim, C. W. 1965. On the autonomy of the tensity feature in stop classification with special reference to Korean stops. *Word, 21,* 339–359.

Kim, C. W. 1968. Review of Lieberman 1967. *Language, 44,* 830–842.

Klatt, D. H. 1973. Discrimination of fundamental frequency contours in synthetic speech: Implications for models of speech perception. *Journal of the Acoustical Society of America, 53,* 8–16.

Klatt, D. H., Stevens, K. N., & Mead, J. 1968. Studies of articulatory activity and airflow during speech in sound production in man. In A. Bouhuys (Ed.), *Annals of the New York Academy of Sciences.* Pp. 42–55.

Kozhevnikov, V. A., & Christovich, L. A. 1966. *Speech: Articulation and perception.* Distributed by U.S. Department of Commerce, Washington, D.C. Moscow-Leningrad.

Krones, R. 1968. Pitch meters. *Monthly Internal Memorandum, Berkeley, July,* pp. 77–88.

Ladefoged, P. 1964. *A phonetic study of West African languages.* Cambridge Univ. Press.

Ladefoged, P. 1967. *Three areas of experimental phonetics.* Oxford Univ. Press.

Ladefoged, P. 1968. Linguistic aspects of respiratory phenomena. In A. Bouhuys (Ed.), Sound production in man. *Annals of the New York Academy of Sciences, 155,* 141–151.

Ladefoged, P. 1971. *Preliminaries to linguistic phonetics.* Chicago Univ. Press.

Ladefoged, P. 1974. Respiration, laryngeal activity, and linguistics. In B. D. Wyke (Ed.), *Proceedings of the International Symposium on Ventilatory and Phonatory Control Systems.* Oxford Univ. Press.

Ladefoged, P., DeClerk, J., Lindau, M., & Papçun, G. 1972. An auditory-motor theory of speech production. *UCLA Working Papers in Phonetics, 22,* 48–75.

Lafage, P., & Hombert, J. M. In preparation. Consonant types, vowel height and tone in Ewe.

Lea, W. A. 1972. *Intonational cues to the constituent structure and phonemics of spoken English.* Unpublished Ph.D. dissertation, Purdue Univ.

Lea, W. A. 1973. Segmental and suprasegmental influences on fundamental frequency contours. In L. M. Hyman (Ed.), Consonant Types and Tone. *Southern California Occasional Papers in Linguistics, 1,* 15–70.

Lee, C. Y., & Smith, T. S. 1972. A study of subglotal air pressure in Korean stop consonants. *Journal of Phonetics.*

Lehiste, I. 1970. *Suprasegmentals.* Cambridge: MIT Press.

Lehiste, I., & Peterson, G. E. 1961. Some basic considerations in the analysis of intonation. *Journal of the Acoustical Society of America, 33,* 419–425.

Li, F. K. 1954. Consonant clusters in Tai. *Language, 30,* 368–379.

Li, F. K. 1966. The relationship between tones and initials in Tai. In N. H. Zide (Ed.), *Studies in Comparative Austro-Àsiatic Linguistics*. The Hague: Mouton. Pp. 82–88.

Lieberman, P. 1967. *Intonation, perception and language*. Cambridge: MIT Press.

Lieberman, P. 1970. A study of prosodic features. *Haskins Laboratories Status Reports on Speech Research, SR-23*, 179–208.

Löfqvist, A. 1975. Intrinsic and extrinsic Fo variations in Swedish tonal accents. *Phonetica, 31*, 228–247.

Maddieson, I. 1974a. A note on tone and consonants. *UCLA Working Papers in Phonetics, 27*, 18–27.

Maddieson, I. 1974b. A possible new cause of tone-splitting evidence from Cama, Yoruba, and other languages. *UCLA Working Papers in Phonetics, 27*, 28–46.

Maddieson, I. 1976a. A further note on tone and consonants. *UCLA Working Papers in Phonetics, 33*, 131–159.

Maddieson, I. 1976b. Tone reversal in Ciluba: A new theory. In L. M. Hyman (Ed.), *Studies in Bantu tonology. Southern California Occasional Papers in Linguistics, 3*, 141–166.

Malécot, A. 1966. The effectiveness of intraoral air pressure pulse parameters in distinguishing between stop cognates. *Phonetica, 14*, 65–81.

Malécot, A. 1970. The lenis–fortis opposition: Its physiological parameters. *Journal of the Acoustical Society of America, 47*, 1588–1592.

Maran, L. R. 1971. Burmese and Jinghpaw: A study of tonal linguistic processes. *Occasional Papers of the Wolfenden Society on Tibeto-Burman Linguistics, 4*.

Maspero, H. 1912. Etudes sur la phonétique historique de la langue annamite: Les initiales. *Bulletin des Ecoles Françaises d'Extrême-Orient, 12*.

Matisoff, J. 1970. Glottal dissimilation and the Lahu high-rising tone: A tonogenetic case-study. *Journal of the American Oriental Society, 90*(1), 13–44.

Matisoff, J. 1971a. The tonal split in Loloish checked syllables. *Occasional Papers of the Wolfenden Society on Tibeto-Burman Linguistics, 2*.

Matisoff, J. 1971b. Review of Maran. *Journal of Asian Studies, 32*, 741–743.

Matisoff, J. 1972. *The Loloish tonal split revisited*, Univ. of California, Berkeley, Center for South and Southeast Asia Studies, 7.

Matisoff, J. 1973a. Tonogenesis in Southeast Asia. In L. M. Hyman (Ed.), *Consonant types and tone. Southern California Occasional Papers in Linguistics*, pp. 71–96.

Matisoff, J. 1973b. *The grammar of Lahu*. Berkeley: Univ. California Press, 75.

Mazaudon, M. 1977. Tibeto-Burman tonogenetics. *Linguistics of the Tibeto-Burman Area, 3*(2).

McGlone, R.E., & Shipp, T. 1972. Comparison of subglottal air pressures associated with /p/ and /b/. *Journal of the Acoustical Society of America, 51*, 664–665.

Mei, T. L. 1970. Tones and prosody in Middle Chinese and the origin of the rising tone. *Harvard Journal of Asiatic Studies, 30*, 86–110.

Mohr, B. 1968. Intrinsic fundamental frequency variation, II. *Monthly Internal Memorandum, Phonology Laboratory, Univ. of California, Berkeley*, June, pp. 23–32.

Mohr, B. 1971. Intrinsic variations in the speech signal. *Phonetica, 23*, 65–93.

Murry, T., & Brown, W. S. 1975. Aerodynamic interactions associated with voiced-voiceless stop cognates. Paper delivered at the 8th International Congress of Phonetic Sciences, Leeds, August 1975.

Nabelek, I. V., & Hirsh, I.J. 1969. On the discrimination of frequency transitions. *Journal of the Acoustical Society of America, 45*, 1510–1519.

Nabelek, I. V., Nabelek, A. K., & Hirsh, I. J. 1970. Pitch of tone bursts of changing frequency. *Journal of the Acoustical Society of America, 48*, 536–553.

Netsell, R. 1969. Subglottal and intraoral air pressures during the intervocalic contrast of /t/ and /d/. *Phonetica, 20*, 68–73.

Newman, P. 1975. The non-correlation of tone and vowel height in Hausa. *Studies in African Linguistics*, 6, 207–213.

Ohala, J. J. 1970. Aspects of the control and production of speech. *UCLA Working Papers in Phonetics, 15*.

Ohala, J. J. 1972. How is pitch lowered? *Journal of the Acoustical Society of America*, 52, 124.

Ohala, J. J. 1973. The physiology of tone. In L. Hyman (Ed.), *Consonant types and tone. Southern California Occasional Papers in Linguistics, 1*, 1–14.

Ohala, J. J. 1974a. Phonetic explanation in phonology. In A. Bruck, R. A. Fox, & M. W. LaGaly (Eds.), *Papers from the Parasession on Natural Phonology*, Chicago Linguistic Society, pp. 251–274.

Ohala, J. J. 1974b. Experimental historical phonology. In J.M. Anderson & C. Jones (Eds.), *Historical linguistics II: Theory and description in phonology*. Proceedings of the 1st International Conference on Historical Linguistics, Edinburgh, 2–7 September 1973. Amsterdam: North Holland. Pp. 353–389.

Ohala, J. 1975. Phonetic explanations for nasal sound patterns. In C. A. Ferguson, L. M. Hyman, and J. J. Ohala, (Eds.), *Nasalfest: Papers from a symposium on nasals and nasalization*. Stamford University. Pp.   289–316.

Ohala, J. J. 1976. A model of speech aerodynamics. *Report of the Phonology Laboratory*, Berkeley, *1*, 93–107.

Ohala, J. J., & Eukel, B. W. 1976. Explaining the intrinsic pitch of vowels. *Journal of the Acoustical Society of America*, 60, S44.

Ohala, J. J., & Ewan, W. G. 1973. Speed of pitch change. *Journal of the Acoustical Society of America*, 53, 345.

Ohala, M., & Ohala, J. J. 1972. The problem of aspiration in Hindi phonetics. *Project on Linguistic Analysis Reports*, Berkeley, *16*, 63–70; *Annual Bulletin*, Research Institute of Logopedics and Phoniatrics, 6, 39–46.

Petersen, N. R. 1976. Intrinsic fundamental frequency of Danish vowels. *Annual Report of the Institute of Phonetics*, University of Copenhagen, pp. 1–27.

Peterson, G. E., & Barney, H. L. 1952. Control methods used in a study of the vowels. *Journal of the Acoustical Society of America*, 24, 175–184.

Pilszcskowa-Chodak, N. 1972. Tone-vowel height correlations and tone assignment in the patterns of verb and noun plurals in Hausa. *Studies in African Linguistics*, 3(3), 399–422.

Pollack, I. 1968. Detection of rate of change of auditory frequency. *Journal of Experimental Psychology*, 77, 535–541.

Pulleyblank, E. G. 1962. The consonantal system of Old Chinese, Part II. *Asia Major*, 9(58), 206–265.

Pulleyblank, E. G. 1970 & 1971. Late Middle Chinese. *Asia Major*, 15, 197–239 and 16, 121–168

Ritsma, R. J. 1967. Frequencies dominant in the perception of complex sounds. *Journal of the Acoustical Society of America*, 42, 191–198.

Rossi, M. 1971. Le seuil de glissando ou seuil de perception des variations tonales pour les sons de la parole. *Phonetica*, 23, 1–33.

Rygaloff, A. 1965. Absence de distinctions tonales dans un dialecte chinois. *Bulletin de la Société Linguistique de Paris*, 60, 173–179

Sarawit, M. 1973. The Proto-Tai vowel system. Unpublished Ph.D. dissertation, University of Michigan.

Schadeberg, T. 1973. Kinga: A restricted tone system. *Studies in African Linguistics*, 4(1), 23–48.

Schuh, R. 1971. Toward a typology of Chadic vowel and tone system. Unpublished manuscript. University of California, Los Angeles.

Sergeant, R. L., & Harris, J. D. 1962. Sensitivity to unidirectional frequency modulation. *Journal of the Acoustical Society of America*, 34, 1625–1628.

Sivertsen, E. 1956. Pitch problems in Kiowa. *International Journal of American Linguistics*, 22(2), 117–130.

Slis, I. H. 1966. A model for the distinction between voiceless and voiced consonants. *IPO Annual Progress Report, 1*, 40–44.

Slis, I. H. 1967. What causes the voiced–voiceless distinction? *IPO Annual Progress Report, 2*, 71–76.

Slis, I. H. 1970. Articulatory measurements on voiced, voiceless, and nasal consonants. *Phonetica, 21*, 193–210.

Snow, W. B. 1936. Change of pitch with loudness at low frequencies. *Journal of the Acoustical Society of America, 8*, 14–19.

Stevens, K. N. 1975. Modes of conversion of airflow to sound and their utilization in speech. Paper delivered at the 8th International Congress of Phonetic Sciences, Leeds, August 1975.

Stevens, K. N. & House, A. S. 1961. An acoustical theory of vowel production and some of its implications. *Journal of Speech and Hearing Research 4*, 303–320.

Stevens, S. S. 1935. The relation of pitch to intensity. *Journal of the Acoustical Society of America, 6*, 150–154.

Subtelny, J. D., Worth, J. H., & Sakuda, T. 1969. Intraoral pressure and rate of flow during speech. *Journal of Speech and Hearing Research, 9*, 498–518.

Taylor, H. C. 1933. The fundamental pitch of English vowels. *Journal of Experimental Psychology, 16*, 565–582.

Trithart, L. 1976. Desyllabified noun class prefixes and depressor consonants in Chichewa. In L. M. Hyman (Ed.), *Studies in Bantu tonology. Southern California Occasional Papers in Linguistics, 3*, 259–286.

Tsumura, T., Sone, T., & Nimura T. 1973. Auditory detection of frequency transition. *Journal of the Acoustical Society of America, 53*(1), 17–25.

Voorhoeve, J. 1971. Tonology of the Bamileke Noun. *Journal of African Languages, 10*, 44–53.

Voorhoeve, J. 1973. Safwa as a restricted tone system. *Studies in African Linguistics, 4*(1), 1–22.

Warren, D. W., & Hall, D. J. 1973. Glottal activity and intraoral pressure during stop consonant productions. *Folia Phoniatrica, 25*, 121–129.

Zürmuhl, G. 1930. Abhängigkeit det Tonhöhenempfinding von der Lautstärke und ihre Beziehung zur Helmholtzchen Resonanztheorie des Hörens. *Zeitschrift für Sinnesphysiologie, 61*, 40–86.

IV

What Is a Tone Language?

JAMES D. McCAWLEY

In this chapter, I will present brief sketches of tonal phenomena in two languages, the one (standard Japanese) generally regarded as a prototype for the notion **pitch-accent system**, the other (Mandarin Chinese) a textbook case of a **true tonal system**. I will then take up some of the typological questions raised by this familiar dichotomy. My remarks on these questions will lead me to reject the dichotomy as a way of dichotomizing languages, though retaining it as part of a more comprehensive typology of tonal phenomena.

1. STANDARD JAPANESE

In standard Japanese, the only distinctive melodic characteristic of a phrase is the location of the syllable, if any, where the pitch drops. For example, the following examples exhaust the tonal possibilities for phrases of two, three, and four short syllables:

1. $\overline{na}\,ga$ 'vegetable' $\quad$ $\overline{kaki}\,ga$ 'oyster' $\quad$ $\overline{makura}\,ga$ 'pillow'
    $na\,\overline{ga}$ 'name' $\qquad$ $ka\overline{ki}\,ga$ 'fence' $\qquad$ $ko\overline{koro}\,ga$ 'heart'
    $\qquad\qquad\qquad$ $ka\overline{ki}\,ga$ 'persimmon' $\quad$ $atama\,ga$ 'head'
    $\qquad\qquad\qquad\qquad\qquad\qquad\qquad$ $sakana\,ga$ 'fish'

Each of these phrases consists of a noun followed by the nominative case marker *ga*. The overline indicates high pitch; syllables without an overline are low pitched. Using ′ (read "accent") to indicate the place where pitch drops, these phrases can be transcribed as:

2. $\qquad$ *na′ ga* $\qquad$ *ka′ki ga* $\qquad$ *ma′kura ga*
   $\qquad\qquad$ *na ga* $\qquad$ *kaki′ ga* $\qquad$ *koko′ro ga*
   $\qquad\qquad\qquad\qquad$ *kaki ga* $\qquad$ *atama′ ga*
   $\qquad\qquad\qquad\qquad\qquad\qquad\qquad$ *sakana ga*

Tone: A Linguistic Survey

A long syllable provides only one possibility for where the pitch might drop, at the end of the first mora but not at the end of the second:

3.   *ka'nsai ga*   'central Honshū'
                            *kan'sai ga
                            hanbu'n ga   'half'
                            *hanbun' ga

The sense of "long syllable" that I understand here is "syllable that counts as two units, as opposed to other syllables, which count as one unit." The syllables that count as long in Japanese (with regard to phenomena to be discussed below) are those of the forms:

4.   (C)VV   *soodan* 'consultation',   **kai**sya 'company'
        (C)VN   *kekkon* 'marriage', *se'nkyo* 'election'
        (C)VC, where the final C is the first segment of a geminate
                gakkoo 'school', **gappei** 'merger'

There is only one workable universal definition of "mora": something of which a long syllable consists of two and a short syllable of one. That is, a long syllable can be divided into something of the shape of a short syllable plus something else, and both of these are moras. Thus the examples in (4) divide into moras as follows:

4'.   *so-o-da-n*   *ka-i-sya*
                            ke-k-ko-n   *se-n-kyo*
                            ga-k-ko-o   *ga-p-pe-i*

Pitches can be predicted from accent marks as follows: The pitch is high up to the first mora of the accented syllable (or up to the end of the phrase, if there is no accented syllable) and low thereafter, except that if the first syllable is unaccented, its first mora is low pitched.[1]

Since the phrases in (1) consist of different nouns followed by the same postposition, the pitch differences among these phrases must be contributed by the nouns, which must accordingly be assigned the following underlying forms:

5.   *na'* 'vegetable'   *ka'ki* 'oyster'   *ma'kura* 'pillow'
        na 'name'   *kaki'* 'fence'   *koko'ro* 'heart'
                             kaki 'persimmon'   *atama'* 'head'
                                                     sakana 'fish'

When these nouns are used without any postposition, they are pronounced with the pitches that are assigned by the rule stated informally in the last paragraph. This will neutralize the distinction between final-accented and unaccented: A final-accented word such as *atama* will be on a high pitch up

---

[1] There is individual variation on one detail of pitch assignment: whether the first mora of an unaccented CVV or CVN syllable is high or low.

to its accented syllable and low thereafter, but since there is no thereafter if there is no postposition, the same LHH pitch will result as in the case of an unaccented word such as *sakana*.[2]

Postpositions can also differ in their contributions to the melody of phrases in which they appear:

6.

'from . . .'	'to . . .'	'only . . .'	'in . . .'	(plural)
ma′kura kara	ma′kura made	ma′kura sika	ma′kura ni	bo′kura (bo′ku 'I')
koko′ro kara	koko′ro made	koko′ro sika	koko′ro ni	
atama′ kara	atama′ made	atama′ sika	atama′ ni	
miyako kara(′)	miyako ma′de	miyako′ sika	miyako ni(′)	kore′ra (kore 'this')

The parenthesized accent mark indicates that the phrase ends on a high-pitched short syllable and hence, in view of the remarks of the last paragraph, might be either final accented or unaccented. The examples in question can be shown to be final accented by adding the topic marker *wa*:

7.   *miyako kara′ wa*   *miyako ni′ wa*

The accentual behavior of *wa* is identical to that of *ga*, and hence the accents in (7) must be contributed by the *kara* and *ni*, not by the *wa*. The various postpositions thus contribute accents that are manifested when they are attached to something unaccented. Accordingly, the postpositions must be assigned underlying forms indicating those accents:

8.   *kara′*
           ma′de
           ′sika
           ni′
           ′ra

and there must be a rule that eliminates an accent that is preceded by another accent in the same phrase:

9.   *atama′ kara′ wa → atama′ kara wa*
           miyako kara′ wa → _____

There are certain postpositions that behave differently from those discussed so far. For example, phrases ending with *gurai* 'to the extent of' (used in comparative constructions) have the accent on the first syllable of *gurai* regardless of the underlying noun, and phrases with *nagara* 'though being'

---

[2] There is considerable variation among dialects on this point. For example, in the dialect of Aomori, whose accentual system is fairly close to that of the standard language, a final-accented phrase is pronounced with a falling pitch on the final syllable.

have the accent on the first syllable of *nagara* or no accent at all, according
as the noun is accented or unaccented:

10.   *makura gu'rai*   *makura na'gara*
                        kokoro gu'rai   *kokoro na'gara*
                        atama gu'rai   *atama na'gara*
                        sakana gu'rai   *sakana nagara*

Postpositions displaying such behavior trigger the application of minor rules:
a rule that wipes out the accent of the preceding matter, in the case of *gurai*
and some other morphemes, and a rule attracting accent, if any, onto the
first syllable of *nagara*.

In compound nouns, generally the accent of the final element predom-
inates, though additional rules (for details, see McCawley 1968, 1977) often
apply to yield surface forms with an accent other than where the second element
is accented in isolation. The predomination of the second element of a compound can be seen in such examples as:

11. *iso'ppu* 'Aesop' + *monoga' tari* 'tale' → *isoppu-monoga' tari* 'Aesop's fables'
     tyu'uka 'China' + *ryo'ori* 'cuisine' → *tyuuka-ryo'ori* 'Chinese cuisine'

Verb and adjective roots display less accentual variety than do nouns:
They either contribute an accent or do not, but they do not differ from one
another with regard to the location of the accent they contribute. For example,
the following illustrate the accentual possibilities for vowel-stem verbs,
consonant-stem verbs, and adjectives:

12.

	Accented		
	'hide$_{intr}$'	'represent'	'correct'
Present	*kakure'-ru*	*arawa's-u*	*tadasi-i*
Past	*kaku're-ta*	*arawa'si-ta*	*tada'si-kat-ta*
Conditional	*kakure'-reba*	*arawa's-eba*	*tada'si-ker-eba*
Provisional	*kaku're-tara*	*arawa'si-tara*	*tada'si-kat-tara*
Adverbial	—	—	*tada'si-ku*

	Unaccented		
	'begin$_{tr}$'	'work'	'sad'
Present	*hazime-ru*	*hatarak-u*	*kanasi-i*
Past	*hazime-ta*	*hatarai-ta*	*kanasi-'kat-ta*
Conditional	*hazime-re'ba*	*hatarak-e'ba*	*kanasi-'ker-eba*
Provisional	*hazime-ta'ra*	*hatarai-ta'ra*	*kanasi-'kat-tara*
Adverbial	—	—	*kanasi-ku*

In vowel-stem verbs and in adjectives, where there is an alternation between stem-penultimate and stem-final accent, what little evidence there is as to which is more basic points to the stem-penultimate accent (McCawley 1968, 1977). I thus take verb and adjective stems as specified [+Accented] or [−Accented] as a whole, with the accent being localized on a specific syllable by the rule

13. $\qquad$ Insert $' / \underline{\quad\quad} (C)(V)]_{[+Acc]}$

Since I take syllables as bearers of accent in standard Japanese, I interpret (13) as putting accent on the syllable containing the position marked by the _____ .

The accent rules for derived and compound verbs and adjectives operate in terms of the accentedness of the constituents rather than in terms of specific places of accent. For example, derived verbs have the same accentedness as the source verbs, and, at least for older speakers, compound verbs have the opposite accentuation of the first member of the compound:

14.

	'write'	'cry'
Basic verb	*ka'k-u, ka'i-ta*	*nak-u, nai-ta*
Causative	*kak-ase'-ru, kak-a'se-ta*	*nak-ase-ru, nak-ase-ta*
Passive[3]	*kak-are'-ru, kak-a're-ta*	*nak-are-ru, nak-are-ta*
Passive of Causative	*kak-ase-rare'-ru, kak-ase-ra're-ta*	*nak-ase-rare-ru, nak-ase-rare-ta*
V + *yam-*	*kaki-yam-u* 'stop writing'	*naki-ya'm-u* 'stop crying'
V + *da's-*	*kaki-das-u* 'start writing'	*naki-da's-u* 'burst into tears'

For younger speakers, compound verbs are generally accented, regardless of the accentuation of the components.

An accent inserted by (13) behaves like any other accent in the action of subsequent phonological rules. Note that accent deletion is involved in many of the forms in (12):

15. $\quad$ *kaku're-ta'ra* → *kaku're-tara*
$\quad$ *tada'si-'kat-ta'ra* → *tada'si-kat-tara*

The forms with stem-final accent are derived by an accent attraction rule that is triggered by a small number of morphemes:

16. *kaku're-ru* → *kakure'-ru*
$\quad$ *tada'si-i* → *tadasi'-i*
$\quad$ *ka'k-nagara* → *kaki-na'gara* 'while writing' (cf. *naki-nagara* 'while crying')
$\quad$ *ka'k-soo* → *kaki-so'o* 'appear to write' (cf. *naki-soo* 'appear to cry')

---

[3] The so-called passive form means 'be subjected to', and thus even intransitive verbs have "passives," e.g., *Tanaka-san wa kodomo ni nak-are-ta* 'Tanaka was subjected to the child crying'.

There are also morphemes whose accents predominate over what they are added to:

17. *kak-o'o*   'let's write'   *nak-o'o*   'let's cry'
    kaku ma'i 'probably won't write'   *naku ma'i* 'probably won't cry'

The morphemes described in (16) and (17) have the same effect on compound derived verbs and adjectives as they do on simple ones.

The bearer of accent in Japanese is the syllable:

1. Accent distinctions, both underlying and superficial, are in terms of which **syllable** provides the place where pitch drops: Long syllables provide only one possible place for the pitch to drop (the end of the first mora), not two.

2. When accent is to be placed immediately before an affix or postposition, it goes on the first mora of the preceding syllable: (*a*) Certain morphemes, when used as the final element of a compound noun put accent on the preceding syllable: *Oosaka'-wan* 'Osaka Bay', *Tookyo'o-wan* 'Tokyo Bay', and (*b*) certain postpositions (as in [6] above) are preceded by an accent, which is realized on the final syllable of a preceding unaccented word: *Oosaka' sika* 'only Osaka', *Tookyo'o sika* 'only Tokyo', and in both cases the pitch drops at the end of the first mora of the syllable in question.

3. Rules that are sensitive to whether an item is "final accented" treat accented short final syllables and accented long final syllables alike: (*a*) Noun compounds whose second member is final accented are accented on the first syllable of the second element: *musume'* 'girl', *hanauri-mu'sume* 'girl who sells flowers', *hanbu'n* 'half', *omosiro-ha'nbun* 'half in jest', and (*b*) the derivational suffix *-zin* puts accent on the preceeding syllable, unless it is attached to a final-accented noun, in which case it takes an accent on itself:

18.   *amerika*   'America'   *amerika'-zin*   'American'
      do'itu   'Germany'   *doitu'-zin*   'German'
      niho'n   'Japan'   *nihon-zi'n*   'Japanese'
      tyoose'n 'Korea'   *tyoosen-zi'n*   'Korean'

However, the unit in terms of which phonological distance is measured is not the syllable but the mora:

1. In Japanese poetry, metric patterns work in terms of moras, e.g., the most common meters involve alternating lines of 5 and 7 moras such as the 5–7–5 of haiku and the 7–5–7–5–7 of waka.

2. The rules for noun compounds treat compounds with a "long" final element differently from those with a "short" final element, where a final element of a compound is "long" if it is 3 or more moras in length or is itself a compound (see McCawley 1968, 1977 for details).

3. Accent in recent borrowings goes on the syllable containing the third from last mora:

19. *bura'ziru* 'Brazil' *reko'odo* 'record' *kuude'taa* 'coup d'etat' *wasi'nton* 'Washington'
    do'rama 'drama' *poke'tto* 'pocket' *mara'son* 'marathon' *rehure'kkusu* 'reflex'

Thus the accent will be on the fourth from last mora in words like those of the last column, in which the third from last mora is the second mora of a long syllable. Note how this rule involves both syllable and mora, each with the function that it in general has in standard Japanese: The bearer of the accent is the syllable, but the distance measured in locating that syllable is in terms of moras.

To sum up, pitch in standard Japanese has the following characteristics:

1. Lexical information: Depending on the morphological category of the morpheme, its dictionary entry will specify either the syllable, if any, on which it contributes an accent (nouns, postpositions, verb inflections) or merely whether or not it contributes an accent (verbs, adjectives).

2. Phonological rules: The rules apply in such a way as to yield outputs in which each phrase has at most one accent. Some accent rules make one accent predominate over others (i.e., wipe out all accents but the first or last in some constituent), others attract accent into a given position. In either case, the action may be at a distance: The accent on a postposition is eliminated after an accented noun, no matter how many syllables away the accent on the noun is, and the accent on the first element of a compound is eliminated no matter how many syllables away from the second element of the compound that syllable is. When a noun is followed by *nagara*, its accent is attracted onto *nagara* even though a large number of syllables may intervene between the accent of the noun and the first syllable of *nagara*. The rules of pitch assignment (which assign high or low pitch to specific moras) also involve action at a distance: Whether a given mora is realized on a high or a low pitch depends on where it is located relative to the accented syllable, if any, of its phrase, which may in principle be any distance away.

3. Units of relevance: In dictionary entries, an accent may be borne either by a specific syllable (not mora) or by an entire lexical item. Prior to the application of phonological rules proper, accents are localized on specific syllables. Rules of accent placement or movement put accents on specific syllables and can be sensitive to the accent of specific syllables, not moras. However, distance and length are measured in moras, i.e., standard Japanese is a "mora-counting syllable language."

2. MANDARIN CHINESE

In Mandarin, each morpheme consists of a single syllable. The dictionary entry of each morpheme must specify which of four "tones" it has. The tones are as follows:[4]

20.   1. *mā* 'mother'   ⌐
       2. *má* 'hemp'   ⌐
       3. *mǎ* 'horse'   ⌐ when phrase final, ⌐ when not phrase final.
       4. *mà* 'scold'   ⌐ when phrase final, ⌐ when not phrase final.

Woo (1969) argues that the third tone is basically a level low tone and that the rise which appears at the end of a phrase-final third tone is inserted by a phonological rule. She then proceeds to represent the four tones as basically sequences of low and high tones:

21.   1. HH
                                      2. LH
                                      3. LL
                                      4. HL

There are in addition unstressed syllables, and the pitch on these is predictable from the pitches on the surrounding syllables:

22. An unstressed syllable is pronounced
       ⌐ when preceded by first or second tone and followed by first or fourth
       ⌐ when preceded by first or second tone otherwise
       ⌐ when preceded by fourth tone
       ⌐ when preceded by third tone and followed by first or second
       ⌐ when preceded by third tone otherwise.

Woo's analysis allows these facts to be described by the following rules:

23. $[-\text{stress}] \rightarrow [-\text{H}]$
       $\rightarrow [+\text{H}]/[+\text{H}] \cdot \underline{\quad} [+\text{H}]$ (. denotes syllable boundary)
       $\rightarrow [+\text{H}]/[-\text{H}][-\text{H}] \cdot \underline{\quad} \cdot \begin{Bmatrix} \text{end of phrase} \\ [][-\text{H}] \end{Bmatrix}$

   There are two rules of tone sandhi: A third tone becomes a second tone when immediately followed by a third tone, and, in rapid speech, a second tone becomes a first tone when preceded by a first or second tone and followed by a stressed syllable:

24.   a. $[] \rightarrow [+\text{H}]/[-\text{H}] \underline{\quad} \cdot [-\text{H}][-\text{H}]$
            b. $[] \rightarrow [+\text{H}]/[+\text{H}] \cdot \underline{\quad} [+\text{H}] \cdot [+\text{stress}]$

---

[4] In the notation used here, devised by Y. R. Chao, the vertical line at the right indicates the scale of pitch (high at the top, low at the bottom), and the other line indicates iconically the level, contour, and duration of the tone.

The characteristics of pitch in Mandarin can then be summed up as follows:

1. Lexical information: The dictionary entry of each morpheme specifies a "tone" (sequence of two pitches, high or low) which that morpheme retains throughout the derivation except as modified by phonological rules.

2. Phonological rules: The phonological rules affecting pitch are assimilations and dissimilations that are conditioned by the immediately adjacent syllables. There is no action at a distance (see Hyman's chapter, this volume).

3. Units of relevance: No distinction is made between "long" and "short" syllables. Syllables of any segmental composition may bear any of the four tones. However, there is a distinction between stressed and unstressed syllables, and unstressed syllables bear a pitch that is predictable from the tones on the surrounding syllables.[5]

3. ENLARGING THE TYPOLOGY

These two sketches illustrate two common clusters of tonal characteristics. However, they do not exhaust the ways that tone can figure in human languages. There are, for example, languages in which there is "accentual" use of pitch, as in standard Japanese, plus some additional tonal phenomenon. For example, in the Japanese dialects of central Honshū (from slightly west of Nagoya to eastern Okayama prefecture, taking in Kyōto and Ōsaka) and most of Shikoku, words differ not only with regard to where, if at all, there is a fall in pitch, but also with regard to whether the word starts on a low or on a high pitch. Thus there are the following pitch distinctions among one-, two-, and three-syllable nouns in the dialect of Befu, Hyōgo prefecture (near Kōbe):

25. $\overline{mi}$, $mi\,\overline{ga}$ 'body' $\overline{kaki}\,(\overline{ga})$ 'persimmon' $\overline{sakana}\,(\overline{ga})$ 'fish'
    nà, $\overline{na}\,ga$ 'name' $\overline{kaki}\,(ga)$ 'fence' $\overline{azuki}\,(ga)$ 'red bean'
    ná, $na\,\overline{ga}$ 'vegetable' $ha\overline{si}$, $\overline{awabi}\,(ga)$ 'abalone'
      $hasi\,\overline{ga}$ 'chopsticks'
      $kaki$, $usa\overline{gi}$,
        $ka\overline{ki}\,ga$ 'oyster' $usagi\,\overline{ga}$ 'rabbit'
          $kab\overline{u}to\,(ga)$ 'helmet'

If an item that begins on a low pitch is preceded by an item that ends on a high pitch (say, a demonstrative), there is a drop in pitch at its beginning:

26. $\overline{ano}\,kab\overline{u}to$ 'that   helmet'
                 $\overline{kono}$ $usa\overline{gi}$ 'this   rabbit'

[5] See Cheng 1973 for a detailed treatment of Mandarin tone. Cheng deals with some important questions that I have ignored here, in particular, the question of what happens when more than two third tones occur in a row. He shows that the result depends on the syntactic structure of the sentence.

It is thus reasonable to use the same symbol for "low initial" as for "drop in pitch" and to assign the nouns in (25) the following underlying forms:

27.
$$
\begin{array}{lll}
mi & kaki & sakana \\
na' & ka'ki & azu'ki \\
'na & 'hasi & a'wabi \\
 & 'kaki' & 'usagi \\
 & & 'kabu'to
\end{array}
$$

The phonological rules in these dialects conspire to give outputs in which each word or combination of word and postpositions has at most one ′ within it and at most one ′ at its beginning, though they allow phrases (such as 'that helmet' in [26]) which do not conform to this restriction. For example, postpositions have underlying accents which are manifested when they are attached to nouns that have no ′ within them (even if the noun has a ′ before its first syllable) and are eliminated otherwise:

28.

	'persimmon'	'fence'	'chopsticks'	'oyster'	
'than . . .'	kaki' yori	ka'ki yori	'hasi' yori	'kaki' yori	/'yori/
'even . . .'	kaki de'mo	ka'ki demo	'hasi de'mo	'kaki' demo	/de'mo/
'from . . .'	kaki kara	ka'ki kara	'hasi kara	'kaki' kara	/kara/

Noun compounds take their high-initial-ness and low-initial-ness from the first element of the compound, and, depending on the length and accent of the second element, take a fall in pitch somewhere in or immediately before the second element, much as in the standard language:

29.   genzi + monoga'tari → genzi-monoga'tari 'the Tale of Genji'
        'isop'pu + monoga'tari → 'isoppu-monoga'tari 'Aesop's fables'
        'abura + musi → 'abura-'musi 'cockroach' (lit. 'oil bug')
        na'nkin + musi → nankin-'musi 'bedbug' (lit. 'Nanking bug')

In the specific dialect under discussion, not only the realization of "fall in pitch," but also that of "low initial" involves action at a distance: A low-initial phrase starts low and stays low until one reaches either an accented syllable or the final mora of the phrase, at which point the pitch rises to high. For example, the initial low of 'Aesop's fables' in (29) extends over the first five syllables. There are other dialects in the area in question, however, where "low initial" affects only the first mora of the phrase, e.g., the dialect of Kōchi on Shikoku, where 'rabbit' is pronounced LHH(H). An accentual system quite similar to that of central Honshū dialects is found in at least one West African language, namely Ịjọ (Williamson 1965).

Okuda (1975) has argued that the tonal system of Proto-Japanese involved not merely a distinction as to whether a word began on a low or a high pitch, but also as to where the pitch of a low-initial word rose to high. See McCawley 1977 for an elaboration and extension of Okuda's analysis, according to which:

(1) In Proto-Japanese the dictionary entry of each noun carries one ⌐ (rise in pitch) and at most one ¬ (fall in pitch), and

(2) The ⌐ and the ¬ can occur at any syllable boundary, except that the ¬ must follow the ⌐. The present central Honshū systems arose from this system via a change whereby all but the last of the syllables before a ⌐ became high-pitched:

30.   *atama⌐ > ata¬ma⌐ > ata¬ma* 'head'
      ino⌐ti > i¬no⌐ti > i¬noti 'life'

The only remaining occurrences of ⌐ were those at the end of the first syllable, and the words of that type then had a distinctive low pitch on the first syllable, contrasting with a distinctive high pitch on the first syllable of other words.

There are also tonal systems in which morphemes contribute melodies that are not tied to specific syllables but distribute themselves over an entire phrase involving the morpheme (see Leben's chapter, this volume). A clear example of this phenomenon is presented by the Japanese dialect of Kagoshima (southern Kyūshū), in which each morpheme that may begin a phrase imposes either a "falling" melody or a "level" melody on the entire phrase, e.g.:

31.

Falling	Level
hi, hi ga 'fire'	*hi, hi ga* 'fire'
hana, hana ga 'nose'	*hana, hana ga* 'flower'
kuruma, kuruma ga 'vehicle'	*abura, abura ga* 'oil'
kamaboko, kamaboko ga 'fish pudding'	*yomikata, yomikata ga* 'pronunciation'

In Kagoshima, the falling melody has a high pitch on the penultimate syllable and low pitches elsewhere, and the level melody has a low pitch on all syllables up to the last, which is high. Other dialects of western and southern Kyūshū have the same opposition of falling and level melodies, though with considerable variation from one locality to another as to the realization of each melody. The status of the melodies as features of the entire lexical item rather than of specific syllables is confirmed by facts about diglossia. Kagoshima speakers generally impose Kagoshima melodies on corresponding words of standard Japanese and, since the standard words often have a different number of syllables, put the high pitches on different syllables in the standard words than in their dialect equivalents:

32.

Dialect form	Kagoshima pronunciation of standard form
agat 'rise'	*agaru*
kanasin 'grieve'	*kanasimu*
akaka 'red' (present)	*akai*
ako 'red' (adverbial)	*akaku*

The falling and level melodies of western and southern Kyūshū correspond to the high-initial and low-initial of Proto-Japanese. The presumable historical development is that all syllables past the first syllable were made low pitched—yielding a two-way opposition between a melody with high on the first syllable and low thereafter and a level low melody, which is the way that the falling/level opposition is realized in the Fujitsu area of Saga prefecture (the northern most part of the area having the falling/level melodic opposition)—and subsequently the high of the falling melody shifted rightwards, to the second syllable of a three-syllable or longer phrase in Nagasaki, and to the penultimate syllable of the phrase in Kagoshima.

There are also languages that have pitch-accent systems as far as dictionary entries are concerned but show surface tonal contrasts greatly in excess of what a pure pitch-accent system could accommodate. For example, in Ganda it suffices to indicate which syllable, if any, of a noun or adjective contributes a distinctive fall in pitch[6] and whether a verb root contributes a distinctive fall in pitch or not:[7]

33.   *mù-límí, ò-mú-límí* 'farmer' /limi/
             mù-sáwò, ò-mú-sáwò 'doctor' /sa′wo/
             mù-góbâ, ò-mú-góbâ 'driver' /goba′/
             mù-lámúzí, ò-mú-lámúzí 'judge' /lamuzi/
             mù-pákàsí, ò-mú-pákàsí 'porter' /pa′kasi/
             mù-wálábù, ò-mú-wálábù 'Arab' /wala′bu/
             mù-gógólô, ò-mú-gógólô 'problem' /gogolo′/
             kù-gúl-á 'buy' /gul/
             kù-láb-à 'see' /la′b/
             kù-sásúl-á 'pay' /sasul/
             kù-wúlìl-á 'hear' /wu′lil/

Assuming that *mu-*, *o-*, *ku-*, and *-a* are all unaccented, one can derive the above pitches via rules that accommodate underlying forms to the template $LH_1('LH_0)$, i.e., the word starts on a low pitch, then goes up to a high until the ′, if any, where it drops to a L and, if any syllables remain, rises up to a H.

The pitch assignment rule just sketched works only for words containing only one "accent." In verb forms involving accented agreement markers and

---

[6] I am ignoring here an important class of nouns (Cole 1967:80–92), in which the first two moras of both the single-prefix form and the double-prefix form are low pitched and the third mora displays a fall in pitch:

                    mù-gòlê, ò-mù-gólè 'bride'
                    mù-sòmésà, ò-mù-sómèsá 'teacher'
                    mù-mànyílìvú, ò-mù-mányílìvú 'experienced'

[7] In citing Ganda forms (and below in Tonga and Kikuyu forms), I use ′ to indicate high pitch and low ˋ low pitch, and cite nouns in both the single-prefix and the double-prefix forms.

tense markers, surface melodies occur that do not conform to the above template, for example:

34.   *bá-làb-à* 'they see' (cf. *bá-gùl-á* 'they buy')
        nágúzéè (= *n-a-gul-yee*) 'I bought' (recent past)
        bà-sàsùl-é 'pay them' (imperative)
        bá-lì-gùl-á 'they will buy' (remote future)
        bá-lì-ràb-à 'they will see' (remote future)

Some of this profusion of surface melodies can be accounted for by allowing multiple accents to appear in a word and taking every mora that directly follows an accent to be low, e.g.:

35.   *bá-làb-à = ba'-la'b-a*
        bá-lì-ràb-à = ba'-lì'-la'b-a

However, it would then be necessary to analyze various tenses as imposing a multiplicity of accents on the verb stem. For example, it would be necessary to analyze the present negative, which ends with a sequence of low pitches, as having accents on all moras of the verb stem past the first (as in Kamoga and Stevick 1968: xxx–xxxi), and thus on all moras of an accented verb stem:

36.   *tálèètà = ta'-le'e't-a'* 'he does not bring'
        Cf. *àléétá = a-le'et-a* 'he brings'
             bálèètá = ba'-le'et-a 'they bring'

The "accent" mark would then no longer mark an accentual phenomenon, i.e., a phenomenon that makes one syllable or mora prominent: It would simply represent a low tone on the following mora.

In one important class of cases, the mora after a ' is not low pitched; namely, those in which that mora is unaccented and there is another accent later in the word:

37.   *tágúlábà = ta'-gu-la'b-a* 'he doesn't see it' (with incorporated object *-gu-*)
      Cf. *tálàbà* 'he doesn't see'

This cannot simply be treated as loss of ' before ', since the first ' plays a role in determining the surface pitches on the individual syllables: It causes the syllable in question to be on a high pitch, whereas an unaccented initial syllable would be on a low pitch. The only way that this phenomenon could be treated in "accentual" terms would be to treat the accented syllables as bearing both ⌐ and ¬ and having rules that eliminate one while leaving the other, e.g.:

38.   ⌐*ta*¬-*gu*-⌐*la*¬*b-a*   ⌐*ta-gu-la*¬*b-a*

possibly by a rule that eliminates the ¬ and ⌐ of a combination ¬X⌐. However, that proposal would provide no natural way of distinguishing among the forms in (36). A more straightforward approach to the phenomenon of (37) is to treat it as simply an assimilation in which a sequence of Ls that is flanked by Hs is assimilated up to the level of the Hs. This assimilation also affects moras that follow an accented mora and thus would otherwise be pronounced low:

39.   *báligúlábà* = *ba'-li'-gu-la'b-a* 'they will see it'
              Cf. *báligùgúlá* = *ba'-li'-gu-gul-a* 'they will buy it'

The only Ganda phenomenon that can be regarded as an accent elimination of the sort found in Japanese is a deaccenting of the head noun in a genitive construction:

40.   *è-m̀-bwâ* 'dog' + possessive marker + *ò-mú-góbâ* 'driver'
              → *èmbwá yóómúgóbâ* 'the driver's dog'

              è-bí-kópò 'cups' + possessive marker + *ò-mú-kázì* 'woman'
              → *èbíkópó byóómúkázì* 'the woman's cups'

Ganda thus can be described as having a pitch-accent system in its deep phonology and a tonal system in its surface phonology. Dictionary entries must include the sort of information that figures in pitch-accent systems. However, with the exception of the rule discussed in the last paragraph, the phonological rules do not operate in such a way as to yield outputs in which each word or phrase contains at most one "prominent" syllable or mora; rather, the phonological rules can be formulated as assimilations and dissimilations of high and low tones (e.g., [37] and [39] involve assimilation of lows up to the pitch of surrounding high tones, and [35] involves a dissimilation in which a high preceded by a high becomes low). There is, however, quite a bit of action at a distance: The high tones to which intervening lows are assimilated can be arbitrarily far apart, and the sequence of unaccented moras at the beginning or end of a phrase that are made high pitched can be arbitrarily long.

Tonga, a Bantu language spoken in Zambia, demands underlying forms like those of the Central Honshū dialects of Japanese, in which nouns differ not only with regard to where, if at all, they contribute a fall in pitch, but also with regard to whether they start on a low or on a high pitch (McCawley 1973):

41.   *i-m̀-bílílá* 'incense' /bilila/
              i-cí-jàtìzyò 'handle' /'jatizyo/
              i-ǹ-gówànì 'hat' /go'wani/
              i-mú-cáyílì 'driver' /cayi'li/
              i-ǹ-'káláyà 'rust' /'kala'ya/

The ' in the form for 'rust' marks "downstep": The high tone on the *ka* of that word is slightly lower than the high tone on the *in*, as contrasted with the word for 'driver', in which the *ca* follows *imu-* on the same high tone. Downstep in Tonga, as in many languages, is derived from HLH sequences: The interval that pitch drops in going from a H to a L in these languages exceeds the interval that it rises in going from a L to a H, and downstep arises when the L of a HLH sequence is assimilated up to the pitch of one of the adjacent H's (here, the following one), leaving a slightly lowered H that immediately follows a H, as in the following derivation:

42.   *í-ň-kàláyà*
          55   2 4 1   Assignment of pitch levels
          55   4 4 1   Assimilation
          í-ň-'káláyà   Reinterpretation of preceding line

Kikuyu, a Bantu language spoken in Kenya, demands underlying forms in which each syllable of nouns is specified distinctively as high or low tone. For three-syllable nouns, seven of the eight logical possibilities of high and low underlying tones on the three syllables are attested:

43.   /héŋgérέ/   *né ké-hèŋgérέ* 'slab'
      /ŋáúrò/   *né ké-ŋàúró* 'person with shaved head'
      /tíŋòrí/   *né gé-tìŋóri* 'large boy not circumcised with his age-mates'
    /CV́CV̀CV̀/
      /rèmérέ/   *né mó-rèmèrέ* 'way of cultivating'
      /bàríítí/   *né mó-bàrììtí* 'anger'
      /bɔbɔɔtɔ́/   *né ké-bɔbɔɔtɔ́* 'downpour'
      /bèrèdì/   *né ké-bèrèdì* 'leaf-shaped spear'

In Kikuyu, each tone is copied onto the following syllable, subject to some restrictions which insure that every underlying high tone will receive a surface realization if at all possible (Harries 1952, Pratt 1972, Ford 1975). In the forms cited above, the noun occurs in predicate position after the copula /né/. The underlying tonal distinction between 'slab' and 'person with shaved head' and between 'way of cultivating' and 'anger' does not manifest itself in the forms given in (43), but the difference does come out when anything follows the noun, e.g.:

44.   *kè-hèŋgérέ né kè-ègá* 'the slab is good'
      kè-ŋàúrò né kè-ègá 'the person with shaved head is good'

I conjecture that Kikuyu, Tonga, and Ganda represent three stages in the development of Bantu tone from a pure tonal system, in which specific syllables had lexical high and low tones, to something which, at least as far as lexical information is concerned, is a pitch-accent system.

For each of the languages discussed in this section, one can ask the question, "Is it a pitch-accent language or a tone language?" However, I think that that is a stupid question to ask, since the material covered in this section makes clear that the various characteristics of pitch-accent systems and of tonal systems are to a fair extent independent of one another and that there is no reason for squeezing the diversity of phonological systems discussed here into a simple dichotomy. The only way that I see in which a tonal/accentual dichotomy can be maintained is to have that dichotomy dichotomize stages of derivations rather than whole languages. I have suggested in my discussion of Ganda that an accentual system can become a tonal system in the course of derivations. I would maintain, in fact, that not only can this happen, but it always happens: A pitch-accent system becomes a tonal system at the point of the derivation at which rules apply assigning pitches to specific syllables or moras as the realization of accents, and Ganda and Japanese differ principally with regard to how deeply in their phonologies they become tonal. Actually, Japanese phonology does not operate exclusively in accentual terms. At least one contraction phenomenon in Japanese depends not on underlying accents but on the pitches that are assigned to individual syllables, namely, the apparent accent observed in *itte'ru* < *itte iru* 'is going'. I have argued (McCawley 1977) that this contraction involves not the insertion of an accent but simply the elimination of a syllable, with the nondistinctive drop in pitch that would otherwise have been spread over two syllables being concentrated on one syllable and perceived as accent.

There remains one way in which an absolute dichotomy between tonal system and a generalized notion of pitch-accent system might be made viable. Suppose that we bring into question an assumption that I have been making gratuitously throughout this paper (and which has been made gratuitously throughout the generative phonological literature on tone and pitch accent), namely, the assumption that "pitch realization rules" attach specific pitches to specific syllables, moras, or segments. There is another possibility that deserves to be taken seriously, namely, that pitch realization rules merely specify details of changes in pitch (i.e., specify the places where rises and falls occur, regardless of whether the change in pitch is distinctive or nondistinctive, and the amount of the rise or fall). The two conceptions of pitch realization rules have different implications as to what sorts of rules could conceivably apply to the output of pitch realization rules. Thus, if downstep is analyzed in terms of specific pitch levels, as in (42), there could in principle be a phonological rule that applied to all syllables of Pitch 3, or to all syllables of pitch greater than 2. I conjecture that no such phonological rule occurs in any language, and that the description of languages such as Tonga that have downstep combined with an opposition of two (rarely, three) level tones should be analyzed in terms of rises and falls, with downstep represented as abutting fall and rise:

45. $i\text{-}n^\daleth\text{-}ka^\ulcorner la^\daleth ya \to i\text{-}n^\daleth\text{-}^\ulcorner kala^\daleth ya$ (reanalysis of [42])

It is thus possible to analyze at least some languages so that tonal information at all stages of derivations is in terms of pitch changes, i.e., so that pitch levels (whether H and L or 5, 4, 3, . . .) play no role in any stage of derivations. Pure pitch-accent systems would be those in which, until some late stage of derivations, only one type of pitch change (say, fall in pitch) need be specified and the rules apply so as to yield at most one occurrence of that pitch change per phrase or per word; additional information needed to yield complete instructions to the vocal tract (in this case, information as to where pitch rises, as to the amount by which it rises and falls, and about "downdrift" in stretches in which there is no other pitch change) is added by rules at a late stage of derivations. In less pure pitch-accent systems, at relatively early stages of derivations, either there is more than one kind of pitch change (say, both rise and fall) or more than one pitch change may occur in a word; this will include systems like that of Ganda, in which dictionary entries can be given in which the tonal information is at most the location of a fall in pitch, but where the pitch movements contributed by the various morphemes of which a word is composed are retained, and predictable rises in pitch must be inserted relatively early in derivations. Under this reanalysis, a pitch accent system need not become tonal at any stage of derivations. Only a "true" tonal system will have pitch levels or sequences of pitch levels attached to the relevant units. The usefulness of this resurrected tonal/accentual dichotomy is weakened, however, by the fact that there is often no clear choice between an analysis in terms of pitches and one in terms of pitch changes, as in the case of Ganda, where there were no strong arguments either way. In addition, Kikuyu, which demands underlying forms in which each syllable of nouns is distinctively high or low in pitch, has downstep, and thus it is not possible to avoid reference to pitch changes in languages that have specific pitches in underlying forms.

4. A POSTSCRIPT ON SYLLABLES AND MORAS

In Section 2, I suggested two oppositions, syllable language versus mora language and syllable-counting language versus mora-counting language, the first opposition relating to what unit bears accents, the second to what unit serves as the standard for measuring lengths and distances. All four combinations of the terms of these oppositions are attested:

46.

	Syllable language	Mora language
Syllable counting	Polish	Beja
Mora counting	Standard Japanese Latin	Lithuanian

I have already presented arguments for Japanese being a mora-counting syllable language. See Jakobson 1937 for arguments that Latin is a mora-counting syllable language. Lithuanian is a clear instance of a mora-language: Long syllables can have either "falling" or "rising" accentuation, but short syllables have only one possible accentuation: The rising but not the falling accent on a stem-final syllable is subject to an accent attraction rule ("Saussure's law") that also affects accented short syllables (examples from Dudas and O'Bryan 1972:88–89):

47.   *áug-u* 'I increase'   *a′ug-u*
              ve͞lk-u → velk-ù 'I pull'   *vel′k-u* → velk-u′
              riš-u → riš-ù 'I tie'   *ri′š-u* → riš-u′

The forms are cited first with the standard orthographic accent marks (´ denotes falling accent, ⁻ rising accent, and ` accent on short syllable) and then in terms of a reanalysis in which falling accent is indicated with an accent mark on the first mora and rising accent with an accent mark on the second mora; in terms of the reanalysis, Saussure's law can be stated as, "Accent is attracted from a stem-final mora onto certain affixes." Stress in Polish goes on the penultimate syllable regardless of the segmental composition of it or of the final syllable; the only respect in which it might be inappropriate to call Polish a syllable-counting syllable language is that Polish, as far as I know, has no rules that are sensitive to a distinction between long and short syllables, and hence it is not clear that a distinction between mora and syllable need be drawn in Polish.

Beja, a Cushitic language of northeastern Sudan (Hudson 1973), distinguishes two accentuations in long syllables (level high versus falling pitch) but has only a single type of accentuation in short syllables. The two accentuations in long syllables can thus be distinguished as accented first mora (= falling) versus accented second mora (= level high). Beja makes a two-way accentual distinction in words: what Hudson calls "final accent," in which the accent is on the final mora of the word, and "penultimate accent," in which the accent is on the final mora of the penultimate syllable, if the word has at least two syllables, and on the first mora if the word has only one syllable. Singulars and plurals are generally of opposite accentual type:

48.

	'camel'	'mother'	'book'	'bride'
Singular	*ka′am*	*dee′t*	*ki′taab*	*doobaa′t*
Plural	*ka′m*	*de′et*	*kita′b*	*doo′baat*

Hudson draws the generalization that the "penultimate" accentual type involves an accent two units from the end and that the choice of units is given by the principle, "Count in syllables if you can, but in moras if you can't [1973: 56]." Beja thus measures distances basically in syllables but assigns accents to the mora, not to the syllable.

My choice of words both in this postscript and in earlier sections suggested that the status of a language as a syllable language or a mora language and as syllable counting or mora counting remained constant throughout the derivation, e.g., that if accent is located in terms of syllables in lexical entries, it will be located in terms of syllables in surface phonology. I will close by pointing out a clear counterexample to the generalization that deep syllable languages are also surface syllable languages. In Kyoto Japanese, dictionary entries need never distinguish between first-mora accent and second-mora accent on a long syllable. However, such a contrast arises through the action of phonological rules. In Kyoto, as in the standard language, certain final elements of noun compounds put an accent immediately before them; however, in Kyoto, unlike the standard language, the accent goes on the immediately preceding mora, even if that happens to be the second mora of a long syllable, thereby creating accented second moras. The phonological rules can thus give rise to derived near-minimal pairs for the mora on which a long syllable is accented:

49.   *si'nkee + syoo → sinkee'syoo*   'neurosis'
        sin + se'ehu → sinse'ehu   'new government'

REFERENCES

Cheng, C. C. 1973. *A synchronic phonology of Mandarin Chinese.* The Hague: Mouton.
Cole, D. T. 1967. *Some features of Ganda linguistic structure.* Johannesburg: Witwatersrand Univ. Press.
Dudas, K., & O'Bryan, M. 1972. Lithuanian verbal accentuation. In M. Kenstowicz & H. Hock (Ed.), *Studies in Baltic linguistics. Studies in the Linguistic Sciences,* 2(2), University of Illinois, Urbana.
Ford, K. C. 1975. The tones of nouns in Kikuyu. *Studies in African Linguistics, 6,* 49–64.
Harries, L. 1952. Some tonal principles of the Kikuyu language. *Word, 8,* 140–144.
Hudson, R. A. 1973. Syllables, moras, and accents in Beja. *Journal of Linguistics, 9,* 53–64.
Jakobson, R. 1937. Über die Beschaffenheit der prosodischen Gegensätze. In *Mélanges de linguistique et de philologie offerts à J. van Ginneken.* Paris. Repr. in *Roman Jakobson: Selected writings,* Vol. 1. The Hague: Mouton, 1962. pp. 254–261.
Kamoga, F. K., & Stevick, E. W. 1968. *Luganda basic course.* Washington: U.S. Government Printing Office.
McCawley, J. D. 1968. *The phonological component of a grammar of Japanese.* The Hague: Mouton.
McCawley, J. D. 1973. Some Tonga tone rules. In S. R. Anderson & P. Kiparsky (Ed.), *A festschrift for Morris Halle,* New York: Holt, Rinehart, and Winston. pp. 140–152.
McCawley, J. D. 1977. Accent in Japanese. In L. Hyman (Ed.), *Studies in stress and accent. Southern California Occasional Papers in Linguistics, 4.*
Okuda, K. 1975. *Accentual systems in the Japanese dialects.* Tokyo: Bunka Hyoron.
Pratt, M. 1972. Tone in some Kikuyu verb forms. *Studies in African Linguistics, 3,* 325–377.
Williamson, K. 1965. *A grammar of the Kolokuma Dialect of Ịjọ.* London: Cambridge Univ. Press.
Woo, N. 1969. Prosody and phonology. Unpublished Ph.D. dissertation, MIT

V

Tone Features[1]

STEPHEN R. ANDERSON

1. INTRODUCTION

According to current views of phonological structure, the task of constructing descriptions of the sound patterns of natural languages can be divided
into three parts: (*a*) providing a set of phonetic representations for utterances
on the basis of the principles of a general phonetic theory, (*b*) providing a set
of phonological representations for utterances in terms of the grammar of a
particular language, and (*c*) determining the properties of the rules which
establish a correspondence between these two levels of representations. Tasks
(*b*) and (*c*) are covered in Chapter VII. This chapter will be confined, then, to
the principled selection and specification of the parameters in terms of which
tonal contrasts are to be described.

1.1 The Role of a Feature System in the Description of Tone

A linguistic phonetic description must be distinguished at the outset from
a direct mechanical record of the physical properties of an utterance, in that
it selects some of these properties as significant to the exclusion of others.
Such a representation must provide a way of characterizing any and all distinctions which may ever be manipulated systematically in a particular language, regardless of whether or not these ever serve directly as the basis of
contrasts within a single language. Any phonetic property, that is, in terms
of which utterances in Language X are systematically different from utterances

[1] The assistance (but not necessarily complicity) of the following people during the writing of
this chapter is gratefully acknowledged: Baruch Elimelech, Vicki Fromkin, Louis Goldstein, Jean-
Marie Hombert, Peter Ladefoged, Will Leben, Ian Maddieson, and Bill Welmers. All of these
people know much more about tone features than I do, but they were all too busy to write this
chapter.

in language Y (as well, of course, as properties in terms of which one utterance differs systematically from another within a single language) must find some reflection in the system of phonetic transcription provided by linguistic theory. This requirement insures the possibility of comparing the representation of one utterance with that of another, whether or not they are part of the same linguistic system.

While linguistic phonetics in thus concerned with establishing the range of linguistically significant cross-language comparisons between utterances, the theory of phonological representations is concerned with the delimitation of those parameters in terms of which the representations of utterances can be structured, compared, or contrasted from the point of view of a single language.[2] As in other domains, the problem of specifying a set of phonological features for tone involves providing representations for tonal properties that allow us to determine what is distinctive about the tonal characteristics of a given element. Phonological representations of tone within a given language, that is, should be constrained so that two utterances can be represented distinctly if and only if the difference between them corresponds to a difference between two distinct signs in the system of the language.

Our choice of descriptive parameters for tone systems, then, is determined by these factors. On the one hand we must provide enough dimensions to satisfy the requirements of general phonetic comparability, without on the other hand allowing for the representation of features of utterances which are never linguistically significant. Since, furthermore, we wish to adhere to the requirement that phonological representations should be natural (in the sense of Postal 1968) in having a more or lest direct interpretation in phonetic terms, we presume that the features appropriate for phonological representation will be (possibly a proper subset of) those appropriate for phonetic representation. This entails that we must recognize a difference between the physical phonetic specification of a given feature, which may involve a considerable range of potentially distinct values determined on the basis of language particular factors, and the categorial interpretation of a feature, which involves basically a binary choice for any given segment of whether the segment does or does not possess the property referred to by the feature. While the same parameters will thus be employed both phonetically and phonologically, with two distinct (though parallel and related) sorts of specification, we recognize that the correspondences between physical phonetic and categorial values for a given feature may be nontrivial, and hence a portion of the grammar of any language is a set of phonetic detail rules which establish this relation. In the domain of tonal phenomena, these detail rules have a somewhat more

---

[2] As represented in Chomsky and Halle (1968), Anderson (1974), and other general references. The discussion below is particularly related to the content of Chapters 1 and 2 of Anderson (1974).

complex role to play (in the description of downdrift and downstep, for example) than is usual for the majority of the "well behaved" segmental features.

Since the requirement of naturalness just noted establishes a phonetic interpretation for phonological forms, it also establishes the possibility of a phonetic interpretation for phonological rules or processes. This, in turn, makes possible the hope that phonetic explanations can be provided for at least some particular phonological processes; but if this hope is to be realized, the phonetic/phonological parameters employed in a linguistic description should be such as to facilitate such explanation. Insofar as possible, therefore, we should attempt to establish a correspondence between the features and the unitary, independently controllable parameters of articulation, acoustics, and/or perception (depending on the view taken of the basis of phonetic representation).

In choosing between two alternative proposals concerning the set of features, then, we consider it an argument in favor of a given feature that it corresponds to a unitary mechanism in one of these domains; and, further, that rules can be exhibited from natural languages whose properties can be seen to follow from other aspects of the relevant mechanism. In particular, if a given choice of features allows processes to be treated as assimilatory (when in fact this seems appropriate), this will generally be taken as an argument for that choice. Other sorts of phonetically explicable or natural processes can also be invoked as arguments for particular features.

We make the further assumption that the system of phonological features will be pervasively reflected in the system of rules. If a given feature does indeed reflect a significant property of linguistic structure, it ought to be the case that segments characterized similarly for that feature behave in similar ways, displaying their possession of this common property. In that case, it would be an argument for a given proposed feature if one could show that the class of elements it groups together function as a group for the purpose of stating a (common?) phonological rule of a natural language. Conversely, if the class of elements grouped together by a given feature never (or hardly ever) function together as a natural class, this must be taken as an argument against the appropriateness of the proposed feature.[3] We may note that this

---

[3] There is a difference among types of phonological opposition which relates to the question of how much weight this kind of argument can bear. As is well known, Trubetskoy distinguished between **privative** oppositions, in which one term has a property which the other term lacks, and **equipollent** oppositions, in which there are two (or more) properties involved that are mutually inconsistent, such that one term of a binary equipollent opposition has some property (or properties) and the other has some other property (or properties). We would take the lack of any rules referring to the class specified by the positive term of a privative opposition, or by either term of an equipollent opposition, to constitute evidence against a proposed feature; however, the absence of rules referring to the negative term of a privative opposition does not need to mean much.

assumption is not made by all phonologists (Lieberman 1977, for example denies explicitly that the phonological rules should be relevant to the choice of a feature system), but it seems appropriate to us as a part of a program for an integrated theory of phonology and phonetics.

1.2 The Phonetic Scope of the Features of "Tone"

A major problem to be addressed at the outset in constructing a theory of tone features is the determination of the phonetic properties that are to be taken to be "tonal." In general (along with the other authors represented in this book) we will take tonal distinctions to be a subset of those corresponding to differences in pitch (a function, in turn, of fundamental frequency or F_0); but there are problems with this definition.

On the one hand, we wish to exclude from consideration here those pitch variations due to intonation: roughly, pitch variations determined by the structure of large syntactic units rather than within a single word. For some recent proposals that seem particularly useful and interesting for the description of intonation, see Liberman (1975). We will in general assume that intonational phenomena can be distinguished from tone, and will have nothing further to say about them.

On the other hand, there are a number of phonetic properties other than pitch that seem to have much in common with tonal features. Distinctions of voice quality often function in much the same way as distinctions in pitch: Thus, breathy voiced vowels are systematically opposed to ordinary vowels in languages like Gujarati (see Fischer-Jørgensen 1970, for a description); "raspy" or "strident" vowels are distinct from plain vowels in several Bushman languages including ≠Hõã (as described by Gruber 1973, and as shown in recorded data provided for me by Gruber); and laryngealized vowels are distinguished from plain vowels in several languages, including the Nilotic languages Ateso and Lango (cited by Ladefoged 1971). In all of these cases, the distinction somewhat resembles in function (though it may be orthogonal to) a tonal distinction. The relation is further reinforced by the fact that it is just these same properties of laryngeal behavior which frequently serve as the historical source of tonal oppositions (see Hombert's Chapter III, this volume and Egerod 1971). The parallelism can be seen in many cases: In Punjabi, for example, the loss of original voiced aspirates and *h* led to the development of tonal distinctions, while the same feature was responsible for the breathy-voiced vowels of Gujarati. Similarly, as is well known, the opposition of syllables with and without glottal stop or laryngealization (the *stød*) in Danish is entirely parallel to, and has the same historical origin as, the tonal accents of Swedish and Norwegian (cf. Gårding 1973 for description and discussion). In some cases, indeed, voice-quality distinctions are completely integrated into tonal systems: In Acoma Keresan (cf. Miller 1965) or Vietnamese (cf. Han

1969), for example, "laryngealized," "glottalized," or "creaky" accents are opposed directly to tonal accents of the usual sort.

Clearly, then, tonal phenomena are closely related to other aspects of laryngeal control, and particularly to voice quality. At least one proposal for the representation of tonal contrasts, that of Halle and Stevens (1971) incorporates this observation directly, by employing the same set of features to describe pitch, voice quality, and aspects of laryngeal control in consonants (voicing, aspiration, glottalization, etc.). We will return to this issue in Section 4, but for the remainder of the discussion in this Chapter we will generally ignore the "tonal" aspects of voice quality and confine our attention to distinctions based primarily on pitch.

Limiting our discussion to the nonintonational uses of pitch in language, then, there is a major distinction which is normally made in the study of tone languages (cf. Pike 1948, for example) between tone levels and tone glides: that is, between the simple specification of pitch values and the description of tonal contours that shift from one pitch to another within the scope of a single tone-bearing element. Pike (and, before him, Sapir) felt there was a fundamental distinction to be made between languages in which such contour tones were simply a consequence of the assignment of more than one level tone to the same element and languages in which it was the glide itself, rather than any particular point(s) on it, that was the distinctive tonal item.

In strictly phonetic terms, it is clear that it is always possible to specify a contour or glide in terms of (some number of) levels which characterize points on it. Independent of the phonological appropriateness of such a description, it is always available to us, and indeed even those authors who argue most forcefully for the basic status of tonal contours consistently describe tones in terms of beginning (middle,) and end points. Pike raises the possibility in his classic work that it might be necessary in some languages to distinguish tonal contours not only in terms of their end points and/or direction, but also in terms of such features as rate of fall or rise, correlation between "time and distance of rise," etc. We might, that is, have to distinguish between tones that could be represented diagrammatically as (1a, b) or (2a, b) below where the beginning and end points of each pair are the same:

1.   a. ⟋   b. ⟋⎤
2.   a. ⟋⎦   b. ⟋

This is indeed a theoretical possibility; and it may well be that languages can differ systematically in this respect, so that the theory of linguistic phonetics will have to ensure that provision is made for such distinctions. Such cases have not been cited in the literature, however, and we do not know of any systematic differences of this sort that have been studied carefully. We will therefore make the simplifying assumption that they can be disregarded, and that any tone can be adequately described in phonetic terms by specifying its beginning point, its end point, and possibly a point of inflection (a point at which it changes direction, in the case of rising–falling or falling–rising tones).

Given this delimitation of the phenomena to be studied, two important areas can be seen which must be treated before an adequate set of tone features can be arrived at: (*a*) the number of tone levels which must be recognized by a feature system (either phonetic or phonological), and (*b*) the question of whether phonological representations must employ features for tone contours which are distinct from the level tone features. These two questions will be dealt with in Sections 2 and 3; Section 4 will return to the relation between tone features and other phonetic properties, and will survey the proposals that have been made for tone feature systems.

2. TONE LEVELS

In physical terms, pitch can vary continuously across a wide range of frequencies, depending on the conjunction of a number of factors. Obviously, much of this variation is not linguistically significant; features of individual voice range, for example, should presumably not be reflected in linguistic descriptions of tone. Emotional and expressive factors, unrelated to any other linguistically determined aspect of an utterance, also play a particularly prominent role in the domain of pitch, but again these factors should presumably be abstracted away from in arriving at a purely linguistic representation of tone. Once we have limited our attention to those variations that are systematically and discretely manipulated by the grammar of the language, we can begin to consider the way they should be represented formally.

2.1 Phonetic Tone Levels

Even when we consider only linguistically significant pitch variations in the sense noted, we do not arrive at a point where only a small finite number of distinct pitch values need to be considered. In a number of tone systems, we find, for example, the phenomenon of downdrift and downstep (cf. Welmers 1973). In such languages, "high" tones within a phrase may not be at the same pitch level, since a high tone following a low tone will have a pitch level lower than a high tone occurring before the low tone; furthermore, subsequent high tones will be at or below this level (cf. Fromkin 1977). Further attention will be given to this phenomenon later; for now, it is sufficient to note that downdrift results in a steadily falling (or rather monotonic nonincreasing) series of pitch levels, which may (in principle) reach any length. Of course, since such "terracing" occurs within the limits of the sentence or the phrase, and phrases are of finite length, there are fairly narrow practical limits to the number of levels that will actually be found in any one utterance; but these limits do not appear to be limits in principle on the possibilities of the tonal system, but rather the consequence of other aspects of linguistic structure. (The question of performance constraints, e.g., the physical pitch limits of the speaker, are additional factors, of course.) It appears that the principles of pitch assignment in a terraced-tone language like Hausa (cf. Meyers 1976) or Akan (cf. Schachter and Fromkin 1968), if allowed to operate without any other constraint, could produce tonal patterns with any required number of distinct levels, and in consequence the phonetic framework for pitch should be able to accommodate this fact. This is not to say that the parameters should take on an infinite number of values, since there are no utterances of infinite length, but rather that there is no value N such that no utterance could ever (in principle) involve more than N levels.

Of course, we could avoid this problem entirely if we could claim that the phenomenon of terracing or downdrift is due to some external, nonlinguistic factor such as the pattern of subglottal pressure over a "breath-group" (cf. Lieberman *et al.* 1970); but this hardly seems likely, since not all tone languages display the phenomenon of downdrift. In Africa, according to Welmers, downdrift is very often found with systems which (otherwise) contrast only two tones, while it is much less common with languages which have three or more contrastive levels. Exceptions of both sorts exist, however; Welmers cites Loma as an example of a two-level language without terracing, as opposed to Hausa, Akan, Igbo, and many others which do have this feature, while Ga'anda (cf. Newman 1971) and Yala (Ikom) (cf. Armstrong 1968) have downstep in a three-level system as opposed to Jukun, for example, with no terracing. Outside of Africa, we can find a downstepping terraced system with two levels in Coatzospan Mixtec (cf. E. V. Pike, n.d.), as opposed to a system such as Navajo, for example, with two levels and no terracing. It is quite clear, then, that the phonetic property involved in a terraced tone system is systematically manipulated by the rules of individual languages, and hence the phonetic theory ought to provide a mechanism for accounting for it.

The character of phonetic tone suggests, then, that we need to provide a dimension which is capable of essentially arbitrary expansion in the number of values assumed. Our argument for this claim, as opposed to a system that posits some small finite number of phonetic pitch values (such as, for instance, the nine values employed by Beach (1924) for Zulu, or the five values of Chao's classic 1920 system of tone letters), derives from the phenomenon of downdrift, by which the tone scale can be expanded arbitrarily downward. We might suggest, then, that phonetic tones can be represented with 0 for the highest phonetic value found, and with progressively higher integers for lower pitch values. Such a system has been employed in several recent treatments of downdrift and downstep, such as Schachter and Fromkin (1968), Williamson (1970), Fromkin (1972), Peters (1973), and Clifton (1976), and permits the required expansion of the low end of the scale. A problem arises, however, when we consider the possibility of systems which are the mirror-image of downdrifting terrace systems. A very few tonal systems have been reported in which the phenomenon of upstepped terracing is found. The classically cited case of this is Acatlán Mixtec (cf. E. V. Pike, n.d.) in which

> the step-up tone contrasts with the three classical tones, high, mid, and low, but it differs structurally from these tones in that it is always higher than any preceding tone. It is not only higher than a preceding high, but it is also higher than a preceding step-up tone. Therefore a sequence of step-up tones is a sequence of progressively higher tones.

Pike goes on to provide examples of up to five consecutive step-up tones, and the rules she gives make it clear that there is no limit in principle to the number of such tones that can appear in sequence. A somewhat similar situation was reported by Elimelech (1974) for the "extreme high" tone in Kru (cf. footnote 4 however, concerning Elimelech's reservations about these data). While exceedingly rare, such systems do apparently occur; thus we must provide in phonetic theory for potentially arbitrary expansion of the tone register upwards, as well as downwards.

Once we have taken account of the existence of these possibilities, it does not seem particularly profitable to pursue the precise numerology of their representation, and this issue has (probably rightly) received little attention. We might suggest, however, that an appropriate representation would be as rational numbers in the interval [0, 1], with the value 1 representing the highest possible tone and 0 the lowest. This would recognize the fact that, while the number of distinct levels may not be limited, the total range of pitch clearly is. A sequence of distinct, progressively lower high tones might then be $1, \frac{2}{3}, \frac{1}{2},$ $\frac{4}{9}, \frac{5}{12}, \frac{2}{5}, \ldots$ (approaching $\frac{1}{3}$ asymptotically as the lower limit of "high" tones), while a corresponding series of progressively lower low tones might be $\frac{1}{2}, \frac{1}{4},$ $\frac{1}{8}, \frac{1}{16}, \ldots$ (approaching 0). In this case, each "low tone" would in fact be lower than surrounding highs, but (in accord with the facts) a tone level which counts as "low" early in the utterance might actually be higher than one which counts as "high" later on. For some discussion of this possibility, see the papers on downdrift referred to above. In a language without downdrift, the distinct registers could be represented as fixed points on this scale, while a language with "upstep" could be represented in terms of a series similar to that given for downdrift, but proceeding in the opposite direction.

Such a system (which clearly lends itself to manipulation by quasi-arithmetic rules of the type generally encountered in the study of phonetic detail) seems to provide a fairly accurate representation of the essential facts of phonetic tone: The levels of tone are discrete, not continuous, but there is no upper bound to the number of such levels, though there is both an upper and a lower bound to the range covered by the total set of levels. Except when considering the phonetics of down- (or up-) drift, however, it is more precise than is generally required, and in the discussion below we will generally employ the Chao five-level system for the phonetic description of tones. On this scale, the number 5 represents the highest tonal level, and the number 1 the lowest. As we remarked at the end of Section 1, it is apparently adequate to represent tones by at most three points on such a scale (for phonetic purposes, at least); thus, a tone 5–5 begins in the highest register and remains level, 3–5 begins in the middle of the scale and rises to high, 2–1–4 begins below mid, falls to low, and then rises to just below the highest value, and so on. While this five-level scale will be seen below to have an obvious relation to the facts of phonological tone inventories, it should be borne in mind that it is in principle simply a notational convenience when interpreted phonetically, similar to the use of segments to abbreviate bundles of distinctive features, and that the actual range of phonetically distinguishable tones is not limited to five values.

2.2 Phonological Tone Levels

When we study real tone systems, we see quickly that the defining principle of a phonological representation yields a much more constrained system than the (potentially) unbounded system of tone levels found in phonetic representations. This point is stressed by Pike (1948), and also by Schachter (1961); in a phonological representation, two items should be distinctly represented only if they can potentially distinguish two signs in the system of the language. What matters in this case, then, is not the precise delimitation of all possible pitch values, but rather the contrast among just those values that could appear in a given position in distinct signs. The multiplicity of levels encountered in the phonetic description of downstep, then, are not significant here. In a typical two-tone system with downdrift (like Hausa), for example, a high tone may be followed by a tone at the same level or by a lower tone, and if these are the only possibilities, we can simply label the higher of the two possibilities phonologically as "high," regardless of its phonetic value or relation to other tones similarly labeled. After a low tone, we can have either another tone at or below the same level (another "low") or another tone at a higher level. This latter we can label "high" regardless of the fact that (due to the phonetic rule of downdrift) it will be phonetically lower than previous instances of tones labeled "high" in the same utterance. We thus need recognize only two phonological tones, "high" and "low," despite the fact that a number of phonetic values may be involved.

Although we have not carefully distinguished "downstep" from "downdrift," the former properly refers to a complication of the situation just discussed. A language with "downstep" behaves roughly as follows. Initially we find only two tones, "high" and "low." After a "low" tone, we have two possibilities: a tone at the same level (a "low") or a tone at a higher level (but lower than a "high" earlier in the utterance, reflecting a downdrift rule). After a "high," however, we may find three possibilities: a tone at the same level (hence "high"), a tone at or below the level of a previous "low" (hence also "low"), or a tone intermediate between these levels—lower than a "high" in this position, but higher than a "low." Typically this intermediate tone has the same effect as a downdrifted "high," in that no other tone later in the utterance can be higher than it is pitch. It is this intermediate tone which is generally referred to as a ("phonemic") downstep tone. As noted by Schuh in Chapter VII of this volume, downstep usually results from the loss of a low tone element (either historically or synchronically) between two highs; when this low tone has conditioned the downdrift of the following high, and is then lost, it results in the appearance of a third potentially contrastive tonal value following a high tone, in addition to "high" and "low."

We can see immediately that the existence of such "downstep" tones need not lead to the enrichment of the system of phonological elements (yet to be developed below) that provides for the specification of ordinary level and contour tones. First of all, in many cases it is possible to identify the downstep synchronically with the deletion of a low tone element. This is frequently the case in Akan, for example (cf. Schachter and Fromkin 1968). Consider the phrase *mé'bó* 'my stone', for example (where 'V represents the downstep tone). This is composed of the high-tone possessive pronoun *mé* and the noun *ɔ-bó* 'stone', which itself contains the low-tone noun prefix *ɔ-*. This prefix element is always deleted after possessive pronouns. In order to describe these facts, then, we need only allow the independently necessary rule of downdrift to apply, lowering the (phonetic) tone of *bó*, prior to the application of the deletion rule for the prefix. One might object that such a phonetic detail rule ought to apply only after the "higher-level" morphophonemic or phonological rules, rather than in the middle of the system of such rules; but it has been established elsewhere (cf. Anderson 1975) that this possibility is frequently attested in the grammars of individual languages. In such a case, then (i.e., whenever a deleted low-tone element can be recovered synchronically as the basis of a downstep tone), we clearly do not need to posit any additional device to account for downstep.

Even in the event that such a low-tone element cannot be plausibly posited synchronically in the grammar of a language, it is not necessary to posit some other novel sort of device to account for downstep. Presumably downdrift has two aspects in a language in which it appears: first, a rule which states that a high tone following a low is (some specified interval) lower than a preceding high tone; and second, a rule that a high tone following another possibly downstepped high has the same phonetic value as the preceding high. But suppose that we have a language in which downstep occurs as a third phonological element. We could then represent the downstep as a mid tone, and say the following. First, a high tone following a low tone is replaced by mid (the downdrift rule). Then, a mid tone has a value intermediate between that of a preceding nonlow and that of a preceding low; and a high tone has the same phonetic value as the immediately preceding nonlow (i.e., high or mid) tone. The downdrift element is now simply a third element of the tone system: a mid, in addition to high and low. Its distribution is restricted, in that it can only appear (distinctively) after a high or mid tone; but this is a fact about the downstep element and is unrelated to our decision to represent it as an intermediate level.

We should observe that the description given here has consequences for the general nature of representations in phonological descriptions. We have assumed, that is, that languages with downdrift and/or downstep contain rules that progressively assign pitch values to tonal elements on the basis of values assigned earlier in the utterance; but note that these rules must have access both to the phonetic pitch value of a previous tonal element (so as to make the current element equal to it, lower, etc.) and also to its phonological categorization as **high**, **low**, etc. (so as to know which operation to perform). We have already seen that the operation of downdrift and/or downstep makes it impossible in the general case to determine either representation (locally) from the other: The correspondence between phonological category and phonetic pitch is one that changes progressively as the utterance gets longer. We must thus assume that both values are simultaneously present: Contrary to a widely held view, the phonetic rules of the language do not serve to **replace** phonological values with phonetic ones, but rather to provide detail in a distinct dimension of representation. This is the view presented in Anderson (1974: Chapter 1), and it is seen here to follow necessarily from the nature of the downdrift/downstep phenomenon, which requires (unavoidably, it would seem) simultaneous access to the phonetic and phonological values of an element in the environment of the rule.

A further assumption of the account above is that the pitch assignment rule(s) must be applied one step at a time from left to right; and this would appear to bear on current controversies concerning the mode of application of phonological rules. In fact, however, this mode of application follows from the intrinsic character of the rules and requires no theoretical assumptions beyond the (surely uncontroversial by now) claim that rules can in some instances reapply to their own output. Pitch assignment rules of the type we have been considering require for their application that both the phonetic and the phonological value of a preceding tone be available. Initially, however, the only phonetic values that are available are those for the **first** high (low, etc.) tone of the utterance, which values are established not by the rules in question but rather as boundary conditions. When the pitch assignment rules first come to apply, then, there is only one place where their environment is defined: immediately to the right of the initial tonal elements. After this first application, a new environment is now defined further to the right, and so on; but the fact that the assignment process "propagates" to the right requires no theoretical descriptive mechanism.

Schuh, in Chapter VII, this volume, cites a case from Dschang-Bamileke (cf. Tadadjeu 1974) in which a downstep tone appears without the presence in the language of a downdrift rule. He notes that after a low (or high), high and downstep tones contrast, as in the pair lòtɔ́ŋ 'feather' and lɔ̀'tɔ́ŋ 'to read'. Schuh feels that the "downstepped HI cannot be interpreted as MID since there would then be a possible phrase LO MID HI. However, after a down-stepped HI, there can be no rise to a high tone [p. 240]." It is not clear that this objection to representing downstep as a mid tone is insuperable, however. We could suggest, that is, that this representation is possible if we reinterpret Schuh's observation that Dschang-Bamileke does not have a downdrift rule; while it does not indeed have a rule that lowers highs after a low, we could suggest that there **is** a rule which lowers highs after a mid tone. The tone rules of the language would then include the following: Mid (downstep) tone has a value intermediate between that of preceding low and preceding high, and high tone has the same value as a preceding nonlow (mid or high). As a result, it will not be possible to have a rise after either high or mid, but we are not thereby compelled to posit a tonal representation for the downstep as other than a mid level tone with somewhat restricted distribution (again, for reasons that have nothing to do with our choice of representation).

Clearly a language displaying three level tones **and** a phonemic downstep could require a somewhat more complicated solution, since it would not do to confuse the downstep with the mid tone. In the two cases known to us, however, such a solution is not required. In Yala (Ikom), Armstrong (1968) describes such a system. Here, a high tone is lower after either a low or a mid than after a high; while a mid tone is lower after a low than after a nonlow. This is simply a natural extension of the terracing principle to a three-level language: Tones are lower after lower tones than after tones of the same level.

In Ga'anda (cf. Newman 1971), we find a more restricted version of this system: Here it is only high tones that are lowered after a preceding non-high (low or mid) tone. In each of these cases the phonetics of the down-drift system, while more complex than in the case of two-level languages, are straightforward and do not call for any new sort of tonal element. Each of these languages also has apparently contrastive downstep tones; but in both cases the descriptions indicate that these are due to tone elements that are present in underlying representation and can be recovered synchronically, as in the simpler Akan case. Even if this were not the case, we could simply posit "lowered high" (and in the case of Yala [Ikom], lowered mid as well) tones as the representation of the downsteps. There is thus no reason to believe that downstep tones in any language require us to posit tonal elements other than ordinary level tones, and hence that the notion "downstep" has any special place in the system of phonological features. As will be evident from the discussion immediately following, this proposal would run into difficulties in the face of a language with a fully productive phonological downstep in a fully downdrifting language with four (or more) tone levels, since it would require us to posit up to seven underlyingly distinct level tones; it is perhaps significant that downstep is not attested in any such language.

Having concluded that downstep does not pose a special problem, we can now turn to the question of how many tonal levels need to be distinguished by a feature system. Systems of two and three distinct level tones are abundantly attested from all of the major groups of tone languages in the world (American, Asian, and African), and their existence is not seriously contested. Systems of four distinct tone levels are somewhat less common, but still firmly established: Examples include the Nikki dialect of Bariba (Welmers 1952), the Miao language Yao-lu (Chang 1972), and Soyaltepec Mixtec (E. V. Pike 1956). The first descriptive feature system for tone proposed within the framework of generative phonology, that of Gruber (1964), in fact provided for the specification of exactly four tone levels, since Gruber was not aware of any languages that contrasted more levels than this. Since that time, however, several languages have been cited as contrasting five level tones (cf. Maddieson, forthcoming, for discussion and references). One of the most famous cases of this sort is "Black Miao" (actually the Black Miao language of Ch'ing Chiang Miao: Cf. Kwan 1971), which has been cited largely on the basis of unpublished field notes of Fang Kuei Li. This language contains five distinct level tones (*11*, *22*, *33*, *44*, and *55* on the Chao scale) as well as two rising tones (*35*, *13*) and one falling tone (*51*). Some contrasting forms include:

3. a. (*11*) *la*	'candle'		e. (*55*) *la*	'short'	
tju	'waist'		*ɬju*	'heart'	
va	'I, me'		*ta*	'to take, use'	
ljoŋ	'green'		*nhaŋ*	'to listen, hear'	
b. (*22*) *la*	'to move away'		f. (*35*) *la*	'to squeeze'	
tɔ	'far'		*ta*	'to break, to kill'	
ɬai	'to enter'		*ɬhai*	'moon'	
ji	'eight'		*ɣau*	'good'	
c. (*33*) *la*	'cave'		g. (*13*) *ɬju*	'to save, rescue'	
tjo	'broom'		*tɔ*	'not'	
khau (*na 13*)	'to kiss'		*fhaŋ*	'to lose'	
xe	'tall, high'		*sho*	'to close'	
d. (*44*) *la*	a classifier		h. (*51*) *la* (*qa 44*)	'to mow'	
ɬjo	'squirrel'		*ta* (*no 33* 'fall')	'to rain'	
xan	'to walk'		*çhaŋ*	'wall'	
ɬhja	'to miss, think of'		*ɣu*	'cage'	

It seems clear that this language does indeed display five contrastive tone levels, as claimed. Another language with this property is the Ivory Coast dialect of Dan studied by Bearth and Zemp (1967), which again displays five levels in addition to two falling tones (*31* and *32*) and one rise (*13*). Forms illustrating the contrast are *gba¹* 'caterpillar (species)', *gba²* 'shelter', *gba³* 'fine (n.)', *gba⁴* '(house-)roof', and *gba⁵* 'antelope', as well as several other minimal or near-minimal quintuplets presented by Bearth and Zemp. Their presentation makes it clear that this language, too, contrasts five tone levels.

A number of other languages also display surface contrasts among five tone levels, although a further consideration of their phonologies makes it likely that one or more of these can be derived from underlying representations containing fewer than five distinct tonal elements. Among these languages are Trique (Longacre 1952, 1959) and Ngamambo Bamileke (Asongwed and Hyman 1977). Systems of this sort do not by themselves demonstrate the necessity of positing five distinct levels of tone, since some levels could be considered merely phonetic; but a consideration of their morphophonemics suggests that the rules responsible for producing these additional levels are of the same type as those manipulating the clearly distinctive tones in Sandhi. Since phonological rules must thus be able to refer to five levels of tone, it would be most appropriate if the feature system provided for this much flexibility; thus such systems provide further support for the claim made by Wang (1967), Woo (1969), Maddieson (1970) and others that five distinct tonal levels must be provided for. A consideration of the range of data from Miao and Yao dialects provided by Chang (1972), some of which have nine or perhaps more distinct tones in contrast, makes it clear that (even where there are not five distinct level tones) a correct description of these systems is extremely hard to provide without five tonal levels.

Our conclusions, then, are as follows: (*a*) Phonetic theory must provide for the description of a potentially unbounded number of distinct tone levels within a restricted range; (*b*) "downstep" does not constitute a phonological element distinct from normal (usually level) tones; and (*c*) a phonological feature system must provide for the description of at least (and apparently at most) five levels of tone.

3. TONAL CONTOURS

At least since Pike's classic (1948) manual appeared, a fundamental issue in the study of tone has been the correct treatment of gliding or contour tones. When the pitch on a single structural unit (vowel, syllable, or other domain of tone assignment) does not remain constant, but rather shifts in value over the course of production of that element, we can always (as noted above) represent this glide phonetically in terms of a sequence of levels; but the appropriateness of such a characterization for phonological systems has been a persistent problem. On the one hand, we might choose to represent, for example, a fall from high to low as the sequence High–Low; on the other hand, we might treat the fall as a unit, describing it with some indication of its "register" (perhaps its beginning, end, or middle point) and a unitary feature such as "Fall" to describe the pitch course.

Before discussing proposals that have been made in this area, we should first make one observation about the scope of the problem. It is not necessarily the case that a tone is to be treated as a phonological contour just because it is not phonetically level. Consider for example, the case of the low tone in Yoruba (cf. Lavelle 1974). This tone is generally realized, at the end of an utterance after another low, not as a level low tone but rather as a fall from low to extralow. Hardly anyone would wish to say that a tone of this sort should be treated phonologically as a contour, however; clearly the fall is a nondistinctive property. Perhaps slightly more controversial is the case of a language like the Chiu-chou, Chia-pa, or Hsin-ch'iao dialects of Miao with the following tonal system: [22], [33], [44], [55], [13], [53], and [21] (cf. Chang 1972). The tones [13] and [53] are clearly a distinctive rise and fall, respectively, but it would seem perfectly plausible to treat the tone [21] as phonologically a low level tone /11/, with the [2] element considered a nondistinctive onglide. Maddieson (forthcoming) reports that it is indeed quite frequent for the "extreme" tones of a system to be preceded by a central onglide ([45] for an extreme high, [21] for an extreme low). Given the evident necessity of recognizing five tone levels, as argued above, it would seem most appropriate to treat the [21] tone in such a system as /11/, thus removing it from the discussion of the treatment of phonological contour tones.

A number of proposals have been made for the phonological description of contour tones. We include here a brief sketch of these proposals.

3.1 Gruber's and Wang's Systems

Both Gruber (1964) and Wang (1967) begin their discussions of feature frameworks for tonal analysis from the position that tone is a property assigned to syllables. Both of these systems were originally designed to deal with the facts of Asian (particularly Sino-Tibetan) languages, and both accept the persuasiveness of Pike's (1948) position that in these languages contours should be treated as unitary tonal elements, rather than as sequences of level tones. Each therefore characterizes contour tones in the following way: first, by some of the same features used in specifying tone levels ("high" and "high2" for Gruber, "high," "central," and "mid" for Wang), which characterize their "register"; second, by associating with some tones the features "rising" and/or "falling," specifying a direction of tone glide. Wang also posits a redundant feature "contour," which is positive for any tone specified either [+rising] or [+falling], and a feature "convex" to specify the relative order of a rise and fall appearing in the same tonal element. Gruber, on the other hand, provides no way to distinguish falling–rising tones from rising–falling tones, since he claims explicitly that these two possibilities never contrast within a single register in any language. Subsequent discussions of tone have in general been more phonetically "realist" than Gruber's, and to our knowledge this question has not been raised again since. The status of Gruber's generalization, to which we know of no counterexamples, is somewhat unclear.

Little explicit discussion is devoted in either of these papers to the principles which determine the register (and consequently the level tone) that is associated with a given contour. These appear to be as follows. For Gruber, there are only four tone levels or registers. Any tone, whether rising, falling, or complex, that does not rise **above** the next-to-lowest of these is associated with the lowest register. Similarly, any tone that does not fall below the next-to-highest level is associated with the highest level. Tones which cross both the next-to-highest and next-to-lowest levels are associated with one or the other of these registers, respectively, depending on whether "most" of the tonal contour is above or below the middle of the tonal range. In the case of Wang's system, which has five tonal registers, contours are apparently all assigned either to the highest or to the lowest of these, in line with Wang's claim that in a single language there can be only two tones with the same shape, one in the upper and one in the lower part of the pitch range. If a contour touches the highest pitch, at any point in the glide, it is assigned to the higher register; if not, it must touch the lowest pitch and is assigned to the lower register. Thus in both of these cases there is no particular point on the tonal contour that determines its register, in line with the position that contours are units, and no particular point is more significant than any other. An alternative view might be to pick either the beginning or the ending of the glide as the determination of the register of a contour tone, but this proposal apparently does not appear in the literature.

3.2 Woo's System

Woo (1969) examined Wang's proposal in some detail and concluded that not only was there no direct evidence in favor of the proposition that contour tones should be treated as units, but that for some languages normally thought to be of the contour type, there were clear arguments in favor of treating them rather as sequences of levels. Woo's basic claim was that the more complex a tonal contour, the more segmental material must be available for it to be realized on. In contrast to Gruber and Wang's assumption that tones are assigned to syllables, Woo claimed that tonal elements are assigned to segmental units (moras), and that the universal system of tone features includes only level tone elements. In such a case, then, it is necessary to posit at least two such units in any syllable bearing a complex tone. She presents several examples which suggest that this is indeed the case; in Mandarin, for example, her measurements indicate that syllables bearing Tone 3 in isolation (with the shape [*315*] or, perhaps more accurately, [*213*]) are phonetically 50% longer than syllables bearing one of the other tones of the language. This is exactly what would be predicted if this tone, which involves three distinct levels and hence three moras in her analysis, is compared with the others; each of them involves two tonal elements ([*55*] for Tone 1, [*35*] for Tone 2, and [*51*] for Tone 4). Gandour (1974) and Leben (1971), though differing on details, reach a similar conclusion for standard Thai. Similar examples and arguments of various sorts from a variety of languages, establish the fact that in many cases tonal complexity is associated with segmental complexity; this in turn makes plausible Woo's hypothesis that tonal elements are always levels and are always associated with units such as the mora in a one-to-one fashion.

3.3 Leben's System

Unfortunately, a detailed examination by Leben (1973) and subsequent authors suggests a conclusion also required by McCawley (1970), namely, that the strong form of Woo's hypothesis is inconsistent with the facts of some tone systems, particularly in Africa. A variety of examples show that a contrastive contour tone is carried by a syllable containing only one vowel mora. This would at first appear to support Wang's contention; tone patterns are associated as a whole with the syllable, not the segment, and there is no reason to decompose contours into unit level tones. The examples presented by Leben, McCawley, and others provide dramatic confirmation of Woo's proposal in one respect, however: namely, in the separation of contour tones into sequences of levels. Leben, for example, demonstrates the existence of a rule of tone copying in Mende which applies in certain compounds. This rule copies the last tone element of the first member of the compound onto the beginning of the second member. The interesting feature of this rule is that it copies a falling tone as a low, and a rising tone as a high. This fact follows directly if one assumes that a rise in represented as the sequence low–high, and a fall as high–low: In that case, it is precisely the last tonal element which is copied, regardless of whether this is part of a contour or not. In a system such as Wang's, however, there is no motivation for this fact: Both the rise and the fall would be assigned in his system to the high register, and there is thus no basis for a register difference in their behavior under tone copying. This process can be related to a vast array of tonal assimilatory (including "spreading") processes, discussed by Hyman and Schuh (1974) and in Schuh's chapter, this volume. All of these examples establish the same conclusion: Wherever the register of a tone is relevant for the operation of an assimilatory rule, contour tones do not behave in the way predicted by Wang's description. They do not, that is, behave as if they had a unitary and homogeneous characterization in terms of register, but, rather, when "seen from the left" (in anticipatory rules), they behave as if their register were determined by their beginning point, while when "seen from the right" (in perseverative processes), their register appears to be determined by their endpoint.

This was actually a point which had been made for some (non-Asian) systems by Pike (1948), as was another, more direct proof for the necessity of regarding at least some contour tones as sequences of levels. McCawley's (1970) analysis of Tiv, for example, shows that each of a set of verbal tense/aspect combinations is associated with a particular tone pattern, specified as a sequence of level tone elements. When such a pattern is realized on a verb with at least as many syllables as there are level tones in the pattern, each level is assigned to a distinct syllable. When there are fewer syllables than tone elements, however, the result is that more than one tone must be assigned to some syllables, resulting in the appearance of contour tones. This treatment, in which a sequence of tones associated with some grammatical category is realized sometimes as a series of simple levels and sometimes as a contour, is familiar from the tradition of Africanist studies. Edmondson and Bendor-Samuel (1966) give an analysis of just this sort for Etung, for example. In this language, tense–aspect combinations are associated with tone sequences as in Tiv. In the Remote Past tense, for example, a series of preroot elements prefixed to verbs are assigned either all high or all low tones while the pattern high–low (–low) is assigned to the root. With a bisyllabic root, we get a form such as à gbómè 'he met'; in the same tense, a monosyllabic root is assigned the pattern of m̀ mân 'I finished'. The contour tone "high–falling" is thus seen to be directly equivalent to the sequence "high–low." Examples of this sort can easily be multiplied, both from synchronic tone systems in Africa and from certain diachronic developments as well.

We conclude, therefore, that for at least some contour tone systems these arguments establish part of Woo's hypothesis and refute another part of it. Contour tones must in at least some cases be treated not as units but as sequences of level tone elements. These level tones are not, however, associated in one-to-one fashion with tone-bearing elements such as the mora; rather, more than one tone element may in some languages be assigned to the same short vowel (or other domain). The issue of segmental versus suprasegmental representations for tone is taken up in more detail in Leben's chapter, this volume, but we should note here that the situation we have just discussed for tonal elements is not entirely isolated in phonological theory. It has recently been shown by Anderson (1976) that the feature [± Nasal] has much the same property, in that a single segment may well be in the domain of more than one specification for this feature. Prenasalized and postnasalized consonants, on this analysis, are treated as precisely the nasal equivalents of contour tones. A similar view of the (even more impeccably segmental) features of vowel quality is implicit in Andersen's (1972) treatment of diphthongization. He views diphthongization as essentially the assignment of more than one vowel

quality specification to a single segment (which may be followed by a reinterpretation of this element as a sequence of two segments, but need not be).
Further, the entire literature which has grown up in the very recent past around
the theory of "Autosegmental Phonology" (cf. Goldsmith 1976) has questioned
the unity of the traditional segment in radical ways. It is clear that there is no
theoretical obstacle to the sorts of representation that are required if we are to
treat contours as sequences of levels, even in the absence of evidence for Woo's
hypothesis of the segmental nature of tone.

3.4 Pike's Arguments for the Unity of Contour Tones

Arguments of the type just reviewed are not in fact particularly new, though
they appeared so within the context of generative phonological discussion when
they were first presented. In fact, Pike (1948) and earlier scholars working on
tone languages had accepted the conclusion that glides also occur in a "register
tone system," where they are analyzable in terms of their end points (together
with a midpoint, if the glide changes direction). Although this property was
widely accepted for tone systems in American and African languages, it was
felt that the tone systems of Asian languages were significantly different in
this regard and that most of these represented a distinct type ("contour systems,"
as opposed to "register systems") in which the contour tones ought not to be
decomposed.

In discussing this point, Pike raises four issues which he feels divide contour
systems from register systems and which, if accepted, would entail the conclusion that contour tones are unitary. This would, in turn, require us to provide
phonological features distinct from those used to specify level tones for their
description. We discuss here the arguments given by Pike (1948: 8).

3.4.1 "The Basic Tonemic Unit Is Gliding instead of Level."

If interpreted to mean that in a contour system all tones glide, this would
indeed establish a typological difference; but as Pike himself notes, no systems
are known in which there is no level tone. This negative finding is further supported by Maddieson's (forthcoming) survey of tonal inventories. If interpreted
to mean simply that the glides are basic units in such a system, this is of course
the point which is to be established, and hence not an argument.

3.4.2 "The Unitary Contour Glides Cannot Be Interrupted by
Boundaries, as Can the Non-Phonemic Compounded Types
of a Register System."

Among the arguments Pike gives for decomposing tonal contours in some
languages is the fact that the beginning point can sometimes be identified with
one morpheme, and the endpoint with another. In Mazateco, for example,
he cites (1948:7) the form *ti 2–4* 'we, but not you, burn', with a glide from the

second highest to the lowest of the four tone levels of Mazateco. This is to be compared with the form *ti 2* 'it burns', showing that the beginning point of the contour *2–4* in the first form is part of the stem, while the endpoint represents the morpheme meaning 'we, but not you'. While this is indeed an argument for decomposing this contour, it is certainly not the only one that can be given for decomposition. When we consider the arguments cited above in Section 3.3. from constant tonal patterns, as in Tiv or Etung, or from the sorts of tone spreading processes cited by Hyman and Schuh (1974) and in Schuh's chapter, this volume, which may well occur within the limits of a single noncomplex form, we can see that the decomposition of surface contours into level tones phonologically in a given language can be supported even without evidence of the sort Pike cites for Mazateco. When we consider that most Asian languages are (independent of their tonal systems) of a type in which the word, the syllable, and the morpheme are virtually coextensive units, it seems exceedingly unlikely that we could find evidence of this kind, but that fact alone does not serve as a positive argument **against** decomposing their contour tones.

3.4.3 *"The Beginning and Ending Points of the Glides of a Contour System Cannot Be Equated with Level Tonemes in the Same System."*

In languages like Mazateco or Yoruba, we find tone glides whose beginning and ending points correspond directly to level tones occurring in the same system. In the Yao language of Hweikang Pa (cf. Purnell 1965), however, the only level tones are [*44*] and [*11*]. In addition to these we find the following contour tones: [*31*], [*453*], [*231*], [*24*]. Clearly we cannot interpret these contours as simply complex combinations of the independently occurring level tones of the language. According to Pike, then, it would be incorrect to analyze them as sequences of level tones.

Again, this argument is less a positive point against tonal decomposition than it is simply the absence in some languages of a particular argument **for** decomposition. As we have seen, it will be necessary for any theory to recognize the existence of five distinct tone levels. In terms of those levels, it appears to be possible to represent contour tones of even the most complex systems, such as those of the Miao-Yao languages. If carried to its logical conclusion, Pike's argument would in fact require us to treat any phonological unit with a restricted distribution as part of a complex unit with the factors which condition it. Thus, in most languages in which it appears, the downstep tone can only appear after a high; in that position, it cannot be identified with any independently occurring level tone. We would not, however, wish to accept the conclusion that the sequence high–downstep forms a single, indissoluble unit "contour tone," which is the conclusion we would be led to if we accepted the form of Pike's argument here as valid. The fact that, in a given language, some of the tone levels are distributionally restricted in that they only occur in certain combinations does not in principle prevent us from recognizing that these sequences are in fact just that—sequences of discrete levels. If we found contour tones which required us to posit levels which never appear alone **in any language** (as, for example, if we found a language with more than five distinct noncomplex tones all beginning at the same level), this could be construed as an argument against the decomposition of contours, but this is not of course the case. We conclude that this argument of Pike's fails to carry conviction.

3.4.4 *"Contour Systems Ha[ve] Only One Toneme per Syllable, Whereas Some of the Register-Tone Languages, like Mazateco, May Have Two or More Tonemes per Syllable."*

This point to some extent begs the question, since what we are trying to decide is whether tone contours assigned to one syllable should be treated as made up of more than one "toneme" or not. There is a real issue here, however, which involves the extent to which the tonal units are tied to particular elements of segmental structure. Pike's argument is that where tones are assigned one-to-one to syllables, and some syllables are assigned contours, this shows that the contours are structurally unitary; there is undoubtedly some force to this observation. The situation is entirely parallel to that of diphthongs, however; we can say that (in any language) each syllable contains exactly one vocalic nucleus, and in a language with the vowel system /a, i, u/ plus the diphthongs /ai, au/, some syllables thereby receive complex vocalism. The rule "one nucleus per syllable" would surely not, all by itself, prevent us from treating the diphthongs as complex sequences of segments. It is a classic problem in phonology to find a way to represent diphthongs so as to reflect both their unitary character and their complexity at the same time, and contour tones are plausibly seen as "tonal diphthongs." Few linguists have argued against the decomposition of diphthongs entirely, however, and the same situation ought to obtain with respect to contour tones.

We can also note that the general problem of how closely tonal units of any size are linked to segmental material is part of the large issue of the suprasegmental aspect of tone (cf. Leben, Chapter VI, this volume). It does not, however, provide a direct answer to the question of whether tone contours should be regarded as units or as sequences. We conclude, therefore, that while Pike has identified certain properties of a certain linguistic type, they are not sufficient to establish his conclusion that contour tones are "basic tonemic units."

3.5 Other Arguments for Unitary Contours

Pike's discussion established at the very outset of serious studies of tone as a general linguistic problem the dichotomy between register systems and contour systems. Since there is a clear typological difference between most Asian tone systems and most American or African tone systems, subsequent discussion has generally assumed that Pike's distinction is the basis for it, and therefore that his conclusion regarding the unity of contour tones is a valid one. Both Wang and Gruber, as noted above, start from this assumption, and it is only recently that it has been questioned. The search for further arguments in favor of Pike's position has not been a particularly fruitful one, however. We summarize below those that have appeared in the literature.

3.5.1 The Argument from Perception

Sapir, in a famous quotation cited by Pike (1948), observed that there is a psychological or perceptual sense in which contours are primitives: "Movement *from* A *to* B (a physical statement) is not really the same thing as movement *in a direction* away from A and toward B. Psychologically, one can have an experience of such movement without being able to 'geometrize' it in terms of fixed points A and B [p. 8]." The work on tone perception reported and summarized in Gandour's chapter, this volume, also supports the claim that contours have a high degree of perceptual salience and that human perception of tone is likely to be heavily dependent not simply on tone levels, but on movements. In part, this is simply because the absolute pitch value corresponding to a given tone may be quite variable, and hence the identification of tone level may be quite difficult, while a rise is always easily distinguishable from a fall, regardless of their relative levels.

In considering the weight to be given to this observation in constructing a theory of tone, however, one must be careful to distinguish between the appropriate linguistic description of a phenomenon and the strategies used by speakers and hearers to identify linguistic elements. It is undoubtedly the case that speakers and hearers use contour, where it is available to them, as an aid in identifying tonal elements. It has not been demonstrated, however, that the perceptual salience of contours is correlated with the extent to which a linguistic structure treats them as units. The tone perception experiment conducted by Gandour (see Chapter II, this volume) failed to show any major difference in the responses of Thai and Yoruba listeners, although speakers of these two tone languages were clearly distinguished from English subjects in their perceptual judgments. There is strong evidence that the surface contour tones of Yoruba must be analyzed as sequences of level tones; yet the evidence shows that contours are neither more nor less salient for these speakers as for Thai speakers, whose contour tones have been analyzed, at least by some, as lexically unitary. The reason for a lack of difference between the Thai and Yoruba speakers may well be, however, because the surface contours in Thai are derived from level tones. This therefore may not be a good test case. If it could be shown that Chinese or Vietnamese speakers bascially categorize tones in terms of contours rather than registers in a generalized perception task, while speakers of Mazatec, Mixtec, Mende, or Yoruba organize their perception in terms of levels, then we could have an argument that contour tones in languages of the Asian type have a special, psychologically primitive status. Failing that, however, all we have is evidence for a general strategy in perception, applicable to languages for which the linguistic evidence shows clearly that contours are phonologically composed of sequences of level tone units as well as to languages for which such evidence is not available. A strict isomorphism between the categorizations yielded in perceptual experiments through multidimensional scaling or similar analytic techniques and the categories of linguistic structure in a particular language should not be expected to obtain, precisely because languages can clearly differ in many more ways from one another than there is reason to believe humans differ in overall perceptual organization.

The situation here is somewhat similar to that in other phonological domains. It is clear, for example, that vowel length is a major perceptual clue in English for the voicing of a following stop. No one (or at least not the majority of linguists) would conclude from this fact that vowel length and not stop voicing is the basic phonological difference between, e.g., *muck* and *mug*. If vowel length were the difference, it is hard to see how the distinction between the final segments of inflected forms (*mucked* versus *mugged*, *mucks* versus *mugs*) could be predicted by anything approaching a natural rule, though everyone would certainly like to treat this difference as a straightforward assimilation.

Similarly it is clear that the direction of formant transitions is an important perceptual clue to the identity of stop consonants in the environment of vowels, but it has not been concluded from that fact that, e.g., stop consonants with similar direction of F_2 transition should be treated as phonologically the same category. To accept this conclusion would be to associate [t] before front vowels, not with [t] before back vowels, but rather with [p] (since both have rising F_2 transitions in this position), while [t] before back vowels would be associated with [k]. Formant transitions are undoubtedly very significant perceptually, but we employ this information in complex and highly structured ways in re-covering the categories of linguistic structure from the perceptual cues we find in the speech signal. We must conclude from this that studies showing the perceptual importance of tone glides do not establish the conclusion that such glides are elementary units of linguistic structure, rather than decomposed into levels in phonological representation.

3.5.2 The Argument from Nonidentity of Contours and Sequences

Elimelech (1974) has given an argument of a rather different sort for the underlying unity of contour tones, based on phonological properties of the tone system of Kru. This language has a tonal inventory consisting of high, low, rise, and fall, as described by Elimelech. The point of interest on which the argument for unitary contour tones is based is the following. Phonetically, a rising tone begins at the same level as a preceding tone, regardless of what tone that is. Subsequent high tones, furthermore, are at the level of the endpoint of the rise and remain thus raised until a low tone causes them to be lowered

by the operation of a downdrift rule. A sequence of tones consisting of high
tones and rising tones, then, has a steadily increasing (or monotonic non-
decreasing) contour,[4] similar to the upstep phenomenon discussed above in
Section 2.1 for Acatlan Mixtec:

4.   kɔ̀ nǎ nḛ̃ṵ̌ téblé kpṵ̌   'The rice is on the table.'
                L R H R H H   R

A tonal sequence consisting of highs and lows, however, does not display this
"upstep" phenomenon:

5.   ɔ́ tḛ̀ bá   'He buys pepper.'
                         H L H
                         [⁻ _ ⁻]   (not *[_ _ ⁻])

Elimelech reasons from these facts to the primitive status of contour tones on
the following basis. If we represent the rising tone as a sequence low–high,
we cannot explain the difference between the behavior of the low–high sequence
which constitutes a rising tone in Example (4) and the low high sequence which
appears directly in Example (5). The tonal element "low" must be set equal
to a previous tone regardless of its identity, that is, if this low is part of a rise;
while an independent low does not follow this rule but is rather set equal to
the level of the next independent low back in the utterance.

It does not follow from this, however, that the contour tone cannot be represented as a low–high sequence. The fact that a low followed by a tautosyllabic
high behaves differently from one alone in its syllable would only motivate
this conclusion if we had no way to write the relevant rules, which would only
be true if we had no way to represent the difference in structure; but this is of
course not the case, since we have the syllabic structure itself on which to base
the statement of the environment for the relevant rule. In general, then, the
fact that we represent contours as sequences does not mean that, when they
are each associated with segmental material, contours and sequences should
be indistinguishable. Since Elimelech's argument assumes this (obviously much
too strong) version of the hypothesis that contours are decomposable, it does
not contradict the version of this hypothesis which is actually in question.

Indeed, we can note in passing that Elimelech's example provides an excellent
argument **for** tonal decomposition. Note that there are two rules that are rel-

----

[4] Elimelech has suggested to me that the data presented on Kru in his paper may not be completely reliable in this respect. The extent to which a true upstep is found in this language is unclear,
and further work with other speakers, as well as instrumental analysis, is required before we can be
sure. The facts cited here should perhaps be taken as hypothetical.

evant: One sets the beginning point of a rise equal to the end of a previous tone, and the other sets the register for high tones equal to the end point of a preceding rise. But it is clear that, in order to state these rules, we must have access independently to the beginning point and to the end point of the rising tone. If we characterize the rising tone in terms of a single homogeneous register, however, as in Wang's or Gruber's systems, this information is not available to us and the rules become unstatable without the introduction of further apparatus which would in effect negate the claim that the contour is a unit. We conclude, therefore, that the facts of Kru support, rather than refute, the hypothesis that contour tones should be decomposed into their component levels.

3.5.3 The Argument from Tone Sandhi in Asian Tone Systems

It is reasonably clear that the phonetic properties of contour tones will not ultimately decide the issue of how they should be represented, and it is only their phonological properties that can be of use here. An important argument would be provided in favor of a set of contour tone features if we could prove that phonological rules operate in terms of natural classes defined by such features. If we found, for example, that rules treating all falling tones as a class (regardless of their beginning and ending points) were at all common in the languages of the world, this would be evidence in favor of the proposition that a feature "fall" should be provided by phonological theory.

In fact, very little evidence for the role of contour tone features in the formulation of phonological rules has been forthcoming. In his original paper, Wang (1967) cites two facts that might be taken to bear on this question. First, he discusses the interrelations of level, rising, and falling tones in the same register in three Chinese dialects. He observes that the level and the rising tone alternate in Peking, the rising and the falling tones in Chaozhou, and the level and the falling tones in Canton. He takes the first of these facts as evidence for his feature [−Falling], the second as evidence for [+Contour], and the third as evidence for [−Rising]. He concludes, then, that the facts of these tonal alternations provide proof that the contour features of his system define natural classes. This seems somewhat surprising, however, since an examination of Wang's argument shows that in fact **any** pair of these tones can alternate, and thus that there are no clear natural classes. This is hardly a significant argument for the phonological reality of Wang's features, therefore.

A second argument rests on Wang's formulation of a rule which describes the basic tone sandhi process in Amoy Chinese. This rule, defining a tone "circle," is obviously remarkably ingenious, but it is not so obvious that it expresses a linguistically significant generalization. As Schuh observes in his discussion of this rule, Chapter VII, this volume, tone sandhi processes such as the one found in Amoy and in other Chinese and Asian systems have a rather different character from ordinary phonological rules. They seem generally to consist in virtually arbitrary substitutions, in environments that have little to do with phonological (particularly tonological) properties. While it is true that (most of) the substitutions in Amoy can be reduced to a single "tone circle" rule in terms of Wang's features, the use of variable feature coefficients in this rule is of a type not normally found in rules of other sorts, and a consideration of Amoy in the larger context of Chinese sandhi systems suggests the rule proposed by Wang is essentially fortuitous. That is, the facts of Amoy are primarily noteworthy for the unusual coherence of the set of alternations they involve. In the general case, no such unitary formulation is available, and indeed the history of these languages makes it unlikely that one will be significant if found. The tone systems involved arose from originally segmental distinctions, as detailed in various chapters in this volume (cf. especially Hombert's chapter, this volume) and after their development, the subsequent histories of individual tones appear to be quite independent of one another. In synchronic terms, then, these alternations are largely arbitrary substitutions, and there is no reason to expect them to be phonologically coherent, given the fact that their environment (usually "nonprepausally" versus "prepausally") is not defined in terms of tonological natural classes. We can suggest that the properties of this sort of rule are as irrelevant to the question of how to represent contour tones as is the general lack of segmental phonology in these languages for the question of whether vowels and consonants should be assigned similar features (or, indeed, separated segmentally from each other). In formal terms, these rules are generally suppletions and hence irrelevant to our question.

We have no doubt, in fact, that it is possible to find just as much evidence in languages of this sort for the decomposition of tones as for contour features. Consider the rule of "rising tone change" in Taishan Chinese, discussed by Cheng (1973). This rule applies in a variety of syntactically defined environments, generally serving to derive concrete nouns from other word classes. The changes performed by this rule are as follows:

6.

Basic tone	Changed tone
[*55*]	(no change)
[*33*]	[*335*]
[*22*]	[*225*]
[*32*]	[*325*]
[*21*]	[*215*]
[*31*]	[*315*]

It is clear that this rule can be stated unitarily as the addition of a Tone 5 element at the end of a contour if tones are decomposed into levels, but it is not clear how to state it in terms of Wang's features. Apparently, we have to make all tones "high" and "rising"; except that the basic tone [*55*], which is already high, must remain unchanged. Obviously it is possible to formulate the rule in Wang's terms, by adroit use of angled brackets and alphas, but it is also clear that its coherence will be obscured if this is done.

Generally we find that insofar as the rules in languages of this type are phonologically (or rather tonologically) conditioned, so that it makes sense to ask whether they are assimilatory or not, any assimilations that can be discerned are in terms of levels. Hyman (1973) points out that the well-known sandhi Rules (7a)—from Mandarin—and (7b)—from Cantonese—have this property:

7.   a. $/35/ \rightarrow [55] / /55/, /35/$ ____ T (where T = any tone except neutral)
     b. $/53/ \rightarrow [55] /$ ____ $/55/, /53/, /5/$

Again, contour tone features will only obscure the assimilatory character of these rules, while decomposition into levels makes it clear. The difference between tonally arbitrary substitutions, which may fortuitously be formulated in terms of contour features but need not be, and phonologically motivated processes, which are generally best stated in terms of tone levels, is clearly correlated with the degree of phonetic motivation provided by the environment and gives no comfort to those who would represent contour tones as units.

Indeed, the absence of rules in which a tone assimilates to the **shape** (as opposed to the beginning or endpoint) of an adjacent tone is striking. If features such as "fall" and "rise" were real, we could expect such processes to occur with approximately the same frequency as level assimilations like (7). Indeed, only one example remotely of this variety has been discussed in the literature, to our knowledge. Gandour (1975) discusses the facts concerning Tone 5 ([*13*] or [*11*], depending on its environment as will be discussed below) in the Tai language Lue. This tone has the shape [*11*] before rising ([*25*]) or falling ([*31*]) tones, and the shape [*13*] before tones [*22*], [*33*], and [*55*]. We are not told what its shape is before another instance of the same tone (which might, indeed, furnish important evidence as to whether its underlying shape is $/11/$ or $/13/$). Gandour's observation is that the tone becomes a rising contour before a level tone, and a level before a contour tone. He shows clearly that there is no particularly satisfying way to formulate this rule in terms of levels, but if it is stated in terms of features such as Wang's, it is straightforward.

It is clear that Gandour's case is just the sort of evidence which would have to be presented if one wished to maintain the necessity of contour tone features. On the other hand, its very isolation in the tone systems of the world, together perhaps with the fact that it is not obviously assimilatory or otherwise phonetically motivated, makes it difficult to support such features on the basis of this one example alone. A rule by which, for example, $/11/$ and $/33/$ were neutralized as *13* after $/13/$ or $/35/$ and as *31* after $/31/$ or $/53/$ would display a much more obvious assimilation to contour properties and would therefore furnish stronger evidence for their reality. If more cases of the same sort should be forthcoming, we would have to consider them seriously, but at present we can only conclude that the support offered for the hypothesis of the unity of contour tones in any language, and hence of the necessity for contour tone features, is extremely tenuous at best.

3.6 An Argument against the Unity of Contours

In a recent survey of the properties of tone systems in the languages of the world, Maddieson (1977) has cited some facts which appear to suggest that a unitary generalization will be lost if contour tones are treated as primitives rather than as sequences of level tone elements. Maddieson observes that the following appear to be true generalizations about tone systems involving level tones in the languages of the world:

8.   a. Languages which permit a sequence of unlike tones on a
         word or morpheme also permit like tones on a word or
         morpheme.
      b. A language which permits successive shifts of tone level in
         opposite directions within a word also permits words with
         only one shift of tone level.

These generalizations can be compared with those about tonal contours:

9.   a. If a language has contour tones, it also has level tones.
      b. A language with complex contours also has simple contours.

The Statements (8a) and (9a), (8b) and (9b) obviously have much in common; if contour tones are always represented as sequences of levels, it is easy to see that (9) is simply a special case case of (8). If contours are treated as elementary, however, these facts are formally unrelated. In the absence of any explanation of why any of these things should be the case, of course, it is hard to use this argument for very much; but most linguists would agree that (8) and (9) appear to be related and hence that they furnish at least some suggestion that contours and sequences of levels are closely related.

3.7 Conclusions Concerning Contour Tones

We have seen evidence above that contour tones must be decomposed into sequences of levels in some languages, particularly in systems of the American or African type. On the other hand, we have seen that there is really no evidence that points clearly to the necessity of representing contour tones as units in any language, with the possible exception of Gandour's argument from Lue, cited above: There is at least a weak reason to believe that such a move would obscure the unity of a broadly applicable generalization about tone systems. We conclude from the discussion above, then, that contour tone features should not be provided by phonological theory, that tonal glides are always to be represented as sequences of tone levels (even where there is no positive evidence to establish this conclusion, in the absence of evidence against it), and that the inventory of features available for the description of tone should be limited to a set sufficient to describe five distinct levels (as argued earlier in Section 2).

4. FEATURE SYSTEMS FOR TONAL ANALYSIS

In the discussion to this point, we have dealt with the range of tonal elements which must be distinguished by a system of phonological features. One remaining issue remains to be dealt with before we can proceed to survey the systems that have actually been proposed to differentiate these elements. While we are now in a position to say which tonal items must be describable by such a system, we have not discussed the connections between tonal and nontonal phenomena. It is well known that consonant type distinctions are related to tone both synchronically and diachronically (cf. Hombert, this volume), and we must address the question of whether the features used to describe tone are actually to be identified with those used to describe some other phonological property as well.

4.1 The Halle–Stevens Feature System

A proposal by Halle and Stevens (1971) is the only one which has appeared in the literature to our knowledge that explicitly identifies the tone features with those used for some other domain. Halle and Stevens start from the classic observations of Haudricourt (1961) and others that voiced consonants are related to low tone, and voiceless consonants to high tone, and construct a unified account of voicing, aspiration, glottalization, and other laryngeal phenomena, as well as tone, in terms of a simple system of four features.

Halle and Stevens base their work on the two-mass model of the aerodynamic and myoelastic properties of laryngeal activity developed by Ishizaka and Matsudaira (1968), Ishizaka and Flanagan (1972), and most recently Flanagan, Ishizaka, and Shipley (1975). This model treats each vocal cord as a pair of masses, representing the upper and lower edges of the vocal fold, which are coupled by a spring force whose tension is variably controllable and which are themselves coupled to the walls of the larynx by springs of specifiable elasticity. The parameters of this model which can be controlled are (*a*) the rest-position aperture between the two vocal folds and (*b*) the amount of coupling or stiffness between the two masses of each vocal fold. Under realistic assumptions about dimensions and airflow, this model achieves a pattern of oscillation which provides an excellent approximation of real vocal cord vibration, and thus it allows the study of the influence of control of glottal aperture and vocal cord stiffness on vibration pattern.

On the basis of this model, it can be suggested that vocal cord vibration is not controlled by one single factor but is rather the result of a complex interplay of transglottal pressure, glottal opening, and vocal cord stiffness. In a three-dimensional space based on these factors, that is, there is a substantial region within which vibration (perhaps of different sorts) is possible. Consequently, it must be emphasized, a value along one dimension which under other conditions would inhibit vibration can be compensated by an adjustment of another parameter which facilitates it. Roughly, however, vibration is facilitated by slackening the vocal cords (reducing the amount of coupling between the two masses in each) and inhibited by stiffening them; similarly, vibration is inhibited by spreading the cords (widening the glottis) or by narrowing the glottis beyond a certain very small value to constrict this opening. On the other hand, the frequency of vocal cord vibration is related in a fairly straightforward fashion to the parameter of tenseness alone; stiffening the vocal cords increases the rate of vibration, up to the point at which vibration stops altogether.

Halle and Stevens propose, therefore, to treat the features of laryngeal activity as parallel to the control parameters of this model. They suggest that the larynx, like other portions of the vocal tract (cf. Chomsky and Halle 1968), has a neutral position for speech, in which the cords are loosely approximated and of moderate stiffness. They can deviate from this position in four ways, corresponding to two dimensions: (a) They can be spread apart, widening the glottis ([+Spread]); (b) they can be approximated more closely, narrowing the glottis ([+Constricted]); (c) they can be tensed, increasing intrafold coupling ([+Stiff]); or (d) they can be relaxed, decreasing intrafold coupling ([+Slack]). Obviously, the values [+Stiff, +Slack] and [+Spread, +Constricted] are impossible (because contradictory); and the resulting system thus defines nine categories of laryngeal type. They then provide interpretations for (most of) these in terms of traditional phonetic categories for obstruents, glides, and vowels:

10.

	1	2	3	4	5	6	7	8	9
Obstruents	b_1	b	p	p_k	b^h	p^h	ɓ	ʔb	p
Glides	w, y				ɦ	h, W, Y			ʔ, ʰw, ʰy
Vowels	V	V̌	V́	Voiceless vowels	Breathy vowels			Creaky voice vowels	Glottalized vowels
Spread glottis	−	−	−	+	+	+	−	−	−
Constricted glottis	−	−	−	−	−	−	+	+	+
Stiff vocal cords	−	−	+	−	−	+	−	−	+
Slack vocal cords	−	+	−	−	+	−	−	+	−

This system provides a straightforward account of most of the interactions that have been observed between consonant type and tone: In general, consonant types that produce high tone, or that facilitate spread of high tones, and so on, have the same features as high tone vowels, while consonants that are similarly related to low tone have the same features as low tone vowels. For a survey of such phenomena, cf. Hombert's chapter, this volume.

4.1.1 Mechanical Problems with the Halle–Stevens System

The most immediate difficulty with this system is that, while it captures the gross relationship between voicing type and tone, it does not provide a good fit in detail between the categories that are relevant for vowels and those relevant for consonants. Most importantly, we have seen that it is necessary to specify at least (and probably at most) five levels of tone, but the parameter Stiff–Slack allows for only three categories along this dimension. Even if the (admittedly small number of) cases of five-height systems could all be analyzed away, there is no question that at least four levels of tone must be recognized, and the conceptual basis of the Halle–Stevens system makes it very difficult to see how to accommodate any more than three, by virtue of its very coherence and internal organization. If we account for the extra two pitch heights by superimposing another feature on the system, we are implicitly saying that another anatomical mechanism than those involved in the dimensions of the Ishizaka, and Flanagan, *et al.* model is responsible (only) for the peripheral pitch values, which seems counterintuitive; while if we say that this additional feature is also relevant for consonants, we are faced with the problem of finding some work for it to do. It seems simply to be the case that there are more phonological categories of tonal elements than there are of consonant types along any homogeneous dimension.

Another more or less mechanical difficulty with the system sketched above in (10) arises when we consider systems in which distinctive voice quality appears superimposed on a tone system. According to this system, breathiness ought to be associated particularly with low pitch: When the same feature is associated with the features for "high pitch" or "mid pitch," we get voiceless or whispered vowels. In some languages, however, this correspondence does not obtain. In Ch'ing Chiang Miao, for example (cf. Kwan 1971), it is precisely the **mid** level tone ([*33*]) of the system of eight, including five levels, which is associated with breathy voice or "murmur." In ≠Hõã the raspy voice quality can appear with any one of the five tones (four levels and a rising glide), as described by Gruber (1973). This phonation type appears to be a form of breathy voice; but in any event, it is a homogeneous property across all tonal registers, and therefore it is difficult to see how it could be dealt with in a theory like that of Halle and Stevens in which phonation types are associated with particular tonal registers. A related case is found in the Tibeto-Burman language Mpi

(Harris and Ladefoged, forthcoming). This language has six tones, including three levels; it also has a coordinate distinction of voice quality, opposing laryngealized or creaky vowels to plain. Laryngealization can cooccur with any of the six tones, so that the syllable whose segmental content is [si] can have 12 distinct meanings. Again, it is hard to integrate this sort of tonally pervasive voice-equality distinction into a system which associates specific voice qualities with specific tonal registers.

4.1.2 Problems for the Halle–Stevens System Posed by Downdrift

When we consider the interaction of consonants with many sorts of tone rules, the Halle–Stevens system makes useful predictions. This is particularly true with respect to "tonogenesis," and also "tone spreading." Consonant types do not, on the other hand, behave at all as predicted with respect to down-drift rules. Recall that the basic property of downdrift systems is that high tone elements are lowered following a low tone. If Halle and Stevens are right, this ought to be formalized by a rule which lowers pitch after a segment that is [+Slack]. Now there are many languages in Africa that contain rules of tone spreading, etc., whose relation to consonant types shows us that the voiced consonants in these languages must indeed be [+ Slack],[5] but to our knowledge there is not a single language in which downdrift has ever been shown to be be associated with the presence of a voiced consonant. The specification [+Slack], when appearing on a consonant does not cause downdrift, which makes us question the identification of (downdrift provoking) low tone with voicing in consonants.

A similar problem concerning downdrift relates more directly to consonant types. In a downdrift system, high pitches tend to be lower at the end of the utterance than at the beginning. If pitch is a function of vocal cord stiffness, this should mean that the cords get slacker as the utterance progresses. But then, in a language with downdrift in which voicing is also related to vocal cord stiffness, we should also notice a tendency for voiceless consonants to become voiced as the utterance progresses, and no such system of consonantal downdrift has ever been presented in the literature.

Yet another problem which arises in downdrift systems has to do with the influence of consonant type on tone spreading and similar rules. Recall that in a downdrift language, a pitch value which counts as "low" early in the

---

[5] We must emphasize here that in the Halle–Stevens feature system, the opposition of voicing could in principle be based in any given language on **either** the dimension Stiff/Slack or Spread/Constricted. Failure to allow for both possibilities weakens somewhat the criticisms leveled by Fromkin (1972) at the Halle–Stevens system. Whenever we observe in a given language, however, that the voiced obstruents favor the spreading, etc., of low tone, we can be sure that the voicing dimension in this language is controlled by the parameter Stiff/Slack, at least if the system is to have any predictive value as intended.

utterance may well be the same as or even higher than one which counts as "high" toward the end of a long sentence. But then, if consonantal manner types are associated with particular pitch values, a problem arises; a value which may have facilitated the spread of **low** tone early in the utterance, when average pitch values were high, might be expected to inhibit low tone spreading (or, at least, to facilitate **high** tone spreading) toward the end of the utterance, where pitch values have sunk considerably. Again, no such case has come to our attention.

Of course, the status of this argument is somewhat tenuous; just as we observed above in connection with Elimelech's argument about contour tones from Kru, we should only expect to find identity of phonological behavior between elements that are categorically indistinguishable. Since we can of course distinguish consonants from vowels, we could simply say that all of the downdrift rules ignore consonantal laryngeal specifications entirely. Doing this, however, substantially weakens the force of the claim that vowel pitch, consonantal voicing, etc. are to be described by the same set of features. What is striking is not only that consonants and vowels generally behave differently, but rather that **no** cases of the predicted isofunction appear to exist.

4.1.3 Other Instances of the Lack of Parallel between Consonant Type and Tone

The Halle–Stevens model predicts that consonantal specifications for laryngeal type and vowel tone specifications ought to be identifiable. While there are certainly instances of consonant type affecting tone (for examples, see Hombert and Schuh, Chapters III and VII, respectively, this volume), there are some important failures of parallelism between the two types which suggest that the strong form of the interaction hypothesis on which Halle and Stevens' system is based is probably an overstatement. For one thing, the assignment of tone to a sequence of segments always seems to consider only the vowel elements as relevant. That is, we do not find systems parallel to those of Tiv and Etung discussed above in which, for example, a high–low–high contour could be assigned to a monosyllable by devoicing the initial, assigning low tone to the vowel, and devoicing the final, as opposed to a low–high–low contour, in which the initial and final would appear voiced, and the vowel have (level) high pitch. When a pitch pattern, whether complex or simple, is assigned to segmental material, we essentially never find that any of it gets assigned to obstruents; furthermore, the consonantal specifications that are present are completely unperturbed by the assignment of pitch. This is in contrast with, e.g., vowel harmony systems based on the feature [± Back] which is applicable to vowels and consonants alike; very often, this sort of vowel harmony is accompanied by some sort of consonant harmony as well (especially involving velars), as in Mongolian or Turkish. Again, the absence of this strong interaction between vowel and consonant specifications does not by itself falsify the Halle–Stevens theory, since the relevant rules can always be formulated, but it does considerably lessen its attractiveness, since a strong prediction of that theory is apparently never confirmed.

4.1.4 Consonant Types and Tone

When we consider the physiology of the larynx, it is clear that there is a wide (often bewildering) variety of possible gestures that could influence the parameters relevant to defining glottis width, shape, vocal cord tension, and so on. (See Ohala, Chapter I, this volume, for a survey.) A great many gestures, furthermore, that could be seen as having one consequence as "primary" also have other consequences. Thus, the geometry of arytenoid cartilage displacement results in the fact that contraction of the posterior cricoarytenoid muscles primarily spreads the cords and widens the glottis; but another, secondary consequence of the same gesture is an increase in longitudinal tension on the vocal ligament. Similarly, lowering of the larynx by the extrinsic musculature expands the vocal tract, perhaps facilitating voicing (as discussed by Ohala), while raising the larynx may be similarly associated with voicelessness; but the lowering gesture also results in a decrease in vocal cord tension, while the raising gesture results in an increase. The primary gestures controlling vocal cord tension (doubtless the primary basis of pitch control) are presumably activity of the cricothyroid muscle (perhaps in combination with the vocalis), but these other gestures also have consequences for this parameter. If we in fact had reason to believe that there were only two dimensions of articulatory control of the laryngeal configuration (corresponding to the parameters Stiff–Slack and Spread–Constricted), the Halle–Stevens unified theory of laryngeal features might well be very plausible, but this is not really the case. There is rather every reason to believe that gestures whose primary function is not the control of pitch might nevertheless have secondary, mechanical consequences for phonetic pitch. The physiology of the larynx, then, suggests that if there were independent features controlling the consonant type and voice-quality distinctions, we might well expect these gestures to have low-level phonetic effects on pitch even though pitch is primarily controlled by a distinct parameter, and in that case the correct way to account for the interactions between pitch and consonant type which Halle and Stevens set out to explain might not be by identifying the features for these two domains.

Support for this view of laryngeal activity comes from the results of Hyman and Schuh's (1974) study of tone rules. As reported there, and discussed also in Schuh, Chapter VII, this volume, it is overwhelmingly the case that consonants influence tone but tone does not influence consonants. Maddieson's (1976) small and somewhat controversial set of apparent counterexamples notwithstanding, this seems to be a substantially true generalization. If the features for consonant type and for tone are identified with one another as the explanation for the effects of consonants on tone, this remains an isolated and unexplained fact; but on the view that tone features are distinct from consonant type features, it is a natural consequence of the properties of each. It is entirely plausible to suggest, that is, that the gestures generally used to control voicing, aspiration, breathiness, laryngealization, etc., in consonants can have (unintended) consequences for the phonetic pitch contour, while the gestures used for primary pitch control have virtually no effect on the presence of voicing, etc. The most recent work in modeling the larynx (Flanagan, Ishizaka, and Shipley, 1975), in which the aerodynamic properties of the supralaryngeal vocal tract were added to those of the two-mass model larynx itself, showed a remarkably good fit between observed pitch perturbations after consonants of various types and the theoretical consequences of the control gestures used in producing those consonants. What remains to be shown is that, in a suitably sophisticated model of total laryngeal function, control of pitch is not possible independent of these consonant-type gestures.

We conclude, then, that the Halle–Stevens model of laryngeal features assumes too close a parallel between distinct aspects of laryngeal control. While it is certainly true that consonant types and tone interact, it is possible to capture this interaction in the theory of general phonetics without requiring that the features for these two domains in phonology be identified. Furthermore, as noted above in Sections 4.1.1–4.1.3, this identification makes predictions which are not, in general, borne out, and which ultimately make as much trouble for phonological description as are solved by this analysis. The primary features for the control of pitch, then, are to be separated from those involved in the control of consonant types and voice quality.

4.2 Systems of Tone Features

We survey here the proposals that have been made in the literature for the pitch-control features which are the basis of tonal distinctions. With the exception of the Halle–Stevens proposal, already noted above, none of these attempts to extend the domain of the tone features beyond pitch into other segmental domains. As we have already observed (in Section 4.1.1), the Halle–Stevens proposal, considered simply as a set of features for tone, is not adequate since it allows for the specification of only three distinct levels rather than the five we have seen to be necessary.

4.2.1 Gruber's Features

As we have already observed, Gruber's (1964) system allows for the specification of only four tone levels. It is probably not adequate in general for that reason; but we describe it here since its organizing principle is somewhat different from other proposals. Gruber primarily distinguishes between pitches above and below some notional mean value, by means of the feature [High]. Within each of these ranges, he distinguishes a relatively high and a relatively low pitch by means of a feature [High2] ("secondary high"):

11.

	⌟	⌐	⌐	⌐
[High]	−	−	+	+
[High2]	−	+	−	+

We have already dealt with Gruber's specification of contour tones.

4.2.2 Wang's Features

Wang's (1967) system allows for five tone levels in terms of three features, and does this in such a way that one of the features comes into play only when all five levels are contrastive. Like Gruber, he distinguishes primarily between tones above and tones (at or) below a notional mean pitch, by means of a feature [High]. He further distinguishes the three levels closest to this mean from the others by means of a feature [Central]; and within this region, a tone at the mean is distinguishable from the other two by means of [Mid].

12.

	⌐	⌐	⊣	⊣	⌟
[High]	+	+	−	−	−
[Central]	−	+	+	+	−
[Mid]	−	−	+	−	−

Wang also details the way these features are to be employed in languages with various numbers of tone levels. His proposals for contours have already been treated above.

4.2.3 Sampson's Features

In a critical discussion of Wang's (1967) paper, Sampson (1969) makes a slightly different proposal about the set of features for tone. He distinguishes tones above the median (by means of [High]), tones below the median (by means of [Low]), and tones at or around the median (by means of [Central]):

13.

	⌐	⌐	⊣	⊣	⌟
[High]	+	+	−	−	−
[Low]	−	−	−	+	+
[Central]	−	+	+	+	−

Sampson prefers this system over Wang's because, while Wang was concerned to reflect the relative rarity of five-level systems in terms of a hierarchy of feature "use," Sampson feels the features provided by the theory ought to be more nearly equally "used." The substance of this issue is somewhat obscure.

4.2.4 Woo's Features

Woo (1969) proposes yet another classification of the five level tones by three features. Her features [High] and [Low] are the same as Sampson's, but instead of his feature [Central], she employs a feature [Modify], which describes the lower tone in the high range and the higher tone in the low range:

14.

	⌐	¬	⊣	⊣	⌐
[High]	+	+	−	−	−
[Low]	−	−	−	+	+
[Modify]	−	+	−	+	−

Since Woo is primarily concerned to reflect the relatively "unmarked" status of a neutral, mid tone she (along with other writers who have been concerned with this issue) interprets positive specifications for any of the tone features as "marked." She provides an assessment of the relative complexity of the various tones in her system. As noted above, Woo does not provide separately for contour tones, since it is her contention that these are always to be analyzed into a sequence of levels (as argued above).

4.2.5 Maddieson's Features

Maddieson (1970, 1972) has proposed another set of features, which are in fact exactly equivalent to those of Sampson (cf. [13] above) except that the feature [Central] is renamed [Extreme] and given opposite values. Trivial as this may appear at first glance, there is a real linguistic issue involved here, which Maddieson was the first to address directly.

Pike (1948) had claimed, and subsequent authors have generally agreed, that all tone languages use essentially the same pitch range, subdividing it into as many registers as required by their tone systems. As a result, the tones in a three tone system will each occupy a larger range than those in a five tone system but a smaller range than those in a two level system. Maddieson contests this; he claims that, in fact, languages with larger tonal inventories generally use larger pitch ranges. In these terms, the three tones of a three-level language will usually be identified with the middle three levels (2,3,4) of a five-level language, rather than with the extreme points and the center (1,3,5). On this basis, Maddieson proposes that the two levels which are furthest from the center of the tonal range are indeed "extreme" tones and are normally an expansion of the usual three tone central range. Besides (a small amount of) data on the actual range of tones covered by languages with varying numbers of distinct tones, Maddieson also cites the fact that the [+ Extreme] tones, in his system, frequently are preceded by central onglides, so that Tone 5 is often phonetically [45], while Tone 1 is phonetically [21].

A consideration of the African tone systems on which Maddieson's work is primarily based suggests that for these systems his interpretation is probably substantially correct, and that Tone Levels 1 and 5 are in some sense "extreme low" and "extreme high." This conclusion is much less obvious for Asian tone systems, however, where the Levels 1 and 5 seem better integrated into the total system as less "marked" relative to the central levels (especially 2 and 4) than in African systems. The generality of Maddieson's conclusion is thus somewhat questionable, though this is certainly an interesting and provocative question for further research.

A further aspect of the issue addressed by Maddieson in the papers cited is the question of the comparability of tones across languages. Do all languages with two levels have, in phonological terms, the same contrast? Does it make sense, on the other hand, to say that (two-level) Language A contrasts Tone 2 with Tone 4, while (two-level) Language B rather contrasts Tone 3 with Tone 5? Maddieson presents some data concerning relative lexical frequency, directionality of assimilation, borrowing, and other factors to suggest that in some languages high tone is more "marked" (e.g., Navajo or Zulu), while in others low tone is more "marked" (e.g., Hausa and Korku). Similarly, three-level systems can be found in which any one of the three levels is the least "marked" in these terms. If we assume that the markedness" of a tone (or indeed, of any phonological feature configuration) is a function only of the features involved, and is not subject to language-internal determinations, then we must conclude that these languages have made, different selections from the inventory of potentially contrastive tonal elements provided by the feature system. Again, this is a question about which much more needs to be learned, but it is potentially a source of considerable help in deciding on an ultimately satisfactory system of features.

4.2.6 Nonbinary Feature Systems

As can be seen from the survey above, virtually any classification of the five tone levels by three features has been suggested by someone. The most troublesome aspect of this situation is the fact that there does not appear to be any very convincing evidence for the superiority of any one system over the others. Most of the discussion of the relative merits of one system over another has been based on considerations of "markedness," or the desire to reflect the comparative complexity of individual tones or tonal inventories, but this area is notoriously difficult to find firm ground in. Judgments about "markedness" tend to be based on unsupported intuition, uncritical use of cross-linguistic statistics, and the like. While there is unquestionably something to the notion that some phonological elements are more complex or less expected than others (*ceteris paribus*, which is seldom the case), no secure foundation for the determination of the markedness of individual elements has ever been presented. It is even less clear how the notion of complexity that is involved, assuming it could be given such a general basis, should be reflected in the design and internal organization of a feature system.

Given this fact, some have felt that any attempt to describe tone levels in terms of a set of features with binary values is misguided. Ladefoged (1971) suggests this conclusion, though he ultimately gives tentative endorsement to the features suggested by Wang (1967). A more recent argument to the same effect is given by Stahlke (1977). Stahlke cites three examples (from Nupe, Igede, and Mixtecan) which he feels establish the need for a single, multivalued feature for tone rather than three cross-classifying binary features. His first point, from Nupe, is that a raised–low tone appears in that language to be more "highly marked" than any of the other three, which he believes supports a system such as Woo's over one such as Wang's. He then cites an alternation from Igede which, he claims, cannot be described satisfactorily in any of the proposed systems of binary tone features. Igede has a system with four levels (identified by Stahlke from highest to lowest as *a*, *b*, *c*, and *d*), and a rule which applies to alter the final tone on a verb before an object pronoun. The generality of this rule is not apparent from Stahlke's discussion, but assuming that this is indeed a rule of Igede phonology, the alternations involved are as follows: Tone *d* is replaced by Tone *c*; (2) Tone *c* is replaced by Tone *a*; and (3) Tone *b* is replaced by Tone *a*. It is not immediately clear what problem this presents for, e.g., Maddieson's feature system. It is clear that the rule can be formulated as follows:

15.
$$\begin{bmatrix} -\text{extreme} \\ \langle -\text{low}\rangle \end{bmatrix} \rightarrow \begin{bmatrix} -\text{low} \\ \left\langle \begin{matrix} +\text{high} \\ +\text{extreme} \end{matrix} \right\rangle \end{bmatrix} \quad \text{(in the appropriate syntactic environment)}$$

This rule assumes the four tones of Igede are phonetically [*55*], [*44*], [*33*], and [*22*], respectively, for *a*, *b*, *c*, and *d*, though nothing in particular hangs on this assumption. We can note, however, that the environment is not a "tonologically natural" one, in the same sense as the environments for tone sandhi in Asian languages discussed above were not, and it is thus not clear that it provides useful evidence about the feature system for tone.

A further fact cited by Stahlke is also of uncertain import for our concerns. He notes that the Igede tone system seems to have developed from an original two-level system, by the splitting of each level into two distinct registers. This, he feels, cannot be described naturally in terms of any of the systems developed to deal with five tone levels. He makes a similar observation concerning the historical development of Mixtecan; here, loss of a glottal stop element resulted in a series of changes that can be roughly described as raisings for any tone affected. Again, systems developed for five tone levels have generally been "center directed," so it is difficult to describe a uniform raising process in a straightforward way. The cases cited, however, involve historical changes, and it is clear that in phonetic terms, we can describe the influence of a glottal stop on a preceding tone as a uniform raising. Note, by the way, that (since we have determined that the features for consonant type are distinct from those for tone) this is precisely where the explanation must be found, in phonetic influence, not phonological "assimilation" or the like. But once the phonetic tone split has taken place, and been given a phonological interpretation, there is no particular reason to expect that the change itself from the system before the split to that after the split can be formulated in terms of a simple, natural, phonological rule. Since the change was not in fact a phonological one (motivated by the system of rules and representations), but rather a phonetic one (motivated by the articulatory and acoustic consequences of various gestures) there is no basis for the expectation that it will have a transparent phonological expression. Thus, the bearing of this sort of example on questions of the framework for phonological description of tone is equivocal at best.

Stahlke concludes from his examples that no system of binary features for tone will permit us to capture all of the relevant generalizations in this domain. He then suggests that the answer is to give up on binary features and to adopt a numerical scale feature instead. This seems somewhat premature, to say the least; until we have a much better understanding of just what evidence exists in general about tone changes (and, more importantly, about just what tone changes count as evidence for features), the lack of any clear arguments in favor of a multivalued tone feature (as opposed to a sort of argument *ex silentio* based on the supposed lack of superiority of any one binary system) should dispose us simply to keep the issue open, rather than to adopt a sort of "null solution."

4.3 Conclusions

Unfortunately, this review of proposals that have been made for the features of tone does not allow us to come to a definite resolution of the question. We have seen that an adequate feature system must allow us to distinguish at least five tone levels, that we probably do not need to recognize more than that, that we do not need to make special phonological provision for downstep or for tone glides (since these can be adequately represented in terms of level tones), and that the features of tone are distinct from those for other segmental distinctions. We are left with the need to cross-categorize five levels along the same dimension, however, and this is obviously a very difficult task to perform in a satisfactory and well-motivated way. On the assumption that tone does indeed represent a unitary, homogeneous dimension, the facts of phonetics, physiology, and so on, are of no help to us. Similarly, the facts of phonological behavior are much less illuminating in this area than in some others, since it is difficult to find well motivated cases of tone rules which are clearly phonological in character (unlike the essentially arbitrary substitutions of Asian sandhi rules), other than cases of tone spreading and related phenomena, which are unfortunately of little help in establishing the naturalness of various groupings of tones into classes. Perhaps considerations such as those raised by Maddieson (see Section 4.2.5) will ultimately shed some light on this question; in the meantime, a comprehensive survey of what evidence there is in phonological rules is clearly in order. At present it can only be said that any of the systems surveyed in Sections 4.2.2–4.2.5 is equally (un)satisfactory.

REFERENCES

Andersen, H. 1972. Diphthongization. *Language, 48*, 11–50.

Anderson, S. R. 1974. *The organization of phonology*. New York: Academic Press.

Anderson, S. R. 1975. On the interaction of phonological rules of various types. *Journal of Linguistics, 11*, 39–62.

Anderson, S. R. 1976. Nasal consonants and the internal structure of segments. *Language, 52*, 326–344.

Armstrong, R. G. 1968. Yala (Ikom): A terraced-level language with three tones. *Journal of West African Languages, 5*, 49–58.

Asongwed, T., & Hyman, L. 1977. Morphotonology of the Ngamambo noun. In L. Hyman (Ed.), *Studies in Bantu tonology*. Los Angeles: Univ. of Southern California.

Beach, D. M. 1924. The science of tonetics and its application to Bantu languages. *Bantu Studies, 2*, 73–106.

Bearth, T., & Zemp, H. 1967. The phonology of Dan (Santa). *Journal of African Languages, 6*, 9–29

Chang, K. 1972. The reconstruction of Proto-Miao-Yao tones. *Bulletin of the Institute of History and Philology*, Academica Sinica, *44*, 541–628.

Chao, Y. 1920. A system of tone letters. *Le Maître Phonétique, 30*, 24–27.

Cheng, T. 1973. The phonology of Taishan. *Journal of Chinese Linguistics, 1*, 93–117.

Chomsky, N., & Halle, M. 1968. *The sound pattern of English*. New York: Harper & Row.

Clifton, J. 1976. Downdrift and rule ordering. *Studies in African Linguistics, 7*, 175–194.

Edmondson, T., & Bendor-Samuel, J. 1966. Tone patterns of Etung. *Journal of African Languages, 5*, 1–6.

Egerod, S. 1971. Phonation types in Chinese and South East Asian languages. *Acta Linguistica Hafniensa, 13*, 159–171.

Elimelech, B. 1974. On the reality of underlying contour tones. *UCLA Working Papers in Phonetics, 27*, 74–83.

Fischer-Jørgensen, E. 1970. Phonetic analysis of breathy (murmured) vowels in Gujarati. *Indian Linguistics, 28*, 71–140.

Fl .agan, J. L., Ishizaka, K., & Shipley, K. L. 1975. Synthesis of speech from a dynamic model of the vocal cords and vocal tract. *Bell System Technical Journal, 54*, 485–506.

Fromkin, V. 1972. Tone features and tone rules. *Studies in African Linguistics, 3*, 47–76.

Fromkin, V. 1977. Some questions regarding universal phonetics and phonetic representations. In A. Juilland (Ed.), *Linguistic studies offered to Joseph Greenberg on the occasion of his sixtieth birthday*. Saratoga, California: Anma Libri & Co. Pp 365–380.

Gandour, J. 1974. On the representation of tone in Siamese. *UCLA Working Papers in Phonetics*, *27*, 118–146.

Gandour, J. 1975. Evidence from Lue for contour tone features. *Pasaa*, *5*(2), 39–52.

Gårding, E. 1973. The Scandinavian word accents. *Lund University Working Papers*, *8*.

Goldsmith, J. 1976. An overview of autosegmental phonology. *Linguistic Analysis*, *2*, 23–68.

Gruber, J. 1964. The distinctive features of tone. Unpublished manuscript.

Gruber, J. 1973. ≠Hõã kinship terms. *Linguistic Inquiry*, *4*, 427–450.

Halle, M., & Stevens, K. 1971. A note on laryngeal features. *Quarterly Progress Report*, MIT Research Laboratory of Electronics, *101*, 198–213.

Han, M. S. 1969. *Vietnamese tones*. Los Angeles: Acoustic Phonetics Research Laboratory, University of Southern California.

Harris, J., & Ladefoged, P. Forthcoming. Voice quality.

Haudricourt, A. G. 1961. Bipartition et tripartition des systèmes de tons dans quelques langues d'Extrême-Orient. *Bulletin de la Société de Linguistique de Paris*, *56*, 163–180.

Hyman, L. 1973. Discussion paper on Sino-Tibetan tone. Paper presented at the 6th International Conference on Sino-Tibetan Languages and Linguistics, Univ. of California, San Diego.

Hyman, L., & Schuh R. 1974. Universals of tone rules: Evidence from West Africa. *Linguistic Inquiry*, *5*, 81–115.

Ishizaka, K., & Flanagan, J. 1972. Synthesis of voiced sounds from a two-mass model of the vocal cords. *Bell System Technical Journal*, *50*, 1233–1268.

Ishizaka, K., & Matsudaira, M. 1968. What makes the vocal cords vibrate? Paper presented to 6th International Congress on Acoustics.

Kwan, J. 1971. Ch'ing Chiang Miao phonology. *Tsing Hwa Journal of Chinese Studies*, New Series, *9*, 289–305.

Ladefoged, P. 1971. *Preliminaries to linguistic phonetics*. Chicago: Univ. of Chicago Press.

Lavelle, C. 1974. An experimental study of Yoruba tone. *Studies in African Linguistics*, Supp. *5*, Pp. 185–194.

Leben, W. 1971. On the segmental nature of tone in Thai. *Quarterly Progress Report*, Research Laboratory of Electronics, *101*, 221–224.

Leben, W. 1973. Suprasegmental phonology. Unpublished Ph.D. dissertation, MIT.

Liberman, M. 1975. The intonational system of English. Unpublished Ph.D. dissertation, MIT.

Lieberman, Phillip. 1977. *Speech physiology and acoustic phonetics: An introduction*. New York: Macmillan.

Lieberman, P., *et al.* 1970. The articulatory implementation of the breath group and prominence. *Language*, *46*, 312–327.

Longacre, R. 1952. Five phonemic pitch levels in Triqué. *Acta Linguistica*, *7*, 62–82.

Longacre, R. 1959. Triqué tone morphemics. *Anthropological Linguistics 14*, 5–42.

Maddieson, I. 1970. The inventory of features. *University of Ibadan Research Notes 3*(2, 3), 3–18.

Maddieson, I. 1972. Tone system typology and distinctive features. *Proceedings of the 7th International Congress of Phonetic Sciences*. The Hague: Mouton. Pp. 958–961.

Maddieson, I. 1976. A further note on tone and consonants. *UCLA Working Papers in Phonetics*, *33*, 131–159.

Maddieson, I. Forthcoming. Universals of tone. *Stanford University Working Papers in Linguistic Universals*.

McCawley, J. 1970. A note on tone in Tiv conjugation. *Studies in African Linguistics*, *1*,

Meyers, L. 1976. Aspects of Hausa tone. *UCLA Working Papers in Phonetics*, *32*.

Miller, W. 1965. *Acoma grammar and tests*. Berkeley: Univ. of California Press.

Newman, R. 1971. Downstep in Ga'anda. *Journal of African Languages*, *10*, 15–27.

Peters, A. M. 1973. A new formalization of downdrift. *Studies in African Linguistics*, *4*, 139–153.

Pike, E. V. 1956. Tonally differentiated allomorphs in Soyaltepec Mazatec. *International Journal of American Linguistics*, *22*, 57–71.

Pike, E. V. n.d. Tone systems of Mexico. Unpublished manuscript, Summer Institute of Linguistics.

Pike, K. 1948. *Tone languages*. Ann Arbor: Univ. of Michigan Press.

Postal, P. M. 1968. *Aspects of phonological theory*. New York: Harper & Row.

Purnell, H. 1965. Phonology of a Yao dialect. *Hartford Studies in Linguistics, 15*.

Sampson, G. 1969. A note on Wang's phonological features of tone. *International Journal of American Linguistics, 35*, 62–66.

Schachter, P. 1961. Phonemic similarity in tonemic analysis. *Language, 37*, 231–238.

Schachter, P. & Fromkin, V. 1968. A phonology of Akan. *UCLA Working Papers in Phonetics, 9*.

Stahlke, H. 1977. Some problems with binary features for tone. *International Journal of American Linguistics, 43*, 1–10.

Tadadjeu, M. 1974. Floating tones, shifting rules, and downstep in Dschang-Bamileke. *Studies in African Linguistics*, Supp. 5, Pp. 283–290.

Wang, W. 1967. Phonological features of tone. *International Journal of American Linguistics, 33*, 93–105.

Welmers, W. 1952. Notes on the structure of Bariba. *Language, 28*, 82–103.

Welmers, W. 1973. *African language Structures*. Berkeley: Univ. of California Press.

Williamson, K. 1970. The generative treatment of downstep. *University of Ibadan Research Notes, 3*,(2,3), 22–39.

Woo, N. 1969. Prosody and phonology. Unpublished Ph.D. dissertation, MIT.

VI

The Representation of Tone

WILLIAM R. LEBEN

1. INTRODUCTION

One of the most challenging tasks in the phonological description of tone involves sizing it up against other phonological units. The problems encountered are immense. The literature, including broad surveys of tone systems and detailed treatments of particular tone languages, manifests virtually every imaginable position that could be taken on the phonological representation of tone. For various languages, linguists have regarded the domain of tone as the phonological word (Edmondson and Bendor-Samuel 1966, Rowlands 1959), the morpheme (Welmers 1962), the syllable (Pike 1948, McCawley 1964, 1970, Wang 1967), the mora (Trubetzkoy 1939, Jakobson 1937), and the segment (Schachter and Fromkin 1968, Woo 1969, Maddieson 1971). The difficulty of separating the points of view that are warranted by fact from those that seem to be reflections of taste arises as much from the quality of the argumentation offered as from the complexity of the tonal phenomena described.

In Leben (1973a, b) I proposed a framework designed to encompass the different types of tonal behavior that had been observed, with the intent of making valid predictions about possible relationships between tones and segments. I proposed that the defining characteristic of suprasegmentals involved their being divorced from segmental representations at some underlying phonological level, and I found evidence for regarding tone in some languages as a suprasegmental in this sense. But I also assumed that in phonetic representations tone was expressed as a segmental feature. For languages with an underlying suprasegmental level of representation, a phonological rule would map the units of suprasegmental tone patterns into segmental tone features. For example, in Mende the tone pattern HL for a word like *kenya* 'uncle' was to be mapped onto the vowels of this word, resulting in the tonal specification [+High] on the vowel *e* and [−High] on the vowel *a*. Prior to this mapping,

177

Copyright © 1978 by Academic Press, Inc.

the independence of tones from segments would explain facts of their distribution and of their behavior in tone rules that defied expression in purely segmental terms. After the mapping, rules referring to tone would be of a type similar to other rules of segmental phonology.

Subsequent work has shown that the suprasegmental framework can be greatly improved if we abandon the assumption that tone is mapped into a segmental feature. Goldsmith (1975, 1976a, b) has shown some advantages that stem from assuming instead that the mapping of suprasegmental tone patterns results in "autosegmental" associations between tones and segments. The mapping can be depicted in the following way:

1.   #kenya#   #kenya#

       # H L # → # H L #

We can express the mapping principles roughly as:

2.   a. Associate the external boundaries of the tonal
                representation with those of the segmental representation.
          b. Assign the first tone to the first vowel,
                the second to the second, and so on.

In both the input and output of (1), tone constitutes a separate level of representation from the segmental level. All that differentiates the two is that the output specifies which segments or syllables each tone is coarticulated with, while in the input the tones simply form a pattern that is a property of the word as a whole.

In this paper, I will draw evidence from three languages whose facts are sufficiently well known to point up the advantages of adopting the proposals just summarized. I will at points reiterate the more familiar arguments that support the phonological independence of tones from segments, such as the facts that when a syllable is lost, its tone can linger on, and that just as tone languages can have toneless morphemes, with just a segmental composition, so they can have segmentless morphemes, with a purely tonal composition. In addition I will provide new support for the suprasegmental hypothesis. For example, I will argue that Etsako has rules which affect tone with no regard for the number or type of syllables in their domain; for example, rules that apply to L apply to LL as well. I will attempt to reinforce this result by considering the past negative form of the Mende verb, in which a level L is assigned to verbs before the ending -nì if the phonological tone pattern of the verb is L, H, or LH, but not if it is HL or LHL. The reason for this is that a suprasegmental deletion rule eliminates a final H in this construction without affecting any other tones. Also in Mende I will show how earlier treatments of the tonal alternation illustrated by *fàndé* 'cotton' versus *fàndè-má* 'on cotton' (where -ma is inherently toneless) can be refined to project the suprasegmental LH pattern of *fàndé* onto *fàndè-má* by means of mapping rules that apply generally in the language. I will further document these proposals with evidence from Hausa and will argue as well that for morphologically assigned tones, of the theoretically possible rule types, only those consistent with the suprasegmental hypothesis are needed, and I will propose an analysis of Hausa feminines that lends further support to the suprasegmental framework developed in this paper.

From my own point of view, the most interesting aspect of this study of the "association" of suprasegmental representations with segmental ones is that it provides explicit criteria and procedures that could be used to strengthen Firth's position that phonetic transcription is not a unilinear string of phones but a set of prosodic levels which the phonology associates with "phonematic units."[1] But I will not here be concerned with the question of the value of prosodic analysis in general.[2] Instead, I will focus on ways in which the distribution and behavior of tones contradict the view that tone is a purely segmental feature. In particular, I will show that in a number of cases language-particular tone rules can be replaced by conventions which, if they are not totally universal, at least can be shown to apply consistently in the languages under examination. In drawing support for this position, I will address some objections to my earlier work in suprasegmental phonology. To the extent that these objections are valid, I will argue that they call for refinements of the suprasegmental model rather than for adoption of a segmental representation of tone.

I propose that at the phonological level, a language may have tone patterns expressed for individual words without specifying which parts of the tone pattern are associated with which parts of the word. Certain phonological operations can apply to this sort of representation. At some stage in a phonological derivation, tones become "associated" with segments or syllables.[3] From this point onward, derivations are subject to what Goldsmith has termed the "well-formedness condition":

3.   Well-Formedness Condition (WFC):
        a. Every tone is associated with some syllable.
        b. Every syllable is associated with some tone.
        c. Association lines may not cross.

The effect of (3) is to prevent surface representations like the following:

4.   a. by WFCa: b. by WFCb: c. by WFCc:

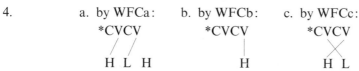

---

[1] See Firth's "Sounds and Prosodies," especially pp. 123 and 137–138, in Firth 1957.

[2] For a brief discussion of the merits, see Leben 1976b.

[3] I will not concern myself with the interesting question of whether tones are more adequately associated with segments or with syllables.

The only way that we can make the structure (4a) well formed without changing either of the association lines already drawn is to convert it into (5a). For (4b), we can make the structure well formed by converting it into (5b):

5.   a. CVCV   b. CVCV
                       / / \   \
                     H L H   H

It will be helpful to regard (3) not only as ruling out the representations in (4) but also as converting (4a, b) into (5a, b).

Certain other aspects of Goldsmith's "autosegmental" model will not be incorporated here. One is the proposal that the tone patterns HHL and HLL are phonologically distinct. I will instead regard these as improper representations of a single tonal "melody" HL. In addition, I will adopt procedures for associating tonal boundary markers with segmental boundary markers which differ somewhat from Goldsmith's. These matters will be discussed at appropriate points in the text. The reader is referred to Goldsmith 1976b for an alternative view.

2. ETSAKO

Etsako is a Kwa language spoken in the Bendel State, Nigeria. In an extensive treatment of the tonal system, Elimelech (1976) argues for representing tone on a level separate from the segmental level on the basis of two facts about the language. First, there are morphemes that have only a tonal realization. As noted in Leben 1973b, such tonal morphemes constitute prima facie evidence against the segmental representation of tone, since in these cases there is no segment that bears the tone phonologically. If one hypothesized that tone must be regarded as a segmental feature lexically, the only way that one could deal with tonal morphemes would be to make the hypothesis empty, by simply inventing some phonological segment to bear the tone. On the suprasegmental hypothesis, on the other hand, the existence of morphemes with a purely tonal realization is precisely what one would expect. Just as some segmental morphemes in a tone language can be inherently toneless,[4] so can some tonal morphemes be inherently segmentless.

A second indication advanced by Elimelech is that when vowels delete or lose their syllabicity, the tone that is normally associated with them remains. Among his examples are:

6.   a. / ówà # ówà / → ówǿ ówà → [ówŏwà]   'every house'
                 'house' 'house'

---

[4] A case in point is Mende postpositions, Section 2.6.1.

b. / ídù # ídù / → *ídʷ̃ ídù* → [ídwĩdù]   'every lion'
'lion' 'lion'

While it would be quite easy to formulate this phenomenon in segmental terms, it would be considerably more difficult to explain it. The suprasegmental hypothesis makes clear why a tone should remain when its vowel is deleted: Tone is phonologically separate from the vowel, and the contraction rule makes no reference to the tone—tone does not enter into its conditioning. For more examples and discussion of the stability of tone patterns, see Goldsmith 1975, 1976b.

Elimelech provides even more dramatic support for the suprasegmental hypothesis, with rules affecting a tone with no regard for the number of syllables in its domain. Before the Etsako associative marker (which occurs between words in possessives, adjectival constructions, and a few others), the final L of a noun becomes H. Here is an example, where A stands for the associative marker.[5]

7.   / únò Aódzí / → *únó ódzí* → [únódzí]   'a crab's mouth'
'mouth' 'crab'

Interestingly, if the first word ends in a sequence of low-toned syllables, the whole sequence is raised to H:

8.   / àmὲ A èθà / → *ámέ èθà* → [ámêθà]   'father's water'
'water' 'father'

From a suprasegmental point of view, this is totally expected. The tone change in (7) is described suprasegmentally in the following way:

9.   Tone Raising: $L \rightarrow H/$ ___ A

This changes ^{HL}uno into ^{HH}uno. By definition there is no distinction between HH and H at the suprasegmental level, since there is no connection between tones and segments. Since HH and H described the same tonal melody, they are one and the same thing. Accordingly, we may guarantee the reduction of HH to H by the following convention, which applies whenever its description is met:[6]

10.   Convention on tone melodies: $[\alpha H][\alpha H] \rightarrow [\alpha H]\ \emptyset$

---

[5] In Elimelech's account, final H is realized as HL by a general rule. This is independent of the associative construction, and I will leave this step out of the account.

[6] The value of this convention is described in Leben 1973b, 1976a. Essentially, it limits the inventory of tonal patterns that can be expressed in a given language. For example, it makes the patterns HHL and HLL equivalent to HL. But more important than this theoretical advantage is the fact that it predicts that the sequence LL in Etsako will behave just like the unitary tone L with respect to Rule (9).

By (9) and (10) we have these derivations:

11.   a. /uno A odzi/   /uno A odzi/   /uno A odzi/

$$\begin{array}{ccc} \text{/uno A odzi/} & \text{/uno A odzi/} & \text{/uno A odzi/} \\ \underset{H\ L}{|\ |}\ \underset{H}{\vee} \xrightarrow{(9)} & \underset{H\ H}{|\ |}\ \underset{H}{\vee} \xrightarrow{(10)} & \underset{H}{\vee}\ \underset{H}{\vee} \end{array}$$

b. /amε A eθa/   /amε A eθa/

$$\begin{array}{cc} \text{/am}\varepsilon\text{ A e}\theta\text{a/} & \text{/am}\varepsilon\text{ A e}\theta\text{a/} \\ \underset{L}{\vee}\ \underset{L}{\vee} \xrightarrow{(9)} & \underset{H}{\vee}\ \underset{L}{\vee} \end{array}$$

To convert these intermediate representations into the correct outputs, we must delete the associative marker A and apply the contraction rule. Deletion of the associative marker could be built into Rule (9); or we might maintain that segmentless morphemes do not interfere with the operation of segmental rules and that they are deleted from surface representations. An initial formulation of contraction would be the following:

12.   Contraction: V V   ∅   V

$$\text{Contraction:}\ \underset{T_1\ T_2}{\overset{V\ \ V\quad \emptyset\ \ V}{|\ \ |\quad\ \ \wedge}}\ \to\ T_1\ T_2$$

We can simplify this rule by omitting any mention of tone. Note that it was assumed that Convention (10) does not delete association lines. Instead, the association line of a deleted tone is transferred to the tone which occasions the deletion. Analogously, we may propose that a rule deleting a segment does not destroy association lines. Instead these lines are transferred to the segment that occasions the deletion. Now Rule (12) can be expressed as (13):

13.   Contraction: V V → ∅ 2

                                     1 2

As a result of contraction, the intermediate representations in (11) become:

14.   a. *unodzi*   *unodzi*   b. *ameθa*

$$\begin{array}{ccc} \textit{unodzi} & \textit{unodzi} & \textit{ame}\theta\textit{a} \\ \underset{H\ H}{\vee\!\vee} \xrightarrow{(10)} & \underset{H}{\vee} & \underset{H\ L}{\vee\!\vee} \end{array}$$

Imagine how a segmental account of tone would proceed. By definition the word *àmè* would have to contain a sequence of two low tones. But it would not suffice to formulate a simple (though perhaps peculiar) rule $L_1 \to H_1/$ ____ A for the tone-raising process, where L_1 denotes a sequence of one or more low tones, since the feature [+Low] does not occur in sequence: There is a segment between the two low-toned vowels. Suppose that, to correct for this fact, one devised a convention which ignores non-tone-bearing segments, for the purpose of applying this rule. It would still count against such an analysis that, though it could describe the process in question, it would yield no prediction, on the basis of (7), that this process would also apply in (8). On the suprasegmental hypothesis, the prediction is automatic. Since the process is indifferent to segmental factors, it applies as in (11), with no regard for the segments or syllables in the tonal domain.

Suppose instead that one attempted to formulate an iterative segmental rule that raised Lows to High one by one—roughly:

15. $L \rightarrow H/ \underline{\quad\quad} H_0\ A$

By this rule, the underlying form in (8) would go through the following stages:

16.   /àmɛ̀ A èθà/ → àmɛ́ A èθà → ámɛ́ A èθà → · · ·

Though the derivation would be successful here, Rule (15) predicts that an initial word with a LH pattern, such as ɔ̀tɛ́, should become ɔ́tɛ́ before the associative marker. Elimelech makes it clear that this does not happen. An example is:

17.   /ɔ̀tɛ́ A ódzí/ → ɔ̀tɛ́ ódzí → ɔ̀tódzí

Mende has a phenomenon that is structurally similar to this one; cf. Section 3.6.4. Unless we find examples that are parallel to these except that they differentiate between L and LL, this stands as striking confirmation of the suprasegmental hypothesis and of Convention (10) in particular.

Another indication that Etsako tones behave without regard for their seg-mental domain comes from an alternation in the future, present progressive, and past habitual tenses and in negatives. The data are illustrated schematically in (18), with sample derivations in (19); cf. Elimelech (1976:94).[7] Rule (20) gives the last step in these derivations.

18.   a. Direct objects: $[\ X\ H\ ]_V\ [\ L_1\ ]_N$
                                                   $\downarrow$
                                                   H_1

                 b. Monosyllabic verbs: $[\ \ H\ \ ]_V\ [\ H\ H\ X\ ]_N$
                                            $\downarrow$
                                            L

                 c. Disyllabic verbs: $[\ H\ H\ ]_V\ [\ H\ X\ ]_N$
                                            $\downarrow\ \downarrow$
                                            $L\ L$

                 d. Disyllabic verbs: $[\ H\ H\ ]_V\ [\ L\ X\ ]_N$
                                            $\downarrow$
                                            L

---

[7] I wish to thank Baruch Elimelech both for supplementing the examples from Elimelech 1976 and for criticizing an earlier version of this section. This should not be taken to mean that he agrees with the revisions proposed here.

19.   a. /ɔ́ dɛ́ àwòθò/ ―(18a)→ ɔ́ dɛ́ áwóθó ―(18b)→ ɔ́ dɛ̀ áwóθó ―(13)→ ɔ́ d ǎwóθó ―(TA)→ ɔ́ d àwóθó
      'he is buying a hoe'

      b. /ɔ́ dɛ́ útsádɛ̀/ ―(18b)→ ɔ́ dɛ̀ útsádɛ̀ ―(18)→ ɔ́ d ǔtsádɛ̀ ―(TA)→ ɔ́ d ùtsádɛ̀
      'he is buying a pot'

      c. /ɔ́ kélé ɔ̀γèdɛ́/ ―(18d)→ ɔ́ kèlé ɔ̀γèdɛ́ ―(13)→ ɔ́ kèl ɔ́γèdɛ́ ―(TA)→ ɔ́ kèl ɔ́γèdɛ́
      'he is looking for a banana'

      d. /ɔ́ kélé útsádɛ̀/ ―(18c)→ ɔ́ kèlè útsádɛ̀ ―(13)→ ɔ́ kèl ǔtsádɛ̀ ―(TA)→ ɔ́ kèl ùtsádɛ̀
      'he is looking for a pot'

20.   Tone Absorption (TA)

$$[\alpha\widehat{H}][-\alpha H]\,[-\alpha H] \to [\alpha H][-\alpha H] \quad \text{i.e.,} \quad \begin{array}{l} \widehat{H}L\ L \to H\ L \\ \widehat{L}H\ H \to L\ H \end{array}$$

Note that in (18b) versus (18c, d), monosyllabic verbs behave differently from disyllabic ones and that the difference appears to call for representation of the sequence HH as distinct from H, in violation of convention (10). Thus either convention (10) or rules (18b, c, d) must be wrong. In fact, I think there is good reason independent of the need to adhere to (10) for reformulating the rules in (18), since despite striking similarities in the operations they carry out, their present formulation says in effect that they have nothing to do with one another. The key to the solution is to order (13) Contraction immediately after (18a). The initial part of derivations will then proceed as follows, assuming that Tone Absorption (20) applies directly after Contraction. Some new forms are illustrated here in addition to those in (19).

21.

	Input string	By Rule (18a)	By (13) Contraction	By (20) TA	Desired output
a.	/ɔ́ dɛ́ àwòθò/	ɔ́ dɛ́ áwóθó	ɔ́ d áwóθó	—	ɔ́ d àwóθó
b.	/ɔ́ dɛ́ ɔ̀γèdɛ́/	—	ɔ́ d ɔ́γèdɛ́	ɔ́ d ɔ́γèdɛ́	ɔ́ d ɔ́γèdɛ́
c.	/ɔ́ dɛ́ úkpò/	—	ɔ́ d úkpò	—	ɔ́ d úkpò
d.	/ɔ́ dɛ́ útsádɛ̀/	—	ɔ́ d útsádɛ̀	—	ɔ́ d ùtsádɛ̀
e.	/ɔ́ kélé àwòθò/	ɔ́ kélé áwóθó	ɔ́ kél áwóθó	—	ɔ́ kèl àwóθó
f.	/ɔ́ kélé ɔ̀γèdɛ́/	—	ɔ́ kél ɔ́γèdɛ́	ɔ́ kél ɔ́γèdɛ́	ɔ́ kèl ɔ́γèdɛ́
g.	/ɔ́ kélé úkpò/	—	ɔ́ kél úkpò	—	ɔ́ kèl úkpò
h.	/ɔ́ kélé útsádɛ̀/	—	ɔ́ kél útsádɛ̀	—	ɔ́ kèl ùtsádɛ̀

The desired outputs are obtained in (21b, c). For the remainder, the discrepancies between the products of the derivations and the desired outputs are all of the same sort: One or two high tones following the pronoun ɔ́ must be lowered. For (21e–h) the tone of the verb *kel-* (from *kele*) is lowered, and the tone of the following syllable, the noun prefix, is lowered just in case the syllable following it is H. These rules are formulated in (22). Assuming that both nouns and noun stems may be referred to by the feature [+N], these may be collapsed into a single rule, (23).

22.   a. Verb Lowering:
$$\begin{array}{cc} V & V \\ | & \\ T & L \end{array} \rightarrow \begin{array}{c} | \\ | \end{array} / \underline{\quad} \ C_0]_V \ [\ \overset{/}{X} \ ]_N$$
$$\qquad\qquad\qquad\qquad\qquad\qquad\qquad\qquad H \ Y$$

        b. Noun Prefix Lowering:
$$\begin{array}{cc} V & V \\ | & \\ T & L \end{array} \rightarrow \begin{array}{c} | \\ | \end{array} / \underline{\quad} \ ]_{N_{Pref}} \ [\ \overset{/}{X} \ ]_{N_{Stem}}$$
$$\qquad\qquad\qquad\qquad\qquad\qquad\qquad\qquad H \ Y$$

23.
$$\begin{array}{cc} V & V \\ | & \\ T & L \end{array} \rightarrow \begin{array}{c} | \\ | \end{array} / \underline{\quad} \ C_0 \ ]_{\left\{\begin{array}{c} V \\ N\,Pref \end{array}\right\}} [+N]$$
$$\qquad\qquad\qquad\qquad\qquad\qquad\qquad\qquad H \ Y$$

This rule, like the rules it replaces in Elimelech's analysis, must be marked as applying only in the future, present progressive, and past habitual tenses and in negatives.

For (21a–d) the same rule suffices. Here the verb has lost its only vowel, making subpart (22a) inapplicable. But subpart (22b) correctly lowers the tone of the noun prefix in (21a, d) without affecting the prefix in (b, c), which is followed by L rather than by H. The derivations in (21) may now be completed:

24.

	Intermediate stage from (21)	By (22a)	By (22b)
a.	ɔ̀ d áwóθó	—	ɔ̀ d àwóθó
b.	ɔ̀ d ɔ́γèdɛ́	—	—
c.	ɔ̀ d úkpò	—	—
d.	ɔ̀ d útsádɛ̀	—	ɔ̀ d ùtsádɛ̀
e.	ɔ̀ kél áwóθó	ɔ̀ kèl áwóθó	ɔ̀ kèl àwóθó
f.	ɔ̀ kél ɔ́γèdɛ́	ɔ̀ kèl ɔ́γèdɛ́	—
g.	ɔ̀ kél úkpò	ɔ̀ kèl úkpò	—
h.	ɔ̀ kél útsádɛ̀	ɔ̀ kèl útsádɛ̀	ɔ̀ kèl ùtsádɛ̀

This analysis, unlike the one illustrated in (19), does not require that HH be regarded as distinct from H and furthermore captures similarities obscured by (18b, c, d). What at first seemed to raise a problem for the strong suprasegmental hypothesis embodied in (10) turns out to have a better formulation in strict suprasegmental terms.

In the remainder of this Chapter, I cite tone processes in Mende and Hausa that argue similarly for the phonological independence of tones from the segments or syllables that bear them, and show how general conventions on tone assignment can be formulated to replace the tone rules of earlier accounts.

3. MENDE

3.1 The Distribution of Tonal Patterns

Mende is a Mande language of Sierra Leone. In Leben 1971b, 1973b, I argued that the distribution of tonal patterns in Mende monomorphemic words provides evidence for the suprasegmental nature of Mende tone. Recently, Dwyer (n.d.) has questioned the synchronic relevance of my claims for Mende tone patterns and has noted that, though true for at least 90% of the vocabulary, they are not true for 100% of the vocabulary.[8] In this section, I will show how the suprasegmental account can be reformulated in the light of Dwyer's data without abandoning the hypothesis that tone is represented suprasegmentally, and I will argue further that this more comprehensive analysis provides additional support for the suprasegmental hypothesis.

First let me summarize the simplified account of the distributional facts in Leben 1971b, 1973b. The majority of Mende monomorphemic words have the tone patterns H, L, HL, LH, and LHL, regardless of how many syllables they have:

25.						
H:	kɔ́	'war'	pɛ́lɛ́	'house'	háwámá	'waistline'
L:	kpà	'debt'	bɛ̀lɛ̀	'trousers'	kpàkàlì	'tripod chair'
HL:	mbû	'owl'	ngílà	'dog'	félàmà	'junction'
LH:	mbǎ	'rice'	fàndé	'cotton'	ndàvúlá	'sling'
LHL:	mbã̌	'companion'	nyàhâ	'woman'	nìkílì	'groundnut'

By regarding the tone pattern as phonologically separate from the segments in these words, we capture the fact that a given pattern can occur regardless of how many syllables a word has. The realization of a given tone pattern on a word can be described by the following rule:

26. Tone Mapping:
   a. Associate the first tone with the first syllable, the second tone with the second syllable, and so on, until all tones or syllables are exhausted.
   b. Tones or syllables not associated as a result of (a) are subject to the well-formedness condition (3).

This gives tone assignments like the following:

27.   a. *pɛlɛ*   *pɛlɛ*   *pɛlɛ*

$$\text{H} \xrightarrow{\text{(26a)}} \text{H} \xrightarrow{\text{(26b)}} \text{H}$$

          b. *nyaha*   *nyaha*   *nyaha*

$$\text{L H L} \xrightarrow{\text{(26a)}} \text{L H L} \xrightarrow{\text{(26b)}} \text{L H L}$$

[8] I wish to thank David Dwyer for making his interesting and informative manuscript available to me.

Dwyer (n.d.) cites the following objections to this analysis:

1. It is not likely that Mende has any monosyllabic words containing short vowels with the tone pattern LHL. The vowel of *mba* 'companion' is long.
2. The chart in (25) does not exhaustively describe the tone patterns of monomorphemic words. There are additional ones, some of which could not be accommodated by (26). In particular, the patterns H'H, H'HL, HLH, HLHL, HHL, and LLH are attested, though rare. The apostrophe in H'H and H'HL signals that the H following it is downstepped. The patterns H HL and LLH contrast, respectively, with HL and LHH illustrated on *ngílà* and *ndàvúlá* in (25).
3. Disyllabic words with the tone pattern LH are actually divided into two classes, one of which has a phonological rise on the second syllable that happens to be realized as level H in isolation. For example, morphotonemic evidence suggests that *fàndé* results from a presurface representation /fàndě/.

I will discuss these objections in the order given.

3.2 Vowel Length

The data available for judging the length of the vowel of *mbà̌* 'companion' and similar words are not reliable. It is possible that any additional length, as compared with the length of the vowel of *mbă* 'rice', is an automatic result of the additional complexity of its tonal pattern. But it is also possible that this vowel is phonologically long. To determine which is the correct description, we must observe vowel duration in environments that neutralize the tonal contrast between *mbà̌* and *mbă*. Before the indefinite plural ending *-ngàa*, the final L of the noun is absorbed by the L of *-ngàa* (e.g., *mbû* 'owl' versus *mbúngàa* 'owls'). Thus, the indefinite plurals for *mbâ* 'companion' and *mbă* 'rice' should both have LH on the noun, followed by the L of *-ngàa*: *mbăngàa*. If this form translates both 'rices' and 'companions', this will be a sign that the lengths are phonologically identical. Similarly, if we find that the vowel of *mbă* 'rice' is somewhat longer than the short vowel of *gbà* 'difference', we will have to determine whether this is due to a phonological length contrast or to the greater complexity of the tone pattern LH as compared to L. Here, too, it is possible to find environments where the tone contrast is neutralized. For example, before the definite marker *-i*, the vowels of *mbă* and *gbà* change to ε, and the H of LH is absorbed by the H of the definite marker; this gives *mbèí* 'the rice' versus *gbèí* 'the difference'. We can again measure the relative durations of the vowels in this environment to determine whether *mbă* and *gbà* contrast phonologically in length.

The available sources are not reliable indications of the length of the vowels in question. For example, Innes 1963 consistently transcribes 'die' with a long vowel (*haa*) while Innes 1967 consistently gives it as short (*ha*). Spears (1967a), who transcribes *mbă* 'rice' as *mbaă*, and *mbâ* 'companion' as *mbaâ*, uses the double vowel as a device for interpreting the tone marks and comments that, "in words such as *mbaă* 'rice', the vowels are not necessarily long (even though there are two). The double vowels . . . are written for the purposes of tonal mapping [p. 176]." Spears employs another device (V. V) for contrastively long vowels, but the use of the word "necessarily" in the preceding extract leaves open the question of whether the simple double vowels also are sometimes contrastively long. This indeed seems to be the case in *ngewɔɔ* 'God', where the double *ɔ* is not needed for tonal mapping. (Compare *pɔnɔ̂* 'tie in a knot', which evidently ends in a short vowel.)

Without information about vowel duration in environments that neutralize the tonal contrast between LH and LHL and between L and LH, it will not be possible to know whether LHL can appear on short vowels.

3.3 Additional Tone Patterns

For the purposes of this discussion, I will assume (with Dwyer) that the preponderance of examples that conform to the patterns illustrated in (25) and to the principles in (26) is not directly the result of the requirements of the suprasegmental hypothesis but that instead it is a result of the historical fact that Mende derives from a protosystem in which the principles (26) were maintained absolutely.[9]

Let us consider cases in which ′H occurs. Dwyer notes that the tone patterns H′H and H′ĤL occur in examples like *tátò* 'start', *wólò* 'listen', and *gɔ́nɛ̀* 'cat'. There are two ways of working this into the suprasegmental analysis. One is to posit that ′H is a separate phoneme. On this account, the mapping principles in (26) work perfectly:

28.   a. *tato*   *tato*   b. *gɔnɛ*   *gɔnɛ*   *gɔnɛ*

$$H\ ′H \xrightarrow{(26a)} H\ ′H \qquad H\ ′HL \xrightarrow{(26a)} H\ ′HL \xrightarrow{(3a)} H\ ′HL$$

In support of the analysis of ′H as a marginal toneme of Mende, there are also marginal examples of ′H on monosyllables: *njè* 'mother' (which contrasts with *njé* 'goat') and *kɛ̀* 'father', a variant of *kɛ̀kɛ́* 'father'. If we accept this, it adds support to the suprasegmental hypothesis, not simply because the mapping of /′H/ proceeds according to the principles in (26), but mainly because the suprasegmental analysis can help to explain the distribution of this toneme. To see this, consider the theoretical possibilities that are opened up by the addition of /′H/ to the tonal inventory of the language. Restricting ourselves

[9] The existence of this protosystem lends support to the suprasegmental hypothesis, though the support is not as dramatic as it would be in present-day Mende, since Dwyer finds no evidence in the protolanguage for three-syllable monomorphemic words.

to patterns with three tones or fewer, we predict the following to be possible. Where these patterns coincide with attested cases, examples are given:

29.   /ˈH/   njè, kè
        /HˈH/   tátò, wólò, ndéwè 'sibling'
        /ˈHˈH/
        /ˈHL/
        /HˈHˈH/
        /HˈHL/   gónè̏
        /ˈHˈHL/
        /LHˈH/   kòóndè̏ 'butterfly'

In determining the theoretical possibilities, I have eliminated cases in which there is no contrast possible with another pattern. For example, /LˈH/ has been omitted, since this is tonally identical with /LH/, due to the fact that H is automatically downstepped after L. Similarly, from a suprasegmental point of view, the patterns /ˈHH/ and /ˈHHH/ are melodically equivalent to /ˈH/.[10]

The attested cases in (29) obey the following restrictions: No contour contains more than one instance of /ˈH/. Given this restriction, which would be difficult to envision if we regarded tone as a segmental feature, only one gap in the pattern is left unexplained: /ˈHL/. This is not a bad record, considering the rarity of /ˈH/ in general.

The alternative to positing the phoneme /ˈH/ is to derive it from /LH/. For example, what was expressed above as /HˈH/ might be regarded instead as /HLH/. The downstepping of the second H to ˈH would be automatic in Mende, by a general rule downstepping any H after L, giving /HLˈH/. And it is normal in Mende to assimilate this L to the following ˈH, giving /HˈH/.[11] One problem with this alternative stems from a contrast in monosyllables. Monosyllables with the pattern /LH/ are typically realized with a phonetic rise: mbǎ 'rice' is an example. If we replace /ˈH/ with /LH/ in our tonemic inventory, we need to formulate a special rule to convert /LH/ into /ˈH/ in the monosyllables njè 'mother' and kè 'father'. But this contrast is too marginal to count heavily against the alternative.

Mende does in fact offer grounds for deciding between the two representations proposed for downstepped High tonemes, but unfortunately the sources do not report on the relevant facts. As will become clear in 3.6.1, toneless postpositions inherit their tone from the preceding syllable. Given this, it is possible to tell whether ndéwè 'sibling' ends in /ˈH/ or in a phonological sequence /LH/ by putting a postposition after it. If nya-ndewe-bu 'under my sibling' is realized as nyá-ndéwè-bú, this will argue for representing the tone

---

[10] Recall Convention (10) in Etsako, which collapses HH into H, etc. This convention is later reformulated for Mende, in (55) in the text.

[11] The operation of this rule can be seen in the definite form of mbû 'owl' and nyápò 'woman': /mbû-í/ > [mbúí]; /nyápò-í/ > [nyápóí].

pattern of *ndéwè* as /HLH/; if, on the other hand, this expression is realized as *nyá-ndéwè-bú*, this will argue for representing the pattern of *ndéwè* as /H'H/.

It is worth noting that if the correct tone pattern for downstepped H is /LH/, this will not affect the formulation of (26) for the suprasegmental analysis. Sample mappings are:

30.   a. *ndewe*   *ndewe*   *ndewe*

HLH $\xrightarrow{\text{(26a)}}$ HLH $\xrightarrow{\text{(26b)}}$ HLH

      b. *gɔnɛ*   *gɔnɛ*   *gɔnɛ*

HLHL $\xrightarrow{\text{(26a)}}$ HLHL $\xrightarrow{\text{(26b)}}$ HLHL

Whether or not the second alternative for representing downstepped H is adopted, Dwyer points out that there are words with the pattern HLH and even words with the pattern HLHL:

31.   *yámbùwú*   'tree (sp.)'
             lánsàná   (proper name)
             náfàlê   'raphia clothed clown'
             njégùlû   'tarantula'
             kónùgû   'centipede'
             dúmbèékà   'star'

Though such words are not numerous, it is true, as Dwyer also notes, that three-syllable monomorphemic words are themselves not numerous in Mende. With this explanation for the rarity of this pattern, there seems to be no point in maintaining a restriction against HLH.

3.4 Irregularities in Tone Mapping

In the next case to be discussed, Dwyer's data forces a more drastic modification of the suprasegmental analysis. Dwyer has noted a contrast between the tonal patterns H L and H ĤL in disyllabic words. This presents a problem for the suprasegmental theory, since both patterns are expressed suprasegmentally as HL. For examples of the contrast, compare *kényà* 'uncle' and *ngílà* 'dog' against *ngɔ́ngɔ̂* 'tooth', *hókpô* 'navel', and *kɔ́nyɔ̂* 'friend'.[12]

---

[12] In Leben 1973b, I suggested that the latter sort of word be treated as a lexicalized compound. Using the hyphen to separate the two elements of a compound, one could analyze the latter words as ᴴ*ngɔ́-ngɔ*, ᴴ*hó-kpô*, ᴴ*kɔ́-nyɔ̂*, and the compound rule (see [57]) would then produce the correct tonal pattern. But this is very ad hoc, since the contemporary language does not contain the free morphemes ᴴ*ngɔ́*, ᴴ*hó-*, and ᴴ*kɔ́-* that would make up these compounds.

The suprasegmental analysis can be modified to accommodate this contrast. The tone H can be lexically associated with some syllable in exceptional words that appear to violate (26). Words like *ngìlà* and like *ngɔ́ngɔ̀* both have a /HL/ pattern, but the latter has a lexically specified association line connecting the H to the second syllable. The well-formedness condition takes care of the rest:

32.

$$
\begin{array}{ccc}
ng\mathit{\jmath}ng\mathit{\jmath} & ng\mathit{\jmath}ng\mathit{\jmath} & ng\mathit{\jmath}ng\mathit{\jmath} \\
\diagup & \diagup\!\diagdown & \diagdown\!\!\!\diagdown\diagdown \\
\text{H L} \xrightarrow{\text{(3a)}} \text{H L} \xrightarrow{\text{(3b)}} \text{H L}
\end{array}
$$

This device handles other tone patterns that were troublesome for the earlier analysis. For example, *lèlèmá* 'praying mantis' and *làsìmɔ́* 'amulet' contrast tonally with *ndàvúlá* 'sling' and *ndèndélí* 'shade', even though all share the tonal melody LH. We can capture the contrast in roughly the following way: By associating H lexically with the last syllable of *lèlèmá* and *làsìmɔ́* but not with the last syllable of *ndàvúlá* and *ndèndélí*,

33. a. /lelema/ *le ema*   b. /ndavula/   *ndavula*   *ndavula*

$$
\begin{array}{cccc}
\diagup \; \diagup & \diagdown\!\!\!\diagup \diagup & & \diagup \; \diagup & & \diagup \diagdown\!\!\!\diagdown \\
\text{L H} > \text{L H} & & \text{L H} \xrightarrow{\text{(26a)}} \text{L H} \xrightarrow{\text{(3b)}} \text{L H}
\end{array}
$$

In *lèlèmá* the unassociated L will be assigned to the first two syllables by procedures outlined in 3.6.3, and the assignment of tones to *ndàvúlá* will be modified at the same time.

Although this represents a weakening of the claims of the original suprasegmental analysis, the facts appear to warrant it. Furthermore, as I attempt to demonstrate in 3.5, this revised account is still superior to a purely segmental one.

3.5 Additional Features of Tone Assignment

Note that the revised analysis makes Mende look more like a pitch-accent system than the original suprasegmental analysis did. The pitch accent is expressed, simply, as a H lexically associated with a syllable in exceptional words. There are two facts about the distribution of tone in Mende that favor this interpretation over a purely segmental account. The first concerns borrowings from English.[13] Words like *pénsù* 'pencil' and *wúndà* 'window', in which the realization of the HL pattern closely matches the intonation of the corresponding citation forms in English, are easy enough to account for in segmental terms. Each syllable of the borrowed word could be said to approximate the features of the corresponding English syllable. Sometimes the English accented syllable is realized as a rise in tone, rather than as a level H. This

---

[13] A number of these may have come from English through Krio.

happens in *klăkì* 'clerk', *plĕtì* 'plate', and *gɔátà* or *gɔ̃tà* 'gutter'; there is not enough data to suggest whether the assignment of H or LH to the first syllable can be predicted on the basis of consonant types or vowel quality or whether indeed some of these words have simply been mistranscribed. Still, both H L and L̂H L conform closely enough to the intonation of the corresponding English words. Where the segmental view runs into trouble is in words like *Yínglísì* 'English', *Íjípì* 'Egypt', *síméntì* 'cement', *Jámáì* 'Germany', *pétíkù* 'spectacles', *Pláimínísà* 'Prime Minister', and perhaps *kábúà* 'cover'. Here the tonal fit with the corresponding English citation forms is less exact, making it difficult for the segmental treatment to regard them as close tonal approximations to the English words. If we adopt the suprasegmental analysis of Mende tone, on the other hand, we can regard the tone pattern HL as an approximation to the English citation intonation contour. The accented syllable in Mende, as suggested above, is denoted by having a H associated with it; for whatever reason, Mende uniformly assigns a penultimate accent in these borrowings.[14] The mapping conventions explain how the remaining syllables get their tone, as shown in the following example:

34.   /pɛtiku/   pɛtiku   pɛtiku

          H L   ——(26a)——→ H L   ——(3b)——→ H L

Neither the segmental nor the suprasegmental analysis is yet in a position to explain why the stressed syllable in English is sometimes rendered in Mende as LH. But, given that the LHL contour must be expressed for *klăkì*, *plĕtì*, and *gɔátà/gɔ̃tà*, the mapping principles explain where the tones are positioned. The example *Pɔ̀tígà* 'Portugal' is handled in the same way:

35.   a. /klaki/   klaki   klaki   b. /pɔtiga/   pɔtiga

      L H L ——(26a)——→ L H L ——(3a)——→ L H L   L H L ——(26a)——→ L H L

The suprasegmental analysis thus helps to account for tone assignment in borrowings. The procedures for placing tones on borrowed words reinforce the principles of tone assignment posited earlier for native words.

     A second advantage of the revised suprasegmental account over a segmental one is the fact that it predicts the surface distribution of rising tones. Rising tones occur on monosyllables, and only on the initial syllable of disyllables:

36.   a. /mba/   mba   mba   'rice'

          L H ——(26a)——→ L H ——(3a)——→ L H

---

[14] The exceptional case *Jámáì* takes the syllable containing the penultimate mora to be the accented one; note that this interpretation is consistent with the examples said in the text to be accented on the penultimate syllable.

b. /bɛsi/   *bɛsi*   *bɛsi*   'pig'

$$\text{L H} \xrightarrow{\text{(3a)}} \text{L H} \xrightarrow{\text{(3b)}} \text{L H}$$

c. /hindo/   *hindo*   *hindo*   'male'

$$\text{L H L} \xrightarrow{\text{(26a)}} \text{L H L} \xrightarrow{\text{(3a)}} \text{L H L}$$

Note that in disyllables, a rise may occur on the first syllable whether the following syllable is H or L. But a rise never occurs on the second syllable, regardless of whether the first is H or L. This peculiarity of distribution, which could not be predicted by a segmental account or by an account that posited a rise as a unit toneme, is a direct consequence of the revised suprasegmental hypothesis. The nonoccurrence of H $\widehat{\text{LH}}$ is a result of the fact that this sequence fits the environment for downstepping the second H and assimilation of L to ′H, as described in 3.3. Thus H $\widehat{\text{LH}}$ is realized as H′H. The nonoccurrence of L $\widehat{\text{LH}}$ is a result of the mapping conventions. If we attempt to derive this pattern, we must start from one of the following forms:

37.   a. CVCV   b. CVCV

                  L H   L H

In either case, the L can only be associated with the first syllable by (26a). Our principles allow no way of placing L on the second syllable!

Though this is a correct prediction about the surface distribution of rising tones, Dwyer and others have proposed that the pattern L $\widehat{\text{LH}}$ is needed in some presurface representations. In section 3.6, I argue that, independently of this proposal's inconsistency with the revised suprasegmental analysis, it is incorrect.

3.6 Mende Morphotonemics

The more carefully we attempt to characterize the behavior of Mende tones in constructions involving more than one morpheme, the more compelling becomes the evidence for regarding tone in Mende as a suprasegmental feature. In this section, I will aim to document this conclusion by considering certain tone alternations in Mende nouns and nominals.

The central issue in the description of Mende morphotonemics involves a choice of procedures to follow in coping with the fact that certain types of behavior on the part of Mende tones are not predictable from the nature of these tones in their citation form. This problem has led to proposals of morphophonemic representations for Mende tones that diverge greatly (and perhaps suspiciously) from their surface realization; examples are Spears 1967a, b, Dwyer 1971, Leben 1971b, Voorhoeve 1975, and Dwyer (n.d.). In

Leben 1973b, I proposed an alternative which can now be considerably refined in light of the revisions developed above.

3.6.1 Basics

In certain cases, falling and rising tones simplify to level ones. Though the exact formulation of the processes having this effect has been the subject of some dispute, it is nonetheless quite easy to characterize the environments in which this occurs. Consider the following data, showing the correspondence between a noun's citation tones and the tones it bears before the indefinite plural marker -*ngàa* and the definite marker -*i*. The change of *a* to *ε* before -*i* is regular:

38.

	Citation form		Indefinite plural	Definite singular
a.	*kɔ́*	'war'	*kɔ́ngàa*	*kɔ́i*
b.	*mbû*	'owl'	*mbúngàa*	*mbúi*
c.	*mbǎ*	'rice'	*mbăngàa*	*mbèi*
d.	*pélé*	'house'	*péléngàa*	*péléi*
e.	*bèlè*	'trousers'	*bèlèngàa*	*bèlèi*
f.	*ngílà*	'dog'	*ngílàngàa*[15]	*ngílèi*
g.	*nyàhâ*	'woman'	*nyàhángàa*	*nyàhêi*

In the indefinite plural, a falling tone simplifies to H before -*ngàa*. Correspondingly, a rising tone simplifies to L before -*i*. These illustrate what Hyman and Schuh (1974) have called Tone Absorption, which converts $\widehat{HL}$ L to H L and $\widehat{LH}$ H to L H:

39.   Tone Absorption: $[\alpha \overset{\frown}{H}][-\alpha H]$ $[-\alpha H] \to [\alpha H][-\alpha H]$

In the definite singular, the H of -*i* is downstepped if a low tone precedes, and a preceding low tone assimilates to the downstepped high. We can begin to describe these processes with the following rules:

40.   Downstep: $H \to {}'H \: / \: L$ ____

41.   Assimilation: $L'H \to {}'HH$

The definite *ngílèi* becomes *ngílèi* by (40) and *ngílèi* by (41). Similarly, *nyàhâ* forms the definite *nyàhêi*, which becomes *nyàhêi* by (40), and *nyàhêi* > *nyàhêi*

---

[15] The interpretation of tone contours in Spears 1967b (p. 184) implies that a sequence H L L will be realized phonetically as H M L, but Spears 1967a (p. 239) gives its phonetic realization as H L L in *kɔ́wùhù* 'in a box', from *kɔ́wù* 'box'. I will assume that this latter realization is correct, at least for polymorphemic forms; it may be that H M L is a fast speech variant of H L L.

by (41). The fact that the behavior of the sequence HL in *ngílà* is matched by the behavior of the falling tone of the second syllable of *nyàhâ*, along with the fact that falling and rising tones behave like mirror images of each other in Rule (39), argues for representing rising and falling tones as sequences of level tones, i.e., as LH and HL respectively, as was proposed in general by Woo 1969. To simplify the exposition, I will omit downstep from the forms below.

Along with tone-bearing suffixes like *-ngàa* and *-i*, Mende has toneless morphemes that can be suffixed to a form. For example, a number of Mende postpositions including *-hu* 'in' and *-ma* 'on' have no inherent tone of their own:

42.

Citation form	Before *-hu*	Before *-ma*
a. *kɔ́*	*kɔ́hú*	*kɔ́má*
b. *mbû*	*mbúhù*	*mbúmà*
c. *mbǎ*	*mbàhú*	*mbàmá*
d. *pɛ́lɛ́*	*pɛ́lɛ́hú*	*pɛ́lɛ́má*
e. *bɛ̀lɛ̀*	*bɛ̀lɛ̀hù*	*bɛ̀lɛ̀mà*
f. *ngílà*	*ngílàhù*[15]	*ngílàmà*
g. *nyàhâ*	*nyàháhù*	*nyàhámà*

There are various ways to assign tones to postpositions, modifying the tones of the preceding nouns accordingly. For the moment, let us attempt to make maximal use of the rules already formulated. We may assign the tones to the postpositions by copying the immediately preceding tone and submitting the output to (39) Tone Absorption. This gives derivations like the following, where TC abbreviates Tone Copying:

43.
    a. *kɔ́ hu* $\xrightarrow{\text{TC}}$ *kɔ́ hú*
    b. *mbû hu* $\xrightarrow{\text{TC}}$ *mbû hù* $\xrightarrow{\text{(3a)}}$ *mbú hù*
    c. *mbǎ hu* $\xrightarrow{\text{TC}}$ *mbǎ hú* $\xrightarrow{\text{(3a)}}$ *mbà hú*

As noted in Leben 1971b, this account strengthens the case for regarding rising and falling tones as sequences of level tones, since the copying rule copies the Tone H from the rise LH and the tone L from the fall HL. If we instead regarded these contour tones as unitary [Rising] and [Falling], there is nothing to prevent us from expecting the contours [Rising] and [Falling] to be copied by Tone Copying.

Another morphotonemic process involves the neutralization of tonal contrasts in noninitial members of certain constructions. The clearest illustration of this is the nominal compound, in which the first element is a noun and the second is either a noun or an adjective. For purposes of illustration, I will choose *hìndâ* 'business, matter' as the second element; the same tone patterns given here would result if the second element were *hàní* 'thing', *nyámú* 'ugly', etc.:

44.

Isolation form of first element	Compound
a. *kɔ́*	*kɔ́-hìndà*
b. *mbû*	*mbú-hìndà*
c. *mbǎ*	*mbà-híndà*
d. *pɛ́lɛ́*	*pɛ́lɛ́-híndà*
e. *bɛ̀lɛ̀*	*bɛ̀lɛ̀-hìndà*
f. *ngílà*	*ngílà-hìndà*
g. *nyàhâ*	*nyàhá-hìndà*

The tone of *hinda* is level L, except in (44a, c, d), where it is HL. To account for this, we may provisionally propose that L is assigned to the second element and that if the first element has a final H (as in [44a, c, d]), this H is copied onto the second element. To make this proposal as consistent as possible with the copying analysis illustrated for toneless postpositions in (43), we may construe copying as (vacuously) copying any final L of a first element onto the second element as well. Subsequently, Rule (39) applies. This gives the following derivations:

45.

L assignment		Tone copying		Tone absorption
a. *kɔ́-hìndà*	→	*kɔ́-hìndà*	⟶	*kɔ́-hìndà*
b. *mbú-hìndà*	→	*mbú-hìndà*	⟶	*mbú-hìndà*
c. *mbǎ-hìndà*	→	*mbǎ-hìndà*	⟶	*mbà-híndà*
d. *pɛ́lɛ́-hìndà*	→	*pɛ́lɛ́-híndà*	⟶	*pɛ́lɛ́-híndà*
e. *bɛ̀lɛ̀-hìndà*	→	*bɛ̀lɛ̀-hìndà*	⟶	*bɛ̀lɛ̀-hìndà*
f. *ngílà-hìndà*	→	*ngílà-hìndà*	⟶	*ngílà-hìndà*
g. *nyàhâ-hìndà*	→	*nyàhá-hìndà*	⟶	*nyàhá-hìndà*

This in essence captures the analysis in Leben 1971b, 1973b for the tonal alternations summarized in (38), (42), and (45), aside from disyllabic nouns with the citation tone pattern LH, to which I now turn.

3.6.2 *LH Nouns*

Disyllabic nouns with the pattern LH are divided into two groups, the first of which behaves in accordance with the rules proposed above, and the second of which does not. Unfortunately, the second group comprises the vast majority of LH nouns.[16] The facts for these two groups are summarized here:

46.

	Group I	Group II
a. Isolation	*nàvó* 'money'	*fàndé* 'cotton'
b. Definite	*nàvóí*	*fàndèí*
c. Postposition	*nàvómá*	*fàndèmá*
d. Compound	*nàvó-híndà*	*fàndè-híndà*

By the rules developed above, we would expect all nouns with the isolation tone pattern of *nàvó* to behave like Group I forms. The addition of the definite marker -*i* should give LH-*i*; the postposition should copy the preceding tone, H, giving LH-*má*; the second element of a compound should have a copy of the final H of the preceding element on its first syllable, giving LH-*híndà*. Instead, Group II has a L in these constructions on the syllable that is H in isolation. The change from H to L is apparently conditioned by a following H, since where Group II nouns appear before a L, they are pronounced LH, just like Group I nouns; for example, adding the indefinite plural marker -*ngàa*, we get *fàndéngàa*, like *nàvóngàa*.

With the exception of Leben 1973b, explicit accounts of this alternation have posited a lexical contrast between the tone patterns of Groups I and II. Examples are Spears 1967a, Dwyer 1971, Leben 1971b, Voorhoeve 1975, and Dwyer (n.d.). In essence, these accounts propose that words like *fàndé* are phonologically *fàndĕ*.[17] The final H is responsible for the appearance of H on a following postposition and on the first syllable of the second element of the compound in (46d). The reason that the postulated L͡H is realized as L before a following H is given by (39) Tone Absorption. All that is needed in addition is a rule to convert this LH into H in cases where (39) does not apply, including the isolation form in (40a) and the indefinite plural form, *fàndéngàa*.

---

[16] Voorhoeve 1975 reports, to the contrary, that the second group is a small minority, based on a count that he conducted with a Mende speaker. This finding is anomalous, for Dwyer reports the opposite for the same dialect (Kɔɔ Mende), and this is in agreement with Innes 1967: "Words like *fandé* are much commoner than words like *navó*, so if you forget whether a word behaves like *fandé* or like *navó*, there is more chance of your being right if you give its definite singular form the tone LLH, like fandeí [p. 18]." Innes bases his statement on the Kɔɔ Mende dialect.

[17] These accounts differed in the status they assigned to the LH postulated for the final syllable of *fàndé*. Spears 1967a regarded it as a morphophonemic tone that was interpreted as L before H and as H before L; Dwyer 1971 derived it by a rule converting final V̌ into V̌V́ when no H tone precedes. Forms like *bèlè* were regarded as exceptions to this process. Leben 1971b considered it an underlying sequence on the final syllable. Voorhoeve 1975 regarded it as a final sequence V̌', where ' is a "floating" tone.

In Leben 1973b I argued against this solution on the following grounds:

1. The proposed contrast between $\widehat{LH}$ and H is here being employed dia-critically, in violation of the constraint originally proposed in Kiparsky 1968.
2. Since words of the type *fàndé* greatly outnumber those of the type *nàvó*, one would expect the grammar to make this distribution apparent by characterizing the *nàvó* class as odd in some way. But the account sum-marized above does just the opposite: It is the common *fàndé* class that requires the abstract $\widehat{LH}$ syllable.
3. The abstract $\widehat{LH}$ has a peculiar distribution: It can occur only finally in a noun whose first syllable is L. This peculiarity is reflected in the rule which takes $\widehat{LH}$ to H, as in *fàndĕ → fàndé*. This rule must be restricted to apply only after L, so as not to convert the real rise of *mbă* 'rice' to **mbá*.

I proposed the following alternative. The alternations summarized in (46) could be captured by regarding both Group I and Group II as containing their isolation tone patterns lexically, but with the members of Group I marked as an exception to the following rule:

47.   Tone Spreading: $H \rightarrow L / L \underline{\quad} H$

Given the two proposals just summarized for expressing the exceptionality of Group I nouns, it is difficult to see how one could seriously prefer the first. The second produces the same alternations, but without positing abstract tonal contrasts. It handles one peculiarity of tonal behavior without introducing new peculiarities into the account. It is worth noting that the second analysis is consistent with either suprasegmental or segmental representation of tone, though it is not surprising that this analysis was first arrived at in the supra-segmental framework—this is due to the fact that most variants of the first analysis are ruled out in principle in the suprasegmental model, since, as noted in Section 3.5, the rules for associating tones with syllables would not permit disyllabic words to have contrasting tonal patterns L H and L LH. The at-tractiveness of the suprasegmental model will become clearer in 3.6.3, where the account of these tonal alternations is refined. Note that the suprasegmental account explains how, even though Mende exhibits the surface tone patterns H L and H HL, it may not exhibit the mirror image of the latter: L LH. The source of the explanation is the principle which permits H but not L to be associated with either of the two syllables in a disyllabic word, as demonstrated in (37).[18]

---

[18] Mende has one common word *pômà* 'behind' whose tone pattern would most economically be described by associating the L of HL lexically with the first syllable. While it would be ques-tionable to amend an analysis on the basis of one example, I am at a loss to suggest how the supra-segmental account can otherwise deal with this word.

3.6.3 Tone Mapping: A New Approach

The account of the tonal alternations just presented does not incorporate the innovations for Mende tone assignment developed in 3.4. In this section, I will show how, with appropriate modifications, these principles of tone assignment lead to some remarkable refinements in the description of the alternations in question. Consider first the matter of differentiating Group I from Group II. Rather than simply marking Group I nouns as exceptions to (47) Tone Spreading, we can distinguish these groups lexically in the following way:

48.   Group I: *navo*   Group II: *fande*

                                      L H   L H

As we will see below, *fàndé* loses its H before *-i* in (46) because this H is not lexically associated with any syllable. It is free to move to any syllable that is in accordance with the tone assignment principles of the language.

Before pursuing the description in (48), we can reconsider the account of the tonal alternations in (38), (42), and (45). It is clear that the operation of Tone Copying is technically unnecessary in many of these cases, since the tone assignment procedures would themselves provide for the correct tone assignment without a rule of copying. For example, rather than treat the assignment of tone to the postposition *-ma* in the way initially proposed, we can use the well-formedness condition:

49.   a. /pɛlɛ-ma/   *pɛlɛ-ma*   *pɛlɛ-ma*

                        H $\xrightarrow{(26a)}$ H $\xrightarrow{(3b)}$ H

              b. /bɛlɛ-ma/   *bɛlɛ-ma*   *bɛlɛ-ma*

                        L $\xrightarrow{(26a)}$ L $\xrightarrow{(3b)}$ L

              c. /ngila-ma/   *ngila-ma*   *ngila-ma*

                        H L $\xrightarrow{(26a)}$ H L $\xrightarrow{(3b)}$ H L

              d. /nyaha-ma/   *nyaha-ma*

                        L H L $\xrightarrow{(26a)}$ L H L

Observe that in the last example, we avoid the need for a separate operation of Tone Absorption; the realization of the H͡L from the isolation form *nyàhâ* as H in *nyàhá-mà* is instead a consequence of the tone mapping rules. The same holds true for *mbû*: In *mbú-mà*, the L component of *mbû* is automatically taken away from *mbû* and assigned to the toneless postposition *-ma*.

A similar treatment is possible for words with a LH pattern. For *mbă*, the tone mapping principles employed above will give the derivation:

50.   *mba-ma*   *mba-ma*

$$\text{L H} \xrightarrow{\text{(26a)}} \text{L H}$$

For words of more than one syllable, we wish Group I nouns to have the pattern LH-*má* and Group II nouns to have the pattern LL-*má*. To do this, all that is necessary is to modify the tone mapping rule so that it associates the rightmost H of a lexical contour with a toneless syllable before associating it with any syllables further to the left. As shown in (51b), this modification permits us to derive the correct tone associations without referring to (47) Tone Spreading.

51.   a. /fande-ma/   *fande-ma*   *fande-ma*   *fande-ma*

$$\text{L H} \xrightarrow{\text{(52a)}} \text{L H} \xrightarrow{\text{(52b)}} \text{L H} \xrightarrow{\text{(52c)}} \text{L H}$$

    b. /navo-ma/   *navo-ma*   *navo-ma*

$$\text{L H} \xrightarrow{\text{(52a)}} \text{L H} \xrightarrow{\text{(52b)}} \text{L H}$$

The revised mapping principles are:

52. Tone Mapping (revised):
   a. Associate a final H with the rightmost syllable.
   b. For any tones that are not associated with any syllables, associate the first tone with the first syllable, the second with the second, and so on.
   c. Any syllable that has no tone is associated with the tone of the preceding syllable, if there is one. Otherwise, tone assignment takes place according to the well-formedness condition.

These change some of the steps taken earlier, but without affecting the outputs. For example, the derivation of (49a) now becomes:

53.   /pɛlɛ-ma/   *pɛlɛ-ma*   *pɛlɛ-ma*

$$\text{H} \xrightarrow{\text{(52a)}} \text{H} \xrightarrow{\text{(3b)}} \text{H}$$

In addition, the lexical contrast between *lèlèmá* and *ndàvúlá* (Section 2.4) is now represented as in the left-hand side of (54), and is realized by the procedure carried out in the rest of (54):

54.   a. /lelema/   *lelema*   *lelema*

$$\text{L H} \xrightarrow{\text{(52b)}} \text{L H} \xrightarrow{\text{(52c)}} \text{L H}$$

    b. /ndavula/   *ndavula*   *ndavula*

$$\text{L H} \xrightarrow{\text{(52a)}} \text{L H} \xrightarrow{\text{(52b)}} \text{L H}$$

Neither word behaves like a Group II noun; i.e., like Group I nouns, both retain their final H in the environments illustrated in (46) where Group II nouns lose their H. Accordingly, we associate the H lexically with the appropriate syllable of these words, as shown in (54).

The new representation in (51) for *fàndé* versus *nàvó* and the new mapping rules (52) suggest a way of dealing with definites *fàndèi* versus *nàvói* (cf. 46b) without Tone Spreading. The lexical tone pattern of *fàndèi* and *nàvói* is #LH#H#, where the final H# is from the definite suffix -*i*. If we assume that the rightmost of a sequence of identical tones is deleted, we can formulate convention (55), which is reminiscent of the one formulated for Etsako in (10), except that it operates over #:

55.   Convention on tone melodies: $[\alpha H]$ (#) $[\alpha H] \rightarrow [\alpha H]$ (#) $\emptyset$

This reduces #LH#H# to #LH##. By (52a), a final H is first associated with the rightmost syllable in the word. Subsequently, any remaining tones are associated by (52b, c). Boundaries from the tonal and segmental representations can be matched up by extending the left-to-right procedure of (52b) to boundaries.[19] This gives the following derivations for *fàndèi* and *nàvói*, and analogous ones for forms with the indefinite plural marker -*ngàa*:

56.

Input strings	Intermediate stages			Output
a. /#fande# i #/	#fande#i#	#fande#i#	#fande#i#	#fande#i#
/# L H #H#/	# L H # #	# L H # #	# L H # #	# L H # #
b. /#navo# i #/	#navo#i#	#navo#i#		#navo#i#
/# LH#H#/	# LH# #	# LH# #		# LH# #
c. /#mbu#ngaa#/	#mbu#ngaa#	#mbu#ngaa#		#mbu#ngaa#
/#HL # L #/	# H L # #	# H L # #		# H L # #
d. /#ngila#ngaa#/	#ngila#ngaa#	#ngila#ngaa#		#ngila#ngaa#
/# H L# L #/	# H L # #	# H L # #		# H L # #

Where boundaries at the margins of tonal representations remain unassociated, we may propose that they are eventually deleted if an adjacent boundary is associated, or alternatively we may draw another line. Note that in (56c, d),

[19] Accordingly, we may redefine (52b) as saying, "For any elements in the tonal representation that are not associated with like elements in the segmental representation, associate the first element of the tonal representation with the first like element in the segmental representation, the second with the second, and so on." The term "like element" is construed to call for the association of tones with syllables and the association of boundaries with boundaries.

the result of applying (52b) violates well-formedness condition (3b), since the suffix -*ngàa* has not received a tone. To assign a tone to this suffix, we move the association line of the boundary immediately following L; otherwise, a new violation of the well-formedness condition would be incurred, since, as (57) shows, this would cause association lines to cross:

57.   *#ngila#ngaa#

$$\text{*\#ngila\#ngaa\#}$$

$$\# \quad \text{H L} \quad \# \ \#$$

If we moved the association line for this boundary to the left, this would obviously compound the violation of (3c); therefore, we must move it to the right:

58.   #ngila#ngaa#

$$\# \quad \text{H L} \quad \# \ \#$$

Now, by (52c) L associates with the final syllable, completing the last step in derivation (56d). For (56c), the discussion of (59) will demonstrate why (52b) does not associate L with -*ngaa*, and the above treatment shows how this situation is remedied.

The forms *pélêngàa* 'houses' and *mbăngàa* 'rices' have the following derivations in this reanalysis; the steps are explained below:

59.   a. /#pɛlɛ#ngaa#/   #pɛlɛ#ngaa#   #pɛlɛ#ngaa#

$$/\# \ \text{H} \ \# \ \text{L} \ \# \xrightarrow{(52b)} \# \ \text{H} \ \# \ \text{L} \ \# \xrightarrow{(52c)} \# \ \text{H} \ \# \ \text{L} \ \#$$

           b. /#mba#ngaa#/   #mba#ngaa#   #mba#ngaa#

$$/\# \ \ \text{L H} \ \# \ \text{L}\# \xrightarrow{(52b)} \# \ \ \text{L H} \ \# \ \text{L}\# \xrightarrow{(3a)} \# \ \ \text{L H} \ \# \ \text{L}\#$$

In (59a), mapping rule (52b) proceeds from left to right. (Rule [52a] does not apply, since H is not the rightmost tone in the tone pattern of the word.) The leftmost boundaries match up, and H is associated with the first syllable, *pɛ*. Since it is impossible to associate the next item in the tonal representation, #, with a syllable, the syllable *lɛ* is skipped over, and the second # of the tonal representation associates with the second # of the segmental representation. L associates with -*ngaa*, and the final #s match up. Next, by (52c) we assign the tone of the preceding syllable to *lɛ*. (59b) behaves similarly. By (52b), the leftmost # and L of the tonal representation match up respectively with the first # and the first syllable of the tonal representation. H cannot be associated with the next element, #, in the segmental representation, and so this H is skipped, and (52b) associates #L# with the appropriate elements of #*ngaa*#. Finally, by (3a), H is associated with the first syllable. Note that in both examples of (59), when a rule would otherwise improperly associate # with a nonboundary, we first locate a boundary for # to be associated with. If, as in

(56d), this results in a violation of the well-formedness condition that cannot be removed without redrawing the boundary association lines, then the boundary association lines are redrawn.

It must now be shown that this analysis extends to the compounds of (44), (46d). For these, the previous analysis had to account for two changes: non-initial members have their inherent tone replaced by L, and if the last lexical tone of the initial member is H, this H is placed on the first syllable of the second member. We can now reexpress the compound rule as:

60.　Compound Rule: $[\text{ X }]_N \;\#\; [\text{ CV Y }]_{\{N,A\}}$　　$[\text{ X }]_N \;\#\; [\text{ CV Y }]_{\{N,A\}}$

$$T_0 \langle H \rangle \# \quad T_0 \quad \rightarrow \quad T_0 \;\#\; \langle H \rangle L$$

Among other things, this rule adjusts the internal word boundary with respect to a final H in the first member, transferring the H of *fàndé* and *nàvó* to the second member. But *nàvó* will still retain the H on its second syllable because the association (which exists lexically) cannot be destroyed by (60). This is a reflex of the condition which permitted the Etsako contraction rule (12) to be reexpressed as (13): Rules which delete or move segments or tones do not destroy association lines. Some derivations follow:

61.

	Input strings	Intermediate stages	Output
a.	/#fande#hinda#/ /# L H#LHL#/	$\xrightarrow{(60)}$ #fande#hinda# # L #H L #	$\xrightarrow{(52b)}$ #fande#hinda# # L #H L # $\xrightarrow{(52c)}$	#fande#hinda# # L #H L #
b.	/#navo#hinda#/ /# LH#LHL#/	$\xrightarrow{(60)}$ #navo#hinda# # L#H L #	$\xrightarrow{(52b)}$	#navo#hinda# # L#H L #
c.	/#pɛlɛ#hinda#/ /# H #LHL#/	$\xrightarrow{(60)}$ #pɛlɛ#hinda# # #H L #	$\xrightarrow{(52b)}$ #pɛlɛ#hinda# # #H L # $\xrightarrow{(3b)}$	#pɛlɛ#hinda# # # H L #
d.	/#ngila#hinda#/ /# H L#LHL#/	$\xrightarrow{(60)}$ #ngila#hinda# #H L# L #	$\xrightarrow{(55)}$ #ngila#hinda# #H L# #	
		$\xrightarrow{(52b)}$ #ngila#hinda# # H L #	$\xrightarrow{(3b,\;52c)}$	#ngila#hinda# # H L # #

Observe that in (61c) the H of #HL is first associated with the initial syllable of the second member. If instead it were assigned to the initial syllable of the compound, the incorrect form **pélè-hìndà* would result. We avoid this latter mapping by specifying that the boundaries of the tonal pattern are mapped onto the boundaries in the segmental representation by the same principle (52b) which governs the association of tones with segments, namely, in left-to-right order on a one-to-one basis. The output of (52b) for this form violates (3b) of the well-formedness condition, since *pɛlɛ* has received no tones. The same is true of (61d): Rule (52b) leaves *hinda* with no tones. In such cases, the procedure illustrated in (57) and (58) above reassigns the word boundaries, permitting condition (3b) to be satisfied.

Table 1 provides additional illustrations of this reanalysis:

TABLE 1

Sample Derivations Not Covered in Examples (56), (59), and (61)

Input strings	Intermediate stages	Output
a. /#fande#ngaa#/ /# L H# L #/ → (52b)		#fande#ngaa# # L H# L #
/#navo#ngaa#/ /# LH# L #/ → (52b)		#navo#ngaa# # LH# L #
/#nyaha#ngaa#/ /#L HL# L #/ → (55)	#nyaha#ngaa# #L HL# # → (52b)	#nyaha#ngaa# #L HL# # → (3a, b)	#nyaha#ngaa# # L HL # #
b. /#mbu# i #/ /#HL #H#/ → (52a)	#mbu# i # #HL #H# → (52b)	#mbu# i # #HL #H# → (3a)	#mbu# i # #HL #H#
/#ngila# i #/ /# HL#H#/ → (52a)	#ngila# i # # H L#H# → (52b)		#ngila# i # # H L#H#
/#mba# i #/ /#LH #H#/ → (55)	#mba#i# #LH # # → (52a)	#mba#i# #LH # # → (52b)	#mba#i# #LH # #
/#nyaha# i #/ /#L HL#H#/ → (52a)	#nyaha# i # #L HL#H# → (52b)	#nyaha# i # #L HL#H# → (3a)	#nyaha# i # #L HL#H#
c. /#mbu#hinda#/ /#HL #LHL#/ → (60)	#mbu#hinda# #HL # L # → (55)		#mbu#hinda# #HL # #
	#mbu#hinda# #HL # # → (52b) ... (3a, b)		#mbu#hinda# # HL # #
/#mba#hinda#/ /#L H#LHL#/ → (60)	#mba#hinda# # L #H L # → (52b)		#mba#hinda# # L #H L #
/#nyaha#hinda#/ /# LHL #LHL#/ → (60)	#nyaha#hinda# #LHL# L # → (52b)	#nyaha#hinda# # L HL# # → (52c)	#nyaha#hinda# # L HL # #

By weakening the original suprasegmental proposal to permit limited lexical associations between syllables and tones, we have expanded the number of contrasting tone patterns that the framework can describe. The treatment of morphotonemic process just illustrated, along with the description of Group I versus Group II nouns, of restrictions on the surface distribution of rising tones, and of borrowings, suggests that the proposal at hand is both workable and interesting. To the extent that this is true, it would be profitable to re-examine the data in Hyman and Schuh 1974 and in other discussions of Tone Spreading and Tone Absorption to see whether these phenomena are not instead reflexes of general conventions on tone assignment, as they appear to be in Mende.

In effect, the revisions suggested here shift the emphasis off the older question of how segmental and suprasegmental tones differ from each other onto a new and perhaps more fruitful question: How can we avoid the awkwardness and vacuity of some segmental treatments of tone in a model that permits a larger number of contrasting tone patterns than the suprasegmental framework of Leben 1973b? The proposals developed above suggest a promising answer to this question. To conclude the discussion of Mende, I will present an example from verbs that reinforces this judgment.

3.6.4 Tone Assignment in Verbs: A Concluding Argument

Because of limitations of space, it is not possible to dwell on verbs at great length here. But the following case will help to illustrate a point. In the past negative, certain tone patterns are neutralized in intransitive verbs. Spears (1967b:408) and Voorhoeve (1975:26) report that intransitive verbs are uniformly level low toned before the marker -*ni* for this tense **unless** they end in the tone pattern HL. These examples are representative:

62.

	Lexical tones	Tones before -*ni* in past negative intransitive	
a.	gɔ̀ndɔ́	gɔ̀ndɔ̀nì	'starve'
b.	nyámú	nyàmùnì	'become bad, ugly'
c.	mὲlí	mὲlìnì	'graze'
d.	gbáwò	gbáwònì	'howl'
e.	hìtɛ̂	hìtɛ́nì	'come down'

From a segmental point of view, it is puzzling why H should become L in *nyámú* and *mὲlí* but not in *gbáwò* and *hìtɛ*. Suprasegmentally, we can differentiate these by specifying in the morphological rule for this construction that a final H of the verb is deleted:

63.   Morphological rule: Past negative $H \rightarrow \emptyset /$ ___ $\# \, nì$

This gives the following results, incorporating the conventions used above:

64.

Input strings	Intermediate stages			Output
a. /#gɔndɔ#ni#/	#gɔndɔ#ni#	#gɔndɔ#ni#	#gɔndɔ#ni#	#gɔndɔ#ni#
/# L #L#/	# L # #	# L # #	# L # #	# L ##
b. /#nyamu#ni#/	#nyamu#ni#	#nyamu#ni#		#nyamu#ni#
/# H #L#/	# #L#	# # L#		# # L#
c. /#mɛli#ni#/	#mɛli#ni#	#mɛli#ni#	#mɛli#ni#	#mɛli#ni#
/#L H#L#/	# L #L#	# L # #	# L # #	# L ##
				#mɛli#ni#
				# L ##
d. /#gbawo#ni#/	#gbawo#ni#	#gbawo#ni#		#gbawo#ni#
/# HL #L#/	# HL # #	# HL # #		# HL ##
e. /#hitɛ #ni#/	#hitɛ #ni#	#hitɛ#ni#		
/#LHL# L#/	#LHL# #	# LHL# #		

(Rule labels appearing between stages: a. (55), (52b), (52c), (3b); b. (63), (52b), (3b); c. (63), (55), (52b), (52c), (3b); d. (55), (52b), (3b); e. (55), (52b).)

This account is possible only if tones are lexically represented as suprasegmentals. A segmental treatment, which would regard *nyámú* as having a sequence HH, is incapable of explaining why the L of *-nì* can spread backward, erasing both Highs, when it cannot spread backward over HL or LHL.

4. HAUSA

Hausa is a Chadic language of Nigeria and Niger. Its monomorphemic words do not exhibit the same degree of independence from segments as Mende's. For example, a syllable cannot bear a rising tone, and only a heavy syllable (i.e., only one containing a long vowel or closed by a consonant) can bear a falling tone. Still, there are indications in Hausa of the independence of tone from segments. One is the stability of the tone pattern when tone-bearing segments are lost. In some cases pronouns can lose their vowel. For instance, the expression *án zàaɓée nì* 'one chose me' can be realized as *án zàaɓân*. (The change of *ee* to *a* in a closed syllable is regular.) As in Etsako, the tone of the deleted vowel is retained. A number of considerations from derivational morphology will be shown later to reinforce the notion that tones are phonologically separate from segments. First, though, I will consider tone assignment in monomorphemic words.

4.1 Distribution of Tones over Syllables

It is relatively rare for a Hausa lexical item to end in a consonant, and most words that do are borrowed: Examples are *máalàm* 'teacher', *àlhàmìs* 'Thursday', *fénsìr* 'pencil', *fâm* 'pound'. Nouns ending lexically in a consonant often have a variant form with the ending *-ii* attached. This variant is commonly employed before the genitival link *-n* and before the definite marker *-ǹ* (hence, *máalàmín* 'teacher of', *máalàmîn* 'the teacher') and in some cases in isolation as well (hence, *máalàmíi* 'teacher'). The tone of *-ii* is not uniform from word to word, but it is predictable. Consider the following examples:

65.

	Form without *-ii*	Form with *-ii*	
a.	*bìyár*	*bìyáríi*	'five' (cf. *bìyárínsù* 'the five of them')
	bàabúr	*bàabúríi*	'motorbike'
	àlján	*àljáníi*	'imp'
b.	*fâm*	*fámìi*	'pound'
	làadân	*làadáanìi*	'muezzin'
	àlhàmîs	*àlhàmíišìi*	'Thursday'
c.	*máalàm*	*máalàmíi*	'teacher'
	fénsìr	*fénsìríi*	'pencil'

(The change of *s* to *š* before *ìi* in *àlhàmíišìi* is regular. The length of the penultimate vowel in *làadáanìi* and *àlhàmíišìi* suggests that these forms have lexically long vowels in this position. The reason that the corresponding vowels in the left column without *-ii* are short is that Hausa does not permit long vowels in closed syllables.)

In all of these cases, we can explain the tone of *-ii* by assigning it on the basis of the preceding tone and subjecting the result to the regular tone rules and conventions of the language. In (65a), *-ii* inherits the preceding H; in (65b), *-ii* inherits the preceding L (and the final HL of the corresponding form in the left column is realized instead as H before *-ii*); in (65c), *-ii* inherits the preceding L, and this assigned tone is raised to H by a general rule of the language described and motivated in detail in Leben 1971a and in Leben and Bagari 1975:

66. Low Tone Raising: $\begin{array}{c} V \\ [+\text{long}] \\ | \\ L \end{array} \rightarrow H\ /\ \begin{array}{c} V \\ | \\ L \end{array} C_0 \underline{\hspace{1em}} \#$

Schematically, this account provides derivations like the following:

67. a. *bìyár* + *ii* → *bìyár* + *íi*
   b. *àlhàmîiš* + *ii* → *àlhàmîiš* + *ìi* → *àlhàmíiš* + *ìi*
   c. *máalàm* + *ii* → *máalàm* + *ìi* → *máalàm* + *íi*

In past work I have attributed the first stage in the derivations in (67) to Tone Copying. One advantage of adopting the revised suprasegmental framework is that it is no longer necessary to posit this rule as such. The required operation is carried out by the well-formedness condition, which extends the tone of the preceding syllable to toneless *-ii*. Thus, the first stage in (67) can be replaced by:

68.   a. *biyar + ii*   *biyar + ii*

$$\text{L H} \quad \xrightarrow{\text{(3b)}} \quad \text{L H}$$

        b. *alhamiis + ii*   *alhamiis + ii*

$$\text{L} \quad \text{HL} \quad \xrightarrow{\text{(3b)}} \quad \text{L} \quad \text{HL}$$

        c. *maalam + ii*   *maalam + ii*

$$\text{H L} \quad \xrightarrow{\text{(3b)}} \quad \text{H L}$$

We can carry this desirable result one step further by maintaining that like Mende, Hausa has lexical representations in which not all tones are associated with segments. This permits us to collapse the first two stages in (67b) into one, making both Tone Copying and Tone Absorption unnecessary. All that we must assume is that the lexical entry for *alhamis* contains the information that the tone pattern is LHL, with H on the final syllable:

69.   /alhamis/   *alhamis*

$$\text{L H L} > \text{L H L}$$

        /alhamiiš + ii/   *alhamiiš + ii*

$$\text{L} \quad \text{HL} > \text{L} \quad \text{HL}$$

One advantage of the use of general conventions here is that they explain the particulars of tone assignment; earlier treatments simply described them. In addition, as noted in Leben 1971a, if we posit a rule of Tone Absorption to carry out the second stage in (67b), we will have to deal with some systematic exceptions to this rule. Verbs show no inclination to undergo the rule which converts HL L to H L, as illustrated by *ɗàukè* 'remove' and *mântà* 'forget', which occur before noun direct objects. Rather than restrict Tone Absorption from applying to such forms, we avoid the problem altogether simply by not positing such a rule for Hausa.

For the analysis sketched in (69) to be tenable, all that must be true of Hausa is that in monomorphemic words the domain of the final L of a tone pattern is predictable as long as we know to which syllable a preceding H is lexically assigned. This is true, since monomorphemic words do not exhibit a contrast between XCV̂CV̀Y and XCV́CV̂Y.[20] In fact, it may be possible to take an even stronger stand, reminiscent of the one sketched for Mende: The distribution of tones over syllables is predictable, except for the lexical associa-

---

[20] The reason that in verbs we get a contrast between CV̂CV̀ and CV́CV̀ (e.g., *ɗàukè* 'remove' versus *ɗàurè* 'tie up' before noun direct objects) is that verb endings are tonally and segmentally independent of their stems. Verbs (except for monosyllabic ones) are never monomorphemic.

tion of H with a given syllable in some forms. The tone patterns below would
be assigned by (52b, c) formulated for Mende:

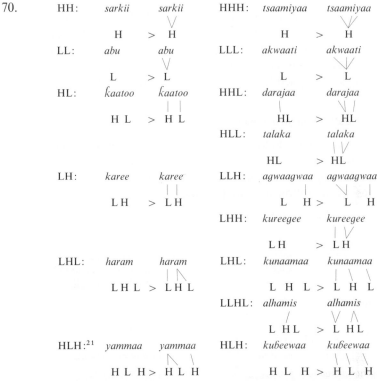

70.   HH: sarkii   sarkii   HHH: tsaamiyaa   tsaamiyaa

                 H   >   H   H   >   H

      LL: abu   abu   LLL: akwaati   akwaati

                 L   >   L   L   >   L

      HL: ƙaatoo   ƙaatoo   HHL: darajaa   darajaa

            H L   >   H L   HL   >   HL

                             HLL: talaka   talaka

                                HL   >   HL

      LH: karee   karee   LLH: agwaagwaa   agwaagwaa

            L H   >   L H   L   H >   L   H

                             LHH: kureegee   kureegee

                               L H   >   L H

     LHL: haram   haram   LHL: kunaamaa   kunaamaa

          L H L > L H L   L H L > L H L

                             LLHL: alhamis   alhamis

                               L HL   > L HL

    HLH:[21] yammaa   yammaa   HLH: kuɓeewaa   kuɓeewaa

         H L H > H L H   H L H > H L H

For four-syllable words with the pattern LHL, it is necessary to add another
provision to the mapping procedure. Words with the distribution LLHL,
like *màjàlísàa* 'council', *bùràbúskòo* '*tuwoo* made from bulrush millet', and
dàgwàlóolòo 'stupidity' can be treated as in (71a). For words with the distribution LHHL, such as *kàdángárèe* 'lizard', *Sàláamátù* (woman's name), and
hàsúumíyàa 'tower', we first associate the first and last tones with the first and
last syllable, respectively. The well-formedness condition takes care of the rest:

71.   a. /majalisaa/   *majalisaa*   *majalisaa*

                L H L   >   L H L   >   L H L

        b. /kadangaree/   *kadangaree*   *kadangaree*

              L H   L   > L H   L   > L H   L

---

[21] The assignment of HLH to disyllables is governed by a constraint against rising tones on
single syllables. This rules out *yàmmàà. Tone assignment in *yámmáa* could be viewed in the
following way: The first H of HLH is assigned to the first syllable, and the last H to the last syllable;
by (3a) L is assigned to the first syllable.

This tone assignment procedure would produce the correct mappings of the three-tone patterns in (70) as well.

I will not proceed further with this suggestion, since, as noted above, all that is needed to permit the analysis of LHL words sketched in (69) is the assurance that the assignment of a final L is automatic once we can identify the last syllable that receives a H, for all tone patterns that end with the sequence HL. Whether the preceding tones are assigned by rule as suggested in (70) and (71), or whether they are assigned lexically is really a separate question.

4.2 Morphologically Assigned Tones

Hausa derivational morphology contains numerous cases in which inherent tone patterns are obliterated by general rules and new tone patterns are assigned. These rules operate without regard for the segments or syllables which bear the tones, as the following examples show:[22]

72.　a. Plurals in -unaa:　$[\,\text{X V}\,]_{\text{sg.}}$　　　　　$\rightarrow [\,\text{X} + unaa\,]_{\text{pl.}}$

$$T_0 \qquad\qquad\qquad\qquad H L$$

tùulúu		túulúnàa	'water pot'
àdíikòo		ádíikúnàa	'kerchief'
àgóogóo		ágóogúnàa	'watch'

　　b. Plurals in -ai:　$[\,\text{X V}\,]_{\text{sg.}}$　　　　　$\rightarrow [\,\text{X} + ai\,]_{\text{pl.}}$

$$T_0 \qquad\qquad\qquad\qquad L \quad H$$

| làabáarìi | | làabàarái | 'news' |
| máalàmíi | | màalàmái | 'teacher' |

　　c. Agent nominals:　$[\,\text{X}\,]_{\text{verb stem}}$　　　　$\rightarrow [\,ma + \text{X} + ii\,]_{\text{N}}$

$$T_0 \qquad\qquad\qquad\qquad H \quad\quad L$$

tàmbáyàa	'ask'	mátàmbàyíi	'questioner'
rúbùutáa	'write'	márùbùucíi	'writer'
bí	'follow'	mábìyíi	'follower'

　　d. Place of origin　$[\,\text{X V}\,]_{\text{N}}$　　　　　$[\,ba + \text{X} + ee\,]_{\text{N}}$
　　　forms in -ee:

$$T_0 \qquad\qquad\qquad\qquad L \quad H \quad L$$

Bàháushèe	'Hausa man'
Bàkátsínèe	'Kàtsínà man'
Bà'ádárèe	'Ádàr man'

[22] As emphasized in Leben 1976c, 1977, this account does not presuppose that the morphologically complex words in (72) are technically derived from morphologically simple ones. In fact there is good reason to suppose that many of them are in the lexicon—in particular, because we cannot always predict which morphological rules a given word can undergo or what the semantic interpretation of the "derived" form will be. For this reason, we may construe these as rules which parse the lexicon, establishing the degree of relatedness between one lexical item and another. Various proposals for implementing this approach are considered in Jackendoff 1975, Aronoff 1976, and Leben and Robinson 1977.

e. Passive participles: $[\text{XC}]_{\text{verb stem}}$ → $[\text{XC} + a\text{CC} + ee]$

$$T_0 \qquad\qquad L \quad H$$

ríɓée	'rot'	*ríɓáɓɓée*	'rotten'
dàamáa	'bother'	*dàamámmée*	'disturbed'

Sample Derivations (using Mapping Rules [52b, c]):

i. /tuul + unaa/   *tuul + unaa*   *tuul + unaa*

        $\xrightarrow{\text{(52b)}}$ $\xrightarrow{\text{(52c)}}$

      H L   H L   H L

ii. /maalam + ai/   *maalam + ai*   *maalam + ai*

        $\xrightarrow{\text{(52b)}}$ $\xrightarrow{\text{(52c)}}$

      L   H   L   H   L   H

It would be technically possible to write rules (72a–e) in a way consistent with treating tone as a feature of syllables or segments. For example, we might replace the derived tonal pattern LH in (72b) with $L_1 H$, with L_1 interpreted to yield as many instances of L as there are syllables in the stem. But this approach would permit morphological rules to specify tone patterns of the following sort for stems as well: $L_0 H$, $H(LH_0)$, and so on. The first pattern would be realized as H on a one-syllable stem, LH on a two-syllable stem, LLH on a three-syllable stem, etc. Yet for all derivational processes of Hausa (outside the verbal grade system),[23] if they replace a tone pattern, the pattern they impose is uniform, regardless of the segmental composition of the stem. The suprasegmental representation of the tonal outputs in (72) makes this a necessary fact, while segmental representation would make this a curious accident.

4.3 Feminines

There are several types of morphological relationship between masculines and feminines in Hausa. For a small minority of adjectives, the masculine and

---

[23] Even within the grade system, this generalization is nearly correct. The tonal realization of Parsons' 1971/72 "primary" Grades 1, 2, 3 is in part dependent on the number of syllables in the stem, but these three grades are basic: There is no semantic or morphological basis for considering any of them to be derived forms. Hence they do not violate the generalization in the text. On semantic grounds, we might consider Grade 4 to be derived, since it normally adds a notion of completeness to the basic meaning, and morphological grounds might support the derived status of Grade 4, since it can be used by any stem whose basic form is in any of the primary grades. Grade 4 stands as a counterexample to the independence of tones from segments in derived forms, since two-syllable forms have the pattern HL, three-syllable forms have the patterns HLH or HLH, and four-syllable forms have the pattern HHLL. But the tone pattern of Grade 4 is the same as that for Grade 1. This situation is analogous to the one described in Section 3.3 for feminines that are formed by replacing a masculine ending. In the present case, we could say that a Grade 4 form is derived by replacing a Grade 1 ending with the corresponding Grade 4 ending. For the remaining grades, the generalization in the text holds true. The Grade 5 (causative) ending *-ár* is preceded by a uniform H; the Grade 6 ending *-óo* is also preceded by a uniform H; and the Grade 7 (passive) ending *-ú* is preceded by a uniform L.

feminine are identical: *bàbbá* 'big', *jáa* 'red'; *tsánwáa* 'green'. Another, some-what larger, set contains nouns as well as adjectives whose stem occurs with either a masculine or a feminine ending: *jàakíi* (m.)/*jàakáa* (f.) 'donkey'; *ràakúmíi* (m.)/*ràakúmáa* (f.) 'camel'; *fáríi* (m.)/*fáráa* (f.) 'white'; *gàjéerée* (m.)/*gàjéeráa* (f.) 'short'. Finally, the greatest number of masculines and feminines are morphologically related by attaching the feminine marker *-aa* onto the masculine form, occasionally with suppletion of the masculine ending by some other syllable. The derivation of feminines of this third type provides additional support for the suprasegmental representation of tone in Hausa.

In general, the tonal relationship between these masculines and feminines is what we would expect from applying the mapping rules (52b, c) and Low Tone Raising (66). The following examples illustrate the point:

73.

Masculine	Feminine	
a. *dóogóo*	*dóogóo + áa > dóogùwáa*	'tall'
b. *ƙáatòo*	*ƙáatòo + áa > ƙáatùwáa*	'huge'
c. *dàbíinòo*	*dàbíinòo + áa > dàbíinùwáa*	'date palm'

We can derive these feminines in the following way, taking the feminine marker *-aa* to be inherently toneless.

74.

a. /doogoo + aa/   doogoo + aa
    \\/ $\xrightarrow{(52c)}$ \\/
    H   H

b. /ƙaatoo + aa/   ƙaatoo + aa   ƙaatoo + aa
   | | $\xrightarrow{(52c)}$ | | $\xrightarrow{(66)}$ \\ \\ |
   H L   H L   H L H

c. /dabiinoo + aa/   dabiinoo + aa   dabiinoo + aa
   | \\ \\ $\xrightarrow{(52c)}$ | \\ \\/ $\xrightarrow{(66)}$ | \\ \\ |
   L H L   L H L   L H L H

Some cases differ from these only in that the masculine ending is replaced by the syllable *-nii-* in the corresponding feminine:

75.

Masculine	Feminine	
a. *màráayàa*	*màráay-nìi-áa > màráynìyáa*	'orphan'
b. *ɓàráawòo*	*ɓàráaw-nìi-áa > ɓàráwnìyáa*	'thief'

Similar to (75), apart from a tonal modification, is the pair *jínjìríi* (m.)/ *jínjírnìyáa* (f.) 'baby'. We could describe the correspondence between the L of the second syllable of the masculine and the H of the corresponding syllable of the feminine with the following rule:

76.   Tone Spreading: $L \to H \mathrel{/} H \underline{\quad\quad} L$ (in feminines)

The correspondence expressed by this rule provides additional support for the suprasegmental representation of tone in Hausa. The reason for this, simply, is that the domain of L which is raised to H by (76) is indifferent to the number or type of syllables over which L ranges. To see this, consider the feminine forms of the agent nominals from (72c):

77.

Masculine	Feminine		
a. *mátàmbàyíi*	*má + támbáy + ìi + áa > mátámbáyìyáa*	'questioner'
b. *márùbùucíi*	*má + rúbúuc + ìi + áa > márúbúucìyáa*	'writer'
c. *mábìyíi*	*má + bí + ìi + àa > mábíyìyáa*	'follower'

The L of the verb stem in the masculine is realized as H in the feminine, whether this stem has two syllables, as in (77a, b) or one, as in (77c). It is possible to express this in the segmental theory, by changing the operation in (76) to $L_1 \to H_1$ in the appropriate environment, but such an account misses a point that comes out clearly on the suprasegmental analysis. Despite the different associations between tones and syllables in masculine/feminine pairs, the tone pattern assigned by Rule (72c) is identical for the masculine and the feminine: It is HL, with a predictable H on the last syllable of both the masculine and the feminine. This identity between masculine and feminine tonal patterns is not simply an artifact of this analysis, for the same claim holds true for the first two types of morphologically related masculine/feminine pairs illustrated in the first paragraph of this section, 4.3.

From a suprasegmental point of view, it is clear why a rule shifting a transition from H to L rightward in feminines should not distinguish between stems of one and two syllables: The number of syllables has no bearing on the representation of tone. A segmental treatment could mimic the empirical effects of the tone shift, but without being able to express why LL and L should behave identically.

The suprasegmental analysis will want to carry out roughly the following operation in deriving the feminine agent nominals and the form *jínjírnìyáa*:

78.   a. /ma + tambay + ii + aa/   *ma + tambay + ii + aa*

$$\text{H} \qquad \text{L} \qquad > \quad \text{H} \qquad \text{L}$$

          b. /jinjir + nii + aa/   *jinjir + nii + aa*

$$\text{H L} \qquad\qquad\qquad > \text{H L}$$

The following reformulation of (76) would work:

79.   Tone Spreading: QCVX   QCVY

                              ╲╲   │ │   in feminines

                              H L → H L

But in light of the Mende result, in which a modification of the tone assignment procedure eliminated the need for Tone Spreading as a separate rule, we might equally well propose the following alternative. A tone pattern that ends in L is assigned to a feminine form by associating L with the syllable in the position of the masculine ending. This is expressed in the following rule:

80.   Tone Assignment: X CV + *aa*   X CV + *aa*

                                              /   in feminines

              T_0 L   → T_0 L

The derivation of examples like those in (78) would now proceed as follows:

81. a. /ma + tambay + ii + aa/   *ma + tambay + ii + aa*   *ma + tambay + ii + aa*

                                          ──(80)──▶   ──(52b, c)──▶

        H   L   H   L   H   L

                                                                ma + tambay + ii + aa

                                                                ──(66)──▶

                                                                    H   L   H

    b. /jinjir + nii + aa/   *jinjir + nii + aa*   *jinjir + nii + aa*

                                          ──(80)──▶   ──(52b, c)──▶

        H L   H L   H   L

                                                                jinjir + nii + aa

                                                                ──(66)──▶

                                                                    H   L   H

The following discussion is neutral with respect to the choice between the alternatives of (79) and (80).

Churma 1975 has argued that it is questionable to maintain that the tone pattern of the feminine is derived from the masculine, both in agentives like (77) and in feminines in general. For agentives Churma proposes instead that masculine agent nominals be assigned the tone pattern $H(L)_1$ and that corresponding feminines be assigned the tone pattern $(H)_1 LL$. Other feminines derived by adding -*aa* to the masculine are divided into two classes. In the first of these, the tone pattern is BLL, where B is the tone pattern of the stem; the first L of BLL is assigned to the syllable corresponding to the final syllable of the masculine, and the second L, assigned to -*aa*, will be raised to H by Rule (66). Churma's second class of feminines consists of forms that are exceptions to the pattern BLL.

This alternative misses the relationship between the masculine and feminine tone patterns in (78). Worse, it misses the fact that this correctly characterizes the relationship between virtually all masculine/feminine pairs in which the feminine is derived by adding -*aa* to the masculine, like those in (73). Here is a more complete table of typical masculine/feminine pairs in the language:

82.   a. Agent nominals (see [77])
    b. Participles

Masculine	Feminine	
ribáɓɓée	ribáɓɓée + áa > ribáɓɓìyáa	'rotten'
rùbùutáccée	rùbùutácc + ée + áa > rùbùutácciyáa	'written'

    c. Place of origin nominals in -*èe*

Bàkátsínèe	Bàkátsín + èe + áa > Bàkátsíniyáa	'Kàtsínà person'
Bànúfèe	Bànúf + èe + áa > Bànúfiyáa	'Núfée person'
Bàdáurèe	Bàdáur + èe + áa > Bàdáurìyáa	'Dàurá person'
Bà'ámíríkèe	Bà'ámírík + èe + áa > Bà'ámíríkìyáa	'person from America'

    d. Simple nouns and adjectives
     (1) Masculine = HL
      (*a*) No suppletion of masculine ending

ƙáatòo	ƙáatòo + áa > ƙáatùwáa	'huge'
shéegèe	shéegèe + áa > shéegìyáa	'bastard'
gúrgùu	gúrgùu + áa > gúrgùwáa	'lame'

      (*b*) Suppletion of masculine ending by *Vnii*

yáaròo	yáarínìi + àa > yáarínyàa	'child'
bírìi	bírínìi + àa > bírínyàa	'monkey'
báràa	báránìi + àa > bárányàa	'servant'
záakìi	záakánìi + àa > záakányàa	'lion'

     (2) Masculine = LHL
      (*a*) No suppletion of masculine ending

dàbíinòo	dàbíinòo + áa > dàbíinùwáa	'date palm'
jàaríirìi	jàaríirìi + áa > jàaríirìyáa	'baby'

      (*b*) Suppletion of masculine ending

màráayàa	màráaynìi + áa > màráynìyáa	'orphan'
ɓàráawòo	ɓàráawnìi + áa > ɓàráwnìyáa	'thief'
ƙànƙánèe	ƙànƙánòo + áa > ƙànƙánùwáa	'small'
hànƙáakàa	hànƙáakìi + áa > hànƙáakìyáa	'crow'

     (3) Masculine = HLH

jínjìríi	jínjírnìi + áa > jínjírnìyáa	'baby'

     (4) Masculine = (L)HH
      (*a*) No suppletion of masculine ending

dóogóo	dóogóo + áa > dóogúwáa	'tall'
tsúntsúu	tsúntsúu + áa > tsúntsùwáa	'bird'

      (*b*) Suppletion of masculine ending

béebée	béebìi + áa > béebìyáa	'deaf mute'
àbóokíi	àbóokìi + áa > àbóokìyáa	'companion'
gàjéerée	gàjéerìi + áa > gàjéerìyáa	'short'

     (5) Masculine = LH

zàabóo	zàabóo + áa > zàabúwáa	'guinea fowl'
ɓàaƙóo	ɓàaƙóo + áa > ɓàaƙúwáa	'visitor'
kàrée	kàrée + áa > kàryáa	'dog'

The same rules employed in (81) generate the feminines in (82).[24] Here are some sample derivations:

83. a. (see [81])

b. /riɓaɓɓee/   riɓaɓɓee
    | (52b, c)
    L H   ⟶   L H

    /riɓaɓɓee + aa/   riɓaɓɓiyaa
    | (52b, c) | V
    L H   ⟶   L H

c. /ba + katsin + ee/   ba + katsin + ee
    | | (52b, c)   ⟍| |
    L   H   L   ⟶   L   H   L

    /ba + katsin + ee + aa/   ba + katsin + ee + aa   ba + katsin + ee + aa
    | | (52b, c) | ⟍| | (66) | ⟍| | |
    L   H   L   ⟶   L   H   L   ⟶   L   H   L   H

d. (1) /yaarinii + aa/   yaarinii + aa   yaarinii + aa   yaarinyaa
                       (80) | (52b, c)   V   V   V   /
        H   L   ⟶   H   L   ⟶   H   L   >   H   L

    (2) /dabiinoo + aa/   dabiinoo + aa   dabiinoo + aa
                       (80)   ⟍   (52b, c) | | ⟍V
        L H L   ⟶   L H L   ⟶   L H L

                                                                dabiinoo + aa
                                                    (66)   ⟍ ⟍⟍ ⟍
                                                   ⟶   L H L   H

    (3) (see [81b])

    (4) /doogoo + aa/   doogoo + aa
                       (52b, c)   V⟍
        H   ⟶   H

    (5) /zaaboo + aa/   zaaboo + aa
                       (52b, c) | V
        L H   ⟶   L H

The last stage in (83d.1) is produced by segmental rules described in Leben 1971a.

The close correspondence between the tonal patterns of the masculines and feminines in the different constructions illustrated above is missed in separate feminine formulas like $(H)_1LL$, BLL, BHLL, etc. Churma attempts to cast doubt on the regularity of the correspondence by citing the cases in (82d 4. *b*) and by considering a construction similar to the one in (82c). For the latter, Churma comments that their structure is too variable to be accounted for by

---

[24] There is some suppletion in the simple nouns and adjectives in (82d). Since it is impossible in general to predict which forms undergo suppletion and what the shape of the suppletive endings is, this argues for the interpretation proposed in footnote 22.

rules. But this is not correct. These forms fall into three separate classes. The first, illustrated in (82c), is derived by (72d). This is the most productive of the three classes. The remaining two are illustrated here:

84.   a. Masculines in *-ii*; feminines in *-aa*

Masculine	Feminine	
Bàgòobíríi	Bàgòobíráa	'Gòobír person'
Bàdàuríi	Bàdàuráa	'Dàurá person'
Bàfàránshìi	Bàfàránsàa	'French person'

    b. Masculines in $\emptyset$; feminines in *-aa*

Bàkánòo	Bàkánùwáa	'Kánòo person'
Bànúfée	—	'Núfée person'
Bàgwáaríi	—	'Gwáaríi person'
Bàtàmbúutùu	—	'Timbuktu person'

Both constructions add prefix *bà-* to a place name. In (84a), the suffix *-ii* is attached to the stem. The tone of *-ii* is derived in precisely the same way described in (68). The feminine form undergoes the same derivation, but with *-aa* in place of *-ii*. (Recall that this is one way of forming feminines; cf. *fárii* [m.]/ *fáráa* [f.] 'white'; *gàjéerée* [m.]/*gàjéeráa* [f.] 'short'.) In (84b), no suffix is attached to the masculine. The only attested feminine I know of is *Bàkánùwáa*, which is formed from the masculine in the regular way.

Thus, forms with *bà-* prefix, far from casting doubt on the regularity of the relationship between masculines and feminines, actually offer additional support for it.

We can conclude from this discussion of Hausa that a suprasegmental treatment of tone is not only feasible but also capable of expressing tonal relationships that are beyond the capacity of a purely segmental account. Furthermore, the analyses of Etsako, Mende, and Hausa proposed in this paper represent quite an improvement over earlier suprasegmental treatments. This demonstrates the value of incorporating Goldsmith's well-formedness condition and autosegmental representations into the suprasegmental framework.

REFERENCES

Aronoff, M. 1976. Word formation in generative grammar. *Linguistic Inquiry*, Monograph 1.
Churma, D. G. 1975. Is Hausa a suprasegmental language? In R. K. Herbert (Ed.), *Proceedings of 6th Conference on African Linguistics. Working Papers in Linguistics*, Ohio State Univ. Department of Linguistics, *20*.
Dwyer, D. 1971. Mende tone. *Studies in African Linguistics*, *2*, 117–130.
Dwyer, D. What is a suprasegmental tone language? Manuscript.
Edmondson, T., Bendor-Samuel, J. T. 1966. Tone patterns of Etung. *Journal of African Languages*, *5*, 1–6.
Elimelech, B. 1976. A tonal grammar of Etsako. *UCLA Working Papers in Phonetics 35*.

Firth, J. R. 1957. *Papers in linguistics, 1934–1951*. London: Oxford Univ. Press.

Goldsmith, J. 1975. Tone melodies and the autosegment. In R. K. Herbert (*Ed.*), *Proceedings of the 6th Conference on African Linguistics. Working Papers in Linguistics*, Ohio State Univ. Department of Linguistics, *20*.

Goldsmith, J. 1976a. An overview of autosegmental phonology. *Linguistic Analysis, 2*, 23–68.

Goldsmith, J. 1976b. Autosegmental phonology. Ph.D. dissertation. MIT. Repr. by Indiana Univ. Linguistics Club.

Halle, M. 1973. Stress rules in English: A new version. *Linguistic Inquiry, 4*, 451–464.

Hyman, L. M., Schuh, R. G. 1974. Univerals of tone rules: Evidence from West Africa. *Linguistic Inquiry, 5*, 81–115.

Innes, G. 1963. *The structure of sentences in Mende*. University of London, School of Oriental and African Studies.

Innes, G. 1967. *A practical introduction to Mende*. University of London, School of Oriental and African Studies.

Innes, G. 1969. *A Mende–English dictionary*. Cambridge: Cambridge Univ. Press.

Jackendoff, R. 1975. Morphological and semantic regularities in the lexicon. *Language, 51*, 639–671.

Jakobson, R. 1937. On Ancient Greek prosody. In *Selected Writings*, vol. 1. The Hague: Mouton, 1971. Pp. 262–271.

Kiparsky, P. 1968. How abstract is phonology? Published as a section of "Phonological representation," by P. Kiparsky. In O. Fujimuria (*Ed.*), *Three dimensions of linguistic theory*. Tokyo: TEC, 1973. Pp. 5–56.

Leben, W. R. 1971a. The morphophonemics of tone in Hausa. In C-W. Kim & H. Stahlke (Eds.), *Papers in African linguistics*. Edmonton, Alberta: Linguistic Research. Pp. 201–218.

Leben, W. R. 1971b. Suprasegmental and segmental representation of tone. *Studies in African Linguistics*, Supp. 2, pp. 183–200.

Leben, W. R. 1973a. The role of tone in segmental phonology. In L. M. Hyman (Ed.), *Consonant types and tone*. Linguistics Program, University of Southern California. Pp. 117–149.

Leben, W. R. 1973b. Suprasegmental phonology. Unpublished Ph.D. dissertation, MIT.

Leben, W. R. 1976a. The tones in English intonation. *Linguistic Analysis, 2*, 69–107.

Leben, W. R. 1976b. On the interpretive function of phonological rules. Paper presented at the 3rd International Phonology Meeting, University of Vienna, September. To appear in *Phonologica Innsbrucker Beiträge zur Sprachwissenschatt, 19*.

Leben, W. R. 1976c. Parsing Hausa plurals. To appear in P. Newman & R. M. Newman (Eds.), *Papers in Chadic linguistics*. Leiden: Afrika-Studiecentrum.

Leben, W. R. 1977. Doubling and reduplication in Hausa plurals. In A. Juilland (Ed.), *Linguistic studies offered to Joseph Greenberg on the occasion of his sixtieth birthday*. Saratoga, California: Anma Libri. Vol. 2, pp. 419–439.

Leben, W. R., Bagari, D. M. 1975. A note on the base form of the Hausa verb. *Studies in African Linguistics, 6*, 239–248.

Leben, W. R., Robinson, O. W. 1977. "Upside-down" phonology. *Language, 53*, 1–20.

Maddieson, I. 1971. Tone in generative phonology. *Research Notes*, University of Ibadan, *3*.

McCawley, J. D. 1964. What is a tone language? Presented at summer meeting, Linguistic Society of America.

McCawley, J. D. 1970. Some tonal systems that come close to being pitch-accent systems but don't quite make it. In *Papers from the 6th Regional Meeting, Chicago Linguistic Society*. Pp. 526–532.

Parsons, F. W. 1971/1972. Suppletion and neutralization in the verbal system of Hausa. *Afrika und Ubersee, 55*, 49–97.

Pike, K. L. 1948. *Tone languages*. Ann Arbor, Michigan: Univ. of Michigan Press.

Rowlands, E. C. 1959. *A grammar of Gambian Mandinka*. University of London, School of Oriental and African Studies.

Schachter, P., & Fromkin, V. 1968. A phonology of Akan; Akuapem, Asante, and Fante. *UCLA Working Papers in Phonetics, 9.*

Spears, R. A. 1967a. Basic course in Mende. Evanston, Illinois: Northwestern Univ.

Spears R. A. 1967b. Tone in Mende. *Journal of African Languages, 6,* 231–244.

Trubetzkoy, N. S. 1939. *Grundzüge der phonologie.* Travaux du cercle linguistique de Prague, 7.

Voorhoeve, J. 1975. Suprasegmental phonology. *York Papers in Linguistics,* Univ. of York, Department of Language, pp. 21–31.

Wang, W. S-Y. 1967. The phonological features of tone. *International Journal of American Linguistics, 33,* 93–105.

Welmers, W. E. 1962. The phonology of Kpelle. *Journal of African Languages 1,* 69–93.

Woo, N. H. 1969. Prosody and phonology. Ph.D. dissertation, MIT. Repr. by Indiana Univ. Linguistics Club.

VII

Tone Rules[1]

RUSSELL G. SCHUH

1. THE FORMALIZATION OF TONE RULES

While significant differences exist between tonal phenomena and segmental phenomena, the general form of tone rules does not differ from that of rules in segmental phonology. Thus, in a transformational–generative phonology, tones are specified in terms of features (binary in most studies), and rules effect changes in feature values in specified environments. Likewise, many of the same theoretical questions which have arisen in generative phonology apply to tonal as well as segmental phenomena, for example: What are the features needed in a universal phonetic feature inventory? Should only binary specifications for features be allowed? What limits should be placed on abstractness of representations? Should the extrinsic ordering of rules be allowed? etc.

A discussion of tone rules must assume a certain set of features needed to specify tone and must further assume an answer to the question concerning whether tone specifications should be part of the segmental matrix or represented, instead, in a separate suprasegmental matrix. Both of these issues are discussed in detail elsewhere in this volume (Anderson and Leben, respectively). I will therefore simply state the framework which I have adopted for my discussion on tone rules.

With respect to tone features, I have adopted a rather pragmatic position. In the discussion, the name by which a tone is generally called will be used, e.g., HI, MID, LO, RISE, etc. In rules for a language with two level tones,

---

[1] Sources for most of the data here are given in the list of references. Data for Bade, Duwai, and, in some cases, Ngizim and Hausa are from my own field notes. Work on Ngizim was done in Potiskum, Nigeria, in 1969–1970 under the auspices of a National Science Foundation grant, GS-2279 (Paul Newman, Principal Investigator). Work on Bade and Duwai was done in Gashua, Nigeria, from 1973–1975 while I was employed as a Senior Research Fellow in the Centre for the Study of Nigerian Languages of Ahmadu Bello University.

221

[±HI] will be used. For languages with three or more level tones, and for "contour" tones (surface or lexical) the meaning of the features used will be made clear at that point in the discussion. Only binary features will be used.

As to the segmental versus the suprasegmental question, my decision requires a little more discussion. Leben (1973:117) notes several types of representations that have been proposed for tone: suprasegmental where tones are features on entire words, morphemes, or syllables, and segmental representations where tones are specified as part of the matrices of segments, usually the [+syllabic] segments. One reason for this variety of proposals is that tone rules in some cases operate independent of any segmental information but in other cases interact with segmental information. For example, in both Ngizim and Duwai, two closely related Chadic languages, there is a rule LO HI HI → LO LO HI. In Duwai this rule operates anytime the tonal configuration is met, but in Ngizim it operates only if the syllable to be lowered begins in a voiced, non-glottalized consonant:[2]

1.	Duwai:	/kəvús ɓái/	→ kəvùs ɓái	'it's not a warthog'
		/mərí ɓái/	→ mərì ɓái	'it's not a beard'
		/ùuɗáu ɓái/	→ ùudə̀ ɓái	'it's not mush'
		/tùnkó ɓái/	→ tùnkò ɓái	'it's not a sheep'
	Ngizim:	/gùbə́s bái/	→ gùbə̀s bái	'it's not a warthog'
		/màrí bái/	→ màrì bái	'it's not a beard'
		/àaɗáu bái/	→ àaɗùu bái	'it's not south'
		/tə̀màakú bái/	→ tə̀màakú bái	'it's not a sheep'

In Duwai, since segmental information is irrelevant, we would like a rule of the form [+HI] → [−HI] / [−HI] ____ [+HI]; but if tones were specified as features on segments (presumably the vowel of each syllable), all the irrelevant intervening consonants would have to be included in the rule as well. The Ngizim rule, on the other hand, will have to make reference to segmental information, so a segmental specification of tone seems necessary.[3]

The Duwai rule illustrates one of the drawbacks of a purely segmental representation for tone, namely, that in a large number of tone rules, a basically simple rule will have to be cluttered with irrelevant segmental information. At least two other arguments against a purely segmental representation for tone can be sated. One involves floating tones (see Section 7 and other examples

---

[2] In citations from African and Mexican languages, the following tones markings will be used: ´ indicates HI, ` indicates LO, ⁻ indicates MID. In languages with more than three level tones, tone markings will be explained in the text. Phonetic falling glide is indicated ^, and rising glide is ˇ. Downstep (lowered HI after HI) is indicated by ' before a HI syllable, e.g., bá'bá (HI Downstep).

[3] If the Ngizim rule uses all segmental features, including the specification of tone, irrelevant segmental information will have to be included there, as well, since the segmental makeup of the environmental syllables is irrelevant, just as in Duwai.

in this chapter) where questionable specifications such as

$$\begin{bmatrix} + \text{seg} \\ + \text{HI} \end{bmatrix}$$

(cf. Schachter and Fromkin 1968) or

$$\begin{bmatrix} - \text{seg} \\ + \text{HI} \end{bmatrix}$$

(cf. Fromkin 1972) have been used (with no other features of the segment specified). A more serious problem with purely segmental features involves languages where a limited number of tonal patterns are used regardless of length of the word (see Section 3.2). For example, a language may have only words with all high tones or with a tone pattern HI LO. The HI LO pattern would be realized as FALL on a monosyllable, HI LO on a disyllable, and HI MID LO on a trisyllable. This generalization could not be captured if tones are represented as features of vowels. It is for reasons such as this, among others, that Leben (1971a, 1973, and Chapter VI, this volume) argues for a suprasegmental representation of tone.

As shown from the examples in Duwai and Ngizim given above, tone is **both** suprasegmental and segmental: It is suprasegmental since a single tone feature can range over several segments, and conversely a single segment can bear more than one tone; it is segmental because tone distinctions can be realized only through pitch and/or amplitude differences between segments or groups of segments.[4] The most desirable approach is clearly to represent this fact about tone as directly as possible. I therefore propose to use the following formalism: Where both tone and segmental features are mentioned in a single rule, vertical slashes will represent the domain of a tone and the segments over which it ranges. For most of the languages discussed below, the domain of a tone will be a single syllable, and in these cases syllable boundaries, represented as $, can serve as well. Thus, for a word/syllable *tám* (with high tone), the representation would be as in (2a), and for *tâm* (with falling tone) it would be as in (2b) or (2c). In a formal statement, the segments would be represented as feature matrices, of course:

2.

    a. *tám* $\left| \begin{matrix} [+\text{HI}] \\ \text{tam} \end{matrix} \right|$ or $\$ \begin{matrix} [+\text{HI}] \\ \textit{tam} \end{matrix} \$$

    b. *tâm* $\left| \begin{matrix} [+\text{HI}][-\text{HI}] \\ \text{tam} \end{matrix} \right|$ or $\$ \begin{matrix} [+\text{HI}][-\text{HI}] \\ \textit{tam} \end{matrix} \$$

    c. *tâm* $\left| \begin{matrix} [\text{FALL}] \\ \text{tam} \end{matrix} \right|$ or $\$ \begin{matrix} [+\text{FALL}] \\ \textit{tam} \end{matrix} \$$

---

[4] Floating tones (see Section 7) might appear to be an exception to this, but even here the existence of tones is realized only by pitch-changing effects on segments.

Using this formalism, the statement of the Ngizim rule illustrated in (1) would be:

3. $[+\mathrm{HI}] \rightarrow [-\mathrm{HI}] / [-\mathrm{HI}] \ \$ \underline{\hspace{3cm}} \$ \ [+\mathrm{HI}]$
$$\begin{bmatrix} -\mathrm{syll} \\ +\mathrm{voice} \\ -\mathrm{glott} \end{bmatrix} \mathrm{X}$$

2. INTERACTION OF TONES AND SEGMENTS

In recent years, there has been considerable interest in the ways in which tones and the segments over which they range interact (see Hyman 1973a, Hyman and Schuh 1974, Mohr 1973, and, in particular, Hombert, Chapter III, this volume). Almost all the examples of interaction of tone and segments involve consonants. The few cases of a connection between tone and vowel height are unconvincing or have alternative explanations (cf. Hombert 1976 and Chapter III, this volume). A few cases of tone correlation with syllable structure are known, e.g., see (52) below. Some of the rules in later sections involve tone–segment interaction, but a general statement of the types of relations seen between tones and consonant types is given here.

2.1 Do Segments Influence Tone or Does Tone Influence Segments?

The major fact that emerges from the study of tone–segment interactions is that it is virtually always segments which influence tone; tone rarely, if ever, influences segments. Maddieson (1974) presents six examples which he claims show the falsity of the statement by Hyman and Schuh (1974) that "**consonants affect tone, but tone does not affect consonants** [p. 108]." Hyman (1976) replies to Maddieson and presents alternative explanations for each of Maddieson's claimed examples of tonal effects on consonants. Presumably, the examples presented by Maddieson are among the best to be found in the literature. Even if all six of these were clear cases of tonal effects on consonants, when compared with the dozens (if not hundreds) of known cases of segmental effects on tones, they would hardly justify Maddieson's statement that "tonal effects on consonants are fairly widespread [p. 21]." It is not clear, however, that any of his examples are cases of tonal influence on segments if tone is understood in the normal sense of "pitch" (cf. Hyman 1976:94). Pitch is often not the only phonetic correlate of a given tone. Thus, low tones are often accompanied by creaky or breathy voice, high tones by greater amplitude. These features accompanying differences in pitch **may** affect segments. In Jingpho, perhaps Maddieson's (1948:18–19) strongest case for tonal effects on segments, a process of gemination in morphemes with low tone produces voiced obstruents from voiceless, whereas obstruents remain voiceless with morphemes having high tone:

4.   *yàk* 'difficult'   *yàggai* 'it is difficult'
       cát 'tight'   *cáttai* 'it is tight'

Hyman (1976:92) points out that low tone in Jingpho is accompanied by breathiness and suggests the voicing is correlated with this feature rather than with pitch.

In Bade, initial *$*C\partial$* has metathesized to *∂C* if the C could permissibly abut with the next consonant except where *$*C\partial$* carried high tone:[5]

5.   *ə̀dgà* < *$*də̀gà$* 'arrow'   but   *də́gà* 'platform'
       ə̀lvú < *$*lə̀vú$* 'sip'   but   *lə́vùwà* 'chaff'

Here the explanation seems to be the extra amplitude associated with high tone which has prevented metathesis.

In summary, virtually no clear cases of tonal influence on segments have been found, whereas the opposite case is common in all areas where tone languages are found.

2.2 Rules in Which Consonants Block or Allow Natural Tone Processes

In Hyman and Schuh (1974) it was argued that a clear distinction must be made between two types of consonantal effects on tones: cases where natural tone processes are **permitted or blocked** by consonants of different types and cases where different consonant types **cause** tonal changes. The former type is discussed in this section, the latter in Section 2.3.

The most commonly found natural tonal process where consonant types may block the process is **tone spreading**, i.e., the tendency for the tone of a syllable to continue into the next syllable (cf. Section 3.1). The most common tone spreading rules are presented schematically as follows:

6.   HI spreading: HI LO X → HI HI X
       LO spreading: LO HI X → LO LO X

The conditions on what X may be vary from language to language (see Section 3.1 for more details).

Typical consonantal interaction with HI spreading can be illustrated with the following languages: In Bade HI spreading takes place unless the LO syllable begins in a nonglottalized voiced obstruent, including prenasalized

---

[5] A better description of this process than "metathesis" is "*ə* weakening." What has actually happened is that the *ə* of *$*C\partial$* weakened and dropped, which occasioned addition of a prothetic *ə* to prevent a word initial consonant cluster from forming. This prothetic *ə* always deletes when preceded by a vowel.

voiced stops; in Bolanci (Lukas 1969) HI spreading takes place unless the LO syllable begins in a non-prenasalized voiced obstruent; in Zulu (Cope 1970) HI spreading takes place unless the LO syllable begins in a "depressor" consonant:[6]

7. Bade: /nə́n kàtáw/   → *nə́n ká'táw*   'I returned'
                /nə́n ɗàmáw/   → *nə́n ɗá'máw*   'I submerged'
                /nə́n làwáw/   → *nə́l lá'wáw*   'I ran'
                /nə́n gàfáw/   → *nə́n gàfáw*   'I caught'

     Bolanci: /kŭm sàawùrà/ → *kŭm sáawùrà* 'ear of a falcon'
                /kŭm nzìmòkì/ → *kŭm nzímòkì* 'ear of an eagle'
                /kŭm zòngé/   → *kŭm zòngé*   'ear of a hyena'

     Zulu: /àɓáyìbónì/   → *àɓáyì'bóni*   'they do not see it'
                /àɓázìbónì/   → *àɓázìbónì*   'they do not see them'

Two points should be noted here. First, those consonants over or through which HI does **not** spread are in all cases the class of nonglottalized voiced obstruents: Second, HI tone **does** spread through sonorants, as well as through voiceless and glottalized obstruents.

Now consider the following cases of LO spreading where consonants play a role: In Ngizim (Schuh 1971) LO spreading takes place unless the syllable which would be affected begins in a voiceless or glottalized obstruent: In Nupe (George 1970) LO spreading operates only through a voiced segment:[7]

8.   Ngizim: /à gáfì/   → *à gàfì*   'catch!'
                       /à ráwí/   → *à ràwí*   'run!'
                       /à ɗálmí/   → *à ɗálmí* 'repair!'
                       /à káčí/   → *à káčí*   'return!'
              Nupe: /èbé/   → *èbĕ*   'pumpkin'
                       /èlé/   → *èlĕ*   'past'
                       /èfú/   → *èfú*   'honey'

For these alternations note that those consonants through which LO does **not** spread are in both cases the voiceless (and, in Ngizim, the glottalized) obstruents; second, note that LO tone **does** spread through sonorants as well as voiced obstruents.

Not all languages which have tone spreading rules have consonantal restrictions such as those illustrated in (7) and (8), e.g., Duwai illustrated in (1). However, all the cases known to me where consonants do interact with tone

---

[6] Cope (1970) describes Zulu depressors as having "the distinctive feature of heaviness, which may be described as glottal friction with heavy voice, a combination of breath ($+$h) and voice ($+$v), neither of which is distinctive in itself [p. 113]."

[7] The LO Spreading rule of Nupe is somewhat different from the others here in that it operates on the pattern LO HI, with nothing following the HI, and it produces a rising glide (LO HI on a single syllable) rather than replacing the HI. This will be returned to in Section 3.1.

show the same partial complementary distribution of consonant classes through which HI and LO tones can spread, namely, HI tones cannot spread through voiced obstruents, and LO tones cannot spread through voiceless obstruents. As shown in Hyman and Schuh (1974), voiced obsturents must be interpreted as **blocking** the spread of HI and voiceless obstruents as **blocking** the spread of LO, rather than the reverse interpretation where voiceless obstruents **cause** the spread of HI and voiced the spread of LO. This is clear since spreading of both HI and LO takes place with sonorants. To quote Hyman and Schuh (1974):

> While we can understand that voiceless obstruents are of a stone raising nature and voiced obstruents are of a tone-lowering nature, [in accepting a "causation" hypothesis for tone spreading] we would be forced to conclude that sonorants are of a raising and a lowering nature simultaneously [p. 108].

The "blocking" hypothesis, on the other hand, says that voiced obstruents and voiceless obstruents are antithetical to HI and LO tones, respectively, and hence hinder the spread of these tones, whereas sonorants are antithetical to neither and allow all tones to spread. Note that "antithetical" does not mean "in direct opposition" but rather expresses a tendency. Hence, there are languages like Yoruba where both HI and LO spreading take place through any consonant. A "causation" account would not be able to explain this at all, except by sone nonphonological process such as analogical spread of the original process to environments where it had not applied.

   Tone assimilation (see Section 4.1) is another type of tonal process where consonant types may be seen as blocking rather than causing the process. In tonal assimilation, tones are raised or lowered in the environment of higher or lower tones, respectively. Examples are found in Ewe (Stahlke 1971a, 1971b), where LO consonant-initial noun stems are raised to MID before HI except where the initial consonant of the noun stem is a voiced obstruent:[8]

9.   /Φù lá/ → Φū lá   'the sea'
             /nyì lá/ → nyī lá   'the cow'
             /dà lá/ → dà lá   'the snake'

   On the other hand, MID tone either preceding or following LO is lowered to LO unless the MID syllable begins in a voiceless obstruent.[9] This lowering

---

[8] Both this and the rule illustrated in (10) are in part morphologically conditioned. Roughly speaking, they apply only to noun stems.

[9] There are probably two processes involved in (10). Lowering of MIDs preceding LO is true assimilation, whereas lowering of MIDs following LO is probably spreading of the LO as described for Ngizim and Nupe above. Stahlke (1971a, b) collapses the two process in a mirror image rule for the Kpando dialect, but in the Peki dialect, described by Ansre (1961), certain differences in the behavior of the lowering processes preceding and following the LO make it impossible to collapse the two rules into one.

rule applied iteratively until its environment is no longer met:

10.　/dà wū āmē/　　→ dà wù àmè　　'a snake killed a person'
　　/āmē wū àfī lá/ → àmè wù àfē lá　'a person killed the mouse'
　　/àfē èvē/　　　→ àfīèvè　　　'two mice'

A similar rule which raises tones iteratively before a HI is seen in Etsako, illustrated in (54) below.

As in the rules for tone spreading, the effect of voiced and voiceless obstruents
on the tonal assimilations must be one of blocking rather than causing, since
syllables beginning in sonorants participate in both raising and lowering
assimilations. Were a causation position adopted, one would again have to
say that sonorants simultaneously cause raising and lowering.

2.3 Rules in Which Consonant Types Cause Tonal Alternations

Tonogenesis (development of pitch as a contrastive feature) and tone splitting
(development of two or more contrastive tones from one) resulting from perturbations in pitch by certain consonant types are discussed elsewhere in greater
detail in this volume (cf. Chapters III and VI, this volume, by Hombert and
Hyman, respectively) and will therefore only be briefly discussed here. Matisoff
(1973), citing the work of Haudricourt, describes how early Vietnamese acquired
mid–level, falling, and rising tones: Words with mid–level tones originally
had no final consonant; those with falling tone originally ended in *h*, which
perturbed pitch downward; and those with rising tone originally ended in
_?_, which perturbed pitch upward. Loss of the final consonants left tone as
the only distinguishing feature for these three classes of morphemes. Later,
these three tones were split into six by exploiting the lowering effect of initial
voiced obstruents. When initial voicing contrast in consonants was lost, the
language was left with six contrastive tones. Similarly, many of the tonal contrasts in modern Chinese languages arose from tone splitting in Middle Chinese,
according to whether the word began in a voiced or voiceless consonant (cf.
Wang 1967:104).

Although differences in pitch perturbations by consonants have given rise
to contrastive tones themselves as well as the development of new tonal contrasts over and over in Asia, I am not familiar with any tonal **alternations**
conditioned by consonant types in Asia (see Section 6.2 for reasons why we
would expect there to be few, if any such alternations). Such consonantally
conditioned alternations do exist in Africa, however.[10] Cope (1970) says that
in Zulu "a high toneme is displaced by a depressor to the following syllable
(CV or CCV or CCCV), whether this syllable is high-toned or low-toned,

[10] Hyman (1973b) states that, to his knowledge, tonal alternations **caused** by consonants are
"unattested in African languages [p. 166]." I believe the example cited below is one such case.

unless this syllable also has a depressor, or unless it is a final syllable [p. 115]." In (11), the alternation does not take place in (a) because the first relevant syllable does not begin in a depressor; it does not take place in (b) because the second relevant syllable begins with a depressor; it does take place in (c) because the first relevant syllable begins in a depressor and the second does not. (The depressors in these data are *z*, *d*, *gq*, *nh*; the nondepressors are *s*, *hl*, and *ny*.)

11.   a. /ìsíhlàlò/ → *isíhlàlò*   'chair'
           /ìsígqòkò/ → *isígqòkò*   'hat'

      b. ìzígqòkò/ → *isígqòkò*   'hats'
           /nhéndòdà/ → *nhéndòdà*   'with a man'

      c. /ìzíhlàlò/ → *izìhlálò* or *izìhlâlò* 'chairs'
           /nhènyònì/ → *nhènyónì* or *nhènyônì* 'with a bird'

I believe there is a more explanatory account of these data than is provided in Cope's statement. It has already been established that Zulu has a HI spreading rule, illustrated in (7). We need simply apply this rule to the underlying forms of (11), then add a rule lowering a syllable beginning in a depressor consonant if it is followed by a HI.[11] Such rules lowering syllables beginning in depressors are found throughout southern Bantu languages, e.g., see Beach (1924:95–97) for Xhosa, and Schachter (1976) for siSwati, and are clear examples of consonants causing tone alternations. The Zulu rules are formalized in (12a–b). They must be applied as ordered:

12. a. *HI Spreading:* $\emptyset \rightarrow [+\text{HI}] \,/\, [+\text{HI}]\ \$\ \underset{[-\text{depressor}]\,X}{\underline{\hspace{2cm}}}\ [\alpha\text{HI}]\ \$\ Y\ \$$
        Condition: $Y \neq \emptyset$
        /nhé \$ nyò \$ nì/ → *nhé \$nyó`\$ nì* 'with a bird'

    b. *Depressor*
        Lowering: $[+\text{HI}] \rightarrow [-\text{HI}] \,/\, \$\underset{[+\text{depressor}]\,X}{\underline{\hspace{2cm}}}\$\ [+\text{HI}]$
        nhé \$ nyò \$ nì → [nhènyônì] 'with a bird'

By describing the Zulu process this way, we account for the fact that an alternate pronunciation for the form in (11c) has a falling tone on the raised syllable. If α in (12a) is −, the [+HI][−HI] sequence may remain, giving falling tone, or may be simplified to [+HI] by tone absorption (see Section 3.1). If α is +, the resultant [+HI][+HI] will be simplified to [+HI].

A similar, but morphologically conditioned, example of tone lowering caused by voiced obstruents is seen in the western dialect of Bade. In this language

---

[11] A problem with this account is that the word for 'chair' in (11a) does not become **isíhlálò* as it should be Cope's (1970:116) own rule, illustrated here in (7). I cannot here say whether 'chair' as given in (11a) is not a phonetic form or if there is some morphological conditioning involved in the rules.

the first syllable of a verb in the subjunctive is LO if it begins in a voiced obstruent, HI otherwise:

13. | *dá gàfì* | 'he should catch' |
     | *dá və̀rnànìyì* | 'he should roll' |
     | *dà tádì* | 'he should release' |
     | *dà háptì* | 'he should lift' |
     | *dà dɔ́bdì* | 'he sould sell' |
     | *dà mə́skə́tì* | 'he should turn' |

3. RULES WHICH DETERMINE THE DOMAIN OF A TONE

There are numerous typologies of tone rules which can be proposed: natural
versus unnatural, phonetic versus grammatical, purely tonal rules versus rules
where segmental information is needed, etc. The major division here is between
rules which change the segmental domain of a given tone versus those where
a tone within a particular segmental domain is changed. To take perhaps the
clearest example of this difference, consider Hyman's (1973b) dichotomy
between **horizontal assimilation** (called **tone spreading** here) and **vertical assimilation** (simply called **assimilation** here). I believe there is a fundamental
difference between these two processes. The first is not assimilation at all, but
rather the extension of a **single** tone beyond its original domain. This process
has already been illustrated in (1), (7), and (8). A typical effect of this extension
will be for the tone which is encroached upon to have its domain restricted,
as in the case of Nupe seen in (8), where an original HI occupies only the latter
part of a syllable after a preceding LO has spread into that syllable. In assimilation (= Hyman's vertical assimilation), tones remain in their original segmental domain but become more like (perhaps identical to) neighboring tones.
A typical example was seen in the Ewe case in (9) where LO was raised to MID
before HI.

A principal reason for making the spreading/assimilation distinction has
to do with phonetic effects of the rules. In segmental phonology, assimilation
involves changes in features, and this is true of tonal assimilations as well.
Thus, in Ewe

$$[+\text{LO}] \rightarrow [-\text{LO}]/\underline{\hspace{1cm}} \begin{bmatrix} +\text{HI} \\ -\text{LO} \end{bmatrix}.$$

However, in many of the cases described here as spreading, tone features on a
given syllable are not changed, but rather the feature of one syllable is extended
to part of another syllable. Thus, LO HI may become LO LO͡ HI (= LO RISE)
as in Nupe. Although I think the spreading/assimilation distinction is important
in understanding and explaining tonal processes, there are cases where it is
not possible to tell which process is involved. In Mandarin, the following rule

is found (Chao and Yang 1962):[12]

14.　　⌐$35 →$ ⌐ $55 / 5$ ____ [– Neutral Tone]

　　e.g., ⌐⌐⌐→⌐⌐⌐　　　*dong nan feng*　'southeast wind'
　　　　⌐⌐⌝→⌐⌐⌝　　　*san nian ji*　'third year class'
　　　　⌐⌐⌐→⌐⌐⌐　　　*Mei Lan-feng*　(a proper name)
　　　　⌐⌐⌐→⌐⌐⌐　　　*guo min dang*　'Kuomintang'

The typology of Chinese languages tends to make me consider this to be a case of assimilation rather than spreading, but I know of no way to prove this one way or the other.

3.1 Spreading, Absorption, and Copying

These three processes are grouped together since in all three, one syllable takes its tone directly from or loses it to an adjacent syllable. In **tone spreading**, a tone moves beyond its original segmental domain to replace or displace the tone of a following syllable or syllables. Hyman (1973b) distinguishes between cases where the tone which spreads completely obliterates the next tone and cases where it only partially displaces the next tone. Examples of complete spreading have already been illustrated in (1) for Duwai and Ngizim, where LO HI HI → LO LO HI and in (7) for Bade, Bolanci, and Zulu, where HI LO LO → HI HI LO. The former type of rule is particularly widespread in Africa, being found not only in the languages already mentioned, but also in Kukuyu (Pratt 1972), Bambara (Leben 1973, citing work by Bird), and Vai (Welmers 1976). An example from Vai follows:

15.　　/mùsú náánì/ → *mùsù náànì* 'four women'
　　　cf. *mùsú fè'á* 'two women', where LO follows the HI

An example of only partial displacement of the original tone by the spreading tone was seen in the Nupe example in (8). In Nupe spreading operates only in the environment LO HI and only if the intervening consonant is voiced. In the Gashua dialect of Bade, on the other hand, spreading operates in a two syllable sequence before pause only with HI LO when the intervening consonant is not a voiced obstruent, e.g., [ákâ] 'fire', [ámâ] 'woman', [ádâ] 'head', but [ábàr] 'puff adder', where in all cases the underlying tones are HI LO. In Yoruba and in Gwari (Hyman and Magaji 1970) spreading operates on both

---

[12] In citing Chinese examples, Chao's tone marking system will be used where a pitch contour is represented as a little graph. The vertical axis is a pitch scale with five points. The horizontal axis represents the direction of movement of the tone, and the numbers accompanying the graph represent the pitches of the endpoints (and in some cases the midpoint) of the horizontal axis, with higher numbers representing higher pitches, e.g., ⌐ *55* is a level tone beginning and ending at Pitch 5, ⟋*13* is a rising tone beginning at Pitch 1 and ending at 3, etc.

LO HI and HI LO, giving LO RISE and HI FALL, respectively. In both these languages, the rule operates irrespective of intervening consonant. Data from Gwari illustrating spreading from LO is given in (16a) and spreading from HI in (16b). Gwari, but not Yoruba, spreads MID into following LO, giving MID MID-FALL, illustrated in (16c):

16.　　　　　a. /òšá/　→ òšǎ　'throat'
　　　　　　　 /òjé/　→ òjě　'cloth'

　　　　　　 b. /súknù/　→ súknû　'bone'
　　　　　　　 /šnínwà/ → šnínwâ　'tree'

　　　　　　 c. /zūkwò/ → zūkw̄ò　'how'
　　　　　　　 /āgyà/　→ āgyā`　'blood'

For languages with more than two level tone contrasts, Hyman and Schuh (1974) observe that if spreading operates at all, it always operates across the greatest interval, that is, between HI and LO or LO and HI. The Gwari MID spreading rule then suggests the implicational universal that "if tone spreading takes place from mid tone into a following low, then tone spreading also takes place from a high tone into a following low tone . . . [pp. 88–89]."

In the data so far cited for tone spreading, there is an almost perfect complementary distribution of "complete" spreading occurring only with HI LO LO and LO HI HI and "partial" spreading only with LO HI or HI LO in word final position.[13] "Complete" spreading in the three-syllable sequences is the result of **tone absorption**. Absorption as illustrated here may be interpreted as a subcase of spreading. For example, in the sequence LO HI HI, the initial LO spreads into the domain of the following HI, partially displacing the latter. That HI then spreads into the following HI, where it is absorbed, leaving only the LO in its original domain. This is the explanation of absorption offered in Hyman and Schuh (1974). Data from Etsako (Baruch Elimelich, personal communication) suggest that tone absorption could have an explanation in perception of tones rather than in production, which the "spreading" explanation implies. Consider the following data from two Etsako dialects:

17.　　　Ekpheli:　/ówà ˊ òɣìè/ → ówôɣyè　'house of the chief'
　　　　　　　　　 /òké ˊ òɣìè/ → òkôɣyè　'ram of the chief'

　　　　　Agenebodɛ:　/ówà ˊ òɣìè/ → ówòɣyè　'house of the chief'
　　　　　　　　　　　 /òké ˊ òɣìè/ → òkóɣyè　'ram of the chief'

In Ekpheli (and other dialects) a falling tone is retained in the contracted forms. In Agenebodɛ this syllable is heard as LO after HI and HI after LO.

---

[13] The only counterexample is Zulu in (11c) where the LO LO of a HI LO LO pattern becomes FALL LO. Note, however, that HI LO is an optional variant.

It may be the case that when the end point of a contour matches an adjacent tone, that end of the contour is interpreted as part of the tone it matches and is absorbed into it. When both ends of the contour match adjacent tones, dialects may differ as to which end is absorbed. In all the languages cited above, it was the latter part of the contour which was absorbed, whereas in Agenebodε Etsako it is the first part which is absorbed where possible.

In the case of tone spreading into the second of three syllables, tone absorption, whatever its explanation, accounts for annihilation of the original tone of the second syllable. In two-syllable sequences the partially displaced tone has no place to go so remains as the latter part of a glide. Complete spreading in such cases is rare (but cf. [35] for Zulu).

So far, spreading to the middle of three tones has been considered only where the second and third underlying tones were identical. Spreading in the sequence LO HI LO is rare. It does take place in Gwari with rather interesting phonetic results, interpreted in Hyman and Schuh (1974:97) as undergoing the following derivational stages:

18. /àsé + sà/ → *àsĕsâ* → *às̀ ēsâ* → [àsēsâ] 'sitting' (lit.: 'sitting sit')

The sequence HI LO HI does frequently involve spreading from the first to the second syllable. There are two common phonetic results: HI FALL HI and HI HI Downstep (DS). The first is easily interpreted as the HI spreading into the LO, with partial displacement of the latter. The second takes place in languages having downdrift (see Section 4.1), where a HI following a LO is slightly lower than a HI preceding the LO. Here, the LO is "squeezed out" by the HI and leaves as its only trace a downstep on the last HI. This type of rule was illustrated for Zulu in (7). Ngizim may give either phonetic result, depending basically on how long the LO syllable is, i.e., whether or not there is "room" for both a HI and LO tone:

19.   /ná ɗàasú/ → *ná ɗâasú*   'I poured (into a bottle)'
         /ná ɗàyú/ → *ná ɗá'yú*   'I got lost'

The tone spreading rules cited so far have generally applied any time the tonal and segmental conditions were met, regardless of grammar. There are cases of grammatical use of tones which must have developed from spreading which has become limited to certain morphological environments. Such morphologization of tone spreading sometimes takes the form of **tone displacement**. In Kanakuru (Newman 1974) in a variety of constructions, words of the pattern HI LO undergo spreading, the result being HI HI, with the LO signaled by downstep on the initial syllable of a following word beginning in HI. This is heard, for example, in noun + possessor (20a) and adjective + noun (20b). When there is a series of possessors the process is repeated for each appropriate tonal sequence, resulting in a series of downsteps (20c). However, in a phrase of the form adjective + noun + possessor, spreading occurs but downstep is displaced to the possessor (20d):

20.   a. /jéwè mónó/   → jéwé'mónó   'my slave'
      b. /mánjè mɔ́ná/   → mánjé'mɔ́ná   'old house'
      c. /yérò mólò jí/   → yéró'móló'jí   'your sister's eye'
                                                      ('eye sister you')
      d. /mánjè mɔ́ná mónó/ → mánjé mɔ́ná'mónó   'my old house'

A language exhibiting a more complex case of displacement is Sukuma (Richardson 1971) where, omitting certain details, a high tone is displaced two syllables to the right of a morpheme marked to cause this displacement. Thus, in (21a) no high tone appears,[14] whereas in (21b), in words of similar or identical segmental structure to those in (21a), a high tone is displaced to the second syllable of the adjective. Hyman and Schuh (1974) speculate that morphemes conditioning this displaced high tone originally bore a high tone which spread progressively to later syllables. Why this spread stopped at two syllables remains a mystery:

21.   a. *n-kolo n-taale*   'big sheep'
                      ba-limį ba-taale   'big cultivators'

                  b. *n-kolo n-taalé*   'big heart'
                      ba-temį ba-táale   'big chiefs'

The final process to be discussed in this section is **tone copying**. In this process, a syllable (usually a grammatical morpheme) which bears no tone of its own takes its tone from a preceding or following syllable. Copying resembles spreading, but unlike spreading which is phonologically motivated, copying is always a morphologically conditioned rule. In Igbo (Welmers and Welmers 1968:121) the applicative extension, with the form rV (where V = preceding vowel), in most environments takes the tone of the preceding syllable. In the following examples, the applicative extension is in boldface italics.

22.   *á nà m̀ èsírí' yá nri*   'I'm cooking food for him'
                  bèéré'm̀ é' gó   'reduce the amount for me'
                  ọ́ cọ̀rọ̀ ịbụ̀rụ ànyị́ ábụ̀   'he wants to sing us a song'
                  ọ́ rụ̀ụ̀rụ̀ há ọ́rụ́   'he worked for them'

For another example of copying, see the Ngizim plurals cited in (27).

----

[14] Richardson refers to the syllables unmarked for tone as bearing "normal tone." This is a tone lower than the tone marked as HI, but since I do not know the details of the Sukuma tonal system, I follow Richardson in simply leaving these syllables unmarked rather than marking LO.

3.2 Mapping

The processes described in 3.1 involve changes in distribution of a tone between consecutive syllables. Many languages have cases where a single overall tone pattern must be "mapped" onto more than one type of syllabic environment. In a number of African languages lexical tone patterns are best described as a property of the word. A single tone pattern can be used with words of one, two, three, or even more syllables. In Etung (Bendor-Samuel and Edmonson 1966), rising and falling tones are found only on monosyllables and the second syllable of disyllables, but not on trisyllables. This distribution of contour tones suggests a word-level lexical analysis for tone patterns in this language with tones mapped onto words, as in the examples below (a few patterns have been omitted):

23.

Pattern	Monosyllabic		Disyllabic		Trisyllabic	
LO	kpè	'even'	ègù	'evening'	èyǜrì	'dress'
HI	kpá	'first'	ńsé	'father'	ékúé	'forest'
LO HI	kǒ	'to'	èkát	'leg'	bìsóŋé	'wife'
HI LO	nâ	'it is'	égòm	'jaundice'	bírɔ̀mɔ̀	'me'
LO LO HI	—		èbĩn	'farm'	òròbé	'bean'
HI HI LO	—		éfô	'cloth'	ésébè	'sand'
LO HI LO	—		òbǒ	'arm'	m̀bútà	'rain'
HI LO HI	—		ábǒ	'they'	édìmbá	'pot'

A number of Mande languages are said to have a similar, though less complex, system. For example, Bambara (see Courtenay 1974 and references cited there) has been claimed to have only "high" and "rising" patterns, the former having all high tones, the latter having a rising tone on monosyllables and all LO with a final HI on longer words. Courtenay disputes this for Bambara and illustrates a large number of other patterns, but even she remarks that "about 85% of the Bambara lexicon is either high or rising [p. 306]."

More widespread than such lexical mapping is mapping of tone patterns onto compounds and derived forms. Examples are cited here from Kanuri (Lukas 1937), Hausa (Abraham 1959), and Bambara (Courtenay 1974), languages from three different language families. Kanuri has an agentive suffix -*ma*, which takes low tone and is simply affixed to a noun ending in HI or LO LO. When the noun ends in HI LO, the suffix takes high tone and all preceding syllables are LO. In Hausa, nouns of place take a prefix *má*- and a suffix vowel -*áa*. The derived noun takes all high tone regardless of lexical tone of the root. In Bambara, compounds are formed by giving the last morpheme in the compound HI tone and all preceding morphemes the tone of the underlying first syllable of the first morpheme:

24. Kanuri *fátkémà*   'trader'   < *fátké*   'trade'
            láràvùmà   'diviner'   < *láràvù*   'divining'
            kàttùgùmá   'liar'   < *kàttúgù*   'lie'

    Hausa: *máfítáa*   'exit'   < *fìtá*   'go out'
            mákáràntáa   'school'   < *kàràntáa*   'read'

    Bambara: *yírísúrúnmánnín*   'very short tree'
              < *yírí* 'tree', *sùrùnmán* 'short one', *nín* 'small'
              dùtèfìnmàndúmán   'good black tea'
              < *dùté* 'tea', *fìnmán* 'black one', *dúmán* 'good one'
              mìrìkìtìbèlèbèlèbá   'very big bloodsucker'
              < *mìríkìtí* 'bloodsucker', *bèlèbélé* 'big one', *bá* 'big'

In order to capture the proper generalizations, the tones in all these cases must be expressed as complete tone patterns rather than tones on individual syllables. Thus, using the formalism proposed above, the Kanuri patterns might be described by the following ordered rules:

25.   a. $_N|\ \underbrace{X - [+HI] - [-HI]}_{1} + \underbrace{ma\ |_N}_{2} \Rightarrow \underbrace{[-HI]}_{1}\underbrace{[+HI]}_{2}$

          b. $_N|\ \underbrace{Y}_{1} + \underbrace{ma\ |_N}_{2} \Rightarrow 1\ \underbrace{[-HI]}_{2}$

Some particularly interesting cases of mapping in compounds are found in Tangsic (Kennedy 1953). One type, with certain details omitted, will be discussed. In two syllable compounds where the first syllable is stressed, the lexical tone of the first syllable is mapped over the entire compound and the lexical tone of the second syllable disappears. Examples where the first syllable is ⊣ *33* or ⟍ *51* and the second syllable is one of the other tones are given in (26). In compounds which take an overall ——⊣*33* from the initial ⊣ *33*, Kennedy says that "[the tones] flow in a continuous line without hiatus [p. 368]." Likewise for compounds where the underlying initial syllable has lexical ⟍ *51*, he says that "the two Tangsic syllables again fall in a continuous line without hiatus [p. 369]."

26.   *kao* 'high'   *sae* 'mountain'   →   *kao-sae* 'high mountain'
        ⊣ *33*   ⊣ *33*   ——⊣ *33*

        pen 'ice'   *sea* 'water'   →   *pen-sea* 'ice water'
        ⊣ *33*   ⟍ *51*   ——⊣ *33*

        ka 'artificial'   *sae* 'mountain'   →   *ka-sae* 'rockery'
        ⟍ *51*   ⊣ *33*   ⟍ *51*

        syao 'small'   *nyin* 'man'   →   *syao-nyin* 'children'
        ⟍ *51*   ⟋ *24*   ⟍ *51*

Addition or subtraction of syllables may cause tone sequences to be mapped as simple tones on separate syllables or as contours on single syllables. In Hausa, the word *mùtûm* 'person' ends in falling tone (= HI LO sequence). When the genitival linking morpheme *-n* is added, an epenthetic *-i-* must be inserted and the HI LO sequence is then mapped over two syllables, e.g., *mùtúmìn bánzáa* 'useless person' (person of uselessness). In Ngizim, a common pluralization process reduplicates the last syllable and adds a high tone suffix *-in*. Usually, the reduplicated syllable copies the preceding tone, but if that syllable bears a falling tone (HI LO sequence), the reduplicated syllable bears the LO and the preceding syllable the HI:

27.

tə̀kà	'body'	pl.	*tə̀kàkín*
kwáará	'donkey'	pl.	*kwáarárín*
wûrjí	'scorpion'	pl.	*wúrjàjín*

If two syllables are contracted to one through vowel elision or some other process, the tones of the two syllables may be mapped onto the new syllable as a contour. Examples were seen in (17) in the Ekpheli dialect of Etsako. Jukun (Shimizu 1971, Welmers 1968) has three phonemic tone levels. When sequences of any two of these tones occur on a single syllable, the resultant glide moves between exactly the same two pitch levels as the original tones, except for cases of LO or HI to MID. Thus, MID MID contracts to MID, MID HI to MID–HI rising, LO HI to LO–HI rising, etc., but HI MID simply becomes HI and LO MID becomes LO.[15]

4. RULES WHICH OPERATE WITHIN A GIVEN SEGMENTAL DOMAIN

4.1 Assimilation

In assimilation, one tone becomes more like (perhaps identical to) another tone. Unlike spreading, which always operates from "left to right," assimilation may be either **anticipatory** (the first tone becomes more like the second) or **perseverative** (the second tone becomes more like the first). Examples of both anticipatory raising and lowering have been seen in Ewe. In (9) a LO was raised to MID before HI, while in (10) MID is lowered to LO before LO. Another example of anticipatory raising is seen in Fe'fe' dialect of Bamileke (Hyman 1972), where a LO is raised to Raised-LO (marked by ' over the vowel) before

---

[15] Note that these facts on contraction correlate closely with the cases where tone spreading does or does not operate in Gwari, illustrated in (16).

any non-LO:

28. *sì* 'without' + *pʉà* 'bag' → [sì pʉ̀à] 'without a bag'
   sì   + *càk* 'pot' → [si càk] 'without a pot'
   sì   + *sāk* 'bird' → [si sāk] 'without a bird'

When appearing as the second of three syllables, the Mandarin "neutral tone" "has (approximately) the pitch of the tail end of the first syllable" in a number of combinations (Chao and Yang 1962:xviii). These pitches for neutral tones are almost the opposite of the pitches they take when appearing phrase final after the same tones:[16]

29. ⌐•⟍ *zhong guo hua* 'Chinese language' cf. ⌐.│ *ta de* 'his'
  ◢•⟍ *xue de hui* 'can learn'   cf. ◢.│ *shei de* 'whose'
  _.⌐ *zou bu kai* 'cannot get away' cf. _│•│ *nii de* 'yours'
  _.│◢ *liang ge ren* 'two people'

The best known and most studied case of perseverative lowering is **downdrift** (cf. Ohala, Chapter I and Anderson, Chapter V, this volume). This is the phenomenon whereby a HI following a LO is lower in pitch than a HI preceding the LO. Numerous formalizations for downdrift have been proposed (see Schachter and Fromkin 1968, Williamson 1970, Fromkin 1972, Peters 1973, Clifton 1976, and other references cited in these articles). I will not attempt to summarize these proposals, nor will I propose a formalization here. However, a general criticism of all the proposals just cited can be made, namely, that they do not approximate the phonetic facts. All these proposals treat downdrift as an overall intonational pattern affecting both HI and LO tones, as schematized in (30a). However, it has been shown that in many, if not all, languages having downdrift, the LO tones descend in pitch much more slowly than intervening highs, if they descend at all (Hombert 1974). This is schematized in (30b). A better formalization than those in the references cited above would seem to be one which progressively lowers HIs while leaving LOs constant.

30.   a. HI⟍ ╱HI⟍   ⟍
       ⟍LO╱ ⟍LO╱HI ⟍

    b. HI⟍   ⟍
       ⟍LO╱HI⟍ ⟍LO╱HI ⎯
           ⟍LO╱

Hombert (1974) also points out that in languages with downdrift, sequences of HIs typically remain level, while sequences of LOs drift down in pitch. How-

---

[16] After the ⟍ *51* tone, "neutral tone" is low in all combinations, e.g., ⟍.│ *da de* 'big one(s)'. Strangely, the assimilation does not apply in some three syllable environments. Chao and Yang (1962:xviii) cite ⌐.│⌐ *ta de jia* 'his home'.

ever, sequences of HIs are sometimes found to drift down as well when the language has no contrast between HI and MID or Downstep (Shona), and the downward drifting of a sequence of LOs can be blocked if there is a contrast between LO followed by LO level as opposed to lowered LO, as in Dschang Bamileke (see [43] below). Hombert concludes that "downdrift is a natural, unmarked intonation with an ultimate but as yet unknown articulatory motivation. But this process can be blocked when it threatens to obscure a tonal contrast [p. 178]." (For a different opinion see Ohala, Chapter I, this volume.) While Hombert's latter conclusion has considerable support, I believe (with Hyman 1973b) that the motivation for downdrift is assimilation of HIs to LOs and that downdrift is not simply an intonation pattern. Hombert presents two arguments against this: (a) In languages like Hausa, a downdrift pattern is used in statements, but downdrift is suspended when question intonation is used. Hence, downdrift appears to be "statement intonation." However, it is equally reasonable to say that in statements the assimilations which result in downdrift operate but when question intonation is **superimposed** on a sentence, the effect is that downdrift is cancelled. (b) If downdrift is assimilation, why are LOs not assimilated to HIs as well as vice versa, giving a rising pattern for LOs together with the lowering pattern for HIs? While no satisfactory explanation for this has yet been given, there is a general tendency for lowering tonal assimilations to be favored over rising assimilations.[17] Thus, in Gwari, a language without downdrift, MID becomes lowered MID after LO but MID is unaffected after HI (see Hyman and Magaji 1970:15). This is an undisputed case of assimilation where tones are lowered but are not raised in the analogous environment. One reason for this is suggested by Ohala (See Chapter I, this volume), that is, that it is more difficult to raise pitch from a neurophysiological or articulatory point of view than it is to lower pitch.

A phenomenon closely related to downdrift is **downstep** (DS). (Cf. Anderson, Chapter V, this volume.) DS is a lowered HI directly following a HI. DS is distinct from MID, since following LO there is only one contrasting tone higher in pitch, whereas in a language with HI, MID, and LO, one could go up to either MID or to HI following LO. The vast majority of languages with DS have only HI and LO tones aside from DS, though there are a few languages with HI, MID, and LO which also have DS, for example, Ga'anda (Newman 1971) and Yala of Ikom (Armstrong 1968). The majority of cases of DS known to me are directly derivable from or are assumed, explicitly or implicitly, to be derived from the loss of a LO tone between two HIs, where the second HI is slightly lower than the first as a result of downdrift (but see example [34] and discussion). In languages with DS, it may appear in lexical

---

[17] This assymetry where lowering takes place but raising does not take place in analogous environments has a parallel in distribution of contour tones. In African languages, falling tones (a lowering effect) are far more common than rising tones (a raising effect).

contrast with HI and LO after HI, e.g., Igbo ọ́'gú 'counting', ọ́gú 'twenty', ọ́gụ̀ 'hoe' (Welmers and Welmers 1968). DS may result from loss of a LO syllable through synchronically motivated rules, or from a "floating LO," presumably having its origin in historical loss of the segments which carried it. Examples of each type of derivation are found in the literature. Some examples of DS have already been seen above, e.g., Bade and Zulu, in (7) as a result of HI spreading to LO, and Kanakuru in (20) through a similar process. One further example of each of the two types of derivation just mentioned for DS will be noted for African languages and one for a Mexican language. In Bade when two vowels come together, they contract to form a single syllable. If one of the original syllables was LO but the resulting contracted syllable is HI, a HI following it is heard as DS:

31.   jà màsú 'we bought' + àfcáan 'mat' → [jà màsə́f'cáan] 'we bought a mat'
      jà gàfáw 'we caught' + àkɬán 'cow' → [jà gàfák'ɬán] 'we bought a cow'

In Akan (Schachter and Fromkin 1968), nonemphasized pronominal subjects are marked by low tone prefixes to the verb; if the subject is a noun, the prefix on the verb is simply LO tone. Evidence for this floating LO is a DS on the verb if it has underlying HI, or on the syllable preceding the verb if the verb is LO. The underlying forms with intermediate derivational stages proposed by Schachter and Fromkin follow:

32.   ní nã̀ ` bà → ńí nã̀ bà → [ní'nã̀ bà]   'his mother comes'
      Kòfí ` bébà → Kòfî bébà → [Kòfí'bébá]   'Kofi will come'

In Coatzospan Mixtec (Pike, n.d.), a "floating LO," called a "process phoneme" by Pike, is a property of lexical items. A word may begin in this process phoneme, in which case the word has HI tone but causes DS on a following HI:[18]

33.   /túʔtú ` kúʔšì-ŏ/ → [túʔtú 'kúʔšì-ŏ]   'we will bury paper'
      cf. kúʔcị kúʔšì-ŏ (phonetic and phonemic)   'we will bury a pig'
      cf. /túʔtú ` kàʔmị̀-ŏ/ → [túʔtú kàʔmị̀-ŏ]   'we will burn paper'

Not all cases of downstep come from downdrift. A clear case is Dschang-Bamileke (Tadadjeu 1974), which has no downdrift but does have downstepped HI as can be seen in contrasts such as lətɔ́ŋ 'feather' and lə́'tɔ́ŋ 'to read'. Though both these tones here appear after LO, the downstepped HI cannot be interpreted as MID since there would then be a possible phrase LO MID HI. However, after a downstepped HI, there can be no rise to a higher tone. Down-

---

[18] I have taken the liberty of representing Pike's "process phoneme" as a floating LO to make this example comparable to the African ones. Unfortunately, Pike does not illustrate all the combinations she mentions.

stepped HIs in Dschang have derived historically (34a) or synchronically (34b) from the sequence HI LO on one syllable:

34.   a. *lə́tɔ́ŋ > lə́tɔŋ 'feather'
               *lə́tɔ́ŋ > lə́'tɔŋ 'to read'
          b. /lə́tɔ́ŋ ´ məsə́ŋ/ → lə́tɔ́ŋ mə́'sə́ŋ 'feather of birds'

(An argument counter to this position is presented in Chapter V by Anderson.)

4.2 Dissimilation and Polarization

The phonetic effect of these two processes will be the same, namely, tones on two (usually contiguous) syllables will be the opposite of each other. Rules for the two are distinct, however. In **dissimilation** the affected syllable has an identifiable underlying tone, requiring a rule of the form $[+HI] \to [-HI] /$ $[+HI]$ ____, whereas in **polarization** the affected syllable has no underlying tone, requiring a rule of the form Tone $\to [-\alpha HI] / [\alpha HI]$ ____.

Besides the similarity in their phonetic effect, these two processes have another thing in common: In all valid cases known to me, both types of rules are morphological rules, i.e., they apply only to morphemes marked to undergo them, rather than applying as general phonological rules. At least one proposed case of dissimilation as a phonological rule has an entirely different explanation. In (11) is illustrated a Zulu rule which moves a HI tone onto a LO if the LO does not begin in a depressor consonant. Cope (1970) says that the syllable taking the transferred HI may have a falling tone "if there is vowel length to accommodate it. If there is not, it results in a change from low to high, which brings about a change from high to low (tonal dissimilation) in a high-toned final syllable [p. 116]" (cf. 35a). The same phenomenon may apply to lexical items (cf. 35b):

35.   a. /ìzíntòmbí/ → ìzìntômbì = ìzìntómbì 'girls'
          b. înjá = ínjà 'dog'

This is not a case of dissimilation. Rather, the LO which is optionally heard as the latter portion of the FALL **spreads** into the last syllable, pushing the original HI off and leaving only final LO.

Hyman and Schuh (1974) suggest that synchronic polarization rules generally will have a diachronic explanation in the natural processes of spreading, absorption, and simplification. They suggest further that synchronic dissimilation rules may have other, more "natural," diachronic explanations as well. Spontaneous dissimilation does occur, however. In the Guddiri dialect of Hausa (Dauda Bagari, personal communication), the words *don* 'because of' and *dan* 'a small . . .' take tones opposite that of the following syllable. In Kano Hausa, both have HI tone. Furthermore, *dan* has independent existence in all dialects with HI tone as *dáa* 'son':

36.

Guddiri Hausa	Kano Hausa	
dòn Állàa	*dón Állàa*	'for the sake of Allah'
dón mèe?	*dón mèe?*	'why?' (because of what?)
dàn ƙáuyèe	*dán ƙáuyèe*	'a little village'
dán ƙàrámíi	*dán ƙàrámíi*	'very small' (son of small)

In the Guddiri dialect, *don* in effect has polar tone since it has no function where it would not appear without polar tone, and since it is only through dialect evidence that we know it was originally HI.[19] The rule regulating *dan* must be regarded as one of dissimilation, however, since we know that it has lexical HI tone because of its independent existence in the meaning 'son'.

Though one may voice skepticism as to the spontaneous historical origin of tonal dissimilation and polarization, there are many known cases where synchronically tone must be assigned to morphemes by a polarization rule. Ngizim subject pronouns in certain aspects are polar to the verb, e.g., *dà káaší* 'that he sweep' versus *dá gɔ̀nyì* 'that he accept' (Schuh 1971). In Igbo, the verbal noun prefix is polar to the verb root, e.g., *à-gá* 'going' versus *á-kpà* 'weaving' (Welmers and Welmers 1968). In all the examples cited so far the first syllable has polarized with respect to the second. In Hausa, direct object pronouns polarize with respect to the preceding syllable, e.g., *náa sàyée tà* 'I bought it' versus *náa rúfèe tá* 'I shut it'.

4.3 Simplification

This term can be applied in two ways: Rules which simplify the shape of individual tones and rules which simplify an overall system by reducing the number of contrasts. In the former case, there is the tendency in African languages for contour tones to be simplified to level tones. Some examples of this can be explained by absorption (see Section 3.1), but this explanation avails itself only where the tone following the contour matches the final portion of the contour. In languages with two tones there are also sequences of FALL HI (= HĪLO HI) and RISE LO (= LÔHI LO), where the contour is simplified

---

[19] The case of *dan* is indisputably one of spontaneous dissimilation. Dissimilation of *don* may have another explanation, however. This word derives from *dòomín*, with which it is in more or less free variation. In the contraction of *dòomín* to *don* a rising tone would be expected, but in Hausa, syllables which would otherwise take rising tones are realized as HI, a fact first noted in Leben (1971b) but supported by considerable further evidence since that time. This would explain the HI tone in Kano Hausa and in Guddiri before LO. In Guddiri, if the HI portion of the LO–HI were absorbed by a following HI, the result would be a LO tone on *dòn* before HI.

but where the explanation cannot be absorption. In languages with downdrift, FALL HI is frequently simplified to HI DS. An example of this from Ngizim was seen in (19). Examples with a different type of derivation for the underlying FALL are found in Etsako (Elimelich 1976). When vowel contraction takes place where the first vowel bears HI tone and the second LO, the resultant FALL may be realized as DS on a following HI but simply as HI if the following tone is LO (because of absorption):[20]

37.   /ɔ́ dɛ́ àtásà/ → ɔ̀ d́ àtásà → [ɔ̀ dá'tásà]   'he is buying a plate'
      /ɔ́ dɛ́ ɔ̀ɣɛ̀dɛ́/ → ɔ̀ d́ ɔ̀ɣɛ̀dɛ́ → [ɔ̀ dɔ́ɣɛ̀dɛ̃́]   'he is buying a banana'

(The final FALL in the second example is the result of a general intonational rule affecting final HIs.)

In the combination RISE LO, the RISE is generally simplified to HI. In Etsako the (optionally) simplified RISE is heard as DS after HI (38a) but as HI after LO (38b):

38.   a. /ówà ówà/ → [ówŏwà] or [ó'wówà]   'every house' (house house)
      b. /áyòxò áyòxò/ → [áyòxǎyòxò] or [áyòxáyòxò]
                                      'every coco-yam' (coco-yam coco-yam)

In Hausa, there is no DS, so underlying RISE simply becomes HI. For example, verbs of the pattern LO HI LO without following object take the tone pattern LO LO HI before objects. In the verb *dauka* 'take' the first two tones are on one syllable giving this pattern:

39.   /náa ɗăukàa/ → *náa ɗáukàa*   'I took (unspecified object)'
      /náa ɗàukée tà/ → *náa ɗàukée tà*   'I took it'
      cf. *náa tàmbáyàa*   'I asked (unspecified object)'
          náa tàmbàyée tà   'I asked her'

In languages with more than two level tone contrasts, contours are sometimes simplified to a "compromise" tone. Thus, in Gwari a RISE (itself a derived tone—cf. [16]) is simplified to MID when followed by MID or HI:

40.   *gwìwyě* 'money' + *dā* 'possessor' → *gwìwyē dā* 'possessor of money'

A similar example of "compromise" simplification was seen in Dschang Bamileke in (34).

In Asian languages, there is no apparent tendency to simplify rising or falling contours, but "concave" or "convex" contours are often simplified in sandhi contexts. Thus, in Mandarin, the "dipping" tone is simplified to LO-level before any tone other than another dipping, where it is simplified to rising

---

[20] Numerous details of Etsako phonology are omitted here. Not all FALLs are simplified in this way since other factors such as the number of syllables following the FALL as well as the morphological environment must be considered.

tone (Chao and Yang 1962). In Foochow the *242* convex tone simplifies to *44* or *52* depending on the following tone (K. Pike 1948:85, summarizing data from Chao and Tao):[21]

41.   Mandarin: ⌐ *213* + ⌐ *55* → ⌐ ⌐   *hao tian*   'good weather'
                213 + ⌐ *35* → ⌐ ⌐   *hao ren*   'good man'
                213 + ⟍ *51* → ⟍   *hao ba*   'all right!'
                213 + *213* →   *hao zao*   'how early!'

      Foochow: ⟍ *242* + ⌐ *44*, etc. → ⌐
                 ⟍ *242* + _ *22*, etc. → ⟍

In African languages the number of phonetic tonal distinctions generally increases when morphemes are put into larger contexts. In Asian languages it is unusual for the number of tonal distinctions to increase in sandhi environments, and in some languages, especially those with complex inventories of tonal contrasts in isolation, the number of distinct tones decreases in number. In the Foochow language just mentioned there are seven contrasting tones in isolation, while in sandhi there are only six (two of which do not occur in isolation). More important is the fact that several tones neutralize to a single tone in some contexts. For example, ⌐, _, ⌐, ⟍ neutralize to ⟍ in certain contexts. A similar but even more complex situation is found in Soochow (Kovitz 1970).

5. TONE AND INTONATION

The processes in the preceding sections have had mainly to do with the influence of tones on each other or the interaction of tones and segments. Another factor frequently influences the phonetic realization of tones, namely, *intonation*. By intonational effects on tone, I mean modifications in pitch which cannot be attributed directly to immediate tonal or segmental environments or to some special morphological marking. The environments for intonation will normally be phrase final or will be determined by overall sentence type (statement, question, etc.). Intonational rules do not specify lexical class, syntactic construction type, etc.

Like tonal processes, intonational patterns can be described as either being general patterns applied over domains of varying size, or as specific modifications of a single syllable in a particular position, usually phrase final. Typical of intonational patterns which may apply to utterances of any length is Hausa

---

[21] This seems to be a different Foochow from that mentioned in Mohr (1973). The tones are different, and Pike makes no mention of the vowel alternations which accompany the tone changes noted by Mohr. Pike cites no actual morphemes in his account.

question intonation. Hausa has downdrift. The effect of question intonation is to suspend downdrift, or reduce it considerably, and to raise the last high tone of the phrase to an extrahigh pitch with a sharp fall. The intonation pitch curves in (42) are schematized from Hombert (1974):

42.

Bàláa dà Shéehù záa sù zóo dà mútàanénsù?
'Bala and Shehu will come with their people.'

Bàláa dà Shéehù záa sù zóo dà mútàanénsù?
'Will Bala and Shehu come with their people?'

Note that the question intonation pattern must make reference to specific tones since it must seek out the last HI in the sentence. While in the majority of sentences this will be the penultimate or the last syllable, one can construct utterances such as *yánàa dà àkwàatì* 'he has box' where the last high tone is quite distant from the end of the sentence but where the same rule applies.

Another common overall intonational phenomenon, also found in Hausa, is the downward glide of a series of LOs (see Hombert 1974 for tracings of a pitch curve of downgliding LOs in Kru). A phenomenon related to this but affecting only a phrase final syllable is lowering of a final LO after LO to extra-low or LO-falling. This takes place in Hausa, and in fact the phrase-final distinction between LO HI and LO LO is phonetically LO LO-level versus LO LO-falling, e.g., *sún ràbú* [⌐ __ __] 'they separated' versus *àbù* [__ __⌐] 'thing'.[22]

In Dschang Bamileke (Tadadjeu 1974), what must have been an intonational downgliding of final LOs has produced a phonological distinction between LO-falling and LO-level after LO. The historical explanation for this is given in (43) (LO-falling is marked ⌐), i.e., LO LO-level originally was followed by a HI, which prevented the intonational downglide rule from operating, whereas LO LO-falling was followed by LO, which allowed application of the rule. With loss of the final LO and HI tones, the intonationally introduced difference

---

[22] Bargery (1934), who uses a phonetic rather than phonemic system for marking tones, uses a special marking for what he calls "low falling still lower." He is not entirely consistent in the way he applies this to final LO LO sequences, e.g., he writes *káarùwà* 'prostitute' as HI LO LO-falling, but *àbù* 'thing' as simply LO LO. He also sometimes marks final LO after HI as LO–falling, e.g., *wánnàn* 'this one'. As can be seen from the schematized tracing in (42), final LOs after HIs do fall.

was all that remained to keep them distinct:

43.   *lə̀tɔ́ŋ > lə̀tɔ̀ŋ   'navel'
                                 *lə̀tɔ̀ŋ > lə̀tɔ̂ŋ   'pay back'

In Mandarin there are two tones which have special phrase final forms (Yen 1970). In the Peking dialect underlying ⌐ 55 is sometimes realized as ⌐ 554. This is indisputably an intonational phenomenon (apparently partly stylistically influenced). The other special phrase final tone is ⌐ 213, which is normally taken as underlying and which is realized as ⌐ 11 or ⌐ 35 depending on context (see [41]). A reasonable alternative account for Mandarin is to take ⌐ 11 as underlying for this tone with ⌐ 213 as a phrase-final intonationally derived variant.

Intonation sometimes interacts with tone rules to produce interesting tonal results. In Dschang, a series of LOs has downglide intonation. If two LO words appear in an associative construction with a floating LO associative morpheme, the result is LO followed by downstepped LO, a process which is potentially infinitely recursive:

44.   /kàŋ ˋ kàŋ ˋ kàŋ . . . / → kàŋ̂ 'kànŷ 'kàŋ . . .
                 'squirrel of squirrel of squirrel . . .'

In Zapotec (E. Pike 1948) there are three contrastive level tones. However, among disyllabic morphemes, which comprise a large majority of morphemes, there are none with final HI. There are two basic tone sandhi rules, formulated and illustrated in (45). The first rule applies only to morphemes marked to undergo it. It applies within words and across word boundaries. The second rule applies whenever the environment is met but applies only across word boundaries. The rules apply as ordered, the first feeding the second in some cases:

45. a. LO → MID / ____ $\begin{Bmatrix} HI \\ MID \end{Bmatrix}$ /yèn nājō/ → yēn nājō 'neck we say'

Condition: Applies to only class B morphemes.

b. MID → HI / $\begin{Bmatrix} LO \\ MID \end{Bmatrix}$ ____ # X /z̧ɪ́s gōlɪ̄/ → z̧ís gōlɪ̄ 'old stick'

X ≠ pause   /gʷăgɪ̄ nɪ̄ʔ/ → gʷāgí nɪ̄ʔ 'that friend'

While many details remain to be explained, it seems not unreasonable to assume that rule (45b) is the reverse of an original intonational rule which lowered final HIs to MID when preceded by another syllable in the same word. This would explain the absence of final HI tones in disyllabic words before before pause. It also explains a tone rule applying to the second member of compounds, namely, if that member of the compound is a monosyllable with lexical HI tone, it is lowered to MID, e.g., ẓá 'skin' + gó 'potato' → ẓágō 'potato skin', dè- (nominalizer) + zíẓ 'sweet' → dèzīẓ 'a sweet'. These compounds are subject to rule (45b). If this explanation for rule (45b) is correct, it may be the case that the intonational rule was more general, lowering all non-LO tones by one step. This would explain rule (45a), and in particular it would explain why only some morphemes undergo (45a), namely, those morphemes marked to undergo (45a) originally ended in MID, while those not marked to undergo it originally ended in LO. This suggestion does not explain why the environments for (45a) and (45b) are different nor why the raising takes place only in certain tonal environments. One can only assume the suggested intonational rule is no longer productive and that the rules here have undergone subsequent developments in their guise as purely tonal rules.

A final intonational pattern which is not well documented but which seems to exist in some languages is upgliding of consecutive HIs. In Zulu this is described as "the crescendo of high tonemes in sequence [Cope 1970, citing Lanham]." When interacting with HI spreading—see (7) and (11) above—the result is an **upstep** (marked as '' before the upstepped syllable) on an underlying HI tone when this HI follows and is followed by LOs raised to HI by HI spreading:

46.   /áɓàfánà àɓáyìfúnì/ → áɓá'fáná á''ɓáyí'fúnì
             'the boys do not want it'

Upstep is also seen in Acatlán Mixtec (Pike, n.d.). Though Pike does not mention that HIs in a series glide upward, certain facts suggest that upgliding of HIs as an intonational feature of the present-day language or of the language at an earlier period can explain the origin of upstep here in a similar way to that of Zulu. First, two syllable morphemes may have any combination of the "classical" tones HI, MID, and LO except for HI HI. These are the only tones typically found in lexical forms. Almost all upsteps (US) are derived from HIs in certain sandhi environments. Since US never occurs after LO or MID, it may be that morphemes which are underlyingly (or historically) HI HI are realized as MID HI because of the phonetic similarity between this pattern and HI HI, which would phonetically be HI US. The second fact suggesting that upgliding of HIs is the source of upstep is that "a morpheme which has an initial high tone in its basic allomorph becomes [US] whenever it contiguously follows [HI or US][pp. 13–14]." (The cedillas under the letters replace Pike's apostrophes before the letters in order to avoid confusion with the tone marks.)

47.   kó   + çí''tú + wá + ní   + ɱéè → kó''çí''tú''wá''ní''ɱéè
             neg. kiss   so   you   baby
             'you don't kiss the baby so much'

This is a general rule in the language. Other rules of tone sandhi are morphologically conditioned. All the rules mentioned by Pike raise tones of morphemes
following morphemes marked as tone raisers. In the following phrase, each of
the first two morphemes are marked lexically to raise a following morpheme
one tonal step above itself. The second syllable of *yàá* 'tongue' is raised to US
by the rule illustrated in (47).

48. ʔā̄   + vīdā + yàá   + ñā   → ʔāvídá "yá"áñā
     ques. wet   tongue   3 fem sing   'is the girl's tongue wet yet?'

6. PARADIGMATIC REPLACEMENT OF TONES

6.1 What Is Paradigmatic Replacement?

Most Africanists, and certainly those working in the transformational–
generative paradigm, conceive of tone rules as changing features on a particular
tone. The fact that a rule $[+\text{HI}] \rightarrow [-\text{HI}]$ results in replacement of one toneme
by another is only incidental in the same way that a rule $[+\text{voice}] \rightarrow [-\text{voice}]$ /
____ # which results in replacement of /d/ by an independent phoneme /t/ is
incidental to the process of final devoicing. In other words, the tonal phonology
of an African language is not viewed as a tonal paradigm with rules which
select one tone from the paradigm and replace another tone with it.[23] Such
an analysis does not seem well motivated for Amerindian languages either,
but I maintain that just such an analysis is required for Asian languages, in
particular those of China.

The generative treatments of Chinese tone sandhi which I have seen use feature changing rules in the same way African languages do. A well-known and
particularly interesting example is the Amoy Hokkien "sandhi circle," formalized in Wang (1967). This language has the contrastive tones shown in
(49a). According to Wang these tones developed from the four tones of Middle
Chinese, where the Roman numbers correspond to the Middle Chinese tones
and the (a) and (b) to whether the words began in voiceless or voiced initials,
respectively. Although Wang does not give a detailed account of environments
for sandhi in Amoy Hokkien, his footnote 37 suggests that sandhi in this language is a general change affecting any non-phrase-final tone, irrespective of
lexical category or contiguous tonal environment. The interesting thing about
Amoy Hokkien sandhi is that if the citation forms are taken as basic and the

---

[23] K. Pike (1948) in fact takes exactly this view. He says, "Under the circumstances appropriate
to a given language a syllable may have its normal toneme removed and a different one substituted
for it [p. 22]." While his system of linguistic analysis demands this viewpoint, he would surely agree
to the difference in principle stated here.

sandhi forms as derived, the sandhi derivations for the "long tones" (I–III) can be formulated as a "circle," seen in (49b). The "short tones" (IV) also form a minicircle, seen in (49c):

49. a. Ia   Ib   II   IIIa   IIIb   IVa   IVb

   ⌐55 ⌐35 ⟍53 ⟍ 31 ⊣ 33 ⌐ 21 ⌐ 5

   b. Ia,b   IIIb   IIIa   II   Ia

   {⌐} → ⊣ → ⟍ → ⟍ → ⌐ → . . .

   c. IVa   IVb   IVa

   ⌐ → ⌐ → ⌐ → · · ·

Using the features proposed in his article, Wang formulates the rule for the circle in (49b) as in (50a). These rules can be collapsed as in (50b):

50. a. $\begin{bmatrix} +\text{HIGH} \\ -\text{FALLING} \end{bmatrix} \rightarrow \begin{bmatrix} -\text{HIGH} \\ -\text{FALLING} \end{bmatrix} \rightarrow \begin{bmatrix} -\text{HIGH} \\ +\text{FALLING} \end{bmatrix} \rightarrow$

   $\begin{bmatrix} +\text{HIGH} \\ +\text{FALLING} \end{bmatrix} \rightarrow \begin{bmatrix} +\text{HIGH} \\ -\text{FALLING} \end{bmatrix} \rightarrow \cdots$

   b. $\begin{bmatrix} \alpha\text{HIGH} \\ \beta\text{FALLING} \end{bmatrix} \rightarrow \begin{bmatrix} \beta\text{HIGH} \\ -\alpha\text{FALLING} \end{bmatrix}$

One must admit that this is a formal tour de force. But what does it mean linguistically? The derived tones for the most part have nothing to do with historical antecedents in Middle Chinese, nor can any process normally considered "natural" (assimilation, dissimilation, simplification, etc.) be discerned. As formulated, the rule does appear to express a systematic relationship between underlying and derived tones, but what has this underlying → derived relationship have to do with a circle? The notion of a circle suggests that the underlying tone on one morpheme is the same as the derived tone on a different morpheme, but the rule in (50b) refers to the tones on a single morpheme.

The Amoy Hokkien data avail themselves of a plausible and relatively simple solution in terms of feature changing rules. Other sandhi systems are not nearly so neat. Both Kovitz (1970) and Yen (1970) have proposed comparable solutions for Chaozhou, a Min dialect closely related to Amoy Hokkien. Kovitz proposes a "circle" solution which, to say the least, is contrived.[24] Yen uses features like Wang, but in order to account for certain discrepancies, such as the fact that ⟍53 becomes ⌐24 rather than an expected ⌐13, he creates

---

[24] Her solution utilizes a principle of "rotation" where rising tones become falling and vice versa. At one point in the "circle," ⟍53 becomes ⌐313. She accounts for this by saying that ⟍ 53 actually rotates to become ⌐13, which then rotates to ⟍31. However, this ⟍31 does not become a new sandhi tone, but is attached to the ⌐13 to give ⌐313.

several new features. In addition to the suspicious formal nature of these solutions, Chaozhou sandhi raises the same linguistic questions as Amoy Hokkien: What have the underlying and derived variants to do with each other historically or in terms of natural processes?

Formulation of systematic feature-changing rules for tone sandhi in other Asian languages which I have seen presents the same sort of problems, all of which make me believe that this is the wrong approach to tone rules in these languages. My suggestion is that, in fact, rules for these languages should be formulated not as feature-changing rules but as **paradigmatic replacements**, i.e., in statements of the traditional type such as "a 3rd-Tone word followed by another 3rd-Tone word is pronounced in the 2nd Tone [Chao and Yang, 1962:xvi]," referring to the Mandarin rule in (41). This difference in formal nature of tone rules between African (and Mexican) languages and Asian languages may be a reflection of typological differences between the types of tone systems (see Section 6.2) and historical origin of tonal alternation. African languages generally have a small inventory of contrastive tones and develop alternations from interaction of contiguous tones, sometimes with the added influence of intervening consonants. Asian languages generally have developed additional tones through consonantally induced perturbations of some tones followed by loss of consonantal distinctions, for example, voiced obstruents devoicing and neutralizing with voiceless, leaving only the tonal distinctions to keep morphemes distinct. Environments for tonal alternations in Chinese languages are often describable simply as prepausal (assumed to be the environment for the basic form in most cases) versus non-prepausal (usually taken as the environment for the derived form). One can imagine how tone sandhi as rules of paradigmatic replacement could develop in Asian languages: (*a*)Tonal perturbations by consonant types differ in prepausal and non-prepausal environments because of stress differences, time allotted for pronunciation of a morpheme, etc.[25] (*b*) The perturbation of Tone X in non-prepausal position happens to make X approximate the prepausal realization of Tone Y, e.g., X in nonprepausal position is perturbed to $\dashv$ *24* whereas Y in prepausal position is $\measuredangle$ *13*. (*c*) Since the perturbed X now sounds like prepausal Y, it is simply replaced by Y, allowing the sandhi rule for X to be stated as "X → Y in sandhi." A possible case where this has happened is the Mandarin rule $\measuredangle$ *213* → $\frown$ *35* / _____ $\measuredangle$ *213*. It is disputed in the literature whether the *35* derived from *213* is phonetically distinct from the underlying *35* or not, e.g., Sampson (1969) cites evidence from Kratochvíl that they are distinct whereas Li and Thompson (1976) state that there is no difference. It may indeed by the case that some speakers do make a difference, reflecting different origins of the two *35* tones, whereas others have simply identified the tone

---

[25] The non-prepausal environment appears generally to have had an inhibiting effect or perhaps a leveling effect in tone perturbations since, as pointed out above, there are usually fewer tonal contrasts in sandhi than in prepausal position.

derived from *213* with the underlying *35* and apply paradigmatic replacement as suggested here.

6.2 Language Typology and Tone Rule Typology

The differing types of tone rules between African and Asian languages (feature changing rules versus paradigmatic replacement rules) may reflect the difference in language typology in the two areas. There are two typological factors of particular importance: lexical root structure and presence or absence of grammatical morphology. Words in Chinese and other Asian languages are for the most part monosyllabic, whereas those in African languages are usually two syllables or longer.[26] As one might expect, tone plays a much greater functional lexical role in Chinese languages than in African languages. Indeed the inventory of distinctive tones or tone sequences in the most tonally complex African languages rarely matches that of the simplest Chinese languages. Were tones in Chinese languages allowed to undergo the variety of syntagmatic influences typical of African languages, where a particular syllable may have a number of tonal realizations depending on tonal environment and other factors, the lexical role of tone would be jeopardized. Chinese sandhi rules almost always involve only two tone variants for a particular word with variation conditioned by very simply stated environments, often just whether the word is prepausal or not. Indeed, some scholars, e.g., Sprigg (1975), prefer not to talk about tone change rules at all but rather to say that a particular morpheme has a **set** of lexical tones. Morphemes are then tonally distinct in the way the set of tonal realizations is distributed, not in the phonetic tones alone.

The second relevant typological difference between Asian and African languages is that Asian languages show an almost total lack of grammatical morphology, whereas African languages often have very complex morphological systems. The role of tone in Asian languages is therefore almost entirely lexical. In African languages tone takes on a heavy grammatical load. In fact there are very few African languages with a full-fledged tonal system where at least one or two grammatical functions are not marked by tonal alternations. This usually arises where the segments of a grammatical morpheme have disappeared, leaving only its tonal effects on neighboring syllables to mark the construction.

To return to the difference in tone rule typologies, then, we see that tonal rules in Africa operate syntagmatically as typical feature-changing rules of assimilation, etc.: They are allowed to do so because tone has a relatively low

---

[26] These may be historical rather than synchronic statements. Many words in modern Chinese languages, because of widespread and productive compounding, must now be taken as disyllabic or longer. On the other hand many African languages have lost syllables, leaving monosyllabic roots. In such languages tone generally plays a greater functional role than in languages where roots are two syllables or longer.

lexical functional load, and they must because grammatical relations are often marked by tonal alternations. Typical Asian language tone rules involve relatively simple replacements from a fixed inventory of tones: The heavy lexical role played by tone limits complex environmentally conditioned alternations, and the lack of grammatical morphology has not led to the marking of syntagmatic relations by means other than word order.

7. GRAMMATICAL TONE AND GRAMMATICALIZED TONE RULES

In Africa particular tones and tone alternations are used in an incredible variety of ways to mark grammatical distinctions. Some grammatical use is made of tones in Mexican languages, but judging from the limited research I have been able to do on this area, it is less than in African languages. As pointed out in the previous section, Asian languages make only marginal grammatical use of tone.

There is no meaningful way to summarize all the grammatical uses of tone. Most grammatical relations shown by tonal alternations, such as alternations affecting nouns in associative noun phrase constructions, can be explained historically by one or a combination of the processes mentioned in Sections 3 and 4, perhaps with subsequent analogical or other changes obscuring the original natural processes. Just two ways in which tones manifest a grammatical function will be discussed here: grammatical tone assignment and floating tones in several functions.

By **grammatical assignment** of tone, I mean the morphological placement of a tone on a particular word or morpheme as the marker of a particular grammatical meaning. Many languages differentiate verb tenses/aspects in this way. In Etsako (Elimelich 1976) the only difference between the present progressive and the present progressive negative is in the tone of the subject pronoun:

51.   Present progressive: ɔ́ dàkpá   'he is buying a cup'
                                          ɔ́ dúkpò   'he is buying cloth'
        Present progressive negative: ɔ̂ dàkpá   'he is not buying a cup'
                                          ɔ̂ dúkpò   'he's not buying cloth'

In Ngizim (Schuh 1971), one of the distinctions between the perfective and the subjunctive is that the verb in the perfective has LO HI tones, whereas in the subjunctive, if the verb has Cə as the initial syllable, it has all LO tone, but it has all HI tone for verbs with other initial syllable types.

52.   Perfective: jà kərú   'we stole'
                                  jà kàasú   'we swept'
               Subjunctive: jà kərì   'that we steal'
                                  jà káaší   'that we sweep'

K. Pike (1948:23) gives the paradigm (53) for Mazatec, where 12 segmentally identical utterances are distinguished solely by tone. Mazatec has four level tones marked here as ` LO, ' lower-MID, ‾ higher-MID, ´HI. Many of the syllables carry complex tones. Both tone levels marked are heard on that syllable.

53.   sì' tē'   'I spin; I will spin'
      sí tē   'he spins'   sì' tē   'he will spin'
                                        sì tē   'we (incl.) will spin'

      sì' tè'   'I widen; I will widen'
      sí tè‾   'he widens'   sì‾ tè'   'he will widen'
                                        sì tè‾   'we (incl.) will widen'

      sì' tè   'I make into 10 pieces;
                I will make into 10 pieces'
      sí tè   'he makes into 10 pieces'   sì‾ tè   'he will make into 10 pieces'
                                        sì tè‾   'we (incl.) will make into
                                             10 pieces'

Welmers (1968:21) gives a similar paradigm of 12 segmentally identical utterances distinguished only by tone for two dialects of Jukun.

    Examples of floating tones have already been seen above, (32), (33), and (44). A few others are given here. In Etsako (Elimelich 1976), a floating HI tone between nouns in an associative construction explains tonal alternations found there. This must be combined with a rule raising all LOs directly preceding the floating HI to HI (cf. the first example). This raising does not apply if the tone preceding the HI associative tone is HI (cf. the last example):

54.   /àmè ´ èθà/ → ámêθà   'water of father'
                 /únò ´ òké/ → únôkê   'mouth of a ram'
                 /ódzí ´ ɔ́mɔ̀/ → ójɔ́mɔ̀   'crab of a child'
                 /ɔ̀té ´ èθà/   → ɔ̀têθà   'cricket of a father'

In Dschang Bamileke (Tadadjeu 1974), the associative marker carries HI or LO tone depending on class of the first noun. In this language the segmental associative marker à/è (for Classes 1 and 9) or á/é (for other classes) may actually be pronounced in carefully speech. However, in rapid speech the segmental disappears, leaving only floating HI or LO. What is particularly interesting in this language is that the effect of the floating tone is not always realized in the same way. Thus, in the first example in (55), the effect of the floating tone is heard on the syllable which follows it, whereas in the second example it is on the tone which precedes it:

55.   /làtɔ́ŋ ´ màsə́ŋ/ → [làtɔ́ŋ má'sə́ŋ]   'feather of birds'
        /m̀'bhù ` màsə́ŋ/ → ["m̆bhù màsə́ŋ]²⁷   'dog of birds'

---

²⁷ The mark "m̆" indicates a "double downstep." Details of its derivation are not important here.

Tadadjeu explains the direction of shift of the floating tone by pointing out that if the HI in the first example shifted to the left it would be absorbed by the preceding HI. In the second example, if the LO shifted to the right, it would be absorbed by the following LO. Thus, the floating tone shifts whichever direction is necessary for it to avoid disappearing and hence obscuring the construction. This phenomenon will be recognized as being the same as that in the Akan example cited in (32).

A somewhat different phenomenon is found in San Miguel Mixtec (Pike 1948), where there is something which one might call a floating "influencer" of sandhi. This language has three level tones. There is a tone sandhi rule which raises the initial syllable of a two syllable morpheme to HI. This rule applies to any initial non-HI except MID in the sequence MID HI; it is a morphological rule, since it applies only after morphemes marked to cause it. Thus, the morphemes *kēē* 'eat' and *ná* 'insist on' cause the change in the following words in (56a) because they are lexically marked to do so, whereas the morphemes *kēē* 'go away' (homophonous with the word for 'eat') and *nā-* 're-' in (56b) do not cause the change:

56.   a. *kēē + kòò*   → *kēē kóò*   'the snake will eat'
                 ná + kìkū-ná → *ná-kíkū-ná*   'I insist I will sew'
             b. *kēē kòò*   'the snake will go away'
                 nā-kìkū-ná   'I will mend (re-sew)'

Exactly the same alternation takes place in verbs in the continuative aspect, but here the verb need not be preceded by any segmental morpheme. Pike brings this alternation into line with the general alternation illustrated in (56a) by including in the continuative construction what he calls a "zero word" (written CON here), which is lexically marked to trigger the alternation just as normal segmental words may be.

57.   /CON + kìkū-ná/   → [kíkū-ná]   'I am sewing'
       /CON + nā + kìkū-nā/ → [nà-kìkū-ná]   'I am mending (resewing)'

REFERENCES

Abraham, R. C. 1959. *The language of the Hausa people.* London: Univ. of London Press.
Ansre, G. 1961. The Tonal Structure of Ewe. *Hartford Studies in Linguistics*, Hartford Seminary Foundation, *1.*
Armstrong, R. G. 1968. Yala (Ikom): A terraced-level language with three tones. *Journal of West African Languages*, 5, 49–58.
Bargery, G. P. 1934. *A Hausa-English dictionary and English-Hausa vocabulary.* London: Oxford Univ. Press.
Beach, D. M. 1924. The science of tonetics and its application to Bantu languages. *Bantu Studies*, 2, 73–106.
Bendor-Samuel, J. T., & Edmondson, T. 1966. Tone patterns of Etung. *Journal of African Languages*, 5, 1–6.

Chao, Y. R., & Yang, L. S. 1962. *Concise dictionary of spoken Chinese.* Cambridge: Harvard Univ. Press.

Clifton, J. M. 1976. Downdrift and rule ordering. *Studies in African Linguistics, 7,* 175–194.

Cope, A. T. 1970. Zulu tonal morphology. *Journal of African Languages, 9,* 111–152.

Courtenay, K. 1974. On the nature of the Bambara tone system. *Studies in African Linguistics, 5,* 303–323.

Elimelich, B. 1976. A tonal grammar of Etsako. *UCLA Working Papers in Phonetics, 35.*

Fromkin, V. A. 1972. Tone features and tone rules. *Studies in African Linguistics, 3,* 47–76.

George, I. 1970. Nupe tonology. *Studies in African Linguistics, 1,* 100–122.

Hombert, J.-M. 1974. Universals of downdrift: Their phonetic basis and significance for a theory of tone. In W. R. Leben (Ed.), *Papers from the 5th Annual Conference on African Linguistics. Studies in African Linguistics,* Supp. 5, Pp. 164–183.

Hombert, J.-M. 1976. Development of tones from vowel height. In J.-M. Hombert (Ed.), Studies on production and perception of tones. *UCLA Working Papers in Phonetics, 33,* 55–66.

Hyman, L. M. 1972. *A phonological study of Fe ?fe ?-Bamileke. Studies in African Linguistics,* Supp. 4.

Hyman, L. M. (Ed.). 1973a. Consonant types and tone. *Southern California Occasional Papers in Linguistics, 1.*

Hyman, L. M. 1973b. The role of consonant types in natural tonal assimilations. In L. M. Hyman (Ed.), Consonant types and tone. *Southern California Occasional Papers in Linguistics, 1,* 151–179.

Hyman, L. M. 1976. On some controversial questions in the study of consonant types and tone. In J.-M. Hombert (Ed.), *Studies on production and perception of tones. UCLA Working Papers in Phonetics, 33,* 90–98.

Hyman, L. M., & Magaji, D. J. 1970. *Essentials of Gwari grammar.* University of Ibadan, Institute of African Studies, Occasional Publications No. 27.

Hyman, L. M., & Schuh, R. G. 1974. Universals of tone rules: Evidence from West Africa. *Linguistic Inquiry, 5,* 81–115.

Kennedy, G. A. 1953. Two tone patterns in Tangsic. *Language, 29,* 367–373.

Kovitz, J. 1970. Chinese tone sandhi and the phonology of tone. Manuscript, MIT.

Leben, W. R. 1971a. Suprasegmental and segmental representation of tone. In *Papers from the 2nd Conference on African Linguistics,* UCLA, March 26–27. *Studies in African Linguistics,* Supp. 2, Pp. 183–200.

Leben, W. R. 1971b. The morphophonemics of tone in Hausa. In C. W. Kim & H. Stahlke (Eds.), *Papers in African Linguistics.* Edmonton, Alberta: Linguistic Research, Inc. Pp. 201–218.

Leben, W. R. 1973. The role of tone in segmental phonology. In L. M. Hyman (Ed.), Consonant types and tone. *Southern California Occasional Papers in Linguistics, 1,* 115–149.

Li, C. N., & Thompson, S. A. 1976. The acquisition of tone in Mandarin-speaking children. In J.-M. Hombert (Ed.), Studies in production and perception of tones. *UCLA Working Papers in Phonetics, 33,* 109–130.

Lukas, J. 1937. *A study of the Kanuri language.* London: Oxford Univ. Press.

Lukas, J. 1969. Tonpermeable und tonimpermeable Konsonanten im Bolanci (Nordnigerien). In *Ethnological and linguistic studies in honor of N.J. van Warmelo.* Department of Bantu Administration and Development, Republic of South Africa, Ethnological Publications No. 52, Pp. 133–138.

Maddieson, I. 1974. A note on tone and consonants. In I. Maddieson (Ed.), The tone tome: Studies on tone from the UCLA tone project. *UCLA Working Papers in Phonetics, 27,* 18–27.

Matisoff, J. A. 1973. Tonogenesis in Southeast Asia. In L. M. Hyman (Ed.), Consonant types and tone. *Southern California Occasional Papers in Linguistics, 1,* 71–114.

Mohr, B. 1973. Tone rules and the phonological representation of tones. Paper presented at the 6th International Conference on Sino-Tibetan Language and Linguistics, University of California, San Diego.

Newman, P. 1974. *The Kanakuru language. West African Language Monographs, 9.* Institute of Modern English Language Studies, University of Leeds.

Newman, R. Ma. 1971. Downstep in Ga'anda. *Journal of African Languages, 10,* 15–27.

Peters, A. M. 1973. A new formalization of downdrift. *Studies in African Linguistics, 4,* 139–153.

Pike, Eunice V. n.d. Tone systems of Mexico. Unpublished manuscript, Summer Institute of Linguistics.

Pike, Eunice V. 1948. Problems in Zapotec tone analysis. *International Journal of American Linguistics 14,* 161–170.

Pike, Kenneth L. 1948. *Tone languages.* Ann Arbor: Univ. of Michigan Press.

Pratt, Mary. 1972. Tone in some Kikuyu verb forms. *Studies in African Linguistics, 3,* 325–378.

Richardson, Irvine. 1971. "Displaced tones" in Sukuma. In C.-W. Kim & H. Stahlke (Eds.), *Papers in African Linguistics.* Edmonton, Alberta: Linguistic Research, Inc. Pp. 219–227.

Sampson, G. 1969. A note on Wang's "Phonological features of tone." *International Journal of American Linguistics 35,* 62–66.

Schachter, P. 1976. An unnatural class of consonants in siSwati. In Larry M. Hyman, Leon C. Jacobson, & Russell G. Schuh (Eds.), *Papers in African linguistics in honor of Wm. E. Welmers. Studies in African Linguistics,* Supp. 6, Pp. 211–220.

Schachter, P., & Fromkin, V. A. 1968. A phonology of Akan: Akuapem, Asante, and Fante. *UCLA Working Papers in Phonetics, 9.*

Schuh, R. G. 1971. Verb forms and verb aspects in Ngizim. *Journal of African Languages, 10,* 47–60.

Shimizu, K. 1971. Contraction of tones and inherent gliding tones. In I. Maddieson (Ed.), Tone in generative phonology. *Research Notes 3*(2-3), 41–49.

Sprigg, R. K. 1975. The inefficiency of "tone change" in Sino-Tibetan descriptive linguistics. Paper delivered at the 8th International Conference on Sino-Tibetan Languages and Linguistics, University of California, Berkeley, October.

Stahlke, H. 1971a. Topics in Ewe phonology. Unpublished Ph.D. dissertation, UCLA.

Stahlke, H. 1971b. The noun prefix in Ewe. In *Papers from the 2nd Annual Conference on African Linguistics,* UCLA, March 26–27. *Studies in African Linguistics,* Supp. 2, Pp. 141–159.

Tadadjeu, M. 1974. Floating tones, shifting rules, and downstep in Dschang-Bamileke. In W. R. Leben (Ed.), *Papers from the 5th Annual Conference on African Linguistics. Studies in African Linguistics,* Supp. 5, Pp. 283–90.

Wang, W. S.-Y. 1967. Phonological features of tone. *International Journal of American Linguistics, 33,* 93–105.

Welmers, W. E. 1968. *Jukun of Wukari and Jukun of Takum.* University of Ibadan, Institute of African Studies, Occasional Publications No. 16.

Welmers, B. F., & Welmers, W. E. 1968. *Igbo: A learner's dictionary.* Los Angeles: UCLA African Studies Center.

Welmers, W. E. 1976. A grammar of Vai. *University of California Publications in Linguistics, 84.*

Williamson, K. 1970. The generative treatment of downstep. In I. Maddieson (Ed.), Tone in generative phonology. *Research Notes, 3*(2–3), 22–39.

Yen, S. L. 1970. A note on the theoretical framework for tonal analysis. *International Journal of American Linguistics, 36,* 290–296.

VIII

Historical Tonology[1]

LARRY M. HYMAN

1. INTRODUCTION

In most respects the concerns of historical tonology are indistinguishable from those of historical phonology. Whether dealing with tones or with segments, the historical linguist seeks the same kinds of explanation and utilizes the same methodologies (comparative method, internal reconstruction, etc.). However, the historical tonologist is at a considerable disadvantage when competing with his segmental colleague. At least two centuries of scholarship have carefully documented segmental changes and have provided general principles underlying the nature of sound change. These principles have related either to structure (e.g., the interaction between a sound change and its pre- and postphonological system) or to substance (e.g., the phonetic motivation of sound changes). In tone, it is not always clear whether a proposed change is plausible or phonetically motivated. The study of tone changes in relation to tonological systems has also lagged behind its segmental counterpart.

In the present study an initial attempt is made to present some principles of historical tonology. Most of the arguments will be based on data from African languages, either cited from published sources or based on the author's field notes and analyses. Although no attempt was made to be exhaustive in covering the rapidly growing literature on tone, the principles proposed in this study are believed to have universal application and will have to be tested against tone languages from all parts of the world. In the following sections

[1] This research was supported in part by a National Science Foundation Grant, SOC 75-16487.

Tone: A Linguistic Survey

I shall address myself first to some preliminary general principles of change, and then to the nature of tone change itself.[2]

2. GENERAL PRINCIPLES

In approaching the subject of historical tonology, three general principles were accepted as essential working hypotheses.

2.1 The Principle of Nonarbitrariness

No tone change is arbitrary. Each tone change, like any other kind of linguistic change, is motivated by some principle, rather than by some whim or fancy. If all nouns begin with L tone, it is not because some speakers decided to lower the first tone of all nouns (but not verbs), but rather because there probably was a L tone noun prefix, since lost, at some earlier stage of the language.

2.2 The Principle of Synchronic and Diachronic Nonequivalence

Any tone change is a possible tonological rule. The converse is not true, that is, there are types of tone rules which, although synchronically valid, could not have taken place as tone changes. Thus, a synchronic rule changing a H tone to L only in the remote past tense could not have been introduced in equivalent form as a tone change. This follows from the principle of nonarbitrariness. Since many synchronic tone rules represent restructuring (telescoping, morphologization, etc.), it is necessary to insist on this nonequivalence. However, since we are at the mercy of synchronic tonology in applying the comparative method and internal reconstruction, we must be careful not to draw any unwarranted conclusions.

2.3 The Principle of Nonviolation of Linguistic Universals

No tone change produces an unacceptable tonal state. There is a necessary relationship between states and processes such that the latter cannot produce

---

[2] All of the African languages cited in this study belong to the Bantu group, except Yoruba, Igbo, and Gwari (which are Kwa languages), and Hausa and Bolanci (which are Chadic languages). The symbols used are as follows:

á	H	(high)	ǎ	R or $\widehat{LH}$, $\widehat{LM}$	(rising)
ā	M	(mid)	â	F or $\widehat{HL}$, $\widehat{ML}$	(falling)
à°	L°	(unreleased low)	'á	'H	(downstepped H)
à	L	(low)	à	'M	(lower-mid)

what is known to be in violation of some linguistic universal. A tone change cannot produce a system of eight phonemic tone levels (or pass through such a system) if such a tone system is universally excluded.

Having established these three principles, we shall now turn to the nature of tone change, which is treated under the following headings: (a) tonally induced change, (b) accentually induced change, (c) boundary-induced change, and (d) segmentally induced change. The term "induced" will be interpreted broadly to include factors which either effect or inhibit a given tone change.

3. TONALLY INDUCED CHANGE

Perhaps the best known type of tone change involves instances where one tone (T_m) causes a change on an adjacent tone (T_a). Let us refer to T_m as the motivating tone and T_a as the affected tone. Two principles are immediately obvious:

3.1 Principle of Adjacency

In all tonally induced change, the motivating tone must be **adjacent** to the affected tone. It is not possible for a L tone to lower any H tone two syllables later. That is, a change converting L–H–H–H to L–H–L–H is ruled out. It may occasionally be the case that mention must be made of a nonadjacent tone, as in the following rule proposed by Austen (1974) for Bukusu:

$$L \rightarrow H / L H \_\_\_\_ T \qquad \text{(where T = H or L)}$$

"A low tone, providing it is not word final, will assimilate to the high tone of the previous syllable, only if that particular high tone is itself preceded by a low tone [p. 23]." However, the motivating tone here is the H tone preceding the affected tone. Even in cases where L–H–H–H becomes L–L–L–H, it is necessary to postulate an intermediate historical stage L–L–H–H, in conformity with the adjacency principle.

3.2 Principle of Nonaccumulation

In order for tonally induced change to take place, it must be the case that $T_m \neq T_a$. Where $T_m = T_a$, no change is possible, since a L tone does not lower another L, and a H tone does not raise another H, etc. That is, like tones cannot be accumulated on the same syllabic unit. It follows, then, that we cannot have an opposition between /á/ with one H on it, and /a̋/ with two Hs. Like tones coalesce or absorb one into the other. It also follows that in a language like Tetela (Jacobs 1957:205), where words with reconstructed initial *V́CV́ begin with [CV́] on a higher pitch than words beginning with *V̀CV́, a lowering process has occurred on the latter, rather than a raising process on the former.

Notice, finally, in a language such as Ngamambo (Asongwed and Hyman 1976:35), where historical *L–H–L becomes L–'M–L ('M = lower-end), a *L–H–H–L sequence may be partially or totally exempt from this lowering process. The two H tones, which may eventually even come together on the same syllable, have in a sense reinforced each other, but not by accumulation.

Most tonally induced changes can be categorized as either **assimilations** or **simplifications** (cf. the synchronic analogues of Hyman 1973, Hyman and Schuh 1974). Two types of assimilation are distinguished. The first, termed **vertical**, occurs when T_a assimilates to or towards the pitch height of T_m. Thus, when L–H becomes M–H, we have an instance of anticipatory vertical raising; on the other hand, when L–H becomes L–M, we have an instance of perseverative vertical lowering, and so forth. The second type of assimilation is termed **horizontal** and involves instances where T_m enlarges its domain to encompass an adjacent T_a. Where the process is perserverative, it is known also as **tone spreading**, as when L–H becomes L–L͡H (low followed by rising tone) and H–L becomes H–H͡L (high followed by falling tone), both changes being attested in Yoruba and Gwari.

Two types of tone simplifications are also distinguished, both of which function to convert contour to level tones. The first type, termed **absorption**, converts L͡H–H to L–H and H͡L–L to H–L. That is, the end point of a contour tone is absorbed into an adjacent (normally following) like tone. Absorption may team up with tone spreading to create a rightward shifting of tones, e.g., L–H–L–L becomes L–L͡H–H͡L–L by two applications of tone spreading, and then L–L–H–L by two applications of tone absorption. The result is that the H of the second syllable has surfaced one syllable to the right, constituting an instance of **tone displacement** (Richardson 1959, van Spaandonck 1971; but cf. Batibo 1976). The second type of simplification, which may be referred to as **contour leveling**, takes place in environments where absorption is inapplicable. The most common inputs for leveling are H–L͡H and H͡L–H, both of which typically simplify as H–'H (H followed by downstepped H) in African languages. Note, however, that these simplifications can also convert L͡H or H͡L to H when adjacent to L or pause, e.g., L͡H–L becomes H–L, L–H͡L becomes L–H, L͡H and H͡L both become H on monosyllables in isolation, etc.

The interplay between assimilations and simplifications can be considerably more complex than the one example resulting in tone displacement. As shown for several Mbam-Nkam languages by Hyman and Tadadjeu (1976), the sequence H–L–H can have different histories, depending on whether the intervening L is affected by vertical or horizontal assimilation. Let us consider two dialects of Igbo. In Standard Igbo, [éwú] 'goat' and [àtó] 'three' combine to form [éwú 'átó] 'three goats'. A change occurs of the following form:

$$H–L–H > H–'H–H$$

Since the second H of the input is subject to intonational downdrift, this means that the phonetic sequence [⁻ _ —] has changed to [⁻ — —] by vertical assimilation. In Aboh Igbo, on the other hand, [éwú] 'goat' and [ètó] 'three' combine to yield [éwú é″tó]'three goats'. In this case we observe a change of the following form:

$$\text{H–L–H} > \text{H–H–'H} \qquad \text{(via H–}\widehat{\text{HL}}\text{–H)}$$

This change, it is claimed, necessarily involves an intermediate H–$\widehat{\text{HL}}$–H stage, where the horizontal nature of the assimilation is evident. This conclusion is borne out by the fact that historical H–L nouns are realized H–$\widehat{\text{HL}}$ in Aboh Igbo, e.g., *úlò > [únô] 'house'. The fact that 'house' is pronounced [úlò] in Standard Igbo illustrates even more clearly that some other kind of assimilation is involved in the two dialects. An implicational universal is proposed as follows:

> If a language has undergone rightward spreading of H in a H–L–H sequence, it has necessarily also undergone rightward spreading of H in the corresponding H–L and H–L–L sequences.

That is, the second H of the H–L–H sequence will, if anything, **retard** the process of horizontal assimilation, because a H–$\widehat{\text{HL}}$–H sequence is a more complex articulation than a H–$\widehat{\text{HL}}$ or H–$\widehat{\text{HL}}$–L sequence. Thus, some languages allow spreading to occur on H–L–L sequences, but not on H–L–H (cf. Hyman and Schuh 1974d).

The above discussion of assimilations and simplifications leads us to distinguish two basic underlying principles governing tonally induced change:

3.3 Principle of Ups and Downs

Tonally induced changes tend to minimize the number of ups and downs over a given stretch. In the case of contour simplification, the "stretch" may be as short as a syllable. When H–L–'H (where 'H is intonationally downdrifted) becomes H–'H–H, a sequence involving two changes in pitch is simplified to only one change in pitch. The principle of ups and downs not only accounts for most instances of vertical assimilations and contour levelings, but also predicts that change will occur first where the ups and downs are the most complex. Thus, a H–$\widehat{\text{LH}}$ or $\widehat{\text{HL}}$–H sequence is much more likely to undergo change than a L–$\widehat{\text{LH}}$ or $\widehat{\text{HL}}$–L sequence. Also, a sequence of interspersed Ls and Hs is more likely to undergo change than a sequence of interspered Ls and Ms, or Ms and Hs, etc.

3.4 Principle of Desynchronization

Tonally induced changes tend to delay changes in pitch in such a way that the tones are desynchronized with respect to their original syllabic support. The result is the rightward horizontal assimilations and absorptions which have been referred to above. Desynchronization is most likely to occur where the ups and downs are maximal. Thus, in some languages *H–L has become H–$\widehat{\text{HL}}$, while M–L has remained M–L.

In the operation of the two principles above, timing factors play a key role. Thus, contour simplifications are in some sense an alternative to lengthening the syllabic support to accommodate the contour. Also, it is interesting to note that when tones and syllables come to be out of phase with one another, it is almost always the case that the tones will last too long, rather than the reverse. Changes such as H–L becoming $\widehat{\text{HL}}$–L and L–H becoming $\widehat{\text{LH}}$–H are not motivated from a phonetic point of view (cf. Section 4).

Needless to say, assimilations and simplifications are more widespread than the African examples might suggest. The simplification of a $\widehat{\text{HM}}$–H (*53–5*) sequence to H–H (*5–5*) in Cantonese is not unlike the contour levelings discussed above. Cases such as Mandarin *214–214* becoming *35–214* can also be seen as minimizing the ups and downs combined with timing factors (cf. Hyman 1975:94), although some scholars have chosen to view this change as one of **dissimilation** (where the *214* contour is considered to be a synchronic underlying L tone). Very few cases of tonal dissimilation can be demonstrated to have occurred as processes (i.e., as historical changes rather than as synchronic reflexes of other changes). Leben's (1971:202) Hausa rule which converts L–L to L–H when the second L is on a long vowel and occurs before pause seems to be a clear example. Other cases where L–L becomes L–H or H–L have been shown to be due to an intervening H tone which was lost historically but which continues to exert a raising effect. Thus, when the two nouns [ŋkù] 'message' and [pɛ̀ɣù] 'strangers' are combined in Bamileke-Babete to form a genitive construction, the result is [ŋkù pɛ́ɣù] 'the message of the strangers' (Hyman and Tadadjeu 1976:60). The L of the prefix of 'strangers' has gone up to H not as the result of a historical dissimilation process, but rather as the result of an intervening H tone genitive (or associative) marker whose only affect is tonal. Since it is not always possible to reconstruct with confidence such historical tones, it is difficult to assess how frequently dissimilation occurs as a historical process.

4. ACCENTUALLY INDUCED CHANGE

Languages from various parts of the world have been described with both (stress-) accent and tone. Often the presence of an accent can be determined only by its effect on tone. This effect is seen in two ways.

4.1 Principle of Accentual Prominence

A tone which occurs under the influence of an accent may change to make that tone (or syllable) more prominent. What this usually means is that a level tone will become a contour, as in Haya and several other Bantu languages, where a final H–L sequence becomes F–L by means of a penultimate accent. Thus, historical *ómùkónò 'arm' has become [òmùkônò] in present-day Haya. In the phrase [òmùkónò gwàŋgè] 'my arm' the historical H is exhibited by virtue of its not being in penultimate position.

4.2 Principle of Accentual Preservation

A tone which occurs under the influence of an accent may be exempt from a tone rule which would have detracted from the prominence of that tone. In such a case the original tone is actually preserved. In Haya there has been a tone change of the following form:

$$L–H–H > L–L–H$$

A L tone spreads into a H tone to the right if the latter is in turn also followed by a H. As an example, *àbóná nyìnà 'he sees his mother' becomes [àbòná nyìnà]. However, when the affected H occurs in penultimate position with respect to the % phrase boundary (cf. Byarushengo, Hyman, and Tenenbaum 1976:193ff.), it is exempted from the above rule. Historical *àmùbóná % nyìnà 'he sees her, his mother', where % separates the main clause from the right-dislocated or afterthoughted noun, comes to the surface without tonal modification. The historical H tone is preserved under accent, since the change from H to L would result in a loss of prominence in penultimate position.

In some cases the accent may be manifested only on the tone of the **following** syllable. In Kombe (Elimelech 1976:120), Chichewa (Trithart 1976), Chasu (Kähler-Meyer 1962:258n), and probably other Bantu languages, a final H–H sequence can or must be realized as H followed by a lowered H. It is tempting to interpret such an occurrence as involving first the change of a H penultimate to a $\widehat{HL}$ falling tone (i.e., F–H), which then simplifies as H–'H (or H–M). When such sequences are no longer in phrase-final position, H–H is obtained, e.g., Kombe [čɛ́'lɛ́] 'sand' versus [čɛ́lé ndîrà] 'that's sand' (Elimelech 1976:116).

4.3 Principle of Accentual Attraction

The tone of an unaccented syllable or syllables can assimilate to the tone of an accented syllable. This usually means that syllables preceding an accented H tone may anticipate that H tone. This appears to be the case in Luganda (Kalema 1977), where all H tonal accents but the last in a phrase are reduced, and then H tone is assigned to all syllables up to and including this accent, e.g., kìkópò 'cup' and mùkázì 'woman' combine and undergo accent reduction to yield intermediate kìkòpò kyàà mùkázì 'the cup of the woman', which then becomes [kìkópó kyáá múkázì].

The accent which is anticipated may under certain circumstances become indistinguishable from the H tone itself. Carter (1973:47) points out that anticipation occurs in areas of the Bantu zone where there has been partial reduction of the proto tonal oppositions. It is possible that the type of anticipation of H tone reported by Schadeberg (1976) can be attributed to the accentlike nature of H tone in such languages. In Kirundi (Meeussen 1959) and Kinyarwanda (Kimenyi 1976), anticipation regularly occurs. Thus, consider the following historical derivations:

$$*kùbónà > kùbônà > kúbônà > kúßònà \quad \text{'to see'}$$
$$*kùdó:tà > kùdô:tà > kúdô:tà > kúrô:tà \quad \text{'to dream'}$$

The two reconstructions involve H tone roots -bón- and -dó:t-, which differ only in that the latter contains a long vowel. The changes involved are: (a) The H tone becomes a F tone, perhaps because it is interpreted as accentlike (see below); (b) the F tone is anticipated as a H on the preceding syllable (cf. L assimilating to H before a following $\widehat{HL}$ tone in Shi [Polak-Bynon 1975:108]); (c) a F tone on a short vowel becomes L after H, a sort of left absorption process. The result is a leftward shift of the H of 'to see' and an anticipation of the $\widehat{HL}$ of 'to dream'.

The generalization which appears to hold across Bantu languages can be stated as follows: "The more accentlike a H tone is, the more likely tonal anticipation will occur." A H tone will be judged to be more accentlike if at some level the language tends towards treating H tone as culminative in nature (i.e., one H per word, etc.). There is phonetic evidence in Kirundi (Stevick 1969:338) and also Kinyarwanda (personal observations with Alexandre Kimenyi) that H is tending to be viewed as accentlike. This is shown by the fact that a word like 'to see', historically L–H–L, can optionally be realized in a number of ways by the same speaker on different occasions:

L–F–L [＿ ⌐＿], R–F–L [⊔⌐＿], H–F–L [⌐ ⌐＿], H–L–L [⌐ ＿＿]

What seems to be important here is not that there is a H tone on a specific syllable (or syllables), but rather that there is a H tone with a drop to L somewhere (anywhere?) in this word. Thus, the whole word stands in opposition to a verb such as kùròrà 'to look', which lacks this drop from H to L. It is as if Kirundi and Kinyarwanda speakers, on their way to the Luganda situation, are no longer asking one by one whether a syllable has H or L tone, but rather whether a **word** has an (accentual?) drop in it somewhere. And it is because of this change from a pure (syllable) tone language to a restricted tone language (Voorhoeve 1973) that tonal anticipation is attested. In stable syllable tone languages such as those found in West Africa (Igbo, Yoruba, etc.), a change of L–H–L to H–H–L is, in the absence of accent, unmotivated.

5. BOUNDARY-INDUCED CHANGE

Tone changes can also be motivated (or in certain cases inhibited) by phonetic and grammatic boundaries. By phonetic is meant pause boundaries; by grammatical, we refer to word and phrase boundaries.

5.1 Principle of Pause as L Tone

A pause boundary can at any time cause a lowering of an adjacent H or other nonlow tone. Adjacent is interpreted here as meaning either (*a*) on a syllabic unit adjacent to the pause, or (*b*) on a syllable adjacent to a pause. The difference is the treatment of CV after pause and (C)V́C before a pause, where the syllabic unit, the vowel, is separated from the pause by a consonant. The first environment is more likely to induce lowering than the second, although both environments have been attested as causing this change. In Haya, as well as many other Bantu languages, a H in final position, passing through a F stage, becomes L, for example, **ábóná* 'he sees' is pronounced [àbónà]. Similarly, the H of the initial vowel or preprefiix is lowered to L immediately after pause; cf. [ókùjùnà] 'to help' + [òmwâ:nà] 'child', which combine to form [òkùjùn ómwâ:nà] 'to help the child'. The H tone initial vowel will have H tone except after pause.

Perhaps related to the effect of pause boundaries on tone is the role of intonation. A number of Bantu languages have been noted to raise a final L to H in certain cases. It is tempting to attribute this to the grammaticalization of an intonation type. Cf. Meeussen (1959) for Kirundi: "En fin de phrase 'non définitive', un ton bas final est souvent réalisé à un niveau plus haut, sans que cette élévation ait une valeur distinctive [p. 18]." The example he gives is *bàràbìmènyà* 'they know it', pronounced [‾‾‾‾‾]. The role of intonation in tone change is as poorly understood as is intonational change itself.

5.2 Principle of Demarcation

A boundary may function to **block** a tonal change from applying across it. As a result, the integrity of the grammatical unit (e.g., the word) is thereby preserved. This is particularly noted in languages where a tonal configuration is generalized to a whole grammatical unit, e.g., the word.

6. SEGMENTALLY INDUCED CHANGE

A tone can undergo modification if it is adjacent to or occurs on a segment of a given type. The effect of consonant types on tone has been studied by a

number of scholars (cited in Hyman 1973, Hombert 1975), who generally agree
that voiceless consonants exert a pitch-raising effect on a following tone, while
voiced consonants (especially breathy and obstruent) exert a pitch-lowering
effect. There is some evidence that all obstruents exert a lowering effect on
preceding tones. As argued by Human and Schuh (1974:108), voiceless consonants can block the spreading of L tone through them, while voiced consonants can block the spreading of H tone (see Hombert, this volume).

A somewhat different situation concerns the affect of syllable structure on
the tone which occurs on them. Asongwed and Hyman (1976:32) have demonstrated that the tone of noun prefixes in Ngamambo is predictable from
their syllabic structure: Nasal prefixes carry L tone, vowel prefixes carry M
tone, and CV prefixes carry H tone. Historical H tone appears to have been
lowered to M on vowel-initial prefixes. Similarly, as pointed out by Newman
(1972:307–308), in Bolanci, verbs ending in -u will have L–H tone if their first
syllable is heavy (CV: or CVC), but H–H if their first syllable is light (CV, i.e.,
with a short vowel). Finally, Meeussen (1955:155) has shown that historical
H–L has surfaced in Shambala as H–L if the vowel of first syllable was long,
but as H–H if it was short.

     cf. *-dó:t- > [-lótà] 'dream'   versus   *-túm- > [-túmá] 'send'

Thus, tonal histories are sensitive to the kind of segmental support on which
the tones reside. A contour tone is more likely to be maintained on a heavy
syllable than on a light syllable (cf. the Kinyarwanda example above).
Meeussen's example suggests that tone spreading may be enhanced if the
spreading tone is on a short vowel (light syllable?). Finally, certain final consonants have a shortening effect on the preceding vowel and may therefore
discourage contour tones from appearing before them. A case in point derives
from Bamileke-Feʔfeʔ. In Feʔfeʔ, as in most Bamileke dialects, there is a L°
tone (unreleased or nonfalling L, deriving from historical L–H by loss of the
final syllable). Nouns which carry this tone in isolation develop a L͡M rising
tone when followed by L: [ǹkɔ́p°] 'finger-nail', but [ŋ̀kɔ́b à] 'my fingernail'
(Hyman 1972:136). However, when the L° noun ends in a glottal stop, a different pattern is observed: [ŋ̀gù̙ʔ°] 'strength', but [ŋ̀gù̙ʔ â] 'my strength'. In
this example, instead of obtaining L͡M–L, we obtain L–M͡L. That is, the M
of the rising contour has been sent to the right of the glottal stop, suggesting
that the vowel-shortening effect of a glottal stop conflicts with the duration
requirements of the rising tone. A segment has thus caused a tone change.

By far the most pervasive effect of segments on tones in African languages
is observed when the syllabic support of a tone is lost historically. As we saw
in the Bamileke-Babete case, a H tone genitive marker occurs without syllabic
support between two nouns in an associative construction. We know from
comparative evidence that this marker used to be on a full syllable of the form
V or CV depending on the noun class of the possessed noun (see Hyman and

Tadadjeu 1976). By loss of that syllabic support, tone changes have been introduced on either the preceding or the following noun. Both grammatical and lexical "floating" tones have been noted in the literature. The stages involved in such historical derivations are as follows (cf. Hyman and Tadadjeu 1976).

6.1 Principle of Tone Grounding

When the syllabic support of a tone drops historically, the tone either drops with the segment or is assigned to an adjacent syllable. Such assignment is termed **tone grounding**. In Hyman and Tadadjeu (1976:62), a number of tendencies were noted in conjunction with determining the direction of tone grounding. These included tonal, segmental, and grammatical factors.

6.2 Principle of Tonal Equivalence

Once a floating tone has been grounded, the resulting sequence behaves equivalently to the same sequence deriving from underlyingly grounded tones. If a floating tone is gounded onto a like tone, coalescence or fusion takes place. If a floating tone is grounded onto an unlike tone, a contour results, and this contour may then be subject to tonal simplifications. Detailed argumentation and derivations are available in the above cited work.

7. CONCLUSION

In the above sections we have surveyed the different types of motivations for tone changes and proposed several principles governing historical tonology. Not treated adequately was the means by which tonal changes may lead to changes in tonal systems. Of particular interest is the development of terraced-level tone systems from discrete-level tone systems, and vice versa. Since a separate paper is now in preparation on this subject, only a few comments will be made here.

There is evidence that a system of tonal dowsteps may come into being as the result of contour simplifications of the type $\widehat{HL}$–H and H–$\widehat{LH}$ becoming H–'H. According to this view, intonational downdrift is **not** the primary source of phonemic downstep, as previously believed, and still believed by some scholars. Downstepped Hs and Ls as well as double-downstepped tones have been demonstrated to be the result of minimizing the number of ups and downs as those become condensed onto shrinking syllabic sequences (cf. the discussion of floating tones above).

A downstep system can undergo a change to discrete-level in one of two ways. First, it can choose to create a new "superhigh" level, as seen in Bamileke-

Fe ˀfe ˀ (Hyman 1976b). The sequence H–'H has been reinterpreted as S–H. A H–'H–'H sequence would emerge today as S–S–H (analyzed as H–H–M in most treatments of Fe ˀfe ˀ). The second alternative is for each H–'H sequence to be reinterpreted as H–L, as has happened in much of Bantu. Consider the following surface realizations of *-bón-* 'see' in Haya:

   tàbálibònà 'they will not see'   *tìbálikìbôna* 'they will not see it'

The second form is straightforward, deriving from historical *-kì-bón-à*. The first form, however, is in terms of motivated tonal assimilations inexplicable— why should *-bón-* go down to L in this future tense only? And why should it not go down to L when there is an object infix pronoun? The answer lies in the reconstruction of the subject marker as **bá˷*, in which case the first form reconstructions as **tì-bá˷-lí-bón-à*. The L of the H̃L subject marker causes a following H to become a 'H, yielding intermediate L–H'–H–H. It is this sequence which later becomes L–H–L–H when the system ceases to permit downstepped tones. The present of the L tone pronoun in the second form serves as further evidence for this reconstruction. The L of the H̃L subject marker is simply absorbed into the **-kì-* pronoun, and its effect is stopped. We therefore must postulate an early stage with tonal downsteps, a later stage without tonal downsteps—and, in some cases, a still later stage with **new** downsteps created in other contexts.

REFERENCES

Asongwed, T., Hyman, L. M. 1976. Morphotonology of the Ngamambo noun. In L. M. Hyman (Ed.), *Studies in Bantu tonology. Southern California Occasional Papers in Linguistics, 3.* Pp. 23–56.

Austen, C. L. 1974. Anatomy of the tonal system of a Bantu language. *Papers from the 5th Conference on African Linguistics. Studies in African Linguistics,* Supp. 5, pp. 21–33.

Batibo, H. 1976. A new approach to Sukuma tone. In L. M. Hyman (Ed.), *Studies in Bantu tonology. Southern California Occasional Papers in Linguistics, 3.* Pp. 241–257.

Byarushengo, E. R., Hyman, L. M., & Tenenbaum, S. 1976. Tone, accent, and assertion in Haya. In L. M. Hyman (Ed), *Studies in Bantu tonology. Southern California Occasional Papers in Linguistics, 3.* Pp. 183–205.

Carter, H. 1973. Tonal data in *Comparative Bantu. African Language Studies, 14,* 36–52.

Elimelech, B. 1976. Noun tonology in Kombe. In L. M. Hyman (Ed), *Studies in Bantu tonology. Southern California Occasional Papers in Linguistics, 3.* Pp. 113–130.

Hombert, J.-M. 1975. Towards a theory of tonogenesis: An empirical, physiological, and perceptually-based account of the development of tonal contrasts in language. Unpublished Ph.D. dissertation, Univ. of California, Berkeley.

Hyman, L. M. 1972. *A phonological study of Fe'fe'-Bamileke. Studies in African Linguistics,* Supp. 4.

Hyman, L. M. (Ed.). 1973. *Consonant types and tone. Southern California Occasional Papers in Linguistics, 1.*

Hyman, L. M. 1975. Review of C. C. Cheng, *A synchronic phonology of Mandarin Chinese. Journal of Chinese Linguistics, 3,* 88–99.

Hyman, L. M. (Ed.). 1967a. *Studies in Bantu tonology. Southern California Occasional Papers in Linguistics, 3.*

Hyman, L. M. 1976b. D'où vient le ton haut du bamileke-fe?fe??. In L. M. Hyman, L. C. Jacobson, & R. G. Schuh (Eds.), *Papers in African linguistics in honor of Wm. E. Welmers. Studies in African Linguistics,* Supp. 6, pp. 123–134.

Hyman, L. M., & Schuh, R. G. 1974. Universals of tone rules: Evidence from West Africa. *Linguistic Inquiry, 5,* 81–115.

Hyman, L. M., & Tadadjeu, M. 1976. Floating tones in Mbam-Nkam. In L. M. Hyman (Ed), *Studies in Bantu tonology. Southern California Occasional Papers in Linguistics, 3.* Pp. 57–111.

Jacobs, J. 1957. Long consonants and their tonal function in Telela. *Kongo-Overzee, 23,* 200–212.

Kähler-Meyer, E. 1962. Studien zur tonalen Struktur der Bantusprachen, II: Chasu. *Afrika und Übersee, 46,* 250–295.

Kalema, J. 1977. Accent modification rules in Luganda. *Studies in African Linguistics, 8,* Pp. 127–141.

Kimenyi, A. 1976. Tone anticipation in Kinyarwanda. In L. M. Hyman (Ed.), *Studies in Bantu Tonology. Southern California Occasional Papers in Linguistics, 3.* Pp. 167–181.

Leben, W. R. 1971. The morphophonemics of tone in Hausa. In C.-W. Kim & H. Stahlke (Eds.), *Papers in African Linguistics.* Edmonton: Linguistic Research Inc. Pp. 201–218.

Meeussen, A. E. 1955. Tonunterschiede als Reflexe von Quantitätsunterschieden im Shambala. In J. Lukas (Ed.), *Afrikanistische Studien.* Berlin: Akademie Berlag. Pp. 154–156.

Meeussen, A. E. 1959. *Essai de grammaire rundi.* Tervuren: Annales du Musée Royal du Congo Belge.

Newman, P. 1972. Syllable weight as a phonological variable. *Studies in African Linguistics, 3,* 301–323.

Polak-Bynon, L. 1975. *A Shi grammar.* Tervuren: Annales du Musée Royal de l'Afrique Centrale.

Richardson, I. 1959. *The role of tone in the structure of Sukuma.* London: School of Oriental and African Studies.

Schadeberg, T. C. 1976. Anticipation of tone: Evidence from Bantu. Paper presented at the 7th Conference on African Linguistics, Gainesville, Florida.

Stevick, E. W. 1969. Tone in Bantu. *International Journal of American Linguistics, 35,* 330–341.

Trithart, L. 1976. Desyllabified noun class prefixes and depressor consonants in Chichewa. In L. M. Hyman (Ed), *Studies in Bantu tonology. Southern California Occasional Papers in Linguistics, 3.* Pp. 259–286.

van Spaandonck, M. 1971. *L'analyse morphotonologique dans les langues bantoues.* Trans. by Luc Bouquiaux. Paris: Société d'Etudes Linguistiques et Anthropologiques de France. Pp. 23–24.

Voorhoeve, J. 1973. Safwa as a restricted tone system. *Studies in African Linguistics, 4,* 1–22.

IX

The Acquisition of Tone

CHARLES N. LI and SANDRA A. THOMPSON

1. INTRODUCTION

The study of the acquisition of tone by children learning their first language is in its infancy, like the tone acquirers themselves. The number of studies available at this writing does not go into double digits, and of these, most are either informal and unpublished or anecdotal and extremely superficial.

The best statement that can be made about tone acquisition at this point, then, is that much more research must be done before any significant generalizations can be proposed with confidence. There are entire language areas for which nothing specific is known about tone acquisition (Africa, Central America, South America, and New Guinea), and even in those language areas for which some data are available, only one longitudinal multisubject study is available at present (for Chinese). Within these limitations, however, a few tentative generalizations do emerge rather clearly; more apparent, however, are the central issues which future studies should address themselves to.

2. THE QUESTIONS

In the area of tone acquisition a number of interesting general questions arise which require answers. Because of the sparsity of research in this area. as mentioned above, few answers can be provided; but it has often been said that in the development of a science the questions one asks are sometimes as important as the answers one has found. The questions direct the course of future research. Thus, in a volume on tone it is important to summarize some of the questions of interest which we will do in this section. We will then follow the list of questions with a summary of the small amount of data which is at present available, data which may provide clues to the full answers we seek.

Tone: A Linguistic Survey

The questions fall into five main groups. All five sets include questions that may be related to the research on the nature of segmental phonology acquisition, in that possible differences between segmental and tonal acquisition have particular bearing on phonological theory.

    I. Chronology of acquisition
        A. What is the relationship between the time when the child has mastered the tone system and the time when E^1 has mastered the segmental system of E's language?
        B. In what order is mastery over the various tones in the system acquired?
    II. Deviations from the adult norm
        A. What range of substitutions do children make for tones which they have not yet mastered or acquired which occur in the adult language?
    III. Variation in the process of acquisition
        A. To what extent is there variation in strategies for tone acquisition among children learning the same language?
        B. To what extent is there variation in the acquisition of tone from one language to another?
    IV. Tone rules
        A. What are the differences in the child's output before, during, and after a tone rule is acquired?
        B. At what stage of the acquisitional process are tone rules acquired?
    V. The child's perception of tone
        A. To what extent is tone perception more advanced than tone production in first language acquisition?
        B. In what way do the child's problems in perceiving tonal contrasts parallel apparent difficulties in the production of these contrasts?

3. THE DATA

In this section all the data available to us will be summarized. The data will be discussed by geographical or language area, by language, and by the specific study conducted.

3.1 Central and South America

The only reference to tone acquisition that we know of concerning this part of the world is a footnote in a paper by Evelyn G. Pike (1949). That paper reports an informal experiment in which the author controlled the intonation

---

[1] We are using "E" for "he or she" and "E's" for "his or her." Thanks go to Donald Mackay for suggesting it.

pattern she used in presenting the words *baby* and *daddy* to her daughter who was just learning to speak English. Of general interest to the study of tone acquisition is the fact that the child mimicked her mother's intonation perfectly, providing support for the by now well-accepted claim that children are sensitive to pitch at the earliest stages of production. The footnote which refers to tone acquisition points out that a Mixteco neighbor child correctly pronounced the falling tone on two of his early words (p. 22).

3.2 Africa

We know of three sketchy sources for data on the acquisition of tone in African languages. Kirk (1973) analyzed imitated utterances from four children 2 and 3 years old. She contrasted 108 imitated utterances with their adult models in terms of rhythm, tone, and segmental phonemes and recorded the number of "units" (i.e., roughly syllables or phonemes) distorted per total number of units. She found that only 13% of the children's total number of distortions involved tonal errors, while 87% of the total involved segmental errors. She concludes that the children "imitate tone most accurately, segmental phonemes least accurately, and rhythm with an intermediate degree of accuracy [p. 273]." It is unfortunate that this study leaves unanswered so many of the questions that we might ask about tone acquisition in Gã.

Apronti (1969) presents a preliminary report on the language of his 2-year-old daughter learning Dangme in Ghana. We judge from the data he cites that, although there are a number of adult consonants either missing or unstable in the child's speech, the tones seem to be essentially correct. In addition, the fact that tone is **not** mentioned, although disappointing from our point of view, suggests that the tones were accurate and thus went unnoticed by the author. This, of course, may be a wrong inference.

Finally, we have some unpublished data on the language of a 2-year old Yoruba girl, collected by Sukari Salone at UCLA. Yoruba has three level tones at the phonological level in the adult language—High, Mid, Low—and a rule which changes the high and low tones into rising and falling tones in certain environments. The rules may be stated informally as:

$$\text{High} \longrightarrow \text{Rising} / \text{Low} \underline{\qquad}$$
$$\text{Low} \longrightarrow \text{Falling} / \text{High} \underline{\qquad}$$

Salone notes that her subject's tones were in general correct but that she did not seem to have internalized this rule. In one expression the child did produce the correct surface contour tone, but one cannot conclude from this that a rule had yet been formed. This is a most interesting finding, since it suggests that the child seemed to attend more to the abstract value of the high and low tones than to their phonetic manifestations. On the other hand, Salone also points out that there is another environment where the child seemed to be aware only of the surface form of a tone: Yoruba has a rule which changes a low tone verb to mid tone before a noun object, but for this child, at least, one low tone verb (*wò* 'look') was sometimes articulated with a mid tone even in sentence-final position.

We look forward to seeing more research on tone acquisition in Yoruba and other languages with similar systems. Further evidence for or against the internalization of tone rules which create surface phonetic forms not present in posited lexical representation (i.e., in the underlying repertoire of contrasts) can contribute to ongoing debates in phonological theory.

3.3 Asia

3.3.1 Thai

The Thai data comes from Tuaycharoen[2] (1977). The dialect studied has five tones, and essentially no tone sandhi. The tones are:

High level	⌐
Mid level	⊣
Low level	⌐
Falling	\
Rising	/

Tuaycharoen reports that her subject used mid and low tones from the age of 11 months, when his first words appeared. At this stage, the Mid and Low tones were substituted for the Falling, High, and Rising tones; the most frequent substitution was Low tone for High and Falling tones. Rising tone was also heard, but only in nonsense syllables which had become familiar during the prelexical stage. At about 14 months the child began to use the Rising tone on lexical items. Falling and High tones did not appear until the end of the fifteenth month, but even then these two tones were not used consistently. Tuaycharoen's subject appears to be an early language acquirer; comparing him to Tse's son (see Section 3.3.2) and the Mandarin-speaking children we studied, this Thai child was about 5 months ahead in reaching each stage. What is interesting is that, like the children in the other studies, he had mastered his tone system fairly well by the time he was beginning to produce two-word utterances (about the end of the fifteenth month).

3.3.2 Cantonese

Tse's (1977) study on the acquisition of Cantonese tone is based on observations of his son. There are six contrastive tones in the Cantonese dialect,

---

[2] Ms. Tuaycharoen was kind enough to make a special copy of her findings for us in advance of the formal submission of her thesis, for which we are most grateful.

including four level tones (High, Mid, Mid–Low, Low) and two contour tones (High Rising, Low Rising), as shown in the following schematic diagrams:

	Level	Rising
High	⌐	⌐
Mid	⊣	
Mid–Low	⌐	
Low	⌐	⌐[3]

Tse reached the following conclusions from his observational study:

1. Perceptual discrimination of tones began in the tenth month.
2. At 16 months, the beginning of his one-word stage, the child has mastered the High tone and the Low tone: ⌐, ⌐.
3. By 20 months, still in the single-word stage, the child had added the Mid tone and the High Rising tone to his repertoire: ⊣, ⌐.
4. The Low Rising tone and the Mid–Low tone ⌐, ⌐ were mastered at the emergence of the first two-word utterances in the twenty-first month. Some confusion between the High Rising and the Low Rising tones was observed briefly during this month as well.
5. The child still had difficulty with a number of segmental sounds at the age when the tone system was completely mastered.

Unfortunately, Tse does not indicate what the child did if he wanted to say a syllable whose tone he had not yet acquired; he does not present substitution data, except for the confusion noted in (4) above.

One factor which might affect the acquisition of a specific tone by children is the distribution of the tone in the language. If the tone rarely occurs, we can predict that its acquisition will be late. However, in Cantonese the Low Rising tone is fairly common. Thus, its late acquisition can not be explained by the frequency factor. There is a possible phonetic explanation, however. Phonetic evidence indicates that rising tones in general are more difficult to produce (Ohala 1973, and Chapter I in this volume) than other tones (see below).

We still have too little data on the kinds of substitution or avoidance strategies used by Cantonese-speaking children for the tones they have not yet mastered.

In a general study of his Cantonese-speaking daughter learning English, Light (in press) noticed that by the age of 19 months, when the child was still in a predominantly Cantonese speaking environment, her Cantonese utterances were tonally correct. The data collected by Light show that the child was producing multiword sentences at this age, so the correlation between mastery of the tone system and the ability to produce sentences matches the results of the Tse study. Another interesting observation in this study is that between

---

[3] There are phonetically conditioned variants of certain of these tones which need not concern us here.

30–36 months, after the family had moved back to the U.S., the child's productive command of tones partially disintegrated; many of her mispronuncia-
tions involved substituting High tone for High Rising tone and Mid–Low tone
for Low Rising tone. These findings suggest that level tones may be easier in
some sense than rising tones for Cantonese children. This lends some support
to Ohala's suggestion regarding the relative difficulty of producing rising tones.
However, since there are no falling tones in Cantonese, these data alone cannot
differentiate between a possible alternative hypothesis which would suggest
that level tones are easier to produce or to acquire than contour tones.

3.3.3 *Mandarin*

It is Mandarin on which the largest body of tone acquisition research has
been done. The Mandarin tone system includes four contrastive tones (High,
Rising, Dipping, Falling):

       High

       Rising

       Dipping

       Falling

There are two relevant tone sandhi rules:

    a. ⋎ → ⌐ before ⋎

    b. ⋎ → ⌐ before { ⌐ / ⋏ / ⋌ }

The pioneering work of Y. R. Chao (1951) concerns the Mandarin spoken
by his granddaughter, Canta, in her twenty-eighth month. He claims that
"Canta acquired tones very early, as most Chinese children do. Isolated tones
of stressed syllables are practically the same as in standard Mandarin [p. 32]."
However, he does not say how early the tones were acquired, nor does he give
any specific data as to the order of acquisition or substitution errors. He does
mention that records from the time Canta was about 16 months old showed
that she had "one instead of two rising tones, so that [hɛ] high–rising was either
shye 'shoe', [i.e., Rising—C.N.L. and S.A.T.] or *shoei* 'water' [i.e., Dipping—
C.N.L. and S.A.T.] which are now distinct in her speech [p. 27]." Interestingly
enough, however, though Canta at 28 months may have produced *xié* 'shoe'
and *shuǐ* 'water' with the correct Rising and Dipping tones, respectively, in
the Cantian lexicon which he provides, out of 51 Rising tone words, 15 of them
are transcribed as Dipping tone words in Canta's speech, though only one
Dipping tone word is transcribed as a Rising tone word. This suggests that
there was still some confusion for Canta between Rising and Dipping tones,
a finding which is strongly supported by our study discussed below. Chao also

reports that the sandhi rule of Mandarin which raises a Dipping tone to a Rising tone before another Dipping tone was only beginning to be learned by Canta.

The Clumeck study and the Li and Thompson study which follows it are complementary in that Clumeck was primarily investigating children's perception of tone while we were looking at their tone production.

For Clumeck (1976), two Mandarin-speaking children served as subjects in a set of phonemic discrimination tests. In each test, the child was given three items, two of which had names which differed only in tone, and the third of which had an entirely different name. The experimenter asked for each of the three objects five times in random order. Results of these tests show that the children had essentially no difficulty with the following four contrasts:

> High versus Dipping
> High versus Rising
> High versus Falling
> Dipping versus Falling

Both of them, however, had slightly more trouble with the Rising versus Falling distinction. Finally, on the Rising versus Dipping contrast, they seemed to be responding randomly. In interpreting these results, however, Clumeck notes that in the last two tests involving the Rising tone, one of the test items was a painted block with a nonsense syllable for a name. Hence, the results for these two tests are not directly comparable to those for the other four tests. However, the results from the last two tests can be compared with each other; they show that when the children were taught a new word with a Rising tone, they had greater difficulty discriminating it from a familiar Dipping tone word than from a familiar Falling tone word.

This is not a surprising finding. An examination of the pitch contours of the tones given schematically above shows that the Dipping tone is to a great extent a Rising tone. Furthermore the first tone sandhi rule (a) changes Dipping tones to Rising tones before Dipping tones. Thus the child does hear these two phonologically contrastive tones as identical, i.e., as rising. Furthermore, if the direction of the pitch change serves as a perceptual cue it is understandable why Rising and Falling tones are more easily discriminated. This finding again coincides with the other two studies reporting on language acquisition of Mandarin-speaking children, where it was also found that at early stages there is a confusion between Rising and Dipping tones.

In our study (Li and Thompson 1977) we investigated the spontaneous speech of 17 Mandarin-speaking children over a period of 7 months in Taipei, Taiwan. The ages of the children at the start of the investigation ranged from 18 to 34 months. Each child was visited approximately once every 2 or 3 weeks. All spontaneous conversations involving the child were recorded. The main method used to collect the data to be analyzed was to show the children pictures in a children's picture book asking the child to name the object shown in the picture. The data collected in this way as well as the data of the children's normal conversation were transcribed and analyzed quantitatively and qualitatively.

We were able to delineate four stages in the tone acquisition process:

Stage 1: The child's vocabulary is small. High and Falling tones predominate irrespective of the tone of the adult form.

Stage 2: The child is still at the one-word stage, but he has a larger vocabulary. The correct four-way adult tone contrast has appeared, but sometimes there is confusion between Rising and Dipping tone words.

Stage 3: The child is at the two–three-word stage. Some Rising and Dipping tone errors remain. Tone sandhi is beginnging to be acquired.

Stage 4: Longer sentences are being produced. Rising and Dipping tone errors are practically nonexistent.

The main results of our study can be summarized as follows:

1. The correct tone system is acquired relatively quickly and is mastered well in advance of the segmental system.
2. The High and Falling tones are acquired earlier and more easily than the Rising and Dipping tones.
3. Confusion persists in the form of substitution errors throughout Stages 2 and 3 between the Rising and Dipping tones.
4. The tone sandhi rules are learned, with infrequent errors, as soon as the child begins to produce multiword utterances.

Our study provides rather extensive documentation supporting the hypothesis that Rising and Dipping tones cause problems for Mandarin-speaking children, which is also confirmed by Chao's report on Canta and by Clumeck's perception study.

4. DISCUSSION

The results from the Asian language acquisition studies, the only ones presenting enough systematic data for consideration, bear on the two questions raised under I (p. 272) above, concerned with the chronology of acquisition.

4.1 Tones versus Segmentals

All the studies confirm the hypothesis that the tone system of a language is mastered before the segmental system. It seems clear that the smaller number of contrasts presented by a tone system as opposed to a segmental system partially accounts for the relative ease and speed with which children learn the tones of their language. Another factor having to do with the salience of pitch will be discussed below.

Support for this conclusion is provided by Tuaycharoen, who points out that her Thai subject had mastered the tone system by the age of 23 months but had not, by that time, acquired diphthongs, triphthongs, or initial consonant clusters.

Similarly, Tse's son learning Cantonese was making very few tonal "mistakes" at 22 months, although he had acquired only one of the last of the three final stops -p, -t, and -k, and was not yet producing l or æ.

The consistent pattern found among the children surveyed in our Mandarin tone project in Taiwan was that the acquisition of tones was always far more advanced than the acquisition of segmentals, and the tone system is always mastered before the segmental system. We have many examples of utterances which are tonally perfect but which are incomprehensible due to the segmental "errors." One of our subjects, for example, at 26 months, was making very few tonal errors, all of which were confined to substitutions of Rising for Dipping tones or vice versa. During this same period her affricates were extremely unstable, usually substituted for by stops, and she did not have l in her segmental inventory. During one taping session, we recorded the following segmental renditions for [čaŋ jiŋ lu] 'giraffe', none of them repetitions:

> [a di du]
> [da di du]
> [da di u]
> [a ži u]
> [ya ǰi wu]
> [za ǰi du]

The tone pattern for this word is ⌐_⌐⟍, which she always produced. (Note that this pattern—Rising–Low Level–Falling—is the result of the second tone sandhi rule.)

It was based on these findings that we reached the conclusion stated at the beginning of this section, that the tone system seems to be acquired quickly and mastered well in advance of the segmental system. On the basis of the data available to date, we can tentatively suggest the following progression. By the time the child is productively using single words, the tones of these words are for the most part correct. Roughly, by the time words are beginning to be combined, the child has already mastered the tone system, but E's consonant and vowel production is still far from standard.

The Tse findings roughly match the Li and Thompson findings as to duration: Tse's son took 8 months from the time he uttered his first word with its correct High Level tone to acquire the complete six-tone system. In our study there were two children who acquired the tone system during the 7 months we were observing them. When we began our taping, one was using only High, Mid, and Low Level tones, and the other only High and Falling tones. We do not know how long they had been at this stage in their linguistic development, but their vocabulary and utterances indicated that they were at the onset of their acquisition process. At the end of 7 months, they were both using all four tones nearly perfectly.

As noted above, the smaller number of tonal contrasts which have to be learned by the child offers one explanation for the differences observed between the acquisition of tonal and segmental contrasts. To this must be added the observation that pitch seems to be highly salient even in languages where it is not used to contrast lexical items. There are, for example, a number of studies suggesting that distinctive intonation patterns can be detected in the young infant's early vocal behavior. Kaplan (1970) shows that normal falling and rising intonation contours in English can be discriminated by 8-month-old children. Lenneberg (1967) cites complementary evidence suggesting that an infant's produced intonation patterns become distinct at 8 months. The early use of prosodic features is also reported by Weir (1966) and Atkinson-King (1973) (also see references cited in these two studies). Crystal (1970) cites studies demonstrating that children from 7–10 months have "primitive lexical items" with a "suprasegmental character" which is more stable and more readily elicited than the segmental character (p. 80). Kaplan and Kaplan (1970) report that most of the literature suggests that at about 5–6 months, the child is primarily processing suprasegmental aspects of speech, while Crystal (1973) states that most observers conclude that 6–7 months is the most likely period for the emergence of such features in production.

Thus, the early acquisition of tone may be seen as a special case of the early acquisition of prosodic features in general.

4.2 Order of Mastery of Tones in the System

Let us summarize the Tuaycharoen, Tse, and Li and Thompson findings on the chronological order in which the tones were acquired:

		Thai	Cantonese	Mandarin
1.	Early	⊣ ⌐	⌐ ⌐	⌐
2.	Intermediate	⟋	⊣ ⌐	⟍
3.	Late	⟍ ⌐	⊣ ⊣	⟋ ⌐

When these results are compared, it is clear that these data do not present an unambiguous, straightforward picture regarding the order of the tones acquired. Across all three languages, however, level tones were acquired before contour tones, i.e., the first tones acquired were level even if the particular level tones differed according to language.

It is interesting that Tse's subject acquired three of the four level tone contrasts in Cantonese relatively early. Furthermore Tse makes no mention of any substitution errors among these four tones, although he does mention some confusion between the High and Low Rising tones approximately one month before the system became stable. The ease with which Tse's son seemed to manage a four-way level tone contrast may appear, at first glance, to cast some doubt on the plausability of our suggestion offered above that the similarity between the Mandarin Rising and Dipping tones plays a role in accounting for their confusion among children acquiring Mandarin Chinese. However, one would first have to show that the four level tones are perceptually more confusable than are the two Rising and Dipping tones. This is not necessarily the case as is shown by perception experiments, the findings of which reveal the ability of the human ear to differentiate between many more than four pitch levels.

It may also be observed that the order of acquisition of Thai tones is nearly a mirror image of the Mandarin tone acquisition order: Falling and High Level tones are acquired last in Thai but first in Mandarin; the Rising tone is acquired earlier than the High Level and Falling tones in Thai, whereas it is acquired last (after the High Level and Falling tones) in Mandarin. It would be very difficult to draw any conclusions regarding relative difficulty or ease of production from such contradictory orders of acquisition.

In trying to make generalizations from these tone acquisition studies a number of points must be kept in mind which confound the picture even more.

1. **Number of subjects:** It is obvious that further research is needed to determine the extent to which the results obtained for any one child will hold for a large number of children before reliable cross-language comparisons can be made. So far there are data for just one Thai child, one Cantonese child, and two Mandarin children (the only two in our study who had not already acquired the basic tone system by the time we began our investigation). The studies in the acquisition of segmental phonology reveal that order of acquisition of segments (and features) varies across children; the same may therefore be true of tone acquisition.

2. **Distribution of tones in the child's lexicon:** This factor may account for some of the discrepancies across languages noted above; a meaningful cross-language comparison can only be made if some control over this variable can be achieved. Thus, while the child's vocabulary is distributed fairly evenly over the four tones in Mandarin, as our study revealed, this may not be the case in other languages. One would suspect that the distribution of tones in the child's lexicon correlates with the distribution of tones in the adult's, but this may not be the case. A statistical survey of tone distribution in both the adult language and in the lexicons of the children's language may be relevant in explaining the order of acquisition of tones in a particular language.

3. **Role of tones within the language:** In addition to the role played by the perceptual similarities and differences of tone in explaining the relative order of acquisition, functional factors may also be responsible. For example, we mentioned above that the neutralization of the Mandarin Rising and Dipping tones before another Dipping tone (see the first Mandarin sandhi rule above) may provide a partial explanation for the fact that this distinction appears to be relatively difficult for the child to acquire. This was suggested to us by Clumeck and Hyman (personal communication). Thus it is not only the lexical contrasts which must be considered, but also the phonetic realization of these contrasts in various contexts. Particularly where two tones are neutralized one might expect greater confusion. It will be of interest to see whether in other languages with similar neutralization rules our Mandarin findings are replicated.

We see then, that the research conducted on tone acquisition to date provides an "answer" to only one question of the five categories I–V (p. 272). The studies discussed above have confirmed that tones are mastered before segmentals in general (Question I.A). As to the order in which tones are learned (Question I.B), there are some data but too little information on the intervening variables. The Li and Thompson study is the only one so far that presents data on substitution errors (Question II), variation among children learning the same language (Question III.A), and the acquisition of tone rules (Questions under IV). Clumeck's work represents the only study on tone perception among children acquiring a tone language (Questions under V). It is clear that Question III.B, regarding variation across languages, must wait for the results of additional research.

5. DIRECTIONS FOR FURTHER RESEARCH

The theme of this chapter has been the meagerness of our knowledge in the area of tone acquisition, due to the dearth of empirical studies. Because of the accepted importance of acquisition studies for linguistic theory in general, it is clearly necessary that this gap in our knowledge be filled. Future research will hopefully address itself to the following issues at the very least.

5.1 Number of Children Studied

It is clear that data from many more children are needed, particularly from those languages where tone acquisition has not yet been studied, and also in those languages which are already represented in the literature surveyed above. Individual variation is not uncommon in any aspect of human behavior. Generalizations can only be made confidently when we see trends across many individuals.

5.2 Early stages

We need more precise information about what is happening during the very early stages of children's one-word period. What, for example, are the strategies children use for dealing with words whose tones they have not yet mastered?

5.3 Order of Acquisition of Tones

It is important that all possible variables which might affect order of tone acquisition be considered (as discussed above). It is highly possible that we do not know as yet what these variables are, but certainly questions of frequency, tone neutralizations, and so on, should be considered.

5.4 Tone Rules

Given the various types of tone rules discussed by Schuh, Chapter VII, this volume, it is important that we investigate the stages in the acquisition of these rules, and the strategies adopted by children in acquiring mastery over them. The Asian languages have fewer complex tone rules than do other languages, such as those in Africa, where tone also plays a heavy functional role in syntax, as, for example, in languages where different tenses are distinguished primarily or solely by tone changes. We have no information available regarding the stages when such tonal variations are acquired, and how they relate to other aspects of acquisition.

5.5 Perception

The Clumeck study suggests a direction for research leading to more information on the relationship between perception and production of tonal contrasts in a given language. Such research should be extended. In addition early childhood perception and production studies should be related to studies of adults such as those discussed by Ohala, Gandour, and Hombert in Chapters I, II, and III, respectively, this volume.

The growing body of child language research in phonology, syntax, semantics, and discourse is invaluable in enhancing our understanding of the nature of language. There is no doubt that we learn more about the acquisition of tones by children, we will learn more about the nature of tone and how it functions in language.

REFERENCES

Apronti, E. O. 1969. The Language of a 2-year-old Dangme. Paper presented at the 8th West African Language Congress, Abidjan, Ivory Coast.

Atkinson-King, K. 1973. Children's acquisition of phonological stress contrasts. *UCLA Working Papers in Phonetics, 25.*

Bar-Adon, A., & Leopold, W. (Eds.) 1971. *Child language: A book of readings.* Englewood Cliffs, N.J.: Prentice-Hall, Inc.

Chao, Y. R. 1951. The Cantian idiolect: An analysis of the Chinese spoken by a twenty-eight-months-old child. In W. J. Fischel (Ed.), *Semitic and Oriental Studies.* Berkeley and Los Angeles: University of California Press. Pp. 27–44. Repr. in Ferguson & Slobin 1973 and Bar-Adon & Leopold 1971.

Clumeck, H. 1976. Acquisition of the tonal contrasts of Mandarin. Unpublished manuscript, University of California, Berkeley.

Clumeck, H. 1977. Studies in the acquisition of Mandarin phonology. Unpublished Ph.D. dissertation, University of California, Berkeley.

Crystal, D. 1970. Prosodic systems and language acquisition. In P. Leon (Ed.), *Prosodic feature analysis.* Montreal, Paris: Didier. Pp. 77–90.

Ccrystal, D. 1973. Non-segmental phonology in language acquisition: A review of the issues. *Lingua, 32,* 1–45.

Ferguson, C. A. & Slobin, D. I. (Eds.) 1973. *Studies in child language development.* New York: Holt, Rinehart, and Winston.

Hyman, L. (Ed.) 1973. *Consonant types and tonè. Southern California Occasional Papers in Linguistics, 1.*

Kaplan, E. 1970. Intonation and language acquisition. *Papers and Reports on Child Language Development,* Stanford University, *1.*

Kaplan, E., & Kaplan, G. 1970. Is there any such thing as a prelinguistic child? J. Eliot (Ed.), *Human development and cognitive processes.* New York: Holt, Rinehart, and Winston

Kirk, L. 1973. An analysis of speech imitations by Ga children. *Anthropological Linguistics, 15*(6), 267–75

Lenneberg, E. 1967. *Biological foundations of Language.* New York: Wiley.

Li, C. N., & Thompson, S. A. 1977. The acquisition of tone in Mandarin-speaking children. *Journal of Child Language. 4,* 185–199. Revised version of paper appearing in *UCLA Working Papers in Phonetics* 1976, *33.*

Light, T. 1977. Clairetalk: A Cantonese-speaking child's confrontation with bilingualism. *Journal of Chinese Linguistics, 5*(2), 261–275.

Ohala, J. 1973. The physiology of tone. In L. Hyman (Ed.), *Consonant types and tone. Southern California Occasional Papers in Linguistics, 1,* Pp. 1–4.

Pike, E. 1949. Controlled infant intonation. *Language Learning, 2*(1), 21–24

Smith, F., & Miller, G. A. (Eds.). 1966. *The genesis of language: A psycholinguistic approach.* Cambridge: MIT Press.

Tse, J. K-P. 1977. Tone acquisition in Cantonese: A longitudinal case study. Unpublished manuscript, Univ. of Southern California.

Tuaycharoen, P. 1977. The phonetic and phonological development of a Thai baby: From early communicative interaction to speech. Unpublished Ph.D. dissertation, University of London.

Weir, R. 1966. Some questions of the child's learning of phonology. In F. Smith & G. A. Miller (Eds.), *The genesis of language: A psycholinguistic approach.* Cambridge: MIT Press

Language Index

Language	Language Family	Country	Pages
Acatlan (Mixtec)*	Oto-Manguean	Mexico	140,156,247ff.
Acoma	Keresan	N. America	136
Akan	Kwa	Ghana	139,142,144,240,254
Amoy (Chinese)	Sino-Tibetan	China	157ff.,248ff.
Aomori (Japanese)	Altaic	Japan	25, 115n,
Arabic	Semitic	Middle East	93,95
Ateso	Nilotic	Uganda	136
Babete (Bamileke)	Grassfields Bantu	Cameroun	262,266
Bade	Chadic	Nigeria	96,225ff.,231,240
Bambara	Mande	Mali	231,235ff.
Bariba	Gur	Benin	145
Befu (Japanese)	Altaic	Japan	121
Beja	Cushitic	Sudan	130
Blimaw (Karen)	Austro-Thai	Thailand	86
Bolanci	Chadic	Nigeria	226,231,258n,266
Bukusu (Luyia)	Bantu	Kenya	259
Burmese	Sino-Tibetan	Burma	93
Cantonese (Chinese)	Sino-Tibetan	China	62,96,159,262,274–276, 279,281
Chaozhou (Chinese)	Sino-Tibetan	China	103,157,249ff.
Chia-pa (Miao)	Sino-Tibetan	China	147
Chichewa	Bantu	Malawi	91,263
Chiluba	Bantu	Zaire	104
Ch'ing-chiang (Miao)	Sino-Tibetan	China	145,163
Ch'iou-chou (Miao)	Sino-Tibetan	China	147
Chinese	Sino-Tibetan	China	14,60,78,93,96,154,157, 228,231n
Chipewyan	Athabaskan	N. America	104
Chuang (Thai)	Austro-Thai	Thailand	87
Coatzospan (Mixtec)	Oto-Manguean	Mexico	139,240
Dan	Mande	Ivory Coast	145ff.
Dangaleat	Chadic	Chad	104
Dangme (Gã)	Kwa	Ghana	273

*If dialect, language given in parentheses.

Language	Language Family	Country	Pages
Danish	Germanic	Denmark	87,97,136
Dschang (Bamileke)	Grassfields Bantu	Cameroun	143,239,240ff.,243,245, 253
Dutch	Germanic	Netherlands	58,89
Duwai	Chadic	Nigeria	222ff.,226,231
English	Germanic	England,U.S.A.	56,61,64ff.,71,86,87,97, 280
Etsako	Kwa	Nigeria	178,180–185,189n,201, 203,217,228,232ff., 237,243,252,253
Etung	Ekoid Bantu	Nigeria	150,152,235
Ewe	Kwa	Togo	98,227,237
Feʔfeʔ (Bamileke)	Grassfields Bantu	Cameroun	237,266,267,268
Foochow (Chinese)	Sino-Tibetan	China	244
French	Romance	France	25,87,97
Gã	Kwa	Togo, Ghana	273
Ga'anda	Chadic	Nigeria	139,144,239
Ganda	Bantu	Uganda	21ff.,124–128,263,264
Gujerati	Indo-Iranian	India	136
Gwari	Kwa	Nigeria	18ff.,231ff.,237n,239,243, 258n,260
Hausa	Chadic	Nigeria	96,139,141,170,179,185, 206–217,235ff.,237, 239,241ff.,243,244ff., 262
Haya	Bantu	Tanzania	9,12,16,263,265
Hindi	Indi-Iranian	India	25ff.,87,89,90
Hsiao-chang (Miao)	Sino-Tibetan	China	91
Hsin-ch'iao (Miao)	Sino-Tibetan	China	147
Hweikang-pa (Yao)	Sino-Tibetan	Thailand	152
Igbo	Kwa	Nigeria	33,139,234,242,258n,260, 261,264
Igede	Kwa	Nigeria	171
Ijō	Kwa	Nigeria	122
Japanese	Altaic	Japan	14,113–119,121–124,128, 131
Jeh	Mon-Khmer	Vietnam	96
Jingpho	Sino-Tibetan	Burma	90,92,93,224ff.
Jukun	Benue-Congo	Nigeria	139,237,253
Kagoshima (Japanese)	Altaic	Japan	123ff.
Kanakuru	Chadic	Nigeria	233,240
Kanuri	Nilo-Saharan	Nigeria	235ff.
Kikuyu	Bantu	Kenya	124n,127,129,231,
Kinyarwanda	Bantu	Rwanda	264
Kirundi	Bantu	Burundi	264,265
Kiowa	Aztec-Tanoan	N. America	96
Kōchi (Japanese)	Altaic	Japan	122
Kombe	Benue-Congo	Cameroun	263
Korean	Altaic	Korea	87,90,97

Language	Language Family	Country	Pages
Korku	Austro-Asiatic	India	170
Kru	Kwa	Liberia	140,155ff.,165,245
Lahu (Burmese)	Sino-Tibetan	Burma	91,93,103,104
Lango	Nilotic	Uganda	136
Latin	Italic	Rome	129
Lisu (Burmese)	Sino-Tibetan	Burma	91,103
Lithuanian	Balto-Slavic	Lithuania	129
Loloish	Sino-Tibetan	Burma	91,103
Loma	Mande	Liberia, Guinea	104
Lue (Thai)	Austro-Thai	Thailand	159,160
Luganda (cf. Ganda)			
Lung Chow (Thai)	Austro-Thai	Thailand	87
Lung Ming (Thai)	Austro-Thai	Thailand	91
Mandarin (Chinese)	Sino-Tibetan	China	45–47,55ff.,61,119–121, 148ff.,159,231,238, 243ff.,246,250,262, 276–278,279,281
Manya (Mandinka)	Mande	W. Africa	104
Mazatec	Oto-Manguean	Mexico	151ff.,154,253
Mbam-Nkam	Grassfields Bantu	Cameroun	260
Mende	Mande	Sierra Leone	149,154,177,178,183,185, 186–206,208ff.,214,217
Miao	Sino-Tibetan	China	79,91,145,146
Mixtec	Oto-Manguean	Mexico	145,154,171ff.,273
Mongolian	Altaic	Mongolia	165
Mpi	Tibeto-Burman	Burma?	163ff.
Navaho	Athabaskan	N. America	139,170
Ndebele	Bantu	Zimbabwe	90
Ngamambo (Moghamo)	Grassfields Bantu	Cameroun	146,260,266,
Ngie	Benue-Congo	Cameroun	91
Ngizim	Chadic	Nigeria	96,222ff.,226ff.,231,233, 237,242,252
Norwegian	Germanic	Norway	54,136
Nung (Thai)	Austro-Thai	Thailand	87
Nupe	Kwa	Nigeria	171,226ff.,230,231
Nyakyusa	Bantu	Tanzania	104
Omei (Mandarin)	Sino-Tibetan	China	96
Polish	Balto-Slavic	Poland	130
Purjabi	Indo-Iranian	Pakistan	26,90
Pu-yi (Thai)	Austro-Thai	Thailand	91
Pwo-Karen	Austro-Thai	Thailand	78,86,87
Saek (Thai)	Austro-Thai	Thailand	87
Sani (Burmese)	Sino-Tibetan	Burma	91,103
San Miguel (Mixtec)	Oto-Manguean	Mexico	254
Serbo-Croation	Balto-Slavic	Yugoslavia	49–53,97
Shambala	Bantu	Tanzania	266
Shan (Thai)	Austro-Thai	Thailand	87
Shi	Bantu	Zaire?	264
Shona	Bantu	Zimbabwe	239

Subject Index

A
B
C   8
D   9
E   0
F   1
G   2
H   3
I   4
J   5

414
T 66

59327